Sharon - I pray you
will be as blessed by
this book as I was

Jamie

# Searching
## for the
# GOD
## of Grace

# ALSO BY STUART TYNER

*The ABZs of Adventist Youth Ministry*

*Summer Ministries: How to Revolutionize Your Town With Targeted, Project Evangelism*

*Walking on the Edge: Thirteen Interactive Bible Studies for Adventist Students in Public High School*

*The Colors of Grace in Our Homes: 100 Creative Ideas to Enrich Family Worship*

# Searching for the GOD of Grace

# STUART TYNER

**Pacific Press® Publishing Association**
Nampa, Idaho
Oshawa, Ontario, Canada
www.pacificpress.com

Edited by David C. Jarnes
Cover design by Mark Bond
Cover photo by iStockPhoto.com
Author photo by Dan Rathbun

ISBN: 0-8163-2152-3
ISBN 13: 9780816321520

Additional copies of this book are available by calling toll free 1-800-765-6955 or by visiting <www.adventistbookcenter.com>.

06 07 08 09 10 • 5 4 3 2 1

*To Karen,*
*the agent of grace in my life*
*and my best friend*
*since September 4, 1960,*
*the day we first met*

# CONTENTS

# ACKNOWLEDGMENTS

Few books, if any, are written in isolation. One's life experiences always produce influences and interactions to the words of those who have expressed themselves in previous times and to the insights of those who are willing to share their current explorations. Robert Frost said about the creative process that it begins with a lump in the throat; a homesickness or a love-sickness. The result is a wondrous blend of hard work and welcome inspiration, strategic planning and sweet surprise.

This is especially true when the subject is a spiritual treasure that lays claim to being the central position in the structure of our faith. Wherever and whenever the treasure is revealed, it captures our hearts and minds, conveys meaning, and instills hope.

## FAMILY

I have seen the revealing of the treasure in my own family. My wife, Karen, who has known me better than anyone else in the world since we were young teenagers long ago, still loves me anyway!

Karen and I have three fantastic kids, now all married to three delightful people: Erin and Steve in North Carolina, with Jacob and Joshua; Matthew and Jennifer here in Southern California with Emma and Sophie Grace; and Ben and Jenny in New York City. They all have had plenty of opportunities to give to me the kiss of forgiveness, and, in doing so, have taught me a great deal about grace.

## COLLEAGUES

I have explored the treasure map with pastoral colleagues in the La Sierra University Church for more than seven years now. Throughout these years, Wednesday mornings have meant staff meeting at La Sierra, and it has been in these administrative gatherings (which often spill over to lunch at local restaurants) that our richest theological discussions on the nuances of grace, as well as the most practical applications of grace in the life of the church have taken place.

To the exemplary, devoted veterans of ministry John Champlin, Art Lesko, Penny Shell, Brad Whited, and Hallie Wilson; to the exceptional ministry specialists Jim Clizbe, Devo Kritzinger, Sam Leonor, Janeen Little, and Dan Smith; to the energetic young scholars and visionaries Raewin Hankins, Steve Hemenway, and Vaughn Nelson; to Chris Oberg, whose pinches of pastoral wisdom speak as sensibly as all our combined blusterings; to Edna Thomas, our able and optimistic administrative assistant; and to Betty, Corinne, Mary Jo, Marilyn, Wanda, and all the steady volunteers in the church office, my heartfelt thanks for making grace the keynote of our church and the foundation of our service together. Throughout these chapters you'll find frequent references to life in the La Sierra church.

FRIENDS

I've discussed the treasure of grace at Adventist gatherings as often as I could. I've tried out these concepts, refined them, and discovered their most compelling elements with camp meeting friends in New Zealand, Australia, and Holland; with the worshipers in the Connections tent in North New South Wales and the young adults at Lake Junaluska in the Carolina Conference and the cowboys at Springtown in Arkansas; with the talented, persevering faculty of Portland Adventist Academy; and with Stephen and Leanne Davies and all the members of their energetic, creative worship-planning team at the Papatoetoe church in Auckland. Thanks to them for all their insights and encouragement.

STUDY GROUP

During the first six months of this past year, the dear friends in the study group that meets weekly in Karen's and my home gave me a lovely gift. This generous group of people agreed to read each chapter in this manuscript in advance and come prepared week by week to probe, scrutinize, investigate, add to, subtract from, and edit these pages. I want you to become acquainted with them.

Nora Burkett brings a young mother's warmth and sweetness to the study, and then goes home to try out our conclusions on David, her rocket scientist husband, a devoted, engaging man who is not a believer in God.

Steve McClain is an analytical high-school math teacher deeply committed to the religious development of his students.

Jenni Subriar is a new Adventist; a superb, experienced editor; a blossoming theologian; and a first-class ministerial student.

Lorelei and Peter Cress are young parents who have rediscovered the value of a church family. Lorelei is an inspiring musician who shares her love of grace in her work for a well-known Adventist ministry; Peter is an electrical engineering student and nascent philosopher who seldom misses a misspelled word or a stray conjecture.

Ryan and Sharilyn Horner are stellar representatives of a new generation of Seventh-day Adventists. I had the honor of officiating at their wedding on a cool Valentine's Day evening. Ryan is a nursing student at Loma Linda; Sharilyn teaches math at La Sierra University. Neither one will allow sloppy thinking or imprecise conclusions.

Debbie Saknit skillfully manages the nurses who care for children in the Loma Linda University Children's Hospital. She comes from a background in which the treasure was hidden. She easily pinpoints the difference grace brings. Debbie's husband, Tom, is an independent video producer with a passion for precise language. Our discussions of what *pagan* means and how the word *obvious* should be used have been classic.

Jeff and Stefani McFarland have been members of our study group the longest. Their commitment to their children, Bryce and Katie, is steady and exemplary. Stefani is a respected accountant, a gourmet cook, and an adroit questioner. Jeff is a creative graphic artist who never lets an exclusive remark go by when an inclusive one better reflects the character of God.

And over all of us Karen has hovered, starting us on time, keeping us on track, feeding us, perceiving the heart of grace in each discussion, and reminding us not to stay up all night talking!

If there is one group of people who represent for me the individuals I hope will read this book, this is that group. I wanted you to meet them, to see their great diversity, and to know their considerable contribution to the process that has made this a better study than I could have made it by myself.

*"The plans of the Lord stand firm forever,
the purposes of his heart through all generations."*
—Psalm 33:11

*" 'Before they call I will answer.' "*
—Isaiah 65:24

*"The angel said to them, 'Do not be afraid.
I bring you good news of great joy that will be for all the people.' "*
—Luke 2:10

*"This grace was given us in Christ Jesus
before the beginning of time."*
—2 Timothy 1:9

*"Jesus Christ our Lord, before all ages,
now and forevermore!"*
—Jude 25

# BEFORE THE BEGINNING:

## *The Primacy of Grace in the Plan of Salvation*

Before our birth, both yours and mine, there was an invitation;[1]
Before we ever sought His face or tried to earn His favor;
Before we knew to worship Him, or righteousness to savor;
Before our praise, before our works, before our pulse, was grace.

Before the fundamental list of doctrinal citation;[2]
Before the founders could retrace the certain steps to Christ;
Before the counsel fixed our gaze on Jesus, sacrificed;
Before we saw, before we knew, before we were, was grace.

Before the mother church fought back with published declaration;[3]
Before the thought was commonplace to work for what was free;
Before the councils ruled the fates with serious decree;
Before the storm, before the veer, before the church, was grace.

Before a hammer helped a monk begin a reformation;[4]
Before a thousand years' erase of venerable creed;
Before the Scripture's common tongue was ever guaranteed;
Before the press, before the creeds, before the monk, was grace.

Before Anselm and Abelard had shaped our speculation;[5]
Before medieval marketplace had bartered with the judgment;
Before uncertainty increased the fearful soul's torment;
Before the fear, before the price, before the words, was grace.

Before "that African" confessed the cross's inspiration;[6]
Before his service would displace the grasp of pagan pride;
Before his battles met the foe and turned religion's tide;
Before the wars, before the deeds, before the crux, was grace.

Before the Romans heard from Paul there is no condemnation;[7]
Before the church could first embrace salvation as a gift;
Before disciples preached the cross as something to uplift;
Before the cross, before the gift, before the Lamb, was grace.

Before the gathered angels sang the wondrous incarnation;[8]
Before the shepherds sought the place where Mary birthed the Child;
Before the manger held our hope and on Him wise men smiled;
Before the star, before the birth, before the song, was grace.

Before young David brought from God a giant cancellation;[9]
Before in dreams the grand staircase a need identified;
Before old Abram learned to trust the Lord who will provide;
Before the trust, before the need, before the stones, was grace.

Before the first pair wakened in a finished new creation;[10]
Before their Maker knelt in space to breathe the breath of life;
Before the garden's vow was made to crush the head of strife;
Before the fall, before the breath, before the world, was grace.

*—Stuart Tyner*
October 28, 2004

---

1. See chapter 1, "The Crimson Stain." For the "invitation," see Revelation 13:8 concerning "the book of life belonging to the Lamb that was slain from the creation of the world."

2. See chapter 15, "The California Conspiracy." "Doctrinal citation" is a reference to the Adventist statement of fundamental beliefs. "Steps to Christ" alludes both to Ellen G. White's 1844 description of Jesus standing at the top of a stairway stretching from earth to heaven as well as to her devotional book of 1892. For the counsel that "fixed our gaze on Jesus," consider this 1915 statement from her book *Gospel Workers* (Washington, D.C.: Review and Herald, 1948): "Let the science of salvation be the burden of every sermon, the theme of every song. Let it be poured forth in every supplication. Bring nothing into your preaching to supplement Christ" (pp. 159, 160). Or this one from the same book (referred to several times in this book): "The sacrifice of Christ as an atonement for sins is the great truth around which all other truths cluster. . . . I present before you the great, grand monument of mercy and regeneration, salvation and redemption—the Son of God uplifted on the cross. This is to be the foundation of every discourse given by our ministers" (p. 315).

3. See chapter 13, "The Boundary Stones." "Published declaration" references the decree from the Council of Trent on justification. "The veer" is the direction the church took away from the presentation of the gospel. "The storm" is the Protestant Reformation.

4. See chapter 12, "The True Treasure." "The hammer" is the one with which Martin Luther nailed the Ninety-five Theses to the door of the church in Wittenberg on October 31, 1517, after "a thousand years" and more of Christianity being defined by simple, "venerable creed." "The Scripture's common tongue" was guaranteed by the invention of the printing press.

5. See chapter 11, "The Scholastic Dance." The medieval theological speculation about purchasing or paying a price for salvation with our works only increased the torment and fear of the everyday church member.

6. See chapters 9 and 10, "The Perfect Church" and "The Second Battle." "That African" was the pejorative name enemies threw at Augustine, who lived in Hippo in North Africa. The phrase "confessed the Bible's inspiration" refers to his autobiographical work, *The Confessions*. Augustine discovered "the crux" of Christianity, its basic and essential point, in its teaching on grace. "Crux" also is Latin for "cross."

7. See chapter 7, "The Justified Sinner." See Romans 8:1 for "no condemnation," and John 3:14 and 12:32 for "the cross as something to uplift."

8. See chapter 6, "The Impossible Camel," for a discussion of the doctrine of grace as it is found in the Gospels.

9. See chapter 4, "The Hebrew Matrix." The "giant cancellation" refers to David's defeat of the Philistine giant Goliath (see 1 Samuel 17). "The grand staircase" was the focus of Jacob's dream at Bethel (Genesis 28) which opened the door for him to understand his need for grace in his life, although he didn't walk through that door for many years. "Abram learned to trust the Lord who will provide" on Mount Moriah (Genesis 22).

10. See chapter 5, "The Finished Work," and chapter 4, "The Hebrew Matrix." For "the garden's vow" to "crush the head of strife," see Genesis 3:15.

*"The grace of God that brings salvation has appeared to all."*
—Titus 2:11

*"It is by grace you have been saved, through faith—
and this not from yourselves, it is the gift of God."*
—Ephesians 2:8

*"If by grace, then it is no longer by works;
if it were, grace would no longer be grace."*
—Romans 11:6

*" 'My grace is sufficient for you,
for My power is made perfect in weakness.' "*
—2 Corinthians 12:9

*"I saw another angel flying in midair,
and he had the eternal gospel to proclaim to those who live on the earth—
to every nation, tribe, language and people."*
—Revelation 14:6

# THE BURIED TREASURE:

## *The Discovery of Grace in the Kingdom of Light*

H EAVEN'S GATES WILL OPEN WIDE TO LET GOOD BOYS AND GIRLS INSIDE." DID you ever hear such a cautionary note from a strict Sabbath School teacher who seemed to follow you from Kindergarten to Juniors to Earliteens? Did you grow up believing that God liked us Adventist boys and girls better than other kids because of the good things we did and the bad things we didn't do? Have you wondered about significant portions of your belief structure because you just cannot continue to accept such a narrow definition of God?

Did your parents ever take you through the ascending hierarchy of guilt? (*"How can you treat me this way?" "Your father is going to be so disappointed in you." "You make Jesus sad when you do that kind of thing."*) Did you sometimes feel like you couldn't pray anymore because you had offended heaven with your disobedience, your bad language, even your unconverted thoughts?

Did you ever look closely at older church members who seemed so firmly "settled into the truth" and wonder why their faces didn't reflect the "good news" they talked about? Or why their heart and their treasure didn't seem to be in the same place at all (Matthew 6:21)? Have you found yourself at a distance from the God we were told about?[1]

This is a story about cautionary notes and narrow definitions. About distances that lead to disbelief. About buried treasure. This is an exploration of where religious people—including some of our parents, our Sabbath School teachers, our pastors, and our church leaders—have gotten off the gospel path and tried to forge their own way to heaven—a futile exercise that inevitably results in dissatisfaction, skepticism, and hostility. This is an examination of deliberate attempts and clumsy processes that end up burying the greatest treasure the human family has ever known—a treasure that, whenever and wherever it has been rediscovered, has transformed the spiritual

---

1. Peter Manseau speaks of "people made anxious by churches" (*Killing the Buddha* [New York: Free Press, 2004]). Steve Rabey describes a "mass exodus" of spiritually hungry young people from "both traditional and contemporary congregations" (*In Search of Authentic Faith* [Colorado Springs: WaterBrook Press, 2001]). Leonard Sweet reports that we live in a culture in which "there is no interest in a 'second-hand' God that someone else (church tradition, church professionals, church bureaucracies) defines for us" (*Post-Modern Pilgrims* [Nashville, Tenn.: Broadman & Holman, 2000]).

experience of the people who have found it.

## MY FIRST ENCOUNTER WITH THE TREASURE

Close to where I grew up on the central California coast was a corner of a tranquil Pacific bay that the locals called Pirate's Cove. Hidden in the cove, below the sloping hill behind my house and just above the tide pools on the shoreline, was a series of cramped, surf-washed caverns that were accessible only at low tide. I used to sneak out of my bedroom on moonlit nights, steal down the slope, and wade into the caverns to explore. Somewhere within them, the story was told, marauding Spanish swashbucklers had hidden chests of gold doubloons and precious jewels plundered in their exploits at sea.

I dreamed those nights of being the fabled Alexandre Dumas's character Edmond Dantès digging in the secret cave on the rocky island of Monte Cristo. Inside the gloomy subterranean grotto, with his knees trembling and his heart beating violently, Edmond uncovered "a casket of wood bound with iron" hidden beneath two feet of earth and rubble.

In an instant he had cleared every obstacle away, and he saw successively the lock, placed between two padlocks, and the two handles at each end. Dantès seized the handles, and strove to lift the coffer; it was impossible. He sought to open it; lock and padlock were fastened; these faithful guardians seemed unwilling to surrender their trust. Dantès inserted the sharp end of the pickaxe between the coffer and the lid, and pressing with all his force on the handle, burst open the fastenings. The hinges yielded in their turn and fell, still holding in their grasp fragments of the wood, and the chest was open.

Edmond was seized with vertigo; he closed his eyes as children do in order that they may see in the resplendent night of their own imagination more stars than are visible in the firmament; then he reopened them, and stood motionless with amazement. Three compartments divided the coffer. In the first, blazed piles of golden coin; in the second, were ranged bars of unpolished gold, which possessed nothing attractive save their value; in the third, Edmond grasped handfuls of diamonds, pearls, and rubies, which, as they fell on one another, sounded like hail against glass. After having touched, felt, examined these treasures, Edmond rushed through the caverns like a man seized with frenzy; he leaped on a rock, from whence he could behold the sea. He was alone—alone with these countless, these unheard-of treasures!

I never found the treasure of Pirate's Cove, though there certainly was a thrill in just imagining the discovery.

If not in my little cave, I reasoned, perhaps I'd find what I was looking for in the other of my childhood fantasies—in Egypt's mysterious Valley of the Kings. Howard Carter had described in his diary what a "magnificent discovery" meant to a seasoned archaeologist "after so many years of toilsome work." About two in the afternoon on Sunday, November 26, 1922, Carter stood before the door into King Tut's tomb.

Feverishly we cleared away the remaining last scraps of rubbish on the floor of the passage before the doorway, until we had only the clean sealed doorway before us. We made a tiny breach in the top left hand corner of the doorway to see what was beyond. Candles were procured—the all important tell-tale for foul gases when opening an ancient subterranean excavation—I widened the breach and by means of the candle looked in.

It was sometime before one could see, the hot air escaping caused the candle to flicker, but as soon as one's eyes became accustomed to the glimmer of light, the interior of the chamber gradually loomed before one, with its strange and wonderful medley of extraordinary and beautiful objects heaped upon one another.

There was naturally short suspense for those present who could not see, when Lord Carnarvon said to me "Can you see anything?" I replied to him, "Yes, it is wonderful." I then with precaution made the hole sufficiently large for both of us to see. With the light of an electric torch as well as an additional candle, we looked in. Our sensations and astonishment are difficult to describe as the better light revealed to us the marvelous collection of treasures.

I didn't know it while I was growing up, but there was available a treasure far more precious than the gold of Monte Cristo, far more spectacular than the extraordinary possessions of King Tut. I'm not sure I knew about the treasure when my kids were growing up, and now that their kids are growing up, I'm just beginning to realize the value of what's been buried time and time again. It's a treasure " 'that will not be exhausted' " (Luke 12:33)—the "incomparable riches" of God's grace "expressed in his kindness to us in Christ Jesus" (Ephesians 2:7).

This is the story of that treasure. This is the record of how God chose us in Christ "before the creation of the world" (Ephesians 1:4),

how we have been adopted to be children of the King to the praise of God's glorious grace, "which he has freely given us in the One he loves" in accordance with the riches of His grace (Ephesians 1:6, 7). It's the story of how the Father has qualified us "to share in the inheritance of the saints in the kingdom of light" (Colossians 1:12). It's about how our names have been written "in the book of life belonging to the Lamb" (Revelation 13:8). It's about how this treasure and this treasure alone can reorient our identity in our deepest reality.

A TRAGIC PATTERN

Unfortunately, however, the story reveals a tragic pattern. We discover that, from the days of antiquity (chapter 3) through the long, turbulent Old Testament times (chapters 4 and 5), the burying of the treasure was done mostly by *religious* people, and as much by those whom we identify as God's chosen ones as by all those who knew of God only from a distance. From the Incarnation (chapter 6) through the early endeavors of the New Testament church (chapters 7 and 8), it was religious *leaders*, who, thinking of themselves as padlocks on the truth, "faithful guardians . . . unwilling to surrender their trust," sealed the treasure behind the discouraging obstacles and rubbish of a legalistic experience. The *theologians* of the Middle Ages (chapters 11–13) told us we could win God's love by our behavior and then left us in our failures to recoil in fear from the righteous presence of God. In more than 160 years of Adventist history (chapters 14–18), the treasure has been uncovered and then buried again numerous times.

Exploring all those centuries of the concealing of the treasure demands diligence, but it's well worth the effort. The secret of a relevant, personal spiritual foundation is revealed in every historical period. If we persevere in our searching, "if you look for it as for silver and search for it as for hidden treasure" (Proverbs 2:4), the riches will be found and will make us wealthy beyond imagination.

I had already written three chapters about discovering the treasure when Philip Yancey's superb study *What's So Amazing About Grace?* was published. I was exhilarated by Yancey's lucid unfolding of the doctrine of grace—and yet, at the same time, discouraged. I thought Yancey had said everything I wanted to say, that there was now no need for me to continue writing. During my third time through his book, however, I realized that an Adventist viewpoint still had something to add to the discussion. While our perspectives on grace are similar, my experience differs enough from Yancey's to make me believe that other Adventists, especially those who also have grown up with the faulty notion that we must contribute something to the salvation process, might resonate with an Adventist journey. I decided to keep writing.

PLEASE NOTE . . .

*Watch for this:* The Thursday night study group that meets at my house played an important role in the development of this book. During our first meeting on this project, Sharilyn confessed to all of us that she didn't like the title I had suggested for the manuscript: *Afraid of Grace.* "It sounds arrogant," she observed, "as if you're saying, 'I've gotten over my fear, why don't you?' " That is *not* at all what I'm trying to say. I want the reader to understand that right here at the very beginning.

I'll admit it: I've been afraid of grace. Fear has characterized my approach to the doctrine of salvation for most of my life. I see that same

fear in religion's common approach to God. I'm now convinced, however, that is not the Bible's message of what our relationship to God should be. Look for the phrase "afraid of grace" in every chapter.

*The tense of the discussion:* Whoever writes about historical matters must live with the challenge of keeping the material fresh and interesting. It is so easy to doubt that people of long ago who may have mattered once upon a time still connect with us today. I read somewhere that when the rabbis repeat the words of the ancient sages, they always do so in the present tense, to further the feeling that they are carrying on a discussion today with those who lived centuries ago. I think that's such a good idea that I've adopted the practice.

So, in addition to people who are alive and well and writing and speaking today, you'll find in these pages references to lots of people who passed off the scene long ago: Paul Tillich, C. S. Lewis, James Moffatt, A. T. Jones and E. J. Waggoner, Luther, Augustine, Paul, Isaiah . . . Try to listen to their voices in the present tense, as if they are in the room and speaking to us today.

*The great central truth:* I have been stirred by Ellen White's declaration that "the sacrifice of Christ as an atonement for sin is the great truth around which all other truths cluster."[2] It seems to me to be a clarion call for a distinctive, systematic Adventist theology built upon grace. Look for references in many of the chapters ahead to this urging that Ellen White voiced.

*Grace in question:* At the conclusion of each chapter, you'll find a page that's intended to spur discussion in small-group study or to give you a little extra focus as you consider the

---

2. Ellen G. White, *Gospel Workers* (Washington, D.C.: Review and Herald, 1915), 315.

various topics. If you use the book in a study group, look at these questions before you read the chapter, and begin your discussion here. You'll also find on these pages a one-paragraph summary of the chapter.

*Grace Notes:* There may come times in your consideration of the doctrine of salvation by grace when you grow weary of slugging through the historical developments and the theological fine points—when you need to rest for a few moments from this pursuit and be rejuvenated by allowing your heart simply to embrace the biblical invitation to be saved by grace and grace alone. If and when this happens to you, turn to the Grace Notes pages in between the chapters.

Grace notes, you remember, are those little added notes that embellish a musical score. As a rule, the Grace Notes in this composition are short, are built on Bible passages about grace, and are more devotional in nature than the chapters they follow, with less commentary and opinion and footnotes. They are directed more to worship and praise than to investigation and analysis. Seems like we all benefit from frequent breaks like that.

At the same time, the Grace Notes follow the theme that already has been sounded in the chapter. The questions that begin the Grace Notes suggest the connection between the chapter's emphasis and each Grace Note's song.

In the end, the treasure already is ours, but it's never forced upon us. We can refuse it, ignore it, trample on it, attempt to obscure it, or lock it up and bury it. We can be afraid of grace, as so many have been throughout history and as so many continue to be. We can try to confuse people into accepting another story of salvation. ("I am astonished," Paul said to the Galatian church members, "that you are so quickly deserting the one who called you by the grace of Christ and are turning to a different gospel—which is really no gospel at all" [Galatians 1:6, 7].)

However, in spite of all the efforts to bury it, the treasure remains. Sometimes it's out in the open for everyone to see. Sometimes it's hidden.

It is my prayer that these pages might clear away a few more obstacles, burst a few more padlocks, and illuminate a few more facets of the inexhaustible riches of God's grace.

"The grace of the Lord Jesus be with God's people. Amen" (Revelation 22:21).

# GRACE NOTES
## PSALM 90—THE LENGTH OF OUR DAYS

"Lord, you have been our dwelling place throughout all generations" (Psalm 90:1).

Q. What benefits are there to unlocking the Bible's treasures of salvation by grace?

It's Moses speaking. He has composed a hymn of praise to the Voice from the burning bush, the great I AM, the Ruler of the universe, the Creator God.

The "generations" he speaks about stretch back in time as far as he can see. Beyond the laborers suffering under the taskmasters' whips. Before the settlers of Canaan: Joseph and his brothers; Jacob, Leah, and Rachel; Isaac and Rebekah; Abraham and Sarah. Back to those who escaped the waters of the great Flood. Back to the original, aged patriarchs. Back to the Garden dwellers, Adam and Eve. There, where humans love to tell the story, Moses finds the presence of God.

Q. What immediate advantage does enduring, unfailing love bring to our lives?

> Before the mountains were born
> > or you brought forth the earth and the world,
> > from everlasting to everlasting you are God (Psalm 90:2).

The "generations" move our direction as well. With prophetic clarity, Moses sees the Promised Land, the Kingdom, the Division, the Exile, the coming of the Messiah. He looks into the future and sees God's people in constant trouble, seeking an identity, a clue to our place in the universe.

> For a thousand years in Your sight
> > are like a day that has just gone by,
> > or like a watch in the night . . .
> The length of our days is seventy years—
> > or eighty, if we have the strength;
> yet their span is but trouble and sorrow,
> > for they quickly pass, and we fly away (Psalm 90:4, 10).

Then the gospel begins to break through. None of us can return to God, "our dwelling place," in our own strength. We are powerless to make the journey. We bring nothing to the endeavor except our confessed weakness, our great need. We are sinners in need of a Savior. Captives in need of a Redeemer. Hostages in need of ransom. We are estranged and in need of reconciliation.

> We are consumed by your anger
> > and terrified by your indignation.

You have set our iniquities before you,
    our secret sins in the light of your presence.
All our days pass away under your wrath;
    we finish our years with a moan (Psalm 90:7–9).

But Moses doesn't end his hymn on a sour note. He continues because the gospel continues. God's goodness overwhelms the terror. We hear the rest of the story, the next verse in the hymn.

Satisfy us in the morning with your unfailing love,
    that we may sing for joy and be glad all our days.
Make us glad for as many days as you have afflicted us,
    for as many years as we have seen trouble (Psalm 90:14, 15).

The affliction of being separated from God melts away in the satisfaction of His unfailing love. "Unfailing love"! The psalmists seem never to tire of singing about this God of grace.

Give thanks to the LORD for his unfailing love (Psalm 107:8).

With the LORD is unfailing love
    and with him is full redemption (Psalm 130:7).

I trust in your unfailing love;
    my heart rejoices in your salvation (Psalm 13:5).

How priceless is your unfailing love! (Psalm 36:7).

Save me in your unfailing love (Psalm 31:16).

Have mercy on me, O God,
    according to your unfailing love (Psalm 51:1).

With joy and gladness, accompanied by the music of lyres and harps, trumpets and cymbals, the God of satisfying mornings and unfailing love will be worshipped by His people throughout the generations. King David adds to the celebration the comforting, enticing aromas of freshly baked bread, date cakes, and raisin cakes (1 Chronicles 16:1–6). He sings of the splendor and wonder of God's deeds (Psalm 90:16; 1 Chronicles 16:9). He joins Moses in giving thanks to the Lord, calling on His name, making known among the nations what He has done (1 Chronicles 16:8), and praising God for remembering "his covenant forever, the word he commanded, for a thousand generations" (1 Chronicles 16:15).

Sing to the LORD, all the earth;
    proclaim his salvation day after day.
Declare his glory among the nations,
    his marvelous deeds among all peoples. . . .
Splendor and majesty are before Him;
    strength and joy in his dwelling place.
Ascribe to the LORD, O families of nations,
    ascribe to the LORD glory and strength,
    ascribe to the LORD the glory due his name.
Bring an offering and come before him;
    worship the LORD in the splendor of his holiness. . . .
Let the heavens rejoice, let the earth be glad;
    let them say among the nations, "The LORD reigns!"
Let the sea resound, and all that is in it;
    let the fields be jubilant, and everything in them!
Then the trees of the forest will sing,
    they will sing for joy before the LORD,
    for he comes to judge the earth.
Give thanks to the LORD, for he is good;
    his love endures forever (1 Chronicles 16:23, 24, 27–29, 31–34).

There is no hesitation in the rejoicing. No exclusion in the invitation to be jubilant. No fear of the coming judgment. God's grace extends the length of our days.

Giotto di Bondone's fresco masterpiece *Lamentation Over Jesus,* in the Arena Chapel in Padua, Italy. Completed by 1306, the painting is a stunning reminder of the absolute incongruity between the everlasting gospel of God's saving grace and any attempt to earn eternal salvation (see chapter 2, pages 39 and 40).

*"There is absolutely no danger of saying too much about the grace of God."*

—WATCHMAN NEE, *GRACE FOR GRACE*

*"Grace is the greatest discovery of my life."*

—MAX LUCADO, *IN THE GRIP OF GRACE*

*"Grace is God's attitude toward us."*

—RICHARD ROHR, *RADICAL GRACE*

*"Grace is reconciliation."*

—PAUL TILLICH, *SYSTEMATIC THEOLOGY*

*"Grace is not something God Himself gives us; it is the way God gives us Himself."*

—ROBERT MCAFEE BROWN, *THE SPIRIT OF PROTESTANTISM*

# CHAPTER 1
# THE CRIMSON STAIN:
*The Foundation of Grace in the Triumph of the Lamb*

**M**Y MOTHER NEVER TOLD ME NOT TO EAT SHRIMP. SHE DID INSTRUCT me to keep away from pork chops, ham-and-cheese sandwiches, and the all-American hot dog. But shrimp escaped the list of prohibited food in the nominal Seventh-day Adventist home of my childhood.

I'm sure the lapse in my mother's Adventist orthodoxy had something to do with my dad's seasoned appetite. He absolutely loved shrimp. With a Louisiana heritage, a Texas Gulf Coast upbringing, and a Southern Methodist mother who loved to cook, Dad had grown up knowing the pleasures of buying and frying the little crustaceans. "God must have put them in the water just to delight our taste buds!" Dad would say in a voice twinged with a Texas drawl. "What other purpose do they serve?"

And so, warm summer Saturday nights in our home in Navasota, Texas, were never more enjoyable than when accompanied by a platter of deep-fried shrimp dipped in ketchup and washed down with an ice-cold Dr Pepper. To this day, if a passenger next to me on an airplane has ordered a seafood meal, the smell of the shrimp transports me back to the Gulf, to happy, stress-free family times. Mom and Dad still enjoyed each other's company in those days, and, for a little while, our family walked together sweetly through the humid Texas evenings.

ADVENTIST SURPRISES

My dad probably had never heard of Seventh-day Adventists (and certainly had never read Leviticus 11) until quite some time after he and my mother married. Returning to the mainland from the shock of Pearl Harbor, Dad, who was a chief petty officer on a navy hospital ship, met and married my mother, then a young navy nurse. After the war, they settled down in Southern California close to her parents, who lived just east of Loma Linda in the sleepy little foothill town of Yucaipa.

Somewhere early in the story of their quickly troubled marriage, Mother began to talk about Adventists. While Mother was still a high-school student, a literature evangelist had introduced her family to the church, and the entire family had been baptized. Mom and her sister (whose name was Grace) attended Glendale Academy. Then, after her graduation, Mom rode the train north all the way to Walla Walla, Washington, to take nursing at the Adventist college there. After her training, in the middle of World War II, Mother joined the navy. The next time she went to church with her parents in Yucaipa, she was wearing a striking, dark blue uniform with silver lieutenant's bars on her shoulders. Unfortunately, the love of the Adventist message was not firmly rooted in Mother's heart, and with the war, my dad, and freedom from her parents, the church became an increasingly distant reality.

Then one day something began to rekindle a little Adventist flame. Mother realized how nice it would be for her and her family (Dad, me, and my two little sisters, Jane and Julie) to have a common and active faith. So, she began talking about her parents' religion. She suddenly refused to go out with Dad on Friday night. She insisted we turn off the TV just before sundown on Friday evening and keep it off until sundown Saturday night. She began driving us seventy-five miles to attend the nearest Adventist church on Saturday morning. And she instituted the rule prohibiting pork chops, ham-and-cheese sandwiches, and hot dogs.

Fifty years later, long after Mother had passed away, Dad was still complaining about Mother's "Adventist surprises." The church issue drove a wedge between them that ultimately led to their divorce when I was twelve.

Not even fried shrimp could keep them together.

### WHERE THEOLOGY BEGINS

In the beginning of his delightful little book *The Alphabet of Grace*, Frederick Buechner makes one of those statements that invites you to put down the book and stare out the window for a few moments of reflection. "At its heart," Buechner proposes, "most theology, like most fiction, is essentially autobiography."[1]

### THEOLOGY AS AUTOBIOGRAPHY

AUGUSTINE: "Augustine conceded that his earlier works . . . should be corrected in the light of his later insights concerning the doctrine of grace. . . . It is clearly important to exclude any writings prior to his elevation to the episcopacy from our analysis of his mature doctrine of justification." —Alister E. McGrath, *Iustitia Dei: A History of the Christian Doctrine of Justification: The Beginnings to the Reformation* (Cambridge: Cambridge University Press, 1986), 24.

MARTIN LUTHER: Luther's reforming doctrine of justification by grace through faith "developed over a period of years, being influenced by various strands of late medieval thought and undergoing several fundamental shifts." —Timothy George, *Theology of the Reformers* (Nashville: Broadman Press, 1988), 69.

CARDINAL NEWMAN: "Newman's copious writings gave ammunition to his foes, since he had moved with agonizing steps, each precisely marked, from one church to another, each stage in effect canceling what was said before so that his words could be pitted against each other in apparent contradiction." —Garry Wills, *Papal Sin* (New York: Doubleday, 2000), 262.

HUSTON SMITH: After several autobiographical paragraphs in the preface to his book *Why Religion Matters,* philosopher Huston Smith says, "Everything in this book should be read in the light of the above paragraphs." —Huston Smith, *Why Religion Matters* (San Francisco: HarperCollins, 2001), xiv.

I certainly can testify to the truth of Buechner's formula. The values and priorities I learned at home conditioned my early lifestyle (includ-

---

1. Frederick Buechner, *The Alphabet of Grace* (San Francisco: HarperCollins, 1970), 3.

ing my diet), my interests, and even my politics. When my dad called Hubert Humphrey and Adlai Stevenson "idiots," I naturally thought they were idiots, too. Only much later, studying political speeches for a college class in political science and hearing things in those speeches that I had accepted as a Christian, did I begin to question my parents' political opinions.

And what was true of diet and politics was also true about the life of faith. Mother had been taught an Adventism that emphasized outward correctness of behavior as the church defined correctness. While she had distanced herself over the years from the church and most of those "correct" behaviors, the emphasis continued to produce guilt in her life: "You should be ashamed of not doing the things you should be doing and of doing things you shouldn't be doing, and unless you quit doing those bad things and start doing the good things, you, and your children as well, will be disciplined by the church—you'll be disfellowshipped from the communion of those who love the truth, and you'll be lost when Jesus comes again." At least that's the way it felt to Mother—the way she spoke of it from that day on.

One summer while I still was in elementary school, Mom and Dad shipped me from Texas to Yucaipa to spend a few weeks with my grandparents. I remember sitting between them in church on Sabbath morning when the pastor held up a newspaper, put it down quickly, and said, "Have you seen this morning's headlines?" Then, pretending to read from the front page of the paper, he reported, "President Signs National Sunday Law." A gasp thundered through the congregation, some people began to weep, and a couple just down the pew from us slipped to their knees and started to pray out loud. One dear sister, sitting near the front of the church,

fainted and had to be carried out of church by the deacons. At that, the pastor apologized profusely and tried unsuccessfully to refocus our attention on his sermon.

I thought the great fuss was over the fact that the pastor had purchased a newspaper on Sabbath morning! Only later did I learn from my very angry grandfather that the pastor had been playing a trick on us, attempting to use the immediacy of the Second Coming to get people back to correct behavior and to avoiding incorrect behavior. That's the Adventism my mother handed to me.

Two years in an Adventist elementary school did nothing to change my perspective. In an Adventist boarding academy, my Bible teacher posed a question to the class about being stranded on a desert island. "What if the only other life form on the island was a pig? Would you kill the pig and eat it in order to survive?" the Bible teacher asked us. "Or would you obey God, starve to death, and wait for God's reward on resurrection morning?" The "right" answer was obvious. If we ate to survive, we'd end up being lost eternally.

In college theology classes, I had my first encounter with the apostle Paul. Studying Romans, Galatians, and Ephesians, I became increasingly frustrated with Paul's emphasis on grace. "Paul clearly is wrong," I concluded. "He just doesn't understand Adventism. If he did, he'd realize how essential is our obedience to our eternal destiny."

DISCOVERING GRACE

It took years and years for me to come to a genuinely biblical—and authentically Adventist—understanding. On November 9, 1990, I made my first discovery of what I would soon refer to as a "grace book." Appropriately, it was Charles Swindoll's *The Grace Awakening*.[2]

---

2. Charles Swindoll, *The Grace Awakening* (Dallas: Word Publishing, 1990).

Though I bought the book for my wife, Karen, I was the one who really needed it. Judging by the message I wrote to her on the inside cover, I didn't have a clue about what grace really was.

What's more, when I did get around to reading the book, I became convinced that Swindoll was seriously mistaken. What could possibly motivate God to offer to us anything not tied specifically to our performance? What good would that do? Where was the essential emphasis on the law that was in the forefront of my young faith? Where was obedience? And overcoming? And cooperation? I determined to prove Swindoll wrong. Certainly, I could make the point from Ellen White, I thought. But even the Bible was clear on the point, wasn't it? (What was that text in James?)

I began buying every book about grace I could find. In the Graduate Union Theological Seminary bookstore in Berkeley, at a time when my collection of grace books still numbered only a handful, I found a dozen new discussions about grace and left with an armload of books to pack into my small suitcase and carry home. But I found no anti-Swindoll ammunition there.

In the delightful mixture of new and used books in the never-disappointing Powell's Book Store in Portland, in the next-to-last row of the religion section, I stumbled across Paul Tournier's classic 1962 work, *Guilt and Grace.* There I discovered an intelligent and riveting discussion of the human "reflex of self-justification," which included the marvelous affirmation that "salvation is not an idea; it is a person."[3] I was perplexed but fascinated. My own grace awakening was under way.

In a musty corner of the Archives Bookshop on East Washington Street in Pasadena, I discovered an almost perfect edition of James Moffatt's *Grace in the New Testament,* published in London in 1931.[4] At the Willow Creek complex outside Chicago, in a Cokesbury bookstore in North Carolina, in a busy publisher's showroom in St. Louis, in the packed aisles of the gift shop beneath the National Cathedral in Washington, D.C., in the stacks in Blackwell's Booksellers in Oxford—wherever I traveled, I searched for more understanding and found one book after another, each one painting the picture of grace in slightly different detail.

Several years ago, someone gave me a gift certificate to one of our local Christian bookstores here in Riverside. On an early Friday afternoon, with the temperature soaring over one hundred degrees and a surprising summer rainstorm about to burst upon us, I drove past the Galleria and the Sportsmart and parked in a space I'd parked in scores of times before. I didn't really expect to find anything I didn't already own, but there in the middle of the Christian Living section was Max Lucado's insightful study on Romans, *In the Grip of Grace*—a typical Lucado treasure.[5] And with the gift certificate, it cost me only four dollars and thirty-six cents!

The titles have multiplied: *The Rest of Grace, The Discipline of Grace, The Parables of Grace, The Sovereignty of Grace, The Riddle of Grace, The Gospel of Grace, Radical Grace, Dangerous Grace, Responsible Grace, Future Grace, What's So Amazing About Grace?, Grace and Faith, Grace and Law, Grace and Truth* . . . You'll see references to all of them in the footnotes.

3. Paul Tournier, *Guilt and Grace* (New York: Harper & Row, 1962), 187.
4. James Moffatt, *Grace in the New Testament* (London: Hodder and Stoughton, 1931).
5. Max Lucado, *In the Grip of Grace* (Dallas: Word Publishing, 1996).

Here's what I concluded from all my study: I'd been wrong about grace. Wrong about Ellen White. Wrong about the Bible. Wrong about what I must do to be saved. Wrong about God.

## WHY KEEP TALKING ABOUT GRACE?

So why shouldn't I just tell you about all those grace books now perched on the walls of my study? With all the chapters already written, with all the articles in all the Christian journals, with all the musical messages about the glories of amazing grace, why try to produce one more sentence on the subject?

The answer is a bit complicated. And fully personal.

I certainly don't think I can be *the final word* on God's immense capacity to forgive and accept us. It seems clear to me that in worship services ten million years from today, the unnumbered host of the redeemed still will be singing praises to the Lamb who was slain from the foundation of the world and to the triumph of His grace (see Revelation 5:12 and 13:8). "In all that shining throng," Ellen White assures us, "there are none to ascribe salvation to themselves, as if they had prevailed by their own power and goodness. Nothing is said of what they have done or suffered; but the burden of every song, the keynote of every anthem, is: Salvation to our God and unto the Lamb."[6]

Nor do I think I can end the debate between those who insist that grace is unconditional and those who believe that faith is the work *we do* in a *process* of justification. I'm convinced that the Lord Himself finally will have to set our theology straight and that in the years of the first post–planet Earth millennium, He will delight in doing just that.

"Remember what you used to preach about grace?" He may very well ask me one day with a celestial twinkle in His eyes. "Well, let Me tell you how We define grace here in heaven." I can hardly wait for His definition!

The reason for this book has more to do with how this one Seventh-day Adventist Christian finally got the good news. In my almost sixty years now of growing up in the Adventist Church, I often have encountered—and at times adopted—certain attitudes about how we are saved, and why we are saved, and what part we play in the salvation dynamic. These feelings tended to make me wary of anyone's single-minded emphasis on what God does for us. I became afraid of grace, fearful that a Paulinelike concentration on grace would be detrimental to Adventism by somehow undermining our commitment to a lifestyle of obedience, to commandment keeping, and especially to the centrality in our experience of the seventh-day Sabbath.

So I struggled for more years than I like to admit *against* the biblical presentation of a free, unmerited, undeserved, unconditional grace. I relied upon James's version of how we are saved—by what we do, not by faith alone (James 2:24). I discounted Ellen White's graphic insistence that the robe of Christ's righteousness "has in it not one thread of human devising."[7] I listened most closely to those who appropriated prophetic power to focus on *our* role, *our* obedience, *our* overcoming, *our* perfecting of character, and *our* faith. Righteousness is *by the work of our faith,* I would have told you.

At a camp meeting during my seventh-grade year, I learned a song that I later sang in church after church. It went like this:

---

6. Ellen G. White, *The Great Controversy* (Mountain View, Calif.: Pacific Press®, 1950), 665.

7. White, *Christ's Object Lessons* (Washington, D.C.: Review and Herald, 1941), 311.

The theme of the Bible is Jesus and how
    He died to save men.
The plan of salvation assures us He's
    coming back again.
Are you ready for Jesus to come?
Are you faithful in all that you do?
Have you fought a good fight?
Have you stood for the right?
Have others seen Jesus in you?
Are you ready to stand in your place?
Are you ready to look in His face?
Can you look up and say, "This is my
    Lord"?
Are you ready for Jesus to come?

The more I sang the song to others, the worse I felt. I was trying my best to be a good Christian boy. But if "the theme of the Bible" and "the plan of salvation" really were about whether or not I was ready, I was pretty sure I wasn't! And the theme and the plan were incalculably discouraging—not at all good news. As with plenty of others who grew up in religious environments where the emphasis was on our readiness and faithfulness, our fighting and standing, two things were lacking in my Christian experience. One was victory. And the other was peace with God.

JESUS PAID IT ALL

One day, in an unsophisticated little Adventist church near Lake Tahoe, the words of a familiar hymn Elvina Hall wrote in 1865 absolutely arrested me:

Since nothing good have I,
Whereby Thy grace to claim,
I'll wash my garment white,
In the blood of Calvary's Lamb.
Jesus paid it all,
All to Him I owe;
Sin had left a crimson stain;
He washed it white as snow.

Unexpected tears streamed down my cheeks as I sang the chorus over and over again, finally listening to the words: "Jesus paid it *all*" the chorus insisted. That Sabbath morning, the gospel began to be an unassailable foundation for me—perhaps because so many authors were so passionate about it; perhaps because I never had needed the assurance of grace more; perhaps because I was tired of fighting unsuccessfully to overcome; perhaps because of the constant discouragement of a Christian experience that never felt good enough or ready enough, loved enough or accepted enough.

I'd like to believe, however, that I finally began to surrender to grace because that's exactly what the Holy Spirit intended for me—for all of us—to do. That's the point of the gospel, isn't it? *"Jesus* paid it all." That *is* the gospel (see Acts 20:24); "the gospel of [our] salvation" (Ephesians 1:13); the good news of God's grace reaching our stubborn hearts, winning our acceptance of our acceptance (Acts 15:8–11; Romans 15:7).[8]

---

8. In what has been called the most important sermon of the twentieth century, theologian Paul Tillich defined grace as "the acceptance of that which is rejected" and makes this impassioned plea: "Grace strikes us when we are in great pain and restlessness. It strikes us when we walk through the dark valley of a meaningless and empty life. It strikes us when we feel that our separation is deeper than usual. . . . It strikes us when our disgust for our own being, our indifference, our weakness, our hostility, and our lack of direction and composure have become intolerable to us. It strikes us when, year after year, the longed-for perfection of life does not appear, when the old compulsions reign within us as they have for decades, when despair destroys all joy and courage. Sometimes at that moment a wave of light breaks into our darkness, and it is as though a voice were saying: 'You are accepted. *You are accepted*, accepted by that which is greater than you, and the name of which you do not know. Do not ask for the name now; perhaps you will find it later. Do not try to do

No longer afraid

Of course, I'm still a long way from understanding all that grace means to us Christians. But what started in that little church and grew with every grace book I studied continues to grow. I love the way Anne Lamott confesses her growth in grace in her engaging little book *Traveling Mercies:* "I know more about grace," she says, "than I did two weeks ago."[9] We should expect and welcome growth throughout our lives. The genius Leonardo da Vinci remarked in his eighty-seventh year, *"Ancora imparo"* ("I am still learning").

I fully realize that a month from now and a year from now, I'll wish I had said something a little bit differently than I've said it here. But there's a powerful difference between my life now and my life before: I'm no longer *afraid* of grace. That's why I'm writing this book.

I want others in the church that I love—others who also grew up in the guilt-laden years when so many of us put ourselves, our achievements, and our obedience at the center of our faith, as well as others who are searching for that center today—to find the peace (Romans 5:1; John 14:27) and the confidence (Hebrews 4:16) that comes from the "abundant provision" of God's incredible saving grace (Romans 5:17). If that describes your experience, please keep reading. Don't be afraid to "set your hope fully" (1 Peter 1:13) on the "incomparable riches of [God's] grace, expressed in his kindness to us in Christ Jesus" (Ephesians 2:7), "who came from the Father, full of grace and truth" (John 1:14)

THE ONLY STREAM

(Jill encounters the Lion, Aslan, C. S. Lewis's Christ figure in *The Chronicles of Narnia*.)

"Are you not thirsty?" said the Lion.
"I'm *dying* of thirst," said Jill.
"Then drink," said the Lion.
"May I—could I—would you mind going away while I do?" said Jill.
The Lion answered this only by a look and a very low growl. And as Jill gazed at its motionless bulk, she realized that she might as well have asked the whole mountain to move aside for her convenience.
The delicious rippling noise of the stream was driving her nearly frantic.
"Will you promise not to—do anything to me, if I do come?" said Jill.
"I make no promise," said the Lion.
Jill was so thirsty now that, without noticing it, she had come a step nearer. . . .
"I dare not come and drink," said Jill.
"Then you will die of thirst," said the Lion.
"Oh dear!" said Jill, coming another step nearer. "I suppose I must go and look for another stream then."
"There is no other stream," said the Lion.
—C. S. Lewis, *The Silver Chair*, pages 16, 17.

and "through whom we have gained access by faith into this grace in which we now stand" (Romans 5:2).

anything now; perhaps later you will do much. Do not seek for anything; do not perform anything; do not intend anything. *Simply accept the fact that you are accepted!'* If that happens to us, we experience grace. After such an experience we may not be better than before, and we may not believe more than before. But everything is transformed. In that moment, grace conquers sin, and reconciliation bridges the gulf of estrangement." —Paul Tillich, "Accepted," in *The Shaking of the Foundations* (London: SCM Press Ltd, 1949), 161, 162.

9. Anne Lamott, *Traveling Mercies: Some Thoughts on Faith* (New York: Pantheon Books, 1999), 138.

# GRACE IN QUESTION

## CHAPTER 1: THE CRIMSON STAIN

The experience of grace is intensely personal. Each of us encounters grace at a different time in our lives, under different circumstances, with different emphases. Here in this chapter is another one of those stories, not a dramatic one, but one that produced a dramatically altered perspective on the Christian experience.

1. Watchman Nee says, "There is absolutely no danger of saying too much about the grace of God." Why is this statement true for you?

2. If "most theology is essentially autobiography," what has been the effect on your theology? Discuss the role your parents played in the development of your theology. Did they teach primarily with their words or with their actions? Who else made significant contributions to how you think about God? Are there aspects of your theology that you feel you should change to make it more biblical?

3. How did your "grace awakening" take place? Can you think of a time when the winning, unquenchable, crimson-stain-removing love of Jesus began to break through in your life?

4. Find a hymnal and sing together all the stanzas of "Jesus Paid It All."

5. Use the sidebar "The Only Stream" from *The Silver Chair* (see page 33) as a script for a short skit. You'll need a narrator, someone to play the Lion, and someone to play Jill. Have Jill read her part with a mixture of fear, respect, and longing. Be sure the Lion is firm and strong, yet kind rather than angry or rough. Remember, the Lion, Aslan, is Lewis's Jesus character. What do you think the stream represents? What does it mean to come and drink?

# GRACE NOTES
## GENESIS 32— THE DANCE OF MAHANAIM

Esau was angry with Jacob again. And with reason. Again. (See Genesis 27:45.)

After mother's favorite son (Genesis 25:28) had manipulated Esau into giving up his birthright (verse 33); after he had stolen Esau's blessing (27:35); after all the lying and deceit, Esau's grudge was so bitter, so deeply founded, that he began to make plans *to kill* his brother (verses 34, 41).

Q. How does Jacob's early life illustrate those who center their faith in their own experience?

Mother steps in again and gets Jacob out of harm's way by sending him to Uncle Laban (verse 43). Jacob runs out of the house, heads north (28:10), and keeps running until he gets all the way to the place we know as Bethel (verse 19). Shortly after sunset, Jacob lies down on the ground, props his head on a rock, and goes to sleep (verse 11). In the middle of the night, Jacob dreams about God. Surely God was as angry with Jacob as Esau was. The characteristics of God's government—as well as His expectations for His children—include fairness and courage and honesty. So, how will He treat a manipulative, cowardly deceiver? Listen to His words: " 'I am the LORD. . . . *I will give you* and your descendants the land on which you are lying. . . . *I am with you and will watch over you* wherever you go, and *I will bring you back* to this land. *I will not leave you* until *I have done* what *I have promised* you' " (verses 13, 15, emphasis supplied).

Q. What difference does it make if we wrestle with God from the inside or the outside?

Don't worry about Jacob. God's amazing grace will turn him around, right? Initially, the prevaricator reacts in awe: " 'Surely the LORD is in this place, . . . this is the gate of heaven' " (verses 16, 17).

Then Jacob thinks about it—and retreats. Rather than take God's promise at face value, Jacob's grasping overwhelms his trust. He thinks of a bargain he can strike with God. Basically, it goes like this: *If* God will be with me, *if* He will watch over me, *if* He gives me food to eat and clothes to wear, and *if* I return safely to my father's house, *then* the Lord will be my God (see verses 20, 21).

Twenty years pass. Jacob takes two wives, Leah and Rachel, and two concubines, Bilhah and Zilpah, becomes the father of eleven boys and a girl, and becomes a wealthy shepherd. And along the way, his harsh, ingrained works-orientation deepens.

His treatment of Leah is nothing less than abominable. After Reuben's birth, Leah pines, " 'Surely my husband will love me now' " (29:32). Two births later, she says, " 'Now at last my husband will become attached to me' " (verse 34). After the birth of her sixth son, she wishes out loud, " 'This time my husband will treat me with honor' " (30:20).

When Jacob quarrels with Laban, he acts in concert with this works-based approach to living and reveals the list he's been keeping of his own good works and of Laban's failures: " 'I have been with you for twenty years now. Your sheep and goats have not miscarried, nor have I eaten rams from your flocks. I did not bring you animals torn by wild beasts; I bore the loss myself. And you demanded payment from me for whatever was stolen by day or night. This was my situation: The heat consumed me in the daytime and the cold at night, and sleep fled from my eyes. It was like this for the twenty years I was in your household. I worked for you fourteen years for your two daughters and six years for your flocks, and you changed my wages ten times' " (31:38–41).

But still God pursues Jacob, treating him just as if he had never sinned. God speaks to Jacob and invites him back to the homeland (verse 3). God speaks to Laban (verse 24), and he responds by giving Jacob his blessing instead of his insults (verse 49).

The next morning, Jacob suddenly is full of self-doubt. News of Esau's approach with four hundred men fills him with "great fear and distress" (32:7). He makes defensive moves, dividing his family and flocks into two groups, hoping that one group might escape if Esau attacks (verse 8). Then he prays: " 'O God of my father Abraham, God of my father Isaac, O LORD, who said to me, "Go back to your country and your relatives, and I will make you prosper," I am unworthy of all the kindness and faithfulness you have shown your servant. I had only my staff when I crossed this Jordan, but now I have become two groups. Save me, I pray, from the hand of my brother Esau, for I am afraid' " (verses 9–11).

"Unworthy." "Afraid." Humble. Mindful of God's promises. Trusting. This is a different man, vulnerable and open. There are no conditions now. Just "save me, I pray."

Jacob called the place where he prayed *Mahanaim* (verses 1, 2). He caught a glimpse of two camps of angels there, guarding, protecting, welcoming. He recognized the angels from his experience twenty years earlier, from the place he called Bethel, *"the gate* of heaven." Now, spiritually, he moves *through the gate* into "the camp of God." From *inside* the camp he prays. From *inside* he makes plans. From *inside* he wrestles with God. From *inside* he approaches Esau and asks for his forgiveness.

" 'God has been gracious to me,' " the once grasping Jacob confesses. " 'I have all I need' " (33:11).

Finally, Jacob says yes to God's grace. The dance of Mahanaim begins (see Song of Solomon 6:13).

The ancient Egyptian god Anubis guides a deceased person into the Broad Hall of the Two Justices to stand before Osiris in the judgment scene known as the Weighing of the Heart. The Egyptians believed that in this ceremony they were examined for worthiness to enter the afterlife (see chapter 3, pages 54 and 55).

*"There always seemed to be a need for reckoning.*
*What came in equaled what went out*
*like oscillating ocean waves. All things had to balance out."*
—JIMMY CARTER, *ALWAYS A RECKONING*


*"Nothing comes from nothing, nothing ever could,*
*so, somewhere in my youth, or childhood,*
*I must have done something good."*
—MARIA AND CAPTAIN VON TRAPP IN *THE SOUND OF MUSIC*


*"What act of goodness did we as humans once commit*
*to deserve such kindness from God?"*
—DOUGLAS COUPLAND, *LIFE AFTER GOD*


*"Good enough never is."*
—DEBBIE FIELDS


*"Christ came to introduce a break with logic*
*that made all other outrage seem as child's play."*
—ROBERT FROST, "A MASQUE OF MERCY"

## CHAPTER 2
# THE AIR WE BREATHE:
### *The Centrality of Grace in the Doctrines of Christianity*

S EVEN HUNDRED YEARS AGO, IN THE VOLCANIC EUGANEAN HILLS OF NORTH-
ERN Italy, a guilt-stricken nobleman approaches God with a proposition.[1]
Moved by a frightening vision of the last judgment, Enrico degli Scrovegni
of Padua bargains for his soul with the King of kings.

In exchange for his own salvation and the redemption of his late father,[2] Enrico
promises to build a beautiful little chapel on the land he had purchased for the construction of his private palace.[3] When the promise is completed six years later in 1306,
the single-nave church is decorated with glorious frescoes that will change the course
of European art. But more importantly, the little votive chapel in Padua had become a
stunning reminder of the absolute incongruity between the everlasting gospel of God's
saving grace and any attempt to earn eternal salvation through human effort.

Scrovegni used his abundant wealth to secure the services of the brilliant young
Florentine painter Giotto di Bondone. In his first mature masterpiece, Giotto adorns
the chapel walls with scenes from the life of Jesus. The revolutionary frescoes break
the stranglehold of the sterile, flat Byzantine conventions of medieval painting and
introduce life, weight, personality, and most of all, emotion to the world of art.

For me, one scene is more striking than all the others. In the middle of the north
wall, just above eye level, is Giotto's bold depiction of the Lamentation. The lifeless
body of Jesus has been removed from the cross and now is sprawled on the ground
in the foreground of the scene. Intense emotional pain is etched deeply on the face
of Mary as she cradles the cold body of her precious Son. To the right, a distraught
Mary Magdalene stares at the feet she so recently bathed with her tears and dried
with her long hair. John, the beloved disciple, throws his arms backward in a violent
gesture of heart-rending grief. Joseph of Arimathea and Nicodemus stand in voice-
less agony at the horror of the scene before them. Above them all, ten small cherubs

---

1. Portions of this chapter originally appeared in "Are We Afraid of the Gospel?" *Ministry,* December
1999, 5–7.

2. Enrico's father, the wealthy Reginaldo, had been placed in hell in Dante's *Inferno* for usury.

3. Because the land included the ruins of an ancient Roman amphitheater known locally as the Arena,
the Capella degli Scrovegni came to be referred to as the "Arena Chapel."

## THE CULTURE OF ACHIEVEMENT

No pain, no gain,
    it's all in a day's work,
    just do it,
    roll up your sleeves,
    work your fingers to the bone,
    keep your nose to the grindstone,
    gain the upper hand,
    don't let the grass grow under your feet,
    pull yourself up by your bootstraps,
    buckle down by the sweat of your brow,
    and work like a dog.
Remember that actions speak louder than
    words,
    give a good account of yourself
    (what did I do to deserve this?),
    work your way up the ladder,
    come out on top,
    and if at first you don't succeed, try, try
    again.
Fish or cut bait,
    make hay while the sun shines,
    leave no stone unturned,
    burn the midnight oil,
    it's the early bird that catches the worm,
    don't lie down on the job,
    don't sleep at your post,
    bring home the bacon,
    you can't have your cake and eat it too.
So, be on your best behavior,
    practice makes perfect,
    practice what you preach,
    welcome to the working class,
    welcome to the rat race—
God helps those who help themselves.

are brutally arrested in flight by the unbearable sorrow of the death of their Friend, Jesus.

I am overwhelmed by this passionate work of art. From across the centuries it speaks to me with a clarity I am unable to avoid. Here is dramatic and convincing evidence of the unquenchable love of God *for me* (Romans 5:8). Here is the Lamb slain from the foundation of the world *for my sin* (Revelation 13:8). Here is Jesus suffering at the hands of His enemies "so that by the grace of God he might taste death" *in my behalf* (Hebrews 2:9). Here is the clearest possible revelation of the unsearchable, incomparable riches of God's grace paying the penalty of *my sin* and purchasing *my redemption* (Ephesians 3:8; 2:7; 1:7). Here is what the ministry of Ellen White points us to over and over and over again: "The sacrifice of Christ as an atonement for sin"—which, she insists, "is the great truth around which all other truths cluster,"[4] the "ground of our steadfastness,"[5] and "the foundation of the Christian's hope."[6]

However, remember the setting. Giotto's powerful masterpiece is even more extraordinary because it shouts the gospel from the walls of a church built *to purchase God's favor.* Giotto shows the red-haired young man kneeling in front of Jesus, the Judge, holding up a model of his little chapel to try to influence a favorable sentence. The irony is so rich. Triumphant grace trampling on self-justification. Abounding grace vanquishing salvation by works. The fullness of the gospel exposing the futility of "co-redemption"—of all attempts to add to the *finished* work of Jesus on the cross.[7]

---

4. Ellen G. White, *Gospel Workers* (Washington, D.C.: Review and Herald, 1948), 315.

5. White, *Testimonies for the Church* (Mountain View, Calif.: Pacific Press®, 1948), 1:438.

6. White, *The Great Controversy* (Mountain View, Calif.: Pacific Press®, 1950; revised edition first published 1911), 256.

7. "Any form of co-redemption destroys grace and annuls gratitude." (Patricia A. Forseth, "Hosea, Gomer, and Elective Grace," *The Reformed Journal,* Nov. 19, 1985, 15–18.) "Self-salvation" is Paul Tillich's phrase for the same flawed endeavor; see his *Systematic Theology* (Chicago: University of Chicago Press, 1957), 2:80–86.

Nevertheless, in the culture of achievement in which we live, my natural reflexes and trained sensibilities persistently resist the good news of grace. The Scrovegni impulse rages in my life. Frequently, like Enrico, I approach God with my hands full of something of my own to use in the bargaining. I present my orthodoxy, my service record, my busy schedule, my latest, best sermon. I am so capable of interposing myself into the transaction: my commitment, my obedience, my high standards, my genuine sorrow for personal failures, my repentance—even my growing faith in God's uncompromising grace.[8]

Paul Tournier, the Swiss physician and counselor, calls this need to bargain with God the "reflex of self-justification."[9] Theologian J. I. Packer refers to it as "the faith that has animated pagan religion ever since there was such a thing—namely, the belief that we can repair our own relationship with God by putting God in a position where he cannot say no to us."[10]

C. S. Lewis observes the same temptation in his life, and, as usual, precisely unmasks the tempter: "Thus, depth beneath depth and subtlety within subtlety, there remains some lingering idea of our own, our very own, attractiveness. It is easy to acknowledge, but almost impossible to realize for long, that we are mirrors whose brightness, if we are bright, is wholly derived from the sun that shines upon us. Surely we must have a little—however little—native luminosity." Then Lewis identifies the remedy: "For this tangled absurdity of a Need, which never fully acknowledges its own neediness, Grace substitutes a full, childlike and delighted acceptance of our Need, a joy in total dependence."[11]

RUNNING AWAY FROM THE GOSPEL

Total dependence is a tough assignment. Obviously, Scrovegni wasn't the first or the last to be overwhelmed by the desire to contribute *something* to the salvation equation. The impulse to try to change God's mind is as ancient as Cain, as persistent as Sarah's laughter, as quick as Moses' grasping credit for bringing water from a rock. Our words betray us. "Make me like one of Your hired servants," we insist, speaking the language of merit so stubbornly that we miss the warmth of our Father's welcoming embrace, the significance of the robe and ring of acceptance, the joy of the opening moments of a resurrection celebration (Luke 15:17–24). It's almost as if we were running away from the gospel, as if we were afraid of grace, not wanting to be *that* rich, *that* forgiven, *that* assured.

We publish our cautions far and wide. "If grace becomes the central focus of our experience," a pastor admonished me with disquieting fear, "the Sabbath may lose its importance in our understanding of the end of the world." Doesn't an emphasis on justification by grace through faith lead to "a neglect of holiness and the fruits of the indwelling Spirit?"[12] Don't we need to be careful to maintain "a balance between God's

---

8. One Adventist minister insisted in print that "faith is a work" and that our obedience was "the condition for reception of God's mercy." ("Salvation: The Great Condition," *Our Firm Foundation,* May 1995.) Such a position directly contradicts Paul's argument in Romans 4:16 ("The promise comes by faith so that it may be by grace.") as well as Ellen White's understanding that "faith is not our savior. It earns nothing." (*The Desire of Ages* [Mountain View, Calif.: Pacific Press®, 1940], 175.)

9. Paul Tournier, *Grace and Guilt* (New York: Harper & Row, 1962), 142.

10. J. I. Packer, *Great Grace* (Ann Arbor, Mich.: Vine Books, 1997), 19.

11. C. S. Lewis, *The Four Loves* (New York: Harcourt Brace Jovanovich, 1960), 180.

12. James M. Hopps, "Needed: Balance in Theology," *Ministry,* February 1999, 16.

## PERFORMANCE-ORIENTED RELIGION

"In an era of performance-oriented religion, the rediscovery of grace presents a profoundly subtle challenge. Teaching a religionist grace is like teaching a workaholic to relax." —Thomas C. Oden, *The Transforming Power of Grace* (Nashville, Tenn.: Abingdon Press, 1993), 17.

"Godlessness appears as the will to live without God, to ignore Him, to be one's own source and beginning, to live without being indebted and forgiven, to be independent and secure in one's self, to be godlike in oneself. . . .

"It appears in the complacency of self-righteously moral and of self-authenticatedly rational men, but also in the despair of those for whom all is vanity. It manifests itself in irreligion, in atheism and antitheism; but also in the piety of those who consciously carry God around with them wherever they go. It issues in desperate acts of passion, by which men assert themselves against the social law with its claims to divine sanction; but also in the zealous obedience of the law-abiding, who desperately need the assurance that they are superior to the lesser breeds without the law.

"Thwarted in its efforts to found divine, enduring empires, the desire to be independent of God's grace expresses itself in attempts to establish godlike churches that have stored up all necessary truth and grace in doctrines and sacraments." —H. Richard Niebuhr, *Christ and Culture* (New York: Harper & Row, 1951), 155.

mercy and His justice?" Isn't the pendulum swinging "too far away from legalism toward grace?" Aren't those who preach grace "cheapening" Christianity just so they can fill their pews in these "member-competitive times"?[13] Don't we "nullify the law by this faith" (Romans 3:31)?

It is important to address these concerns and put them to rest. But in the process, we must never allow our focus to shift from Jesus onto *anything else.* In our sincere efforts to respond to God's call to be peculiar, distinctive people, we must not rush past the core definition of our existence or push it into the periphery of our experience. "When all the shouting dies away, when all the issues are laid on the table, when all the doctrines have been discussed, when all the policies have been voted, the only thing that matters is Jesus and our relationship with Him."[14] Whenever we stray from our foundation in the everlasting gospel and make any other ground our central position, we come perilously close to missing completely the point of *the truth as it is in Jesus.*[15]

Not long ago a theologian publicly reminded me that Adventists have been called to be a people of the end time. "It is not grace, but our eschatology that makes us unique," the gentleman instructed, "and what does grace have to do with the Second Coming?" I was so shocked by his question that for a moment I couldn't speak. Tears rose to my eyes. Beyond the obvious answer that grace has *everything* to do with our salvation, even his question was wrong. It would have been much more accurate and in-

---

13. Reo M. Christenson, "Salvation: Faith versus Works," *Ministry,* February 1999, 28.

14. David Newman, "Farewell," *Ministry,* September 1995.

15. To use Ellen White's lovely phrase, which she repeats frequently, as in *Gospel Workers,* page 154, and to which she often adds such admonitions as: "No discourse should ever be preached without presenting Christ and Him crucified as the foundation of the gospel." (Ibid., 158.) "Let the science of salvation be the burden of every sermon, the theme of every song. Let it be poured forth in every supplication. Bring nothing into your preaching to supplement Christ." (Ibid., 160.) "The atonement of Christ should be the great substance, the central truth." (MS 156, 1898; quoted in *Evangelism* [Washington, D.C.: Review and Herald, 1946], 223.)

finitely more Adventist to ask, "What does the Second Coming have to do with grace?"[16]

## SALVATION BY GRACE ALONE

The doctrine of salvation by grace begins with God's realistic evaluation of humanity's complete inability to earn eternal life by works or deeds, by obedience or service—even religious service, by trying to conform perfectly to His will. With His heart full of pain, God concludes that "every inclination" of the young human race was "only evil all the time" (Genesis 6:5, 6). Over the next several thousand years the conclusion would remain the same. "There is no one who does good, not even one," David observes in Psalm 14:3. Paul repeats David's observation and then goes on to describe fallen humanity in the bleakest of terms: "worthless," "vipers," "powerless," "ungodly," "God's enemies," "dead in transgressions," "disobedient," "by nature objects of God's wrath" (Romans 3:10–23, 5:6–10; Ephesians 2:1–3).

Paul is not talking about "them," he's speaking of you and me. And he's not talking about good things like volunteering to go on a mission trip or helping a little old lady cross the street or taking out the trash without being asked. He's referring to being good enough to *merit* eternal life. The stark conclusion of the Bible is unmistakable: *None of us* can earn or merit salvation. It is *impossible*. (See Matthew 19:26.) *Nothing* we can do will change the situation. *"No one* will be declared righteous in [God's] sight by observing the law" (Romans 3:20, emphasis supplied). "By observing the

---

### OPEN-HEART SURGERY

Suppose you need open-heart surgery and don't have a dime to your name. A wealthy friend learns of your plight and takes care of all the expenses. He makes it clear that there are no strings attached; he just wants to see you alive and well.

How would he feel if you sent him twenty dollars as "your part of the cost"? Would he appreciate it? Not likely. This paltry sum is nothing compared to the magnitude of his gift, and your sending it would only indicate that you don't understand the value of what he did for you. Only one response is appropriate: sheer gratitude. Any effort on your part to defray the expense would only insult the giver.

For Paul, salvation is entirely the gift of God; there is nothing about us that deserves it. The only appropriate response is to accept it with a full and grateful heart.
—Richard Rice, *The Reign of God* (Berrien Springs, Mich.: Andrews University Press, 1985), 240, 241.

---

law *no one* will be justified" (Galatians 2:16, emphasis supplied).

The Adventist Church fully accepts the consistent biblical testimony that humans cannot contribute to their own salvation. "We profoundly believe that no works of the law, no deeds of the law, no effort however commendable, and no good works—whether they be many or few, sacrificial or not—can in any way justify the sinner."[17] "We can contribute

---

16. Perhaps, like Enoch, who learned from Adam "the dark story of the Fall, and the cheering one of God's grace," (White, *Patriarchs and Prophets* [Mountain View, Calif.: Pacific Press®, 1958], 84, 86, 87), we need periodically to withdraw from the demands of our culture of achievement in order to renew our souls with the refreshment of the grace of Christ, which is "like a spring in the desert, welling up to refresh all, and making those who are ready to perish eager to drink of the water of life." (White, *The Faith I Live By* [Washington, D.C.: Review and Herald, 1958], 99.)

17. *Questions On Doctrine* (Washington, D.C.: Review and Herald, 1957), 142.

nothing to Christ's gift of righteousness."[18] "It was possible for Adam, before the fall, to form a righteous character by obedience to God's law. But he failed to do this, and because of his sin, our natures are fallen, and we cannot make ourselves righteous. Since we are sinful, unholy, we cannot perfectly obey the holy law. We have no righteousness of our own with which to meet the claims of the law of God."[19]

Thankfully, the doctrine doesn't end there!

Since time on earth began, the message of the "grace of God that brings salvation" has been given to us to provide the motivating "hope of eternal life" (Titus 2:11; 3:7). From the tree of life in the center of the Garden of Eden to the dry ground in the middle of the Jordan River, from the jubilant worship in Solomon's temple to the quiet reflections in Paul's prison cell, the "precious truth"[20] has been set before us. The good news of God's grace (Acts 20:24) is the theme into which the prophets "searched intently and with the greatest care" (1 Peter 1:10) and was the favorite subject of Christ's teaching here on earth.[21] "So surely as there never was a time when God was not, so surely there never was a moment when it was not the delight of the eternal mind to manifest His grace to humanity."[22]

Here is the matchless truth, expressed in one book of the Bible, but with an abundance of creative pictures: God has put all our sins behind His back (Isaiah 38:17). He has graven us on the palms of His hands (49:16). He has clothed us with garments of salvation (61:10). Our sin is atoned for (6:7). We are ransomed (35:10). Healed (53:5). Chosen (49:7). Redeemed (63:9). Forgiven (33:24).

"Christ has made a way of escape for us. He lived on earth amid trials and temptations such as we have to meet. He lived a sinless life. He died for us, and now He offers to take our sins and *give us* His righteousness. If you give yourself *to Him,* accept *Him* as your Saviour, then, sinful as your life may have been, for *His sake* you are accounted righteous. Christ's character stands in place of your character, and you are accepted before God just as if you had not sinned."[23]

This is the gospel of our salvation (Ephesians 1:13), the Bible truth about how we are saved—by grace *alone,* through faith *alone,* in Jesus Christ *alone.* There are no exceptions. "We are saved by grace through faith in the Saviour's merits, or we are not saved at all."[24]

THE AIR WE BREATHE

Grace is the divine acceptance that seeks and saves sinful human beings, doing for us that which we are powerless to do for ourselves. "Grace is not earned," Dr. Gerald May reminds us, "not accomplished or achieved. It is not extracted through manipulation or seduction. It is just given."[25]

---

18. *Seventh-day Adventists Believe* . . . 2nd ed. (Silver Spring, Md.: General Conference Ministerial Association, 2005), 146.

19. White, *Steps to Christ* (Mountain View, Calif.: Pacific Press®, 1956), 62.

20. White, *Selected Messages* (Washington, D.C.: Review and Herald, 1958), 1:384.

21. "Christ's favorite theme was the paternal tenderness and abundant grace of God."(*Christ's Object Lessons* [Washington, D.C.: Review and Herald, 1941], 40.)

22. White, *Signs of the Times,* June 12, 1901.

23. White, *Steps to Christ,* 62, emphasis supplied.

24. Helmut Ott, "Another Look at Valuegenesis," *Ministry,* February 1994, 20.

25. Gerald G. May, *Addiction & Grace* (San Francisco: HarperCollins, 1988), 126, 127.

Grace is not merely one of the fundamental doctrines of a denomination. It is "the great truth around which all other truths cluster;"[26] "the one great central truth to be kept ever before the mind in searching the Scriptures."[27] Grace is "the absolute truth by which the church stands or falls. It is this truth that makes Christianity Christian and the church really the church, preserving it from idolatry, preventing its secularization, providing the charter of its career, and offering believers a solid basis and direction for their daily life."[28]

We must not write off grace as just somebody's new idea or the current theological darling of west coast liberals. Grace is "the *everlasting* gospel" that God has commissioned *all of us* to take to every nation, tribe, language, and people (Revelation 14:6, NKJV, emphasis supplied). "The substance and the essence of the true gospel are the doctrine of God's grace. If you take away the grace of God from the gospel, you have extracted from it its very lifeblood, and there is nothing left worth preaching, worth believing, worth contending for. Grace is the soul and the music of the gospel; without it, the gospel is silent."[29]

Grace is not the beginning point of the Christian journey; it is the road upon which journeying Christians walk day by day, moment by moment. Grace is not a robe Christians put on in order to be correctly dressed; it is the air Christians breathe in order to live.

26. White, *Gospel Workers,* 315.
27. White, MS 31, 1890.
28. Carl E. Braaten, *Justification* (Minneapolis: Fortress Press, 1990), 82.
29. Charles Spurgeon, *Grace Abounding in a Believer's Life* (Lynnwood, Wash.: Emerald Books, 1994), 99.

# GRACE IN QUESTION

## CHAPTER 2: THE AIR WE BREATHE

Chapter two presents the doctrine of salvation by grace alone as the everlasting gospel, the fundamental truth of Christianity, the central doctrine of the church. It defines grace as an essential, life-sustaining, hope-producing dynamic in the experience of growing Christians.

1. Watch the scene in the 1965 movie *The Sound of Music* in which Maria and Captain von Trapp are singing to each other in the gazebo. Pretty romantic stuff, right?—even today! While the romance is strong, however, what do you think of the theology in the words? How does "somewhere in my youth or childhood, I must have done something good" get us into trouble, theologically speaking?

2. Carefully examine Giotto's "Lamentation" (on page 25). Notice the emotion on the faces and in the posture of each of the characters. With which person in this great piece of art do you identify?

3. Read the sidebar "The Culture of Achievement" (page 40) around your circle, each person taking just one line, until the last line ("God helps those who help themselves"), which all of you should read together. Start out reading slowly, but try to read each line a little faster than the previous line, until, by the end of the passage, you're flying through the phrases. Discuss how these American truisms get into our theology.

4. In the third paragraph on page 44 are nine pictures from the book of Isaiah about how God saves us. Which picture do you like best? What picture would you like to add?

5. Think of the Bible doctrines you hold dear. How does each of those doctrines depend upon the "one great truth" of grace?

# GRACE NOTES
## 2 SAMUEL 14—THE WISE WOMAN OF TEKOA

In the story of King David's reign over the united kingdom (2 Samuel 5:1–5; 1 Chronicles 12:38) appears a remarkable woman we know only as the wise woman of Tekoa. Joab, David's nephew, the son of David's sister Zeruiah and the commander-in-chief of David's army (1 Chronicles 2:16; 2 Samuel 20:23), summons this woman to Jerusalem. Joab has conceived a plan to alleviate David's depression, which has overpowered the king ever since his third son, Absalom, murdered his eldest son, Amnon. David has banished Absalom, who now has been away for three years (2 Samuel 13:38, 39).

Joab's idea is to improvise a situation similar to David's that would draw out David's wisdom and help him see how beneficial it would be to bring Absalom back home and end the estrangement. So, Joab finds this wise woman in the little village of Tekoa and asks her to play the part that will awaken David's compassion.

In a secret meeting, Joab counsels, " 'Pretend you are in mourning' " (2 Samuel 14:2). Pretend you are a widow who had two sons. Pretend that one day the boys were out in a field and got into a fight. One of the brothers struck the other, accidentally killing him, and then ran home to your house. Now the entire clan has determined that revenge demands the death of the remaining son (verses 5–7). Joab has the entire story figured out, and he "put the words in her mouth" (verse 3).

So, the wise woman of Tekoa goes to the king, as any citizen of the realm has the right to do. When it is her turn to bring her request to David, she tells the story just the way Joab told her to. " 'They would put out the only burning coal I have left,' " she concludes, a bit dramatically, " 'leaving my husband neither name nor descendant on the face of the earth' " (verse 7).

The throne room of the kingdom is packed, and the people there have heard the whole story. They turn to watch David deliberate. Now the drama becomes really interesting. We have the transcript of the entire conversation in 2 Samuel 14; there's nothing else like it in the entire Bible.

David sympathizes with the woman and makes a quick executive decision, announcing his decision and then dismissing the woman: " 'Go home, and I will issue an order in your behalf' " (verse 8). I've heard your case. I think the boy should live. I'll write up the necessary order and send it to your village. Now you can go home.

David has taken in the entire situation, realized immediately what should be done, and reacted in fairness. He's only missed one thing—he has no clue that the made-up story is really about him and his son Absalom. That part goes right over his head.

Q. What contributions do Old Testament stories make to the definition of grace?

Q. What does the following Old Testament gospel story reveal to us about the plan of salvation?

The woman from Tekoa realizes that Joab's great idea hasn't worked at all. She knows she has to buy a little more time to let the connection sink in.

" 'My lord the king,' " she starts in again, surprising the people in the room by speaking after she has been dismissed, " 'let the blame rest on me and on my father's family' " (verse 9). In other words, if anyone gets mad at you for your decision, you can blame me. It's really not your fault.

David replies politely, " 'If anyone says anything to you, bring him to me, and he will not bother you again' " (verse 10). I'm still the king. I know what I'm doing. Don't worry about it. Now you can leave. (There's still no recognition of what this is all about.)

The woman speaks again, doubling her demerits for speaking after the king has moved on. Would you mind making this a *spiritual* issue and not just a *civil* one? she asks. Would you invoke the name of God to show my relatives how serious you really are? (See verse 11.)

You can almost hear David's impatience in his restrained answer. " 'As surely as the LORD lives,' " David says, granting the woman's request for a spiritual dimension to the decision, " 'not one hair of your son's head will fall to the ground' " (verse 11).

Now David has dismissed her the third time, but still he hasn't figured it out. She must press on. "May I say one more thing to my lord the king?" the woman requests.

"Speak!" David thunders (see verse 12). As if he could do anything to stop her!

The woman can stifle the object lesson no longer. With everyone in the room leaning forward to catch every word and David now standing in exasperation, the woman goes directly to the point David's been missing all this time. " 'Why then have you devised a thing like this against the people of God?' " she accuses, comparing David to the pretend clan members who want to execute her remaining son. " 'When the king says this, does he not convict himself, for the king has not brought back his banished son?' " (verse 13).

The onlookers would have gasped except they all were holding their breath already. David glares at the woman. She stares back at the king.

Then the woman continues—and what she says now is the most amazing part of the story. Here, in the middle of the Old Testament, the wise woman of Tekoa reveals a mature understanding of the gospel that few in her time can equal. In spite of what others believe about God, this woman knows His grace. She knows the length to which God will go in His pursuit of guilty sinners. She knows that God's kindness leads us to repentance (Romans 2:4). So, she says God does not take away life. Instead, He devises ways so that banished people may not remain estranged from Him (2 Samuel 14:14).

There is absolute silence in the room. The woman ventures a few more words of explanation. Then David steps toward her. "Now I'm going to ask you a question," he says, "and I want you to be completely honest with me when you answer." (See verse 18.)

"Whatever you say," the woman wisely responds.

"Do I detect the hand of Joab in all this?"

Everyone in the room turns to find Joab, and there he is, way over there against the wall, looking every way except forward, trying his best to be inconspicuous.

" 'My lord has wisdom like that of an angel of God,' " the woman answers (verse 20).

Joab comes forward sheepishly, kneels before his king, and waits for the retribution to fall. David focuses his gaze on his nephew, pauses for a few moments, and then says, "Thank you, my friend. You're right. Go and bring back the young man Absalom" (see verse 21).

This is a story about human beings, so it isn't perfect. Some time must still pass for the reconciliation to take place. But at the end of the chapter we find a gospel moment. Absalom at last appears in his father's throne room. He kneels before David and bows low. "And the king kissed Absalom" (verse 33). The estrangement of the banished person has ended. Grace wins again.

"Even if you have been banished to the most distant land under the heavens, from there the LORD your God will gather you and bring you back" (Deuteronomy 30:4).

*"The story seems to me to be about the breakdown of justice and rationality and the triumph of grace."*

—Mary Gordon, *Genesis: A Living Conversation*

*"In the ancient world at large it would have been typical to believe that the deity was inattentive because he or she had been offended."*

—*The IVP Bible Background Commentary, Old Testament*

*"It would be a mistake to ignore the relation of the church to the Jewish thought out of which it came and to the pagan thought which it sought to correct."*

—Jaroslav Pelikan, *The Christian Tradition*

*"A procession of Canaanite priests and fivescore Canaanite pilgrims approached to consult the oracular tree . . ."*

—Naomi H. Rosenblatt, *Wrestling With Angels*

*"From fruit-eating to fratricide to wholesale vengeance, the world of God was on a slippery slope to disaster."*

—Michael Williams, *The Storyteller's Companion to the Bible*

# CHAPTER 3
# THE RESTLESS TREASON:
## *The Scarcity of Grace in the Myths of Antiquity*

As LONG AS THERE HAVE BEEN human beings on the earth, there has been *religion*.

Religion is from our perspective. It is a human attempt to make some sense of what happens in this world, to bridge the chasm between the experienced and the unknown, to forge some sort of relationship with whatever force or being or god exists out there. Religion seeks to answer questions such as these: Can I talk to the god? Can I expect any communication in return? Is there a way to please it, make it happy, honor it, do its bidding? What if I make it angry? What if it becomes impatient, short-tempered, or mean-spirited? What if it accepts me at first but then raises its expectations of me?

And what happens when this existence is over? After the fire burns up or the earth closes over or the wild animals drag away, what then? Is there an afterlife? Who or what are the inhabitants? Can I prepare for whatever it is? Can I influence what happens to me? Can I barter with or bribe the ruler of the realm? Will I be welcomed or turned away?

### Can I Please It? Make It Happy?

"He's watching you (He just does!) and He's keeping track. If you're wanting Him to be there for you, 'to give you the gift of salvation,' like they tell you in church, then it's up to you to be deserving of it. He's not up there handing out goodies!" —Twelve-year-old Matt, in Robert Coles, *The Spiritual Life of Children* (Boston: Houghton Mifflin, 1990), 215.

### What If I Make It Angry?

"Did I not offer enough to my ancestors during the last New Year's Day? Was there not wine in the cups, and chopsticks on the meat and vegetable, and spoons in the soup bowls? Did the woman and I not stand and kneel, stand and kneel, and bow low and strike our heads three times against the floor? Did not the flames of the candles flicker as the cold drafts blew across the table, indicating the spirits were present and partaking of the food? Did I not feed properly the suffering ghosts of our village, those tormented dead who wander without peace, who haunt the trees from which they fell and the river in which they drowned?" —The Old Man, in Chaim Potok, *I Am the Clay* (New York: Alfred A. Knopf, 1992), 38, 39.

Religion answers the questions of restless souls about the supernatural, the eternal, the spiritual. The further away from the Garden of Eden humans wandered and the more the first fear of being separated from God receded into the background (Genesis 3:10), the more complex and original the religious answers became. As humans gathered together in cities and societies, they began to shape their religious answers into teachings, to organize their teachings into belief systems, and to demand that others believe exactly as they believed—that they share the same religion (see Genesis 11:1–9).

Paul Tillich observes that the history of religion "is the history of man's attempts and failures to save himself."[1] Religious humans, whether they are monarchs or everyday people like you and me, consistently have attempted to influence the good will of their god. They have tried by obeying, by contributing to the established religion, and by praying and giving praise, reckoning that "human achievements in this world—some concrete human behaviour or disposition—constitute a claim to the favour of God"[2] that He must reward. Even the sophisticated Roman pagan "regarded religion as a precise code of rites, designed to establish the correct relationship of the community to its God (or gods)."[3]

In Christian terminology, this approach to religion is known as a *works orientation*— "the belief that our place in God's kingdom is awarded to us, either in whole or in part, in exchange for, or in reward for, or because of, our obedience, our proper behavior, our correct belief, the strength of our faith, the merits of our Christian life, our acceptance of Christ's offer of grace, or *anything* else, other than the wholly undeserved favor of God,"[4] which we know simply as grace. In fact, we set a *works* orientation over against a *grace* orientation, which is the good news that our place in God's kingdom is assured because of *God's* undying, unquenchable love for us and not because of our merit or our good works[5] (see Romans 3:20–24 and Ephesians 2:4–9). Though this works orientation formed the robust foundation of the pagan religious systems in ancient times, it didn't die in antiquity or lose its grasp on religion. It persists among religious people to this day!

---

1. Paul Tillich, *Systematic Theology* (Chicago: The University of Chicago Press, 1957), 2:80. Tillich goes on to write, "Most conspicuous and important for the history of religion are the legalistic ways of self-salvation. Man, seeing what he ought to be, driven by the anxiety of losing himself, believing in his strength to actualize his essential being, disregarding the bondage of the will, tries to attain again what he has lost" (81).

2. Karl Barth, *The Epistle to the Romans* (London: Oxford University Press, 1933), 111.

3. Peter Brown, *Augustine of Hippo* (Berkeley, Calif.: University of California Press, 1967), 219.

4. Stuart Tyner, "Grace Orientation," in *The ABZs of Adventist Youth Ministry* (Riverside, Calif.: The Hancock Center for Youth and Family Ministry, 2000), 127.

5. "The gospel reverses all human understanding and endeavors. By nature we operate on the principles of achievement: the reward should match the performance. But the good news is that 'the gift of God is eternal life through Jesus Christ our Lord' (Romans 6:23, KJV). 'For where sin abounded, grace did much more abound' (Romans 5:20, KJV). God is generous in His love, extravagant beyond our comprehension." (J. Robert Spangler, "The Dynamics of Salvation," *Ministry*, February 1988, 24.)

## "REJECTED AS TREASON"
### Ellen White on Grace vs. Merit

"Jesus imparts all the powers, all the grace, all the penitence, all the inclination, all the pardon of sins, in presenting His righteousness for man to grasp by living faith—which is also the gift of God. If you would gather together everything that is good and holy and noble and lovely in man and then present the subject to the angels of God as acting a part in the salvation of the human soul or in merit, the proposition would be rejected as treason." —*Faith and Works* (Nashville, Tenn.: Southern Publishing Association, 1979), 24.

"The idea of doing anything to merit the grace of pardon is fallacy from beginning to end." —*Faith and Works,* 24.

"Money cannot buy it, intellect cannot grasp it, power cannot command it; but to all who will accept it, God's glorious grace is freely given. . . . Those who enter heaven will not scale its walls by their own righteousness, nor will its gates be opened to them for costly offerings of gold or silver, but they will gain an entrance to the many mansions of the "Father's house through the merits of the cross of Christ." —*God's Amazing Grace* (Hagerstown, Md.: Review and Herald, 1973), 179.

"Divine grace is the great element of saving power; without it all human effort is unavailing." —*The Faith I Live By,* 94.

"The heathen looked upon their prayers as having in themselves merit to atone for sin. Hence the longer the prayer the greater the merit. If they could become holy by their own efforts, they would have something in themselves in which to rejoice, some ground for boasting. This idea of prayer is an outworking of the principle of self-expiation which lies at the foundation of all systems of false religion. The Pharisees had adopted this pagan idea of prayer, and it is by no means extinct in our day, even among those who profess to be Christians. The repetition of set, customary phrases when the heart feels no need of God is of the same character as the 'vain repetitions' of the heathen." —*Mind, Character, and Personality* (Nashville: Southern Publishing Association), 1:276.

"It is not possible to effect anything in our standing before God or in the gift of God to us through creature merit. Should faith and works purchase the gift of salvation for anyone, then the Creator is under obligation to the creature. . . . Salvation, then, is partly of debt that may be earned as wages. If man cannot, by any of his good works, merit salvation, then it must be wholly of grace, received by man as a sinner because he receives and believes in Jesus. It is wholly a free gift. Justification by faith is placed beyond controversy. And all this controversy is ended, as soon as the matter is settled that the merits of fallen man in his good works can never procure eternal life for him." —*Faith and Works,* 19, 20.

"The salvation of the human race has ever been the object of the councils of heaven. The covenant of mercy was made before the foundation of the world. It has existed from all eternity, and is called the everlasting covenant. So surely as there never was a time when God was not, so surely there never was a moment when it was not the delight of the eternal mind to manifest His grace to humanity." —*Signs of the Times,* June 12, 1901.

I was traveling a few years ago in the Middle East with a group of church members, exploring the rich biblical backgrounds in Israel, Egypt, Italy, and Greece. In front of the Lion's Gate at Mycenae, deep in the Peloponnesian peninsula south of the Gulf of Corinth, a dear sister on the tour sat on a bench for a moment's relaxation before climbing the pathway to the acropolis of the ancient city. Later that afternoon, the same woman ran into the dining room of our hotel out of breath and announced to us that she had left her purse at Mycenae, complete with her passport, her traveler's checks, and a diamond she had purchased in Israel as a gift for her daughter. "My husband and I have ordered a taxi to take us back to Mycenae," the woman said. "We're going to hunt for the purse. Please pray that we will find it."

Hours later, the taxi returned to the hotel, and when the couple got out, they were all smiles. "We found it," the woman reported gleefully. "It was under the bench, right where I left it. *God has rewarded me for being faithful to Him.*"

It was an uncomfortable moment—it was difficult not to draw conclusions about the basis of this dear woman's relationship with God. Surely, without realizing it, she had established her religion on "a system of reciprocity in which the honour of giver and recipient are engaged."[6] For that moment, at least, her religion could be reduced to an orderly exchange of items of value—"I'll give You this, and You give me that"—just as surely as if she had said, "Here's my devotion in exchange for

my purse." I couldn't help but see the irony of this "Christian" commerce taking place at a site that tradition holds was founded by Perseus, the son of Zeus!

## The Negative Confession

Perhaps no single belief of antiquity more clearly captured the works orientation of the ancient religions than the ceremony known as "The Weighing of the Heart." The 125th chapter of the Egyptian funerary text called *The Book of the Dead* explains the ceremony in full detail. The ancient Egyptians believed that, when they died, they would be judged in the afterlife on the basis of their behavior during their lifetime on earth. In the judgment, the deceased Egyptian was guided by the god Anubis, the jackal-headed god of cemeteries and embalming, into the Broad Hall of the Two Justices, to stand before the throne of Osiris, the chief god of the dead and the afterlife, and forty-two other almighty judges. "The divine tribunal had the power to stamp the seal of eternity on the personhood of the defendant, provided of course that he or she was not found wanting."[7]

Anubis placed the heart of the deceased on one side of a giant scale, to be weighed against the feather of truth from the goddess Maat, who was intimately connected with the Egyptian understanding of truth and justice.[8] The deceased then was asked to make a series of thirty-six statements, with Thoth, the god of wisdom and scribes, who was represented as a man with the head of an ibis, recording every word. French professor of Egyptology

---

6. Marcel Mauss, *The Gift: The Form and Reason for Exchange in Archaic Societies,* W. D. Halls, trans. (New York: W. W. Norton, 1990), viii.

7. Jan Assmann, *Ägypten. Eine Sinngeschichte* (Munich: Carl Hanswer Verlag, 1996), translated into English as *The Mind of Egypt: History and Meaning in the Time of the Pharaohs* (New York: Metropolitan Books, Henry Holt and Company, 2002), 161.

8. Richard H. Wilkinson, *Reading Egyptian Art* (London: Thames and Hudson, 1992), 37.

Jan Assmann calls the religious rationale for this ceremony "the Osirian doctrine of self-justification."[9]

> "I have not blasphemed a god.
> "I have not made anyone sick.
> "I have not made anyone weep.
> "I have not killed.
> "I have not taken milk from the mouths of children.
> "I have not driven cattle away from their pasturage," etc.[10]

While the defendant recited his protestations of innocence—his "negative confession"—his heart reacted on the scale. With every truthful statement of innocence, the heart became lighter. But with every admission of wrongdoing, it became heavier. "If in the final reckoning the heart was found to be too heavy, it was devoured by a monster,"[11] the horrible Ammit, the gobbler, which had the head of a crocodile, the body of a lion, and the hindquarters of a hippopotamus, and who "lurked in the judgment hall to devour any who failed the test."[12] But if the person was found worthy and declared free from sin, the heart was put back into the body, and the deceased was rewarded with passage to the realm of the dead, the Field of Hetep, to enjoy eternity in the Egyptian paradise.

The ancient model is unmistakable. Entrance into the afterlife is based on judgment. The judgment is based on the behavior of each individual in his or her life on this earth. If the behavior is acceptable as the religion defined acceptability, the individual had *earned* or *merited* or *won* or *purchased* the eternal reward.

THE RESULTS OF A WORKS ORIENTATION

The religious establishment became so powerful in the ancient societies, and the works orientation so pervasive, that the worshippers, to earn the favor of their gods and ensure their own place in the afterlife, were led to the most horrific practices—activities the Bible calls "detestable" (see Deuteronomy 18:9; 20:18). As difficult as it is to comprehend, people actually became willing to meet the ultimate demand of an exacting god by offering their own precious children as human sacrifices.

After the death of Ahab, King Mesha, the shepherd king of Moab, rebelled against Joram, Ahab's son. Joram forged an alliance with Jehoshaphat, king of Judah, and attacked the Moabites. Under the pressure of the devastating attack and the reality of having only boys and old men to defend his border, Mesha summoned his own firstborn son, the very son who was to succeed him as king, took him up to the city wall, and sacrificed him to the Moabite god. Mesha would attribute peace to his action, to behavior he believed merited the blessing of a change of military fortune. (See 2 Kings 3. First Kings 16:34 may also refer to an instance of child sacrifice.)

THE BACKDROP OF THE OLD TESTAMENT

This world that included child sacrifice is the religious world on which we must overlay the Old Testament story. It's never very far beneath the surface.

Genesis introduces us to the beginnings of the human race, but it focuses on the lineage of a very, very small group of people. By the

---

9. Assmann, 159.
10. Pritchard, 34.
11. Assmann, 161.
12. Sue H. D'Auria, "Preparing for Eternity," in *Pharaohs of the Sun* (Boston: Museum of Fine Arts, 1999), 162.

beginning of the second book of the Bible, we are following the lives of only seventy individuals (Exodus 1:5; Genesis 46:26, 27). *Seventy!* Granted, these few lives are essential to the story the Bible is trying to tell us. But if we are going to apprehend the full meaning of that story, we must see the Old Testament played out against the backdrop of powerful, densely populated nations, complete with their well-formed, works-oriented religious systems. These pagan systems taught their adherents how to "bring the gods down" to them. "If we make the surroundings comfortable enough and magnificent enough," James Kugel describes in his book *The God of Old,* "if our priests offer them the choicest of our precious livestock and flocks and fill their palace with the scent of our sweetest incense, and if we build this prospective god-house on our highest mountain so that the heaven dwellers will not have far to travel, perhaps they will indeed consent to come and sojourn in our midst. Thus was born the ancient Near Eastern temple, in an age before the dawn of history."[13]

The Bible draws a direct line from Noah through his great-grandson Nimrod to the establishment of Babylon, Akkad, and Nineveh (Genesis 10:1–12). Abraham begins his life in the land that will be ruled by Hammurabi (Genesis 11:27–31). Joseph comes to power among the pharaoh-gods of ancient Egypt (Genesis 37:28). The children of Israel conquer their Promised Land when it already is inhabited by "Hittites, Girgashites, Amorites, Canaanites, Perizzites, Hivites and Jebusites" (Deuteronomy 7:1) and surrounded by Midianites, Edomites, Ammonites, Arameans, Phoenicians, and Philistines. From the building of Solomon's temple a thousand years

### A CONFUSION OF GODS

Laban's household gods didn't just end up in Rachel's camel's saddlebag (Genesis 31:34). Those gods, with her from childhood, also were kept in the heart of Jacob's second wife.

When Pharaoh bestowed on a thirty-year-old Joseph the new name of Zaphenath-Paneah and married him to Asenath, the daughter of Potiphera, a priest of On (Genesis 41:45, 46), little Ephraim and Manasseh must have felt grandfather Potiphera's religious influence (Genesis 48:5).

The ten plagues aimed at Egyptian deities (Numbers 33:4) didn't dissuade the Israelites for long from begging, " 'Make us gods' " (Exodus 32:1), nor keep Aaron from fashioning a young cow as an answer to their plea.

As Solomon grew old, he began worshipping the gods of the women he had married from among the Moabites, Ammonites, Edomites, Sidonians, and Hittites. "He followed Ashtoreth the goddess of the Sidonians, and Molech the detestable god of the Ammonites, . . . [and] Chemosh the detestable god of Moab" (1 Kings 11:1–7; 2 Kings 23:13). The practitioners of these religions were notorious for seeking the favor of their gods through child sacrifice (Leviticus 18:21; Jeremiah 32:35).

before Christ to the destruction of Herod's temple in A.D. 70, the Israelites were in close contact—either at war, under domination, or in alliance—with all the major powers of the ancient world: Egyptians, Syrians, Assyrians, Babylonians, Persians, Greeks, and Romans.

Should it surprise us then that in the oldest book in the Bible, Eliphaz the Temanite

---

13. James L. Kugel, *The God of Old* (New York: Free Press, 2003), 82.

lectures Job with words that reek of the pagan retribution principle embedded in the ancient works-oriented religious systems?[14] Listen to Eliphaz: " 'Who, being *innocent,* has ever perished? Where were the *upright* ever destroyed?' " (Job 4:7, emphasis supplied).

Should we be shocked when Bildad the Shuhite explains to Job with all sincerity, " 'Surely God does not reject a *blameless* man or strengthen the hands of *evildoers'* " (8:20, emphasis supplied)? " 'If even the moon is not bright and the stars are not pure in [God's] eyes, how much less man, who is but a maggot—a son of man, who is only a worm!' " (25:5, 6).

Should we wonder where Zophar the Naamathite got the undergraduate theological degree that would lead him to say things such as the following to Job? " 'If [God] comes along and confines you in prison and convenes a court, who can oppose him? Surely he recognizes deceitful men; and when he sees evil, does he not take note? . . . Yet *if you devote your heart to him* and *stretch out your hands to him, if you put away the sin* that is in your hand and allow no evil to dwell in your tent, *then* you will lift up your face without shame; you will stand firm and without fear. . . . Life will be brighter than noonday, and darkness will become like morning' " (11:10–17, emphasis supplied). Or should it surprise us when God finally steps into the discussion and characterizes the theology the entire group has been spouting as "empty headed nonsense" (38:2, New Jerusalem Version)?

No wonder that the patriarch Abraham so easily confused the lesson God really was try-

ing to teach him (the lesson that *God,* not we, provides the sacrifice—Genesis 22:14), and mistakenly thought that, after all, child sacrifice might be the ultimate way of winning God's approval. We must not miss the point that God is drawing His eager follower out of the quagmire of the contemporary religious scene.

When the psalmist writes, "They shed innocent blood, the blood of their sons and daughters, whom they sacrificed to the idols of Canaan" (Psalm 106:38), he is writing not about the Israelites' pagan neighbors but about the Israelites, who had copied those practices themselves!

If Yahweh, the God of heaven, was going to prove to be any different from Molech, the detestable god of the Ammonites, or Chemosh, the vile god of the Moabites, then He, Yahweh, was going to have to make a very strong statement, make it believable, and make it soon.

GOD RAISES THE STANDARD

Was it Moses who first recognized Yahweh's statement for what it was?

Old by today's standards, halting by his own admission, insignificant in comparison to the place he once occupied in Egypt, Moses stands in front of what seems at first just to be a curious natural phenomenon. Then he begins to listen to the words. By the time he gets back to Egypt, this is the message Moses carried from Yahweh: " ' "I am the LORD, and *I will bring you out* from under the yoke of the Egyptians. *I will free you* from being slaves to them, and *I will redeem you* with an outstretched arm and with mighty acts of judgment. *I will take you* as

14. The Retribution Principle portrayed God as an exacting accountant. In order to be just, God must reward and punish in this lifetime in proportion to the righteousness or wickedness of each individual. Prosperity is a reward for righteousness. Suffering is a punishment for wickedness. Great prosperity is a sign of great righteousness. And great suffering reveals great wickedness.

my own people, and I will be your God. . . . *I will bring you* to the land I swore with uplifted hand to give to Abraham, to Isaac and to Jacob. *I will give it to you* as a possession. I am the LORD" ' " (Exodus 6:6–8, emphasis supplied).

The Hebrews who heard that message had been living as aliens in a foreign country for 430 years (12:40, 41), most of those years as slaves to the oppressive Egyptians. Worked ruthlessly by their taskmasters, the Hebrews endured bitter, violent lives of hard labor (1:11–14). While their numbers had increased greatly during their years in Egypt (12:37), they were still a weak, unorganized group of people who had no leadership; even the Canaanites, to say nothing of the Egyptians, were "nations larger and stronger" (Deuteronomy 7:1). Under the cruel oppression of slavery, the Hebrews' culture had diminished, and they were forced into the role of distant spectators to the art, music, writing, and religion of the Egyptians. So, the instructions had to be simple and clear—the consequences of those next few days not only would determine the status of the Hebrew nation but also would establish the type of god the Hebrews would worship.

How's this for simple and clear: " 'The LORD will fight for you; you need only to be still' " (Exodus 14:14).

During that long night that none of them would ever forget, God keeps His promise. As the Hebrews "stand still," the waters of the Red Sea pile up to the left and to the right. A strong wind from the east turns the seabed into dry ground. The cloudy pillar shields their escape. "The entire army of Pharaoh that had followed the Israelites into the sea" perishes before morning (verse 28).

The Hebrew response to the work of God is immediate: " 'The LORD is my strength and my song; he has become my salvation. . . . Who among the gods is like you, O LORD? Who is like you—majestic in holiness, awesome in glory, working wonders? . . . In your unfailing love *you will lead* the people *you have redeemed*. In your strength *you will guide* them to your holy dwelling' " (15:1–13, emphasis supplied).

To this day, thousands of years after the event, when the Jewish people celebrate their Passover meal, the father explains his behavior in the light of God's *prior* work: " ' "I do this *because of what the* LORD *did for me*" when I came out of Egypt" ' " (13:8).

Yahweh is different from Molech, who demands that we sacrifice our children. *Yahweh provides* the sacrifice (Genesis 22:14). Yahweh is not Osiris, who requires our heart to be weighed on his scale. *Yahweh gives* us a heart to know Him (Jeremiah 24:7). Yahweh "shows no partiality and *accepts no bribes*" (Deuteronomy 10:17, emphasis supplied).

This is what the LORD says:

"Let not the wise man boast of his wisdom or the strong man boast of his strength or the rich man boast of his riches, but let him who boasts boast about this: that he understands and knows me, that I am the LORD, who exercises kindness, justice and righteousness on earth, for in these I delight" (Jeremiah 9:23, 24).

This is what God the LORD says—he who created the heavens and stretched them out, who spread out the earth and all that comes out of it, who gives breath to its people, and life to those who walk on it: *"I, the* LORD, *have called you* in right-eousness; *I will take hold of your hand. I will keep you* and *I will make you* to be a covenant for the people and a light for the Gentiles, to open eyes that are blind, to free captives from prison and to release from the dungeon those who sit in darkness. I am the LORD; that is my name! I will not give my glory to another or my praise to idols" (Isaiah 42:5–8, emphasis supplied).

The religion of Yahweh begins at a different place. It's about what *He has done,* not about what we must do. It's about accepting *His acceptance* of us, not about trying to make ourselves acceptable (" 'You did not choose me, but I chose you' " [John 15:16]). It's about drinking from the wells of *His salvation* (Isaiah 12:3). It's about receiving *His gifts:* "Large,

flourishing cities *you did not build,* houses filled with all kinds of good things *you did not provide,* wells *you did not dig,* and vineyards and olive groves *you did not plant"* (Deuteronomy 6:10, 11, emphasis supplied). It's about realizing that "our heart is restless till we find rest" in Him.[15]

It will take millennia before God's people fully grasp this truth. Before we at long last quit trying to establish our religions on our own behavior and start worshipping God for what He already has done. Before we finally stop being afraid of grace.

# GRACE IN QUESTION
## CHAPTER 3: THE RESTLESS TREASON

Before the time of Israel, other cultures created religious systems—ways to contact and influence their gods. Chapter 3 surveys antiquity to reveal the absence of grace in those religious systems, and it points out how Yahweh's approaches to humans differ from them.

1. Recall a time when religious language you've heard or used sounded like you were bartering with God for His favor.
2. Do a Web search on the word *treason.* Repeat two or three stories of acts of treason. Clarify the definition of the word. In what respects can presenting that which is "good and holy and noble and lovely" be considered treason in the government of God? (See the first *Faith and Works* quotation in the sidebar on page 53.)
3. Read "The Negative Confession" section in this chapter and look carefully at the hieroglyphic depiction of "The Weighing of the Heart" (on page 37). How does your understanding of the way in which our eternal destiny is decided resemble what that picture portrays? How does your belief differ?
4. Read Exodus 14:14 in a number of Bible versions. What difference would this biblical strategy make in your life if you fully adopted it?
5. Explain how Yahweh differs from Molech and Osiris and what difference it makes that Yahweh "shows no partiality and accepts no bribes."

---

15. Augustine, *Confessions,* 1.1.1.

# GRACE NOTES

## JOSHUA 6—THE INCLUSION OF THE FORBIDDEN

Q. Restate the fundamental differences between worshipping Yahweh and worshipping Molech.

Q. How does Rahab's story reveal God's grace?

Nothing in the Old Testament is clearer. "When the LORD your God brings you into the land you are entering to possess and drives out before you many nations—the Hittites, Girgashites, Amorites, Canaanites, Perizzites, Hivites and Jebusites, seven nations larger and stronger than you—and when the LORD your God has delivered them over to you and you have defeated them, then you must destroy them totally. Make no treaty with them, and show them no mercy. Do not intermarry with them. Do not give your daughters to their sons or take their daughters for your sons, for they will turn your sons away from following me to serve other gods" (Deuteronomy 7:1–4).

There is no question about what to do. No wiggle room in the instructions. No loopholes.

Nor is there a chance to misinterpret how God wants to remove the people who are living in Canaan: *He* will drive the people out in front of the Israelites.

> The LORD your God will send the hornet among them until even the survivors who hide from you have perished (verse 20).

> But the LORD your God will deliver them over to you, throwing them into great confusion until they are destroyed (verse 23).

> The LORD your God is the one who goes across ahead of you like a devouring fire. He will destroy them; he will subdue them before you (9:3).

> The LORD hurled large hailstones down on them from the sky, and more of them died from the hailstones than were killed by the swords of the Israelites (Joshua 10:11).

> "The LORD your God is the one who goes with you to fight for you against your enemies to give you victory" (Deuteronomy 20:4).

If there was anyone left after God drove the people out, if any of the Canaanites survived the hornets and the hailstones, the confusion and the fire, if any of them somehow escaped the work God promised to do ahead of His people, the Israelites were to eliminate them. No treaties. No intermarrying. No polite hospitality. No international exchange students. No mercy.

So what do you think the Israelites do in their very first battle inside the Promised Land?

They do just what God told them to do. " 'The LORD has given you the city,' " Joshua tells the people (Joshua 6:16). So, they march around in circles and then go home and go to bed (verses 8–11). The next day they repeat the process. Finally, on the seventh day, they march around the city seven more times. Then they blow their trumpets and shout as loudly as they can (verses 15, 16). They follow God's instructions right down to the letter, right up to the moment when the walls fall down.

Then orders come to forget the clearest instructions in the Old Testament. The Israelites walk into the city, find Rahab, the Canaanite prostitute, her father and mother and brothers and all who belonged to her—her entire family (verse 23)—rescue her, welcome her, "and she lives among the Israelites to this day" (verse 25). An Israelite man named Salmon marries Rahab. They have a baby boy they name Boaz, who, when he grows up, follows his father's example and intermarries with a Moabite woman named Ruth. Their son is named Obed, who becomes the father of Jesse, who becomes the father of David.

OK, what just happened?

Here's what I think happened. God's righteous judgment rightfully separates His followers from detestable religious influences. God's clear instructions protect us from very real danger: "When you enter the land the LORD your God is giving you, do not learn to imitate the detestable ways of the nations there. Let no one be found among you who sacrifices his son or daughter in the fire, who practices divination or sorcery, interprets omens, engages in witchcraft, or casts spells, or who is a medium or spiritist or who consults the dead. Anyone who does these things is detestable to the LORD, and because of these detestable practices the LORD your God will drive out those nations before you" (Deuteronomy 18:9–12).

But God is full of grace. He hates the sinful things sinners do, but He doesn't hate *sinners*. He hates their evil influence. He hates the hurt they cause. He hates seeing children suffer. But He loves the people who do those terrible things. They are His children too. He longs to change their hearts. His grace extends to all sinners, to all of us, even to the Canaanites and the Moabites, even to people and nations who don't know who He is. " 'I revealed myself to those who did not ask for me; I was found by those who did not seek me. To a nation that did not call on my name, I said, "Here am I" ' " (Isaiah 65:1).

Grace delights in opening eyes that are blind, in freeing captives from prison, and in releasing " 'from the dungeon those who sit in darkness' " (42:7). The next time we see Rahab the Canaanite and Ruth the Moabite, they are appearing as star exhibits in the genealogy of Jesus (Matthew 1:5–16)!

" 'I will record Rahab and Babylon among those who acknowledge me—Philistia too, and Tyre, along with Cush—and will say, "This one was born in Zion" ' " (Psalm 87:4).

*"If grace is unmerited favor, it gets into the biblical story very early. In the first chapter of Genesis, to be specific."*
—J. Ellsworth Kalas, *Grace in a Tree Stump*

*"The revelation of what God is like— in both Old and New Testaments— comes speedily and unmistakably to center in the word 'grace.' "*
—Ronald Hals, *Grace and Faith in the Old Testament*

*"At the center of the biblical revelation stands the doctrine of grace."*
—Kenneth Kinghorn, *The Gospel of Grace*

*"The biblical story is supremely the story of grace."*
—James Logan, *Grace Upon Grace*

*"God's character is grace. We can know nothing more important about God."*
—Thomas Langford, *Grace Upon Grace, A Study Companion*

# THE HEBREW MATRIX:

## *The Introduction of Grace in the Old Testament*

WITH PROFOUND SIGNIFICANCE, THE BIBLICAL STORY OF THE HUMAN race begins without one human being anywhere in sight. Deliberately, the story informs us, God waits to create Adam and Eve until the entire physical world is ready to be given as a thoughtful, bountiful, sustaining gift.

It didn't have to be that way.

It could have started out with a lot of hard work on our part. God could have decided that what we needed most was to have nothing given to us, nothing free, nothing except what we worked and sweated for, what we earned and deserved. "Here are your supplies," God might have said to Adam and Eve at the beginning of the Creation week. "Here is a stockpile of raw materials: carbon, hydrogen, a puff of oxygen, a pile of dirt, a shovel, a hammer, and a bucket of nails. What you put together is what you get to live with. An urban jungle or an Edenic garden—it's up to you. That's the way your world is going to work. Might as well get used to it from day one."

God might have said that to Adam and Eve. But He didn't.

Instead, He did all the work. "God saw all that he had made, and it was very good" (Genesis 1:31). " 'The hand of the LORD has done this; the Holy One of Israel has created it' " (Isaiah 41:20). "Without him nothing was made that has been made" (John 1:3). "All things were created by him" (Colossians 1:16).

If you accept the Bible's assertion that "all these things . . . were written for our admonition" (1 Corinthians 10:11, NKJV) and that the Bible's stories are able to make us "wise for salvation" (2 Timothy 3:15), then seizing the salvific significance of the Creation story becomes crucial: God saves us the same way He creates us—without our help! "Creation is already redemption."[1]

While no single illustration can "lay claim to exhaust, nor adequately characterize in itself, the richness of the biblical understanding of salvation in Christ,"[2] the first

---

1. Richard Rohr, *Radical Grace* (Cincinnati, Ohio: St. Anthony Messenger Press, 1993), 137.
2. Alister McGrath, *Iustitia Dei, A History of the Christian Doctrine of Justification: The Beginnings to the Reformation* (Cambridge: Cambridge University Press, 1986), 2.

three chapters of Genesis effectively place the entire great controversy in the forefront of our thinking. The spirit of the Christian doctrine of salvation by grace alone through faith alone in Jesus Christ alone hovers over the structure and content of the Creation story.

1. God does all the work (Genesis 1:1, 31).
2. God gives His work as a gift (Genesis 1:27–30).
3. The recipients of the gift disobey and then run away and try to hide from God (Genesis 3:1–8).
4. God pursues the ones who are running away (Genesis 3:9–13).
5. God promises to take care of the problem caused by separation (Genesis 3:15).

For me, nothing in the rest of the Bible improves on this initial story as an explanation of how the plan of salvation operates.

OVER AND OVER AGAIN

Nevertheless, the Bible writers try. Over and over again, they come at the theme in a new way, with a fresh perspective, an untried approach, an original angle, a new window, so that more and more of us might be able to access the salient points of the doctrine of grace.

"The subtext of the entire Old Testament," says Scott Hoezee in his book *The Riddle of Grace,* "its basic, underlying theological tenet, is that God is first and last a gracious God whose lovingkindness is the spring both for creation and for redemption."[3]

"The substance of the doctrine is there," Thomas Torrance assures us. "The one thing of which all the Old Testament writers are certain is that God's love for Israel was not because of anything that Israel had or was," but because of "the persistent and unshakable love of God."[4]

"The evidence is found," Jon Dybdahl insists, "not in a few isolated proof texts, but in the very structure of the Old Testament itself. Grace is heralded in story, ritual, song, and descriptions of God. It is not a minor, secondary theme but an all-pervasive, dominant melody ringing loudly throughout the pages of the Old Testament."[5]

In his careful survey of the theology of salvation, *By Faith Alone,* Norval Pease agrees, calling saving faith in Christ *the theme* of the Old Testament. "In direct revelation, in prophecy, in song, and in allegory, God endeavored to reveal to his ancient people the great truth that 'salvation is of the Lord.' "[6]

"The theology emerges through the stories," William Placher observes.[7] The "presupposition of Paul's message," can't be ignored.[8] "By the time we come to the end of the Old Testament, the entire story of Christ has been prewritten," Henry Halley proposes in an early twentieth-century Bible handbook.[9]

---

3. Scott Hoezee, *The Riddle of Grace* (Grand Rapids, Mich.: Wm. B. Eerdmans Publishing, 1996), 19.

4. Thomas F. Torrance, *The Doctrine of Grace in the Apostolic Fathers* (Grand Rapids, Mich.: Wm. B. Eerdmans Publishing, 1959), 11, 12, 14.

5. Jon Dybdahl, *Old Testament Grace* (Nampa, Idaho: Pacific Press®, 1990), 16. Alister E. McGrath wrote, "The conceptual foundations of the Christian doctrine of justification may be sought in the Old Testament, in a milieu quite different from that of western Europe, where it received its systematic articulation. The transference of the concept from this Hebraic matrix to that of western Europe has significant consequences." (*Iustitia Dei,* 5.)

6. Norval F. Pease, *By Faith Alone* (Mountain View, Calif.: Pacific Press®, 1962), 21.

7. William C. Placher, *A History of Christian Theology* (Philadelphia: The Westminster Press, 1983), 10.

8. Carl E. Braaten, *Justification, The Article by Which the Church Stands or Falls* (Minneapolis: Fortress Press, 1990), 81.

9. Henry H. Halley, *Bible Handbook* (Chicago: Halley, 1924), 346.

Theologian Karl Rahner puts it dramatically: The Old Testament, he says, is "the immediate pre-history of Christ himself."[10] Professor Stephen Farris summarizes: "Grace arches over the older testament like a rainbow."[11]

## A NEW OLD TESTAMENT

Admittedly, that's not the way most of us have looked at the Old Testament, and especially at the God of the Old Testament. When Jimmy Carter's father died, the future president found his death hard to understand. It seemed to him a harsh act, Carter admits in his book *Living Faith,* "one I could only attribute to what I thought of as the God of the Old Testament, a stern, judgmental figure, very different from the loving, forgiving Jesus I knew from the Gospels."[12]

Honestly, haven't you felt that way as well? "I hate the God of the book of Judges," a church member recently told me. "And as long as we're at it, I might as well throw in the cruel God of the Flood, the revengeful God of the tenth plague, the arbitrary God of the battles of Jericho and Ai, and the wrathful God of the Minor Prophets."

It's not difficult to come to a tacit acceptance of this picture of a mean-spirited Old Testament God. We hear God shouting from the ancient mountaintops. We see Him hurling thunderbolts against defenseless men, women, and children who happened to have grown up in the wrong neighborhoods in Egypt, Sodom, and Babylon. We watch the River Nile turn red. We tremble as the earth opens up to swallow irreverence. We count the Assyrian bodies around the walls of Jerusalem.

Yet Jesus says the Scriptures testify about Him (John 5:39)! And of course, He's talking about the Old Testament scriptures. On the road to Emmaus, Jesus opens the pages of the Old Testament and explains "what was said in all the Scriptures *concerning himself*" (Luke 24:27, emphasis supplied). John tells us that Jesus applied Old Testament stories to His own ministry, such as when He was helping Nicodemus understand that " 'just as Moses lifted up the snake in the desert' " [see Numbers 21:4–9], so He would be " 'lifted up, that everyone who believes in him may have eternal life' " (John 3:14, 15).[13] A few years later the noble believers in Berea can be found poring over the Old Testament on a daily basis to check the accuracy of Paul's gospel theology (Acts 17:11).

So who's right? Is the Old Testament a description of a wrathful, unapproachable God who is doing His best to ratchet up the standard, punish people for their shortcomings, and keep them out of heaven? Or does the Old Testament testify about Jesus, as He seemed to believe? Is the Old Testament best understood as a history of the fearful judgments of God against persistent sinners or as a stage in "the

---

10. Karl Rahner, *Foundations of Christian Faith: An Introduction to the Idea of Christianity* (New York: Crossroad, 2002), 167.

11. Stephen Farris, *Grace: A Preaching Commentary* (Nashville, Tenn.: Abingdon Press, 2003), 16.

12. Jimmy Carter, *Living Faith* (New York: Random House, 1996), 24.

13. At the end of her chapter in *Patriarchs and Prophets* that repeats the story of Moses and the bronze serpent, Ellen White makes this application: "Nothing but the righteousness of Christ can entitle us to one of the blessings of the covenant of grace. There are many who have long desired and tried to obtain these blessings, but have not received them, because they have cherished the idea that they could do something to make themselves worthy of them. They have not looked away from self, believing that Jesus is an all-sufficient Saviour. We must not think that our own merits will save us; Christ is our only hope of salvation." (*Patriarchs and Prophets* [Mountain View, Calif.: Pacific Press®, 1958], 431.)

one history of salvation" provided by grace alone?[14]

The answer begins at the very beginning. "As soon as there was sin, there was a Saviour," Ellen White points out. "As soon as Adam sinned, the Son of God presented Himself as surety for the human race, with just as much power"—note this astonishing assertion—"with *just as much power* to avert the doom pronounced upon the guilty as when He died upon the cross of Calvary."[15] The invitation not to be afraid of grace is as clear in the Old Testament as it is in the New Testament: "This is what the LORD says—he who created you, . . . who formed you, O Israel: 'Fear not, for I have redeemed you; I have summoned you by name; you are mine' " (Isaiah 43:1).

God summons a young Abraham from a far country and pursues him across a lifetime until Abraham's body is "as good as dead" (Romans 4:19)—and even then, God has to rescue him from the thicket of a legalistic experience (Genesis 22:14). Jacob wrestles against grace until the Angel of the Lord finally dislocates his stubborn works-orientation (Genesis 32:25–30).[16] The sacrificial lamb, slain on the night before the Israelites leave Egypt, represents the Lamb of God, "in whom is our only hope of salvation"[17] (see 1 Corinthians 5:7). Gideon keeps adding and multiplying while God is subtracting so that the Israelites won't boast that their strength saves them (Judges 7:2).

How many ways can the Old Testament tell us the good news?

Hear the gospel according to Jehaziel: " ' "The battle is not yours, but God's. . . . You will not have to fight in this battle. Take up your positions, stand firm and see the deliverance the LORD will give you" ' " (2 Chronicles 20:15, 17). Listen to the sons of Korah report how God takes enemies and writes their names on the register of His cherished children: "This one was born in Zion" (see Psalm 87:4–6). Catch the delight in the voice of Isaiah as he assures the redeemed, "You will be called [God's] Sought After" (Isaiah 62:12). See the setting for salvation's story as Hosea repeats God's command: " 'Go, show your love to your wife again, though she is loved by another and is an adulteress. Love her as the LORD loves the Israelites' " (Hosea 3:1). Feel the flood of emotional relief sweep over the accused as Zechariah repeats the words of the Judge: "These are the purchase of my blood, brands plucked from the burning" (see Zechariah 3:2).[18]

"God has chosen you as a cherished personal treasure," Moses underlines the point, "not because you were more numerous than other peoples" or "because of your righteousness or your integrity," but "because He loved you" (see Deuteronomy 7:6; 9:5; 7:8). "We are

---

14. Paul Tillich, *A History of Christian Thought* (New York: Simon and Schuster, 1967), 44.

15. White, *Special Testimonies*, March 12, 1901, emphasis supplied.

16. "God thus taught His servant that divine power and grace alone could give him the blessing he craved. Thus it will be with those who live in the last days. As dangers surround them, and despair seizes upon the soul, they must depend solely upon the merits of the atonement. We can do nothing of ourselves. In all our helpless unworthiness we must trust in the merits of the crucified and risen Saviour." —White, *Patriarchs and Prophets,* 203.

17. Ibid., 277.

18. "He who was the hope of Israel then, their defense, their justification and redemption, is the hope of the church today. . . . Jesus, our Advocate, presents an effectual plea in behalf of all who by repentance and faith have committed the keeping of their souls to Him. . . . All who have put on the robe of Christ's righteousness will stand before Him as chosen, and faithful, and true. Satan has no power to pluck them out of the hand of the Saviour." (White, *Prophets and Kings* [Mountain View, Calif.: Pacific Press®, 1943], 583–591.)

not consumed," Jeremiah adds, "for his compassions never fail. They are new every morning" (Lamentations 3:22, 23). David breaks into song: "As far as the east is from the west, so far has he removed our transgressions from us" (Psalm 103:12). Micah paints the picture graphically: God "tread[s] our sins underfoot and hurl[s] all our iniquities into the depths of the sea" (Micah 7:19). One prophet after another speaks God's words to us: " 'I have swept away your offenses like a cloud. Return to me, for I have redeemed you' " (Isaiah 44:22). " '[I] will remember [your] sins no more' " (Jeremiah 31:34). I have "taken away your punishment" (Zephaniah 3:14–17). "I forgive you for everything you have done" (Ezekiel 16:63, New Jerusalem Bible).

No wonder Peter can say that the Old Testament prophets "spoke of the grace that was to come" (1 Peter 1:10) and Paul can report that the gospel had been announced "in advance to Abraham" (Galatians 3:8).

STORIES OF GRACE

***Abraham—against all hope:*** Listen to Abraham testify. After a lifetime of "meddling, managing and manufacturing" (to use Richard Rohr's picturesque wording),[19] in a personal crisis that is "against all hope" (Romans 4:18), the solid, steadfast picture of God's reliable grace finally cracks through Abraham's thick skull. At the end of the story, Abraham steps back from that horrible place where he thinks he is going to have to sacrifice Isaac to prove himself to a demanding, tyrannical God, and announces that, indeed, nothing *is* too hard for God (Genesis 18:14). He has the power to do whatever He promises to do (Romans 4:21), and, most significantly for Abraham (and for us), He is the One who provides the

---

19. Richard Rohr, *Radical Grace*, 15.

---

### ABRAHAM'S STORY MAKES US WISE UNTO SALVATION

**1. God does all the work**: " '*I will make you* into a great nation and *I will bless you*; *I will make* your name great' " (Genesis 12:2*). " '*I have made you* a father of many nations. *I will make you* very fruitful; *I will make* nations of you, and kings will come from you. *I will establish* my covenant . . . between me and you' " (17:5–7).

**2. God gives His work as a gift**: " 'All the land that you see *I will give to you* and your offspring forever. . . . Go, walk through the length and breadth of the land, for *I am giving it to you*' " (13:15, 17).

**3. The recipients of the gift disobey, run away, and try to hide from God**: " 'When the Egyptians see you . . . say you are my sister' " (12:12, 13). " 'I remain childless and the one who will inherit my estate is Eliezer' " (15:2). " 'Go sleep with my maidservant; perhaps I can build a family through her' " (16:2). "For a while he stayed in Gerar, and there Abraham said of his wife Sarah, 'She is my sister' " (20:1, 2). "Abraham stayed in the land of the Philistines for a long time" (21:34).

**4. God pursues the ones who are running away**: "So Abram left, as the LORD had told him. [He] was seventy-five years old when he set out from Haran" (12:4). " 'Do not be afraid, Abram. I am your shield, your very great reward' " (15:1). "When Abram was ninety-nine years old, the LORD appeared to him" (17:1). "The LORD appeared to Abraham near the great trees of Mamre" (18:1).

**5. God promises to take care of the problem caused by separation**: "The LORD said to Abraham, 'Why did Sarah laugh and say, "Will I really have a child, now that I am old?" Is anything too hard for the LORD? I will return to you at the appointed time next year and Sarah will have a son' " (18:13, 14). "The LORD did for Sarah what he had promised" (21:1). " 'On the mountain of the LORD it will be provided' " (22:14).

*All emphasis in this box is supplied.

sacrifice (Genesis 22:14), including the sacrifice that gives us eternal salvation (Hebrews 11:13–16)—doing for humans that which is impossible for us to do for ourselves. " ' "Stand still and see the salvation of the Lord" ' " (2 Chronicles 20:17, NKJV).

***Gideon—a reluctant warrior:*** Gideon also needed to learn the principle. Hiding in fear in the wine press, destitute of weapons and without courage, the son of Joash bitterly reports on his situation: " 'The Lord has abandoned us. . . . My clan is the weakest in Manasseh, and I am the least in my family' " (Judges 6:13–15).

That's exactly the predicament the Angel of the Lord was looking for! Not bigger, stronger, and swifter, but smaller, weaker, and slower. " 'You have too many men for me to deliver Midian into their hands,' " the Lord informs the reluctant warrior, " 'in order that Israel may not boast against me that her own strength has saved her' " (7:2). Gideon leaves twenty-two thousand Hebrew soldiers behind. Still there are too many! Another ninety-seven hundred are subtracted, until only three hundred remain. Now God can do all the work and give His work as a gift to Israel: " *'I will save you* and *give* the Midianites into your hands' " (verse 7, emphasis supplied).

Gideon's story is able to make us wise unto salvation. It's not a story about what God can do with three hundred soldiers. It's about the total impossibility of the situation, the stark reality of a reduced force armed with only trumpets, pots, and torches being absolutely unable to defeat an oppressive multitude that defies numbering, "thick as locusts. Their camels could no more be counted than the sand on the seashore" (verse 12). The story goes out of its way to stress the weakness of Gideon and

his army, observes Ronald Hals. "The theology of the wars of the Lord is extremely simple and consistent: God does it all. This is a prominent setting of grace in the Old Testament. . . . The deliverance of God's people comes by grace alone."[20]

Gideon's story is not about a brilliant military strategy or a courageous, dedicated fighting force; it's about grace—about God doing for humans that which is impossible for us to do for ourselves. God saves us the same way He delivers Israel from the Midianites—without the help of our numerical superiority. "Stand still and see the salvation of the Lord."

***David—a boy in battle:*** The theology of grace is repeated in 1 Samuel 17. A young shepherd boy named David picks up five smooth stones from the dry riverbed and thrusts them up in front of Goliath, the giant champion of the Philistine army. David's action is reported to us not as an example of the important role humans have to play in their salvation but so that we can hear his confession of utter helplessness. In effect, David is saying to us, "This is all we had to defeat the giant and the Philistine horde; this is what the situation had boiled down to—five little rocks against a vast veteran army. We were in an *impossible* position. There was no hope of overcoming Goliath, no hope for our winning the battle. We were afraid and dismayed. Not one of our soldiers had drawn his sword or shot one arrow at the Philistines. For forty days, all we had managed to do was to stand there on the sidelines and yell at the enemy."

David knows from experience the impossibility of winning by himself. He also knows that confessed weakness is the secret of victory, and he shouts the secret in the ears of everyone observing the battle—everyone then and there, and everyone here and now: " 'You come

20. Ronald M. Hals, *Grace and Faith in the Old Testament* (Minneapolis: Augsburg, 1980), 24.

against me with sword and spear and javelin, but I come against you in the name of the LORD Almighty. . . . This day *the LORD will hand you over* to me, . . . [and] all those gathered here will know that it is not by sword or spear that the LORD saves; for *the battle is the LORD's,* and *he will give* all of you into our hands' " (1 Samuel 17:45–47, emphasis supplied).

It's no contest! In a moment the battle is over. Accepting the victory that had been given to them, the soldiers of Saul surge forward and chase the Philistines all the way back to the feeble gates of their walled cities.

The story of David and Goliath is able to make us wise unto salvation. The salvation lesson looms larger than Goliath's shadow: In a moment, Christ, our Champion, wades into earth's dry riverbed, defeats the enemy, and then turns to all of us standing on the sidelines and gives us the victory. In this Old Testament story, God once again tries to teach us the definition of grace: God doing for humans that which is impossible for us to do for ourselves. God saves us the same way. He defeats the Goliaths and then gives us the victory. "Stand still and see the salvation of the Lord."

GRACE DRIPPING LIKE HONEY

God's grace is available for them all! For Adam and Eve running away from God. For Abraham pursuing his offspring without hope. For the Hebrews complaining in the wilderness. For Gideon hiding in fear. For David facing the giant. And for everyone in between. While the theological nuances of the word *grace* are developed "only in the New Testament writings of Paul, ideas and examples of grace drip off the pages of the Old Testament like honey."[21]

"God's actions on behalf of Israel are not necessary, not coerced, and not earned by something Israel has done. God freely chooses to reach out to Israel, to grace the people in many ways, and to stand by them always."[22] "Throughout their history the Israelites experienced the unconditional, unrelenting love of God," points out Richard Rohr in the Old Testament volume of his book *The Great Themes of Scripture.* "Little by little they discovered that worthiness is not the issue. The only real issue in life is the steadfast love of God. And the only real difference in people is between those who can believe this and those who cannot."[23]

Sing, O daughter of Zion; shout aloud, O Israel! Be glad and rejoice with all your heart, O daughter of Jerusalem! The LORD has taken away your punishment, he has turned back your enemy. The LORD, the King of Israel, is with you; never again will you fear any harm. On that day they will say to Jerusalem, "Do not fear, O Zion; do not let your hands hang limp. The LORD your God is with you, he is mighty to save. He will take great delight in you, he will quiet you with his love, he will rejoice over you with singing" (Zephaniah 3:14–17).

"Though the mountains be shaken and the hills be removed, yet my unfailing love for you will not be shaken nor my covenant of peace be removed," says the LORD, who has compassion on you (Isaiah 54:10).

---

21. Scott Hoezee, *The Riddle of Grace,* 19.

22. Elizabeth Dreyer, *Manifestations of Grace* (Collegeville, Minn.: The Liturgical Press, 1990), 48.

23. Richard Rohr and Joseph Martos, *The Great Themes of Scripture: Old Testament* (Cincinnati, Ohio: St. Anthony Messenger Press, 1987), 12.

We have read these old pages wrong. Yahweh is not the God we have made Him out to be. From the freshness of the first mornings in the Garden of Eden, through the interminable years of wandering, through the human successes and failures of the kingdom united and divided, to the closing of Malachi's pages at the end of the Testament, we have been God's "treasured possession" (Malachi 3:17), written with indelible ink in the "scroll of remembrance" (verse 16). " ' "Stand still and see the salvation of the LORD" ' " (2 Chronicles 20:17, NKJV).

There is no refuge here for those who are afraid of grace.

---

# GRACE IN QUESTION
## CHAPTER 4: THE HEBREW MATRIX

The Old Testament frequently is cited as a source for the notion that God is a harsh, cruel, unreasonable, judgmental being, hard to please and difficult to relate to. Chapter 4 suggests that this is an inadequate picture, one we have unfortunately accepted without study or confirmation, contrary to the New Testament understanding of the Old Testament and to the Old Testament's revelation itself.

1. When Paul reminded Timothy that the Scriptures were able to make us "wise for salvation" (2 Timothy 3:15), he was talking about the Old Testament, wasn't he? Which stories or portions of the Old Testament have you already thought of in this light?

2. If we really are going to read the Old Testament as "an invitation not to be afraid of grace," for which stories are you going to need some further explanation? How will approaching those stories expecting God's grace result in a different understanding than approaching them looking for a God of wrath and harshness?

3. How does it make you feel to know you are "born in Zion" (Psalm 87:4–6), God's "Sought After" (Isaiah 62:12), and a "brand plucked from the burning" (Zechariah 3:2)?

4. To " ' "stand still and see the salvation of the LORD" ' " (2 Chronicles 20:17, NKJV) doesn't mean to do nothing at all! In obeying the command to "stand still," the Israelites cross the Red Sea and the Jordan River, Gideon lights a torch and blows a trumpet, and David crosses a dry streambed. What is involved in "standing still and seeing salvation"? What part of us needs to stand still? What do we see when we see salvation? How do you obey the command in your life?

5. Contrast "human worthiness" and "the steadfast love of God" as candidates for the "real issue in life." Which are you voting for?

# GRACE NOTES
## EZEKIEL 16—THE SIN OF GOD'S CHILDREN

This time God is the storyteller. He wants us to know what it's like to be the Father of His people, so He tells us a story about a little girl born in the land of Canaan. It's a tough story to get through, but the punch line is well worth the effort.

" ' "Your father was an Amorite and your mother a Hittite," ' " the story begins (Ezekiel 16:3). In the Old Testament record of God's dealing with nations, you can get a good feel for a nation's relation with Yahweh, God of heaven, by tracing the nation's ancestry. The Moabites and Ammonites, for example, forsake God and worship vile gods with "detestable practices" (Ezra 9:1; 1 Kings 11:33). Their ancestry goes all the way back to Moab and Ben-Ammi, the sons born to Lot's two daughters after drunken, incestuous nights in a cave—not at all a righteous beginning (Genesis 19:36–38). The Edomites, whom the Israelites are constantly fighting, are descendants of Esau, the more violent and unspiritual of the two sons of Isaac and Rebekah (Genesis 36:9).

Likewise with the Amorites and the Hittites, who are among the nations God promises to drive out of Canaan ahead of the Israelites (Deuteronomy 7:1; Joshua 3:10): Their ancestry begins with Noah's youngest son, Ham, the one who disgraces his father, and it continues through Ham's son, Canaan (Genesis 10:15). In other words, when in His story God names an Amorite and a Hittite as the little girl's parents, He is saying in the strongest possible way that this little girl was born on the wrong side of the tracks.

What's more, from the day of her birth, her pagan parents don't want her, don't care for her, don't care if she lives or dies. " ' "On the day you were born your cord was not cut, nor were you washed with water to make you clean, nor were you rubbed with salt or wrapped in cloths. No one looked on you with pity or had compassion enough to do any of these things for you. Rather, you were thrown out into the open field, for on the day you were born you were despised" ' " (Ezekiel 16:4, 5).

When God passes by and sees the baby kicking about in her blood (verse 6), getting dirty in the hot desert sand, and about to die, He has compassion for her and rescues her. As she grows, He watches over her, protects her, and becomes the Father she had never had.

"I gave you My solemn oath and entered into a covenant with you, declares the Sovereign LORD, and you became mine.

"I bathed you with water and washed the blood from you and put ointments on you. I clothed you with an embroidered dress and put

Q. Which Old Testament stories illustrate for you that we are God's treasured possession?

Q. What words do you most need to hear God say to you?

leather sandals on you. I dressed you in fine linen and covered you with costly garments. I adorned you with jewelry: I put bracelets on your arms and a necklace around your neck, and I put a ring on your nose, earrings on your ears and a beautiful crown on your head. So you were adorned with gold and silver; your clothes were of fine linen and costly fabric and embroidered cloth. Your food was fine flour, honey and olive oil. You became very beautiful and rose to be a queen. And your fame spread among the nations on account of your beauty, because the splendor I had given you made your beauty perfect, declares the Sovereign LORD" (verses 8–14).

Unfortunately, in spite of the unprecedented love and unparalleled attention, the little girl turns away from her Rescuer. First of all, she fails to acknowledge that God has given her the gifts she possesses. God reminds her of the fine jewelry that *I gave you,* made of *my* gold and silver; the food *I provided* for you, *my* children (see verses 14, 17, 18, 21). And second, she acts as if those very gifts are her creations, her achievements, the work of her own hands. You trusted in *your* beauty, God points out, you used *your* fame, *your* favors, *your* clothes, *your* sons and daughters (see verses 15, 16, 18, 20).

Turning away from God frequently involves these same two dynamics: failing to affirm God as the Source of the good in our lives, and taking credit for that good ourselves.

When the focus of our religion becomes what we do instead of what God does, we lose the high standard. The kingdom of light becomes fuzzy and distant, and we turn instead toward the kingdom of darkness. So, the young woman flings herself headfirst into an attempt to outstrip her pagan neighbors in immorality. Neither the Egyptians nor the Assyrians nor the Babylonians can keep up with her promiscuity (verses 26, 28, 29). The Philistines "blush at your lewd behavior" (verse 27, New Jerusalem Bible). The Samaritans " ' "did not commit half the sins you did" ' " (verse 51). The people of Sodom seem righteous in comparison to you (verse 52). There is no holding back of God's judgment on the girl's sin. He calls her behavior degrading (verse 25), lewd (verse 43), depraved (verse 47), detestable (verse 51), disgraceful (verse 52), shameful (verse 54), and wicked (verse 57).

And then in the story, these horrible words: " ' "You will bear the consequences of your lewdness and your detestable practices, declares the LORD" ' " (verse 58). " ' "I will deal with you as you deserve" ' " (verse 59). God is angry about it, even while He's telling the story. What she deserves is to have a mob of all her lovers gathered before her to let them see the reality of the situation, to let them take the fancy clothes and fine jewelry and burn the great houses—to allow them to mete out the appropriate punishment in wrath and anger (verses 37–41). As God tells the story, His voice grows louder and louder and increasingly agitated. He wants this wickedness to stop!

Then God takes a deep breath. He remembers that this little girl whom He's talking about belongs to Him. He recalls that He gave her a solemn oath (verse 8). He thinks about the covenant He made with her in the days of her youth (verse 60). He remembers that He is a God of grace, and that grace hates the sin but loves the sinner. He knows what He must do to help her remember her past life, face the shame of it, and be properly contrite (verse 61). The solution will leave her speechless (verse 62, *The Message*).

God looks her straight in the eyes. He embraces her, and then He speaks. She listens, and she hears the voice of grace say the words she most needs to hear: "I forgive you for everything you have done" (verse 63, New Jerusalem Bible).

*"Many who speak of the finished work of Christ
prove by their own actions
that they do not believe it to be finished."*
—HENRY SOLTAU, *THE TABERNACLE*


*"We easily lose our sense of dependence on God
and our always and ever increasingly desperate need for grace."*
—EUGENE PETERSON, *LEAP OVER THE WALL*


*"Sabbath implies a willingness
to be surprised by unexpected grace."*
—WAYNE MULLER, *SABBATH*


*"God leads. We follow.
Whether you are a Jew or a Christian, that is grace."*
—ATHOL DICKSON, *THE GOSPEL ACCORDING TO MOSES*


*"This is a radical departure from accustomed religious thinking."*
—ABRAHAM JOSHUA HESCHEL, *THE SABBATH*

CHAPTER 5

# THE FINISHED WORK:

*The Celebration of Grace in the Old Testament*

THE HEBREW PEOPLE WALK HESITANTLY OUT OF THE LAND OF THEIR SLAVERY (Exodus 19:1). Grumbling at every step along the way, they cross the Red Sea (Exodus 14), taste sweet water from the bitter springs at Marah (Exodus 15), gather bread from heaven (Exodus 16), watch water gush from the rock at Rephidim (Exodus 17), and defeat the attacking Amalekites (Exodus 17) while Aaron and Hur hold up Moses' hands. They stop ten times in the desert (Numbers 33), and then camp near Mount Sinai.

At the mountain of God, they receive the Ten Commandments twice (Exodus 20 and 34), are sidetracked by a golden calf (Exodus 32), and grow accustomed to Moses' face being radiant from his visits with God (Exodus 34). Now, with all those events packing the last few months, they turn their full attention toward a surprising, unlikely project with instructions from God: "Build a sanctuary for Me," God tells Moses, "that I might live among them" (see Exodus 25:8).[1]

When the detailed blueprints for the wilderness sanctuary are set out, the people realize how much work lies ahead. Ultimately, the complex enterprise will take 8,580 Levites to perform the tabernacle ministry, to pack up the entire sanctuary and carry it from camp to camp, and to unpack it all again at the end of the traveling day (Numbers 4:46–49). For a full seven months, the task of building the sanctuary consumes all the energies, talents, offerings, and time of the Hebrew people.

Finally, the task is completed and inspected. For the very first time, Moses sets up the tabernacle, from the awe-inspiring ark of the covenant in the center of the Most Holy Place to the last bronze tent peg in the far corner of the courtyard. It is the first day of the first month of the second year out of Egypt (Exodus 40:17). In Exodus 40:33, the Bible succinctly summarizes the end of the building project: "So Moses finished the work."

The last time we heard biblical words like these was when God completed the Creation week and rested on the seventh day: "God had finished the work," the

---

1. The sanctuary is also referred to in the Bible as the tabernacle, the tent of meeting, and in Hebrew, the *Mishkan*.

Bible says (Genesis 2:2). It won't be long before we hear the words again, this time from an old rugged cross on Golgotha: " 'It is finished,' " Jesus said (John 19:30).

Is it possible to draw a closer connection than we have realized before between the finished work of Creation, the finished work of sanctuary building, and the finished work of salvation? Let's examine four dynamics that seem to indicate the connection is strong.

## 1. CELEBRATING

**Sabbath:** The finished work of Creation is celebrated with the first Sabbath (Genesis 2:3) and with God coming to walk in the Garden with Adam and Eve.

**Sanctuary:** The finished work of the sanctuary is celebrated by a consecration service (Numbers 7:1) and by God coming in the cloud to cover the tabernacle (Exodus 40:34; Numbers 9:15).

**Salvation by grace:** When the finished work of salvation, planned from before the creation of the earth, was announced to the angels, "inexpressible joy filled heaven. The glory and blessedness of a world redeemed, outmeasured even the anguish and sacrifice of the Prince of life. Through the celestial courts echoed the first strains of that song which was to ring out above the hills of Bethlehem"[2] with the coming of God to earth, the incarnation of Jesus: "Glory to God in the highest heaven, and on earth peace for those He favors" (Luke 2:14, New Jerusalem Bible). "With a deeper gladness now than in the rapture of the new creation" the salvation celebration began.[3] "The morning stars sang in chorus and all the angels shouted praise" (Job 38:7, *The Message*).

Biblical celebrations tend to be large, noisy gatherings accompanied by days and days of feasting (1 Chronicles 12:39, 40; Esther 9:17, 18, 22), lots of singing and dancing (Exodus 15:20), brass instruments (2 Chronicles 5:13), harps, lyres, cymbals, tambourines, rams' horns, songs of praise from large choirs (1 Chronicles 15:16, 28; Nehemiah 12:31), and giving presents to each other and gifts to the poor (Esther 9:19, 22).

When the children of Israel cross the Red Sea, when Samuel confirms the choice of Saul as king in Gilgal, when David is made king in Hebron over a united kingdom, when the ark is returned to Jerusalem, when Solomon and Nehemiah dedicate their temples, and when Hezekiah and Josiah celebrate the Passover with the people of Judah, there is "great rejoicing" (2 Chronicles 30:21), "fig cakes, [and] raisin cakes" (1 Chronicles 12:40), and lots of "amen-ing" and "praising the Lord" (see 16:36). These are times of "joy and gladness . . . with feasting and celebrating" (Esther 8:17).

Karen and I were talking recently about family celebrations, and we began to recall the fun we've had through the years celebrating her birthday. One year we were in Paris, and we ate a little birthday pastry at a sidewalk café. Another time we were on a cruise ship in Canadian waters with a group of dear friends we'd known since high-school days. Once I secretly flew our daughter Erin from North Carolina to surprise Karen. I picked Erin up at the airport, and, just before we got home, stopped by the side of the road, and Erin jumped out of the car and into the trunk. When I asked Karen to help me empty the trunk, she had a wonderful surprise, complete with screaming, laughter, and tears!

---

2. Ellen G. White, *Patriarchs and Prophets* (Washington, D.C.: Review and Herald, 1958), 65.
3. Ibid.

On another birthday occasion, Erin and our son Ben (from New York City) flew in late one evening, spent the night nearby with our son Matt and his family and then slipped into our house the next morning while Karen was out running. When she returned, I told her that Erin had sent some birthday greetings by email and that she should go to the computer and read them. Karen walked into my study and was met by raucous "Happy birthday!" shouts from Erin and Ben, Matt and Jenn, and Emma and Sophie. It was *days* before she got over the shock and joy of the surprise!

Like biblical celebrations and family birthdays, we are invited to experience the newness, the joy, the rich surprise of God's grace with enthusiasm, delight, fullness, and rejoicing.

## 2. RESTING

But there's more to the connection between the Sabbath, the sanctuary, and salvation by grace alone.

*Sabbath:* The Sabbath in the Garden is all about resting in the immediate presence of God. Of course, God has been there all along during the Creation week. But on this first blessed-and-made-holy day of the earth's existence, God commemorates His own creative work by inviting Adam and Eve to cease their work and to rest in His presence.

*Sanctuary:* The sanctuary in the wilderness is all about learning to be at ease in the central presence of God. Of course, God has been there all along with the children of Israel—in the land of bondage, in the escape from pharaoh's army, in the desert. But on this first anointed and consecrated day of the sanctuary's existence, God illustrates His own redemptive work by inviting the Hebrews to put Him at the center of their life and to rest in His presence.

*Salvation by grace:* The gospel of grace is all about resting in the saving presence of Jesus in the cosmic battles of the great controversy. Of course, God is there throughout our earthly journey—in the wakening desire to accept His love, in the daily struggles of our everyday existence, in our growing realization

---

### THE SABBATH

"We are obsessed with work. Six days each week we rest so we can go back to work. But one day each week there is a day devoted to being present, the seventh day. On that day, we do not have to go anywhere or do anything. Everything is done and we are already here." —Rabbi Lawrence Kushner, *The Book of Words* (Woodstock, Vt.: Jewish Lights Publishing, 1993), 24.

"Sabbath resting strengthens our faith in the totality of God's grace." —Marva Dawn, *Keeping the Sabbath Wholly* (Grand Rapids, Mich.: Eerdmans, 1989), 203.

"Sabbath challenges the theology of progress by reminding us that we are already and always on sacred ground. The gifts of grace and delight are present and abundant; the time to live and love and give thanks and rest and delight is now, this moment, this day. Feel what heaven is like; have a taste of eternity. Rest in the arms of the divine. We do not have miles to go before we sleep. The time to sleep, to rest, is now. We are already home." —Wayne Muller, *Sabbath* (New York: Bantam Books, 1999), 79.

"The Sabbath is endowed with a felicity which enraptures the soul, which glides into our thoughts with a healing sympathy. It is a day on which hours do not oust one another. It is a day that can soothe all sadness away." —Abraham Joshua Heschel, *The Sabbath* (New York: Farrar, Straus and Giroux, 1951), 20.

that we don't have to be afraid of grace. But in that first dawning understanding that we are a blessed, chosen people (Deuteronomy 7:6; 14:2), we realize that it is so because God has freely given us His glorious grace and guaranteed our salvation (2 Samuel 23:5). We hear His gentle voice inviting us to enter into His rest and to be at peace in His presence. "He who dwells in the shelter of the Most High will rest in the shadow of the Almighty. I will say of the LORD, 'He is my refuge and my fortress, my God, in whom I trust' " (Psalm 91:1, 2). "Be at rest once more, O my soul, for the LORD has been good to you" (Psalm 116:7).

Biblical rest envelops us, makes us feel secure (Psalm 16:9), and gives us a sustaining realization of God's unfailing love (Psalm 33:22). "My soul finds rest in God alone," David reflects, "my salvation comes from him" (Psalm 62:1). "My people will live in peaceful dwelling places," Isaiah reassures us with the words of God, "in secure homes, in undisturbed places of rest" (Isaiah 32:18). We rest because "[our] Redeemer is strong" (Jeremiah 50:34). Every Sabbath should be like that. Every time we move forward with God at the center of our lives, that's what it's supposed to be like.

The Old Testament repeats the theme in story after story, asking us to imagine how God's rest can bless our lives. After reeling from the swells of the great storm, the ark of Noah finally comes to rest on the mountains of Ararat (Genesis 8:4). What can God do for you and me in the daily storms we encounter? After producing a bountiful harvest year after year, the farmland of Israel enjoys a sabbatical rest from agricultural production (Leviticus 25:4, 5). How much more productive would our lives be if we rested in God's embrace?

After fighting every enemy along the way, the people of Israel finally are quieted as God gives them safety in the Promised Land, with

## THE SANCTUARY

"In Israel's story the sanctuary was a means of thinking about God's presence, of envisioning what God's presence might mean." —John Goldingay, *Old Testament Theology: Israel's Gospel* (Downers Grove, Ill.: InterVarsity Press, 2003), 393.

"God has chosen many illustrations to help His people to understand the person, mission, and ministry of Jesus. The clearest and most important of them is the tabernacle." —Leslie Hardinge, *Shadows of His Sacrifice: Studies in the Sanctuary* (Brushton, N.Y.: TEACH Services, 1996), 5.

"When the people of Israel lived in the wilderness, they discovered that God wanted to have a home among them. The tabernacle gave the people a visual picture of how God wanted to be in the very center of their lives. God had His people arrange their lives, physically and spiritually, around the tabernacle. The entire community was built around the tabernacle." —John Ortberg, *Old Testament Challenge: Discussion Guide* (Grand Rapids, Mich.: Zondervan, 2003), 69.

"Symbols have their place in the outer court of religion. What is found in the inner sanctuary is neither speculative nor artistic pageantry but the simplicity and immediacy of insight, faith and dedication." —Abraham Joshua Heschel, *Quest for God: Studies in Prayer and Symbolism* (New York: Crossroad, 1990), 134.

rest from all their enemies (Deuteronomy 12:10) and from war (Joshua 11:23). How peaceful would our experiences be if we let God do the fighting for us? After gleaning in the fields of Boaz, Ruth experiences shelter and a release from all her work (Ruth 2:7). How safe would we feel if we fully understood that we didn't need to work for God's acceptance? The gospel of grace comes to us in all our reeling, producing, fighting, and working and asks us to be still and rest.

## 3. DISTINGUISHING

Celebrating and resting, however, are only half the Sabbath-sanctuary-salvation by grace picture.

**Sabbath:** The original Sabbath draws a distinction between the work God finishes when He creates the world and the work Adam and Eve continue to do in the place in which they live. God creates the Garden; Adam and Eve tend the Garden. Both God and Adam and Eve are at work, but the nature of the work is fundamentally different. Certainly, there remains much work for Adam and Eve to do, but it isn't the same work that God does. God creates life. We don't create life. From Creation forward, the Sabbath is to be a weekly reminder of the distinction between God's work and our work. The two are fundamentally different.

**Sanctuary:** The sanctuary in the wilderness asks the Hebrew people to distinguish between what is at the center of their lives and what is at the periphery. The Israelites could become the people of Moses, place *his* tent in the middle of their encampment, and follow *him* through the desert. They could pay a Midianite guide to steer them around the dangers and the potholes and follow *him* to the Promised Land. They could make a map the center of their existence and follow *it* through the wilderness. But they don't! They put the sanctuary in the center of their lives and follow *God!* From that day forward, the sanctuary is to be a daily reminder that God's place and the place of everything else are intrinsically different.

**Salvation by grace:** The gospel of grace asks us to distinguish between two views of the Christian life. One view understands Christian behavior as a heartfelt response to the wholly unmerited gift of salvation. The other view of the Christian life suggests that what we do contributes to the process of salvation—a process that hopefully, if we work hard enough and make enough right decisions, will result in God rewarding us for our good work. From the biblical perspective, we must choose a salvation based on grace or choose an attempt at salvation based on works. Grace is a moment-by-moment reminder that God's role in our salvation is to save us, and our role is to quit trying to save ourselves.

The ancient Israelites are immersed in this idea of distinguishing. The God they serve is *one* God; the gods of the nations around them are *many* (Deuteronomy 6:4). Israel's God is the Creator; worthless idols create nothing (Isaiah 42:5–8). During the Creation week, God separates the light from the darkness, the water from the dry ground. " 'Six days you shall labor and do all your work, but the seventh day is the Sabbath' " (Exodus 20:8–11). "I set before you blessing and cursing" (see Deuteronomy 11:26; and chapters 27 and 28). " 'You must distinguish between the holy and the common, between the unclean and the clean' " (Leviticus 10:10). "You will lend to many nations but will borrow from none. The LORD will make you the head, not the tail. . . . You will always be at the top, never at the bottom. . . . Do not turn . . . to the right or to the left" (Deuteronomy 28:12–14). "See, I set before you today life and prosperity, death and destruction" (30:15).

Week after week, day by day, moment by moment, the Sabbath, the sanctuary, and the gospel of salvation by grace alone help us remember to distinguish between who we are as God's chosen, treasured people and who the world says we might become if we'd just buy their cars, wear their clothes, eat their food, drink their drinks, watch their shows, and vote for their candidates. God's people have a distinct perspective on where we've come from, what our purpose is here on planet Earth, and where we're going to spend the next ten million years.

## 4. CEASING

There's one more dynamic to the Sabbath-sanctuary-salvation by grace perspective.

***The Sabbath and the sanctuary:*** The God of the Sabbath, we are told, blesses the seventh day and makes it holy "because on it he rested from all the work of creating that he had done" (Genesis 2:3). To honor that "work of creating," God commanded us to remember the Sabbath day by ceasing from all our work (Exodus 20:8–11). What exactly is the work referred to by the commandment—the work from which we are to cease?

In a fascinating discussion about this question, rabbinic literature points out that the Hebrew word translated "work" in the Sabbath commandment is not the word often used in the Bible for sweat-producing labor. Rather, this term refers to thirty-two specific skilled activities necessary to constructing and maintaining the wilderness sanctuary![4] The rabbis contend that there is a strong, purposeful, meaningful connection between the Sabbath and the sanctuary.

What the Sabbath commandment prohibits, they insist, is the kind of work the Israelites do in the desert to create the sanctuary: the building of a structure, the lighting of a fire to help in the construction process, the carrying of building materials from one place to another. Hunting the animals whose skins they will use to cover the sanctuary is not allowed on the Sabbath. Shearing the fur from a live animal and skinning an animal after it is slaughtered are also forbidden on the seventh day. Setting up a loom is perfectly permissible any other day of the week, but on the Sabbath, it is not to be done. Tying yarn, dyeing material, and sewing material together are all part of the Sabbath prohibition.

The disallowed Sabbath work also includes all the efforts that go into making the bread for the table of shewbread. Plowing a field to improve the soil, sowing the seeds that later will produce grain, harvesting, threshing, grinding, kneading, baking—all are part of the "you shall not do any *work*" on the Sabbath.

According to the rabbis, there is a crucial understanding here. The work we are commanded to cease doing on the Sabbath encompasses those acts that show human mastery over the world—the things we do to take one substance and turn it into something else (a tree into two-by-four lumber, a grazing sheep into a hanging curtain, a measure of flour into a loaf of bread, etc.). In each of these works, we are in charge, we are the superior power, we make the ultimate decisions. The days of our weeks are filled with these controlling activities that make us the authority and give us the supremacy. And then the sun goes down on Friday night, and the Sabbath comes and changes all that.

"Once every seven days," says Rabbi Noah Weinberg, "we step back from the world and make a statement to ourselves and humanity

---

4. Not, for example, the word used for the work of the Hebrew slaves in Egypt, *maaseh*, as in Exodus 5:13: "The slave drivers kept pressing them, saying, 'Complete the *work* required of you for each day' " (emphasis supplied); or the word *abodah*, as in: " 'Make the *work* harder for the men' " (verse 9, emphasis supplied). Either of these words, the rabbis say, might imply that it is mere physical exertion that is prohibited. But the prohibited work of the fourth commandment is the Hebrew term *av melacha*, or, in the plural form, *avot melachot*.

that we are not in charge of this world. We stop all creative work and acknowledge that it is God's world, not ours. We can manipulate the world, but we don't own it. When we refrain from work on Shabbat, we regain clarity and understanding as to Who is the true Creator."[5]

**Salvation by grace:** If the rabbis are correct, God hasn't given us the Sabbath just so we can take a day off from whatever it is we do to earn a paycheck. That's an important feature of "keeping the Sabbath," but it's not the end of the story. The Sabbath isn't intended just to give us a twenty-four-hour period free from studying school subjects or shopping for groceries or watching a Laker game on television. On the Sabbath, we do the things we do—and don't do the things we don't do—not because doing and not doing are the essence of Sabbath observance, but so that we can stay in touch with what the essence of Sabbath really is. What we are supposed to cease doing on the Sabbath has always been so much bigger than not washing dishes and not riding bicycles and not wading into the water past our knees. The Sabbath is about ceasing our attempts to be God!

To "remember the Sabbath day to keep it holy," is to lay down our works, our authority, our control over our own schedules and futures—all those things that necessarily operate in the other realms of our lives, but that, in the spiritual realm, tend to make us believe that we also are in charge of our salvation. "Keep my Sabbaths as holy rest days," God says to us, "they are signposts between me and you, sig-

naling that I am GOD" (see Ezekiel 20:20, *The Message*). Ceasing work on the Sabbath is about declaring our acceptance of grace, about celebrating that God has given us the gift of eternal life, about resting in the assurance of salvation, about distinguishing between God's work of giving grace and our work of receiving grace.[6]

Henry Soltau has it right in his nineteenth-century classic *The Tabernacle, the Priesthood and the Offerings* when he says: "Cease from your own works. Cease from expecting improvement or amendment by your own efforts. Cease from hoping to feel better or to be better. Cease from doubting or mistrusting God or His love. Behold the wonderful manner of His love and hear the universal proclamation of His love, 'that whosoever believes in Him shall not perish but have everlasting life'—shall have it at once, and shall have it for ever."[7]

Imagine what true Sabbath keeping could mean to the thousands of people in New York City on their way to work each morning crammed into every last inch of the subway. To the immigrant workers huddled by the hardware stores waiting to be employed for just one day. To the unending line of commuters inching into Los Angeles on the 91 freeway. To the single moms working three jobs to hold things together. And to the schoolteachers about to face another classroom full of noisy kids. OK—*to all of us in whatever it is that we do!* Imagine what Sabbath as God intended it to be could mean for you and me. Not just a day off. Not just a morning to sleep in. Not just a change in the

---

5. Rabbi Noah Weinberg, "Shabbat—Heaven on Earth," <http://www.aish.com/shabbatthemes/explorations>.

6. And if that's what *the Sabbath* is supposed to be about, is it not also what *worship on the Sabbath* should be about? Whenever two or more of us gather together on the Sabbath, our Sabbath Schools and church services should be about celebrating grace.

7. Henry W. Soltau, *The Tabernacle, the Priesthood and the Offerings* (Grand Rapids, Mich.: Kregel Publications, 1998), 470.

work-a-day routine. But a fresh, invigorating, reassuring, cleansing, re-infusion of grace—a day that puts a smile on our face that lasts for a week. A day we hate to see end.

Then imagine what it must be like for God to give His people this essential gift, only to see those very people turn the gift into something they dread, something that puts a frown on their faces, something they hate to see begin. How in the world did Sabbath-keepers manage to turn the Sabbath into the badge of righteousness by works? How did God's chosen people transform the tabernacle into a fearful symbol of judgment? How did the already redeemed redefine the gospel of grace and make salvation something we could earn?

LEARNING FROM THE NAHUSHTAN

Hezekiah might be able to answer these puzzling questions.

Hezekiah is a young man when he becomes king in Jerusalem. By the end of his reign, the Bible will refer to him as Judah's best king of all time: "There was no one like him among all the kings of Judah, either before him or after him" (2 Kings 18:5). The secret of Hezekiah's success is found in his unflagging commitment to God: "Hezekiah trusted in the LORD, the God of Israel. . . . He held fast to the LORD and did not cease to follow him; he kept the commands the LORD had given Moses. And the LORD was with him; he was successful in whatever he undertook" (verses 5–7).

In the first month of the first year of Hezekiah's reign, he orders the Levites to "purify the temple" (2 Chronicles 29:3, 15, 16). " 'Consecrate yourselves now,' " the young king tells the Levites, and then " 'remove all defilement from the sanctuary' " (verse 5). It takes them two weeks to remove everything unclean that clutters the temple (verse 17).

Sometime during those two weeks, Hezekiah becomes curious about how the Levites are progressing with their assignment. When Hezekiah walks into the temple courtyard, he's probably met by a Levite who has been assigned to explain to him the work that is being done. They walk together among the piles of foreign objects that are being taken out of the sacred rooms—Hezekiah asking questions, the Levite giving answers.

In one corner of the courtyard, Hezekiah notices something he had never seen before. Leaning up against a wall is a long pole that has a bronze sculpture of a snake wrapped around the top of it.

"What is this?" Hezekiah asks.

The Levite answers, "Do you remember this story of our forefathers? In the fortieth year after leaving Egypt, while they were wandering through the desert, many of them were bitten by venomous snakes and died. The rest of the people began to complain to Moses." (We read the story in Numbers 21:4–9.)

Hezekiah remembers.

"Do you remember," the Levite continues, "that God instructed Moses to make a bronze snake, attach it to a pole and hold it up for the people to see? He said that if the people who had been bitten looked at this bronze symbol, they would live. Believe it or not, this is that very snake."

Hezekiah knows the story. What Hezekiah couldn't have known was that hundreds of years after his time, Jesus will claim that this symbol represents His own redemptive ministry to our "snake-bit" world (see John 3:1–15).

In spite of its sacred origin and its historical significance, the bronze snake is on the trash heap of defiling clutter because the people of God have forgotten the God behind the symbol and have started worshipping the symbol itself! "Up to that time the Israelites had been burning incense *to it*" (2 Kings 18:4). They have even given the symbol a name: It is called "the Nahushtan."

Hezekiah, the young king, trusting and holding fast to the Lord, picks up the Nahushtan—this ancient sacred symbol commanded by God, shaped by Moses, later referred to by Jesus—and breaks it into pieces. The only worship Hezekiah will permit in his kingdom is the worship of Yahweh, the God of heaven. The worship of symbols must cease.

How often have we turned our sacred symbols into Nahushtans—into objects of worship? How many Sabbaths—this cherished, sacred symbol of God's enduring love, this symbol commanded by God, shaped by our spiritual ancestors, honored by Jesus—how many Sabbaths have we worshipped instead of worshipping the God to whom the Sabbath was intended to direct us?

The sanctuary is a stunning visual presentation of everything God does for us—ministering to us, dying for us, being our Bread of life, the Light of our world, the fragrant offering ascending to the throne of God in our behalf. It's a stunning spiritual symbol of what it means to rest in the presence of Jesus in our life. How often have we made the sanctuary the object of our worship in place of God?

And what would it mean for us to smash the symbols?

Some friends of mine have concluded that smashing the symbol means abandoning the Sabbath altogether, forgetting what God has invited us to remember. In my opinion, that's an altogether unwarranted, unproductive, unnecessary action. Other friends have decided there is no truth in the Old Testament sanctuary, that it was merely an imperfect attempt of an ignorant people who weren't smart enough to develop a more sophisticated theology. Or worse, the unfortunate command of a perplexed God who couldn't think up any other way to make a point. How sad to miss the richness of the symbol and its ability to cause our eyes to open to an involved God, revealing His primary nature to a consistently stubborn people.

For us, instead, the answer lies in smashing the *worship of the symbol,* not the symbol itself.

It is there, behind the symbols, that we discover the wealth of the tabernacle, the delight of the Sabbath (Isaiah 58:13). There we sing for joy, "How great are *Your works,* O Lord, how profound *Your thoughts.* . . . How good it is to proclaim *Your love* in the morning, and *Your faithfulness* at night." It is there the righteous "will grow like a cedar of Lebanon; *planted in the house of the Lord, they will flourish in the courts of our God.*" [8]

---

8. See Psalm 92; a psalm for the Sabbath day.

# GRACE IN QUESTION

## CHAPTER 5: THE FINISHED WORK

This chapter continues the examination of Old Testament themes, especially the Sabbath and the wilderness sanctuary. These powerful symbols reveal the enduring strength of God's grace and help us understand salvation by grace alone.

1. Recall a project you have completed, and tell about the satisfaction, the joy, and the pleasure that particular finished work brought to you. How is your experience like that of God when He came to the end of the Creation week and instituted the Sabbath?

2. What are your best family celebration memories? When have your Sabbaths been like those celebrations? What keeps Sabbath from being more like biblical and family celebrations?

3. Christians continue to engage in activities that distinguish between " 'the holy and the common, between the unclean and the clean' " (Leviticus 10:10). Buy a poster board and invite all the members of your study group to bring tasteful illustrations from newspapers or magazines that show the Christian task of distinguishing. How does having grace at the center of your life make that task easier?

4. Discuss the rabbinical understanding of what work is prohibited on the Sabbath. What do you think of the idea that "the Sabbath is about ceasing from our attempts to be God"?

5. Read the story of the Nahushtan in 2 Kings 18. What does it mean for you to smash the worship of the symbols and return to the worship of the God behind the symbols?

# GRACE NOTES
## JOEL 2—THE DAY OF THE LORD

If there is one subject about which the Old Testament prophets agree, it is what they called "the day of the Lord." Knowing full well that God's people are in no condition to face judgment, understanding that the surrounding nations are a long ways away from accepting Israel's God, the prophets speak of the end of human history in the most frightening terms.

Q. How does the Old Testament "day of the Lord" reveal our need for grace?

" 'The day . . . of the LORD is near—
a day of clouds,
      a time of doom for the nations' " (Ezekiel 30:3).

"The great day of the LORD is near—
    near and coming quickly.
Listen! The cry on the day of the LORD will be bitter" (Zephaniah 1:14).

Q. What assures us that we are standing in the place of deliverance?

Why do you long for the day of the LORD?
    That day will be darkness, not light.
It will be as though a man fled from a lion
    only to meet a bear,
as though he entered his house
    and rested his hand on the wall
    only to have a snake bite him (Amos 5:18, 19).

Listen, a noise on the mountains,
    like that of a great multitude!
Listen, an uproar among the kingdoms,
    like nations massing together!
The LORD Almighty is mustering
    an army for war.
They come from faraway lands,
    from the ends of the heavens—
the LORD and the weapons of his wrath—
    to destroy the whole country.
Wail, for the day of the LORD is near;
    it will come like destruction from the Almighty.
Because of this, all hands will go limp,
    every man's heart will melt.
Terror will seize them,
    pain and anguish will grip them;

they will writhe like a woman in labor.
They will look aghast at each other,
    their faces aflame (Isaiah 13:4–8).

Blow the trumpet in Zion;
    sound the alarm on my holy hill.
Let all who live in the land tremble,
    for the day of the LORD is coming.
It is close at hand—
    a day of darkness and gloom,
    a day of clouds and blackness.
Like dawn spreading across the mountains
    a large and mighty army comes,
such as never was of old
    nor ever will be in ages to come.

Before them fire devours,
    behind them a flame blazes.
Before them the land is like the garden of Eden,
    behind them, a desert waste—
    nothing escapes them (Joel 2:1–3).

They rush upon the city;
    they run along the wall.
They climb into the houses;
    like thieves they enter through the windows.
Before them the earth shakes,
    the sky trembles,
the sun and moon are darkened,
    and the stars no longer shine.
The LORD thunders
    at the head of his army (verses 9–11).

Doom. Bitterness. Darkness. Wrath. Destruction. Wailing. Terror, pain, and anguish. Trembling. Earthquakes. Thunder. Really makes you long for the Second Coming, doesn't it? Another strike against the Old Testament picture of God!

Or is it? Jesus talks like this about the same subject: " 'You will be handed over to be persecuted and put to death, and you will be hated by all nations because of me. . . . There will be great distress, unequaled from the beginning of the world until now— and never to be equaled again. . . . There will be weeping and gnashing of teeth' " (Matthew 24:9, 21, 51). " 'Then he will say to those on his left, "Depart from me, you who are cursed, into the eternal fire prepared for the devil and his angels" ' " (25:41).

Peter quotes Joel 2 about darkness and blood (Acts 2:20). Paul refers to the day of the Lord as coming like a thief in the night (1 Thessalonians 5:2). John's depictions of the coming of the Lord are no less terrifying:

> The kings of the earth, the princes, the generals, the rich, the mighty, and every slave and every free man hid in caves and among the rocks of the mountains. They called to the mountains and the rocks, "Fall on us and hide us from the face of him who sits on the throne and from the wrath of the Lamb!" (Revelation 6:15, 16).

> The armies of heaven were following him, riding on white horses and dressed in fine linen, white and clean. Out of his mouth comes a sharp sword with which to strike down the nations. "He will rule them with an iron scepter." He treads the winepress of the fury of the wrath of God Almighty (19:14, 15).

> I saw an angel standing in the sun, who cried in a loud voice to all the birds flying in midair, "Come, gather together for the great supper of God, so that you may eat the flesh of kings, generals, and mighty men, of horses and their riders, and the flesh of all people, free and slave, small and great" (verses 17, 18).

This is not an Old Testament/New Testament conflict. There's something else going on here. Something fundamental. Something basic. Something the prophets want us to grasp. Perhaps the clue is here in the questions that follow the description of destruction: "The day of the LORD is great; it is dreadful. Who can endure it?" (Joel 2:11). "Who can endure the day of his coming? Who can stand when he appears?" (Malachi 3:2). " 'Who can stand?' " (Revelation 6:17).

In reality, there are just two places to stand in the great day of the Lord. Some will choose to stand on their own laurels. They will actually look up into the face of the One coming in the clouds and say, "No, thank You. I'd rather be judged on my own merits than accept any gifts. I'd rather try to endure Your coming in my own strength." God's appeal to them is, " 'Even now, . . . return to me with all your heart, with fasting and weeping and mourning.' Rend your heart and not your garments. Return to the LORD your God, for he is gracious and compassionate, slow to anger and abounding in love" (Joel 2:12, 13).

The other place to stand is on the place of deliverance, "on Mount Zion and in Jerusalem" (verse 32). That's the place where grace demonstrates God's love for us (Romans 5:8) from Calvary, where Jesus holds out His arms in an astonishing embrace. There is no fear in grace. No doom or destruction. No wailing and trembling. Only compassion and welcome. Only "abounding love."

Who can endure? Who will stand?

"Everyone who calls on the name of the LORD will be saved" (Joel 2:32). Everyone who says yes to the grace of God.

*"The gospel is Christ's voice."*
—Augustine, *Sermon XXXV*


*" 'There's more joy in heaven over one sinner's rescued life
than over ninety-nine good people in no need of rescue.' "*
—Luke 15:10, *The Message*


*"Wherever the assertion that Jesus is the Christ is maintained,
there is the Christian message.
Wherever this assertion is denied, the Christian message is not affirmed."*
—Paul Tillich, *Systematic Theology*


*"The religion which underlies the New Testament writings
is a religion of grace, or it is nothing."*
—James Moffat, *Grace in the New Testament*


*"Grace is the willingness of God to initiate and accomplish
what is necessary to salvation."*
—Edwin Zackrison, "A Theology of Sin, Grace and Forgiveness"

# CHAPTER 6
# THE IMPOSSIBLE CAMEL:
## *The Incarnation of Grace in the Life of Jesus*

BREATHLESS WAS THE AIR OVER BETHLEHEM."
With these ten charged syllables, C. S. Lewis opens his poem "The Turn of the Tide"[1] about that moment two thousand years ago when, in a little town in the Middle East, "the hopes and fears of all the years" were met in a borrowed stable around the corner from a packed hotel. Lewis continues:

> The romp and war of beast in swamp and jungle ceased
> The forest grew still as though it slept.
> So it ran about the girth of the planet. From the Earth
> A signal, a warning, went out
> And away behind the air. Her neighbours were aware of change.

Was this the moment the Old Testament people had longed for? " 'My righteousness draws near speedily, my salvation is on the way, and my arm will bring justice to the nations' " (Isaiah 51:5). Had the " 'sun of righteousness' " finally risen " 'with healing in its wings' " (Malachi 4:2)? Had the Wonderful Counselor, the Mighty God, the Everlasting Father, the Prince of Peace (Isaiah 9:6), the " 'ruler over Israel, whose origins are from of old, from ancient times' " come at last to the people walking in darkness, searching for a great light (Micah 5:2; Isaiah 9:2)?

> And a rustling, a relaxing began,
> With a rumour and noise of the resuming of joys,
> On the nerves of the universe it ran.
> Then pulsing into space with delicate, dulcet pace
> Came a music, infinitely small
> And clear. But it swelled and drew nearer and held
> All worlds in the sharpness of its call.

---

1. C. S. Lewis, *Poems* (New York: Harcourt Brace Jovanovich, 1964), 49.

Our picture of the moment is well drawn and familiar. From the amazing Florentine Sandro Botticelli at the end of the fifteenth century to Harry Anderson, the gifted Adventist illustrator who died in 1996 at the age of ninety, great artists have made the parts of the scene come alive for us. The stable. The straw. The curious donkey and cow. A hopeful father. A wondering young mother. A star overhead, and angels hovering just out of sight, about to burst into jubilant song.

> Such a note as neither Throne
>     nor Potentate had known
> Since the Word first founded the abyss,
> But this time it was changed in a
>     mystery, estranged,
> A paradox, an ambiguous bliss.
> Heaven danced to it and burned. Such
>     answer was returned
> To the hush, the *Favete*, the fear
> That Earth had sent out; revel, mirth
>     and shout
> Descended to her, sphere below sphere.

Patriarchs, prophets, and kings had dreamed of such a moment. Mothers and fathers of Israel had longed for the coming of a Messiah. "Oh, that salvation for Israel would come out of Zion!" (Psalm 14:7). The earth, "dark through a misapprehension of God,"[2] groaned to its core for deliverance. Elizabeth and Zechariah had listened to the angel's voice (Luke 1:17). Joseph and Mary had responded to the heavenly invitation, " 'Do not be afraid' " (Luke 1:30).

> A shiver of re-birth and deliverance on
>     the Earth
> Went gliding. Her bonds were
>     released . . .
> So death lay in arrest. But at Bethlehem

> the bless'd
> Nothing greater could be heard
> Than a dry wind in the thorn, the cry
>     of the One new-born,
> And cattle in stall as they stirred.

## A SAVIOR HAS BEEN BORN

The New Testament makes a direct connection between Jesus and salvation. The connection begins before His birth. When the angel informs Joseph about Mary's pregnancy, the heavenly messenger also gives Joseph a name for the Baby: " 'You are to give him the name Jesus,' " the angel says, " 'because he will *save his people* from their sins' " (Matthew 1:21, emphasis supplied in this and the following passages). Old Zechariah's response to the news is heartfelt and to the point. "Filled with the Holy Spirit," he speaks up. " 'Praise be to the Lord, the God of Israel, because he has come and has redeemed his people. He has raised up *a horn of salvation* for us' " (Luke 1:67–69). " 'A *Savior* has been born to you,' " the angel reports to the shepherds in the Bethlehem hills (2:11).

Quickly, this issue of saving becomes central to how the story of Jesus is communicated. Jesus says His mission is "to save." " 'The Son of Man came to seek and *to save* what was lost,' " He explains to Zacchaeus, pointing out who does the seeking and the saving (Luke 19:10). John tells us, "The Father has sent his Son to be *the Savior* of the world" (1 John 4:14); " 'God did not send his Son into the world to condemn the world, but *to save* the world through him' " (John 3:17). Even when Jesus is hanging on the cross, people throw the issue of saving into His face: " 'He saved others,' " they say, " 'but he can't save himself!' " (Matthew 27:42).

In fact, the New Testament refers to the good news that Christianity has to offer, the

---

2. Ellen G. White, *The Desire of Ages* (Mountain View, Calif.: Pacific Press®, 1940), 22.

good news we call "the gospel"—the "gospel about Jesus" (Mark 1:1), "the gospel of Christ" (2 Corinthians 10:14; Philippians 1:27), the "gospel of God's grace" (Acts 20:24)—as "the gospel of your salvation" (Ephesians 1:13). It tells us that salvation is the goal of our faith (1 Peter 1:9). " 'Salvation is found in no one else,' " Luke reports Peter's words (Acts 4:12). John adds, " 'Salvation belongs to our God, who sits on the throne, and to the Lamb' " (Revelation 7:10). "By this gospel you are saved," Paul concludes (1 Corinthians 15:2).

*Salvation* is one of the Bible's larger-than-life words. It connotes full deliverance from all the ravages of sin we experience in this enemy-held territory we call planet Earth—all the pain and sorrow and destruction, all the atrocities, the guilt, the hopelessness (Revelation 21:4); all the sorrow we feel at the graveside of a friend or loved one who has died too young; all the helplessness we feel when we watch the dissolution of a once-cherished relationship; all the anger that rises up when we're reading a newspaper report about another senseless suicide bombing, another neglected or abused child, another deadly natural disaster; all the discouragement that almost overwhelms us in this world. Salvation delivers us from all of that. *Jesus* delivers us from all of that. When you hear the word *salvation,* think big—think Second Coming clouds and thunder and lightning, think heaven, think eternity.[3]

And, oh, how we long to be delivered! We are blessed at the La Sierra University Church to have a big church full of wonderful people. But sometimes, with such a large congregation, it seems we lose a dear friend to death almost every week. Our pastoral staff deals with these tragedies professionally, doing all the right things at the right time, but, frankly, none of us is ever fully prepared for the awful reality.

One recent Sabbath morning, as we were waiting to go onto the platform, listening to the prelude just before our worship service, someone came and whispered the dreadful news that one of the dearest men any of us had ever known, Leonard Moore, had died suddenly that morning. We were stunned. It was difficult for Sam to make the announcement, and almost impossible for Dan to preach.

Leonard had been in the hospital before. Years earlier, he had survived a heart attack. We had discussed what happens when people die. He was so grateful to have lived to see a strong grace orientation in the church he loved. We had read together the metaphors of salvation in the book of Isaiah: "We have a strong city; God makes salvation its walls"

---

3. We frequently talk about salvation as if its chief purpose is to deliver us from *immediate* temptation. As if John the Baptist has said to us, "Behold the Lamb of God who takes away the desire to eat too much *Special K* loaf on Christmas Day and drink too much eggnog on New Year's Eve." As if the primary purpose of the life and death of Jesus is to assist us in not driving too fast on the freeway or yelling at our dog at home. Assuredly, deliverance from immediate temptation is also a work of God's grace in our lives. But the salvation we're speaking of in this chapter, *biblical* salvation, is big-picture salvation, capital "S" Salvation, the act of God and God alone that by His grace gives us an *eternal* home in heaven. Knowing we have been given eternal salvation is what motivates us in the cooperative sanctification process. It's eternal salvation we'll be talking about in that moment when we look up and say, " 'Surely this is our God; we trusted in him, and he saved us. This is the Lord, . . . let us rejoice and be glad in His salvation' " (Isaiah 25:9). "My salvation will not be delayed," God promises. "I will grant salvation to Zion" (46:13).

It is important that we make the distinction. If we don't, we slip down the slippery slope into the fallacy of basing our salvation, in whole or in part, on the progress of our sanctification: We believe easily that if we drive the speed limit, and don't yell at the dog, we'll be fit candidates for heaven, "safe to save." Such a perspective diminishes our reliance on the grace of Christ alone for eternal salvation.

(Isaiah 26:1). Leonard knew the Architect of that city. "I know where I'm going," he had told me. "I'm absolutely sure."

For Leonard and for all of us, salvation began when Jesus accepted us into His family long before we knew Him (Romans 5:6–10; Ephesians 2:1–5). It continues in the present as we stand assured of our place in His kingdom (1 John 5:11–13). It will have a glorious fulfillment in the future when Jesus takes us to heaven to live eternally with Him (John 14:1–3). The book of Revelation tells us that the redeemed will give all the honor and glory and praise to Jesus for making our salvation a reality (Revelation 5:9–12).

PARABLES OF GRACE

So if salvation is such a big deal in the New Testament, shouldn't we expect to hear about it directly from Jesus? In fact, we do.

We hear His interest in salvation in the stories He tells. In the parables, "grace is how the wrong are righted," Scott Hoezee reminds us, "how the crooked are made straight, how the guilty are made innocent, how the sooty are made to shine like stars—in short, how the damned are saved."[4]

Grace is the tiny mustard seed planted by a wise farmer that grows and grows until it becomes the largest tree in the field. Grace is the strong branch that supports all the creatures that live in our gardens (Matthew 13:31, 32). Grace is the yeast the woman mixes into her flour until it penetrates all the dough. Grace is the ingredient that makes our daily bread so satisfying and nutritious (verse 33).

Grace is the merchant on a journey to purchase fine pearls—pearls unaware of their own value. Grace is the joy of selling everything to purchase that one pearl, so it can be his (verses 45, 46).

---

4. Scott Hoezee, *The Riddle of Grace* (Grand Rapids, Mich.: Wm. B. Eerdmans Publishing, 1996), 14.

Grace is the net cast deep into the water in order to catch " 'all kinds of fish' " (verse 47).

Grace is the good Samaritan who knows no national boundary or cultural bias, but who rescues and heals because our need is so immediate and real. Grace is the bandage that binds the wounds when we can't stop the bleeding. Grace is the oil and wine that heal the hurts when we can't even dull the pain. Grace is the donkey that carries us to the place where we can heal, the place we can't reach by ourselves. Grace is the money that pays the expenses for us when we don't have even a pocketful of change (Luke 10:30–35).

Grace is the shepherd who leaves the secure flock and goes off into the wild to rescue that one lost sheep that can't save itself, can't find its way back home, can't even admit it's lost. Grace raises us to Christ's shoulders and carries us home in the dark (Luke 15:3–7).

Grace is the woman searching intently throughout her house, sweeping into the corners and lighting the darkness to find that one lost coin that rolled away and can't get back to where it's supposed to be. Grace is the joyful call to friends and neighbors to join the celebration that the lost is found (Luke 15:8–10).

Grace is the king who takes pity on the debtor who is in way over his head and can never repay what he owes—the king who cancels the debt and lets the debtor go (Matthew 18:23–27).

Grace is the father who runs down the hill at the sight of his son who " 'was dead and is alive again; [who] was lost and is found.' " Grace is the kiss of acceptance, the ring of belonging, the music and dancing, the feast and celebration (Luke 15:11–32).

"In none of these parables is *anything* (except the will of God) portrayed as necessary to the new life in joy," points out Robert Capon in his book, *The Parables of Grace.* "There is in them not one single note of earning or merit,

---

GRACE, PRODIGALS, AND ELDER BROTHERS

"Grace is the celebration of life, relentlessly hounding all the non-celebrants in the world. It is a floating, cosmic bash shouting its way through the streets of the universe, flinging the sweetness of its cassations to every window, pounding at every door in a hilarity beyond all liking and happening, until the prodigals come out at last and dance, and the elder brothers finally take their fingers out of their ears." —Robert Farrar Capon, *Between Noon and Three: Romance, Law, and the Outrage of Grace* (Grand Rapids, Mich.: Wm. B. Eerdmans Publishing, 1997), 72.

---

not one breath about rewarding the rewardable, correcting the correctable, or improving the improvable. There is only the gracious, saving determination of the shepherd, the woman, the king, and the father—all surrogates for God—*to raise the dead.*"[5]

"God loves us with a 'first' love, an unlimited, unconditional love," observes Henri Nouwen in his stunningly beautiful meditation on Rembrandt's magnificent painting *The Return of the Prodigal Son.* "During all this time God has been trying to find me, to know me, and to love me. The question is not 'How am I to find God?' but 'How am I to let myself be found by Him?' . . . In all three parables which Jesus tells in response to the question of why He eats with sinners, He puts the emphasis on God's initiative." Nouwen concludes, "Each time we touch that sacred emptiness of non-demanding

---

5. Robert Farrar Capon, *The Parables of Grace* (Grand Rapids, Mich.: Wm B. Eerdmans Publishing, 1988), 39.

love, heaven and earth tremble and there is great 'rejoicing among the angels of God.' It is the joy for the returning sons and daughters."[6]

## WHAT MUST I DO TO BE SAVED?

We hear Christ's concern for how we are saved in the conversations He has with the people He meets every day. To a paralyzed man in Capernaum, He says, " 'Your sins are forgiven' " (Matthew 9:2). To a group of Pharisees at Levi Matthew's house, He says, " 'I have not come to call the righteous, but sinners' " (Mark 2:17). To the seventy-two He sent door to door, He says, " 'Rejoice that your names are written in heaven' " (Luke 10:20). To Nicodemus, He says, " 'Whoever believes in [God's one and only Son] shall not perish but have eternal life' " (John 3:16).

Of the disciples, He asks, " 'What can a man give in exchange for his soul?' " (Matthew 16:26). To the people who tried to keep children away from Him, He warns, " 'Anyone who will not receive the kingdom of God like a little child will never enter it' " (Mark 10:15). To the one who asks Him, " 'Are only a few people going to be saved?' " He replies, " 'People will come from east and west and north and south, and will take their places at the feast in the kingdom of God' " (Luke 13:22–30). To the Samaritan woman at the well, He promises, " 'The water I give . . . will become . . . a spring of water welling up to eternal life' " (John 4:14).

With a child standing nearby, He says, " 'Your Father in heaven is not willing that any of these little ones should be lost' " (Matthew 18:14). While walking with His disciples, He explains that He has come " 'to give his life as a ransom for many' " (Mark 10:45). While having a meal at the home of Zacchaeus in Jeri-

---

6. Henri Nouwen, *The Return of the Prodigal Son; A Story of Homecoming* (New York: Doubleday, 1992), 106, 133.

cho, He says, " 'Today salvation has come to this house' " (Luke 19:9). While standing in Solomon's Porch in the temple in Jerusalem, He says to a group of Jews, " 'I give them eternal life, and they shall never perish; no one can snatch them out of my hand' " (John 10:28).

Mike Yaconelli observes, "Jesus scandalized an intimidating, elitist, country-club religion by opening membership in the spiritual life to those who had been denied it. What made people furious was Jesus' 'irresponsible' habit of throwing open the doors of his love to the whosoevers, the just-anyones, and the not-a-chancers like you and me. Nothing makes people in the church more angry than grace."[7]

To the questioner we call "the rich, young ruler," Jesus carefully crafts an answer that will lead to an unmistakable conclusion (Matthew 19:16–30; Mark 10:1–31; Luke 18:18–30). "What must I do to be saved?" the young man asks—to "get," or "inherit," eternal life?

"Perfect obedience plus perfect motivation equals perfect righteousness" is the essence of the answer Jesus gives. And perfect righteousness is what salvation demands.

When the young man realizes he can never attain to such a level of perfection, instead of falling at Jesus' feet and confessing his great need, he walks away sorrowful. Jesus watches him go away, knowing that "the rich" are likely to walk away from salvation by grace alone. The rich are all of us who rely on our own goodness, our own merit, our own works for salvation—all of us who say, " ' "I am rich; I have acquired wealth and do not need a thing," ' " all of us who don't realize we are " 'wretched, pitiful, poor, blind and naked' " (Revelation 3:17), all of us who are afraid of grace, who find it difficult to accept Christ's gift of salvation, all of us who follow the example of the young ruler.

" 'It is easier for a camel to go through the eye of a needle,' " Jesus says, picturing an utterly impossible feat by contrasting the largest animal any of the disciples ever would have seen with the smallest opening with which they would have been familiar.

The disciples, watching the entire episode unfold before their eyes, are "greatly astonished." " 'Who then can be saved?' " they ask in discouraged wonder (Matthew 19:24, 25).

The answer Jesus gives turns despair into joy. " 'With [humans] this is impossible,' " Jesus declares. Not "difficult," or "unlikely," or "improbable," or "only if you work really hard at it." It's *impossible,* He says—and then quickly adds, " 'but with God, all things are possible' " (verse 26)![8]

"Grace is all on God's side," Niebuhr summarizes.[9] Edward Heppenstall teaches the same thing: "Salvation by grace means being shaken loose from the folly of implanting our ego at the center with the belief that we must arrive at sinless perfection to be sure of salvation."[10]

Max Lucado states it like this:

> You may be decent. You may pay taxes and kiss your kids and sleep with a clean conscience. But apart from Christ

---

7. Michael Yaconelli, *Messy Spirituality* (Grand Rapids, Mich.: Zondervan, 2002), 47.

8. "He who is trying to become holy by his own works in keeping the law, is attempting an impossibility. All that man can do without Christ is polluted with selfishness and sin. It is the grace of Christ alone, through faith that can make us holy." (Ellen White, *Steps to Christ* [Mountain View, Calif.: Pacific Press®, 1956], 60.) Jesus' answer "shows further the opposition of Jesus to the popular merit-religion of his day," James Moffatt states. Jesus taught us "that to gain a foothold in the Life or New Age was not an achievement of obedience to the Torah." (*Grace in the New Testament* [London: Hodder and Stoughton, 1931], 77.)

9. H. Richard Niebuhr, *Christ and Culture* (New York: Harper & Row Publishers, 1951), 152.

10. Edward Heppenstall, *Salvation Unlimited* (Washington, D.C.: Review and Herald, 1974), 82.

you aren't holy. So how can you go to heaven?

Only believe.

Accept the work already done, the work of Jesus on the cross.

Only believe.

Accept the goodness of Jesus Christ. Abandon your own works and accept His. Abandon your own decency and accept His.

Stand before God in His name, not yours.

It's that simple? It's that simple. It's that easy? There was nothing easy at all about it. The cross was heavy, the blood was real, and the price was extravagant. It would have bankrupted you or me, so He paid it for us. Call it simple. Call it a gift. But don't call it easy.

Call it what it is. Call it grace.[11]

---

# GRACE IN QUESTION
## CHAPTER 6: THE IMPOSSIBLE CAMEL

In the first four books of the New Testament, we come suddenly to the incarnation of all the hopes and longings of the Old Testament believers and to the unmistakable revelation of God's grace in the ministry and teaching of Jesus. In parables and sermons and in His relationship with the sinners He came to save, we discover grace in action.

1. Do you approach the biblical story of Jesus with
   a. a relatively high level of confidence that the events actually took place?
   b. a feeling that the event probably occurred?
   c. a serious question about the event's historical accuracy?
   d. a certainty that the event did not take place at the time or in the manner the Bible reports?
2. How does your answer to question 1 impact your view of the doctrine of inspiration, your place in the two-thousand-year flow of church history, and your understanding of salvation?
3. Read the sidebar (on page 94) about Adventist authors writing about salvation through Jesus alone. Count the different pictures the authors present to help us understand the connection between Jesus and salvation. Discuss the different pictures. Is there one you feel drawn to? What other pictures are you aware of from Adventist authors?
4. Read the parable of the Good Samaritan again (Luke 10:30–35). How is grace represented by "the bandage which binds the wounds, the oil and wine which soothe the hurts, the donkey which carries us to the place where healing can take place, the money which pays the expenses"?
5. The section "What must I do to be saved?" (beginning on page 94) contains three rounds of quotations from Matthew, Mark, Luke, and John. Ask four people in your study group to read these Bible verses (they can read them right from this chapter), one person reading Matthew, the next person reading Mark, etc. Discuss what is consistent about the testimony presented in these verses. How and why do you think some of the details differ?

---

11. Max Lucado, *A Gentle Thunder* (Dallas: Word Publishing, 1995), 136, 137.

# GRACE NOTES
## MATTHEW 2—THE WISDOM OF THE GENTILES

Luke, the Gentile, gives us the part of the Christmas story about the Hebrew shepherds (Luke 2:8–20). Matthew, the Hebrew, adds the story of the Gentile wise men (Matthew 2:1–12).

We know they were wise because they were looking for Jesus (Matthew 2:2). We don't know their names—although by the third century we were calling them Gaspar, Melchior, and Balthazar. We don't really know how many of them there were—the "three" comes from the number of gifts they brought: gold, frankincense, and myrrh (Matthew 2:11). Artists throughout the years have painted one of them as young, one of them as middle aged, and one of them as older. They've been depicted ever since the sixth century as a European, an African, and an Asian. The "Magi" have become symbols of the inclusive nature of Christianity: all ages, all races, all searching for the Christ-Child.

They came to Jerusalem "from the east" (Matthew 2:1). Their probable route coiled through the desert along an ancient caravan trail as rich in lore as the gifts they brought.

For the past four thousand years, from just before the time of Moses, one of the most precious commodities in the world has been the hardened sap of a squat, unassuming, bushlike tree—a substance the locals call *bakhoor*. The substance was coveted by Old Testament prophets, Egyptian pharaohs, Persian kings, and the queen of Sheba. We know it as frankincense.

The trees that produce frankincense grow only in a few places in the world. One of those places is in the region known as Dhofar, along the southern coast of the sultanate of Oman. North and east of Dhofar stretches the driest part of the Sahara Desert, the Rub' al Khali, the "Empty Quarter," which some have called the most brutal desert in the world. But Dhofar itself is a tropical paradise, with mountains looming above the shores of the Arabian Sea.

Long ago, as the great camel caravans from India and China—sometimes numbering a thousand camels and stretching out for miles—wound their way around and through the deserts, and as the locals began selling frankincense, cities began to spring up along the route. Some of these cities became strategic centers of the frankincense trade—fortresses for protection.

One such oasis was Iram, capital of the ancient kingdom of 'Ad. Iram became a great city, fabulously wealthy. Then, suddenly, around A.D. 100, it disappeared completely. The Qur'an says the desert sands swallowed the city after the people turned their backs on God.

Archaeologists have been searching for the city ever since, but it remained hidden for two thousand years. Many had begun to wonder if the stories about

Q. In what way is "the cry of the One new-born" in Bethlehem the greatest sound we've ever heard?

Q. What is there about grace that makes you want to worship?

its existence were just fables, even though the Bedouins still talked of the disappeared city to which all caravan trails at one time led. They called the lost city Ubar.

In the 1980s, archeologist Nicholas Clapp was doing research in the Huntington Library in Pasadena. He found there an ancient map of the Arabian Peninsula complete with the old caravan trails leading to Ubar. Clapp convinced NASA to provide him with satellite images of the area. When the images were delivered, there beneath the sands were the old trails (identified by centuries of camel droppings), and they matched the trails on the map.

Clapp assembled an archeological team and began digging. On February 5, 1992, newspapers around the world announced: "The fabled lost city of Ubar, called 'the Atlantis of the Sands' by Lawrence of Arabia, has been found in remote southern Oman." Remains of the frankincense trade were everywhere. The archaeologists also found that the city had been built over a limestone cave, which had become larger and larger as the city had grown and become heavier until the roof of the cave collapsed under all the weight, and the city disappeared.

Perhaps the wise men from the east at the time of Christ's birth traveled through the desert on the frankincense trail. Perhaps they stopped in Ubar. But by the time they arrived in Bethlehem, one thing was certain: Already they were connected to the Child. They couldn't have known it, but earlier in the story, Joseph and Mary had taken Baby Jesus to the temple in Jerusalem "to do for him what the custom of the Law required" (Luke 2:27). In Jerusalem lived a good, old man named Simeon, who, like the Magi, was looking for the coming of the Messiah (verse 25). Moved by the Holy Spirit, Simeon had gone to the temple (verse 27). When Joseph and Mary arrived, Simeon went to them, took Jesus in his arms and praised God, saying, " 'Sovereign Lord, as you have promised, you now dismiss your servant in peace. For my eyes have seen your salvation' " (verses 29, 30).

Listen to what Simeon says next. This salvation, which the old man believes came through Jesus, has been prepared by God " 'in the sight of all people, a light for revelation to the Gentiles and for glory to your people Israel' " (verse 31, 32). The Magi are in the thoughts of the Christ-Child before the Christ-Child is in the thoughts of the Magi!

" 'Rejoice, O Gentiles, with [God's] people,' " Paul quotes the psalmist as saying (Romans 15:10). " 'Praise the Lord, all you Gentiles, and sing praises to him, all you peoples' " (verse 11). " 'The Root of Jesse will spring up, one who will arise to rule over the nations,' " Paul reflects on Isaiah. " 'The Gentiles will hope in him' " (verse 12). Christ "redeemed us in order that the blessing given to Abraham might come to the Gentiles through Christ Jesus" (Galatians 3:14). "This mystery is that through the gospel the Gentiles are heirs together with Israel, members together of one body, and sharers together in the promise in Christ Jesus" (Ephesians 3:6).

When the Magi see the star over Bethlehem, they are "overjoyed" (Matthew 2:10). When they see the Christ-Child, "they [bow] down and worship" (verse 11). Grace has a way of doing that to you. It fills you with joy. It makes you want to worship.

Caravaggio completed his stunning and focused *Conversion of Saint Paul* in 1601. The blustery, punishing, obsessive Saul doesn't know it yet, but grace is exactly what he needs (see chapter 7, page 103).

" 'My grace is sufficient for you.' "

—2 CORINTHIANS 12:9


"The Bible is a witness, and at its center it attests the sovereign,
liberating grace of God in Christ."

—DANIEL MIGLIORE, *FAITH SEEKING UNDERSTANDING*


"There remains no other possibility of justification than this—
that God does not 'reckon,' does not impute the sin and its guilt,
'not counting their sins against them.' "

—HANS KÜNG, *JUSTIFICATION*


"Justification is an act of God's free grace through which the sinner
is absolved from guilt and accepted as righteous
on account of the Son's atoning work."

—THOMAS ODEN, *THE JUSTIFICATION READER*


"Nothing of human merit precedes the grace of God."

—AUGUSTINE, LETTER 186

# The Justified Sinner:
## *The Crescendo of Grace in the Theology of Paul*

I N THE FERTILE GREEK LEGENDS OF THE TROJAN WAR LIVES A REPUGNANT figure named Hephaistos.[1] Although a son of Zeus and Hera, the deformed and clumsy Hephaistos early in his life becomes an object of derision and wrath and is indignantly expelled from his home among the gods. There are two versions of the expulsion story. In one, father Zeus flings his meddling son from the top of Mount Olympus, and Hephaistos falls heavily onto a rocky island in the Aegean Sea far below.[2] The second version implicates the mother: Embarrassed by her crippled son, Hera disowns Hephaistos, drags him to the sea, and tries to drown him.

From such an inglorious beginning, Hephaistos plunges into a series of desperate attempts to secure lasting love and to work his way back to Olympus. "The heart of Zeus is hard to appease," he whines in self-pity.[3] Driven by rage, haunted by derisive laughter, frustrated in romance, Hephaistos labors day after day in a "hot and horrid workshop, full of noise and sweat and hissing irons."[4] Hating his own remarkable skills,[5] he beats his hammer on a great anvil in his fiery forge beneath the eruptions of a volcano. Aphrodite, the goddess of love and beauty, is unfaithful to him. Mighty Athena rejects his advances. His vengeful plot to punish his mother fails when he gets "obliviously drunk."[6]

In the midst of the majestic legends of heroic champions and intrepid explorers, the squalid Hephaistos rises from the pages of Homer and Aeschylus (525–456 B.C.) as particularly unlovable. "Among the perfectly beautiful immortals," Edith Hamilton observes, "he only was ugly."[7] His huge, limping bulk, sweaty and hairy

---

1. Often spelled Hephaestus. *The American Heritage Dictionary* pronounces his name Heh-FES-tus.

2. "From morn to noon he fell, from noon to dewy eve, A summer's day, and with the setting sun Dropt from the zenith like a falling star, On Lemnos, the Aegean isle." (Milton.)

3. Aeschylus, *Prometheus Bound,* line 34.

4. Nigel Spivey, *Greek Art* (London: Phaidon Press Limited, 1997), 8.

5. "I hate my craft, I hate the skill of my own hands. . . . I wish some other had been given my skill." (Aeschylus, *Prometheus Bound,* lines 45, 48.)

6. Spivey, 9.

7. Edith Hamilton, *Mythology* (Boston: Little, Brown and Company, 1942), 36.

and unrepentant, repulses us. His stubborn unworthiness reminds us too clearly of our own unsuccessful graspings.

Then, suddenly, in this dark chapter of mythology, a woman of remarkable redemptive character appears. In full knowledge of Hephaistos's sordid past, she approaches him intentionally. Seeing through his unattractiveness, she embraces him. Desiring what is best for him, she marries him. She speaks in his behalf and sweetly invites her husband once again to occupy a place of importance.[8] In Greek, her name is *Charis*.[9]

In English, we know her as Grace.

### Enter Saul of Tarsus

Centuries pass from the first telling of the story of Hephaistos.[10] The Greek nation moves off the center of history, but its language remains the highway for the commerce of civilization. And in the Mediterranean city of Tarsus in Cilicia, a Hebrew child is born and given the name Saul. The boy grows up in a multicultural setting; an observant Jew, he speaks the languages and enjoys all the privileges of a citizen of the Roman-controlled empire. By his own telling, Saul becomes ferociously Jewish, "advancing in Judaism beyond many Jews of my own age and was extremely zealous for the traditions of my fathers" (Galatians 1:13).

Somewhere along the way, Saul's parents move to Jerusalem (Acts 22:3) and enroll him in one of the two leading academies of learning in the Jewish world[11]—the School of Hillel, founded by the great Babylonian-born scholar Hillel himself. The leadership of the school has been passed down to Rabbi Simeon, Hillel's son, and then to Simeon's son, Gamaliel, who came to be known as Rabban Gamaliel the Elder.[12]

In his "intellectual biography" called *Rabbi Paul,* author Bruce Chilton refers to Gamaliel as "the most famous patriarch of the Pharisees," "the most famous rabbi of his generation," "the greatest patriarch in the whole movement," and a master of "discreet force, moral persuasion, and brilliant argument." "Gamaliel's influence on the Pharisaic movement is so great," Chil-

---

8. Homer, *The Iliad,* book 18.

9. "Fair Charis of the shining chaplet." (Homer, *The Iliad,* book 18.)

10. The Greek myths are mostly from the period of Classical Greece, around five hundred years before Christ, although many of the stories are from a much earlier period, from the time of Homer, about 800 B.C. The myths were added to and adapted until around 400 B.C., when they finally were written as the versions with which we have become familiar.

11. According to the *Pirkei Avot,* the "Ethics of the Fathers" in the *Mishna* (a collection of Jewish regulations, ethics, and commentary on biblical laws and the Jewish oral tradition), the Torah was given by Moses to Joshua, by Joshua to the Elders, then to the Prophets, and then to the men of the Great Assembly. This group of 120 wise leaders, brought together by Ezra, included the prophets Haggai, Zechariah, and Malachi as well as certain priests and sages, such as Mordecai from the story of Esther. (Today's Israeli Parliament, the *Knesset,* has 120 members in imitation of the Great Assembly.) When Shimon HaTzaddik, the last member of the Great Assembly died in 273 B.C., a period of Jewish history began known as the period of the *Zugot,* "pairs," in which there were always two rabbis leading the discussion of Jewish tradition. One of the two rabbis was given the position of *Av Beit Din,* the head of the Sanhedrin; the other rabbi was made the *Nasi,* or president of the Sanhedrin. By the time of Paul, there were two prominent schools of Jewish thought, which followed the two paths of interpretation of the Zugot—the Hillel school, which had the reputation of being liberal, humane, and practical, and the school of Shammai, which was more conservative and legalistic.

12. *Rabban* is a higher title than *Rabbi* and was given to only a few distinguished leaders of Judaism, teachers of great influence and reputation. Gamaliel, who came into prominence about A.D. 20, earned a seat on the Sanhedrin, presiding over that council during the reigns of Tiberius, Gaius (Caligula), and Claudius.

ton tells us, "the Mishnah conveys his teaching not only by what he said to disciples but also by arrangements in his household and by what he did. The patriarch's every act could be taken as an example."[13]

Gamaliel's son, another Rabbi Simeon, tells us that two types of students came to the Hillel school under his father: One type came to learn the Torah, and the other type came to study Greek wisdom. Surely Saul was one of those students who studied the Torah. But just as certainly, Saul would have, at the minimum, caught the conversations that swirled around Greek philosophers, poets, and gods. One easily can imagine Saul standing just outside a circle of students in which the topic of Homeric legends is being pursued. We can see him absorbing all the majesty of the epic poems, the emotions and passions of the myths, the beauty and tragedy of the tales. And could it be possible that one day, years later, when the now apostle Paul is struggling to find just the right word to describe God's enduring love to sinful people—a concept that in Hebrew doesn't have quite the full force of what he wants to say—that he dips back in his memory of those school discussions? "What was the name of that woman?" Paul may have asked himself. "That intentional, redemptive, embracing wife of Hephaistos? Oh yes, it was Charis—Grace. What a perfect word!"

## DARKNESS IN A STRANGER'S HOUSE

But back to the earlier Saul. He doesn't know it yet, but grace is exactly what he needs. This blustery, punishing, obsessive man (Acts 26:9–11) finds himself sitting in a stranger's house in Damascus. Uncharacteristically, he is quiet, unprotected, almost fragile, having been blinded by an intense vision of where his life is

heading. "About noon, . . . I saw a light from heaven, brighter than the sun, blazing around me" (Acts 26:13). Caravaggio paints the moment of the blinding light with Saul flat on his back on the road. The sword, recently employed in his violent pursuit of the followers of Jesus, has now fallen, useless, to his side. The eyes that have been searching so successfully to discover the hiding places of the Christians now are closed and unseeing. The hands that held the garments of those throwing stones at Stephen now are thrust out in a gesture that at first glance seems defensive, but on a closer examination appears almost welcoming, as if Saul is embracing what the eyes of faith have seen.

But the house in Damascus is dark. Saul can see nothing (Acts 9:8). He must be led about by the hand. He refuses to eat or drink. Night and day are indistinguishable. The darkness overwhelms him, and the emotions of the experience of blindness will never leave him.

Later he will express his mission to the Gentiles as being " ' "to open their eyes and turn them from darkness to light" ' " (Acts 26:18). He will say to the church at Ephesus, "I pray also that the eyes of your heart may be enlightened" (Ephesians 1:18). To the Colossians he will explain that the Father "has rescued us from the dominion of darkness and brought us into the kingdom of the Son he loves" (Colossians 1:13), "the kingdom of light" (verse 12).

"You were once darkness," he will preach, "but now you are light in the Lord. Live as children of light" (Ephesians 5:8). "The night is nearly over; the day is almost here. So let us put aside the deeds of darkness and put on the armor of light" (Romans 13:12). "God, who said, 'Let light shine out of darkness,' made his light shine in our hearts to give us the light of the knowledge of the glory of God in the face

---

13. Bruce Chilton, *Rabbi Paul, An Intellectual Biography* (New York: Doubleday, 2004), 33–41.

of Christ" (2 Corinthians 4:6). "The grace of God that brings salvation has appeared to all" (Titus 2:11).

In the darkness of the stranger's house, Saul struggles for insight. "We fix our eyes not on what is seen, but on what is unseen," he comments later. "For what is seen is temporary, but what is unseen is eternal" (2 Corinthians 4:18). What becomes clear to him, he explains later to Timothy, is that God's gift of salvation to us is "not because of anything we have done but because of his own purpose and grace . . . given us in Christ Jesus before the beginning of time" (2 Timothy 1:9).

God's love for humans is not a reaction to anything we do; it is original, self-initiated, unforced. "Grace would not be grace if it were a response to resources in us. Grace is grace because it highlights God's own overflowing resources of kindness. Grace is eternal because it will take that long for God to expend inexhaustible stores of goodness on us. Grace is free because God would not be the infinite, self-sufficient God he is if he were constrained by anything outside himself."[14]

God does not give grace because of our goodness or our attempts at being good, Saul realizes, even when our behavior is zealous (Galatians 1:14). God does not like us better because we belong to the right group, even when we claim membership among His chosen people (Philippians 3:5). God's perfect love keeps no record of what we do, right or wrong (1 Corinthians 13:5), even when legalistic righteousness would pronounce us "faultless" (Philippians 3:6).

When it comes to salvation, God does all the work. "Praise be to the God and Father of our Lord Jesus Christ," he will say to the church at Ephesus, *"who has blessed us* in the heavenly realms with every spiritual blessing in Christ. For *he chose us* in him before the creation of the world to be holy and blameless in his sight. In love *he predestined us* to be adopted as his [children] through Jesus Christ, in accordance with his pleasure and will—*to the praise of his glorious grace,* which *he has freely given us* in the One he loves. *In him* we have redemption *through his blood,* the forgiveness of sins, in accordance with *the riches of God's grace* that *he lavished on us* with all wisdom and understanding" (Ephesians 1:3–8, emphasis supplied).

UNEXPECTED ACCEPTANCE

Suddenly, unfamiliar hands grasp Saul's shoulders (Acts 9:17), and a voice he has never heard before greets him with unexpected words: "Brother Saul." With these two unpretentious words, Ananias begins an explanation to Saul of the nature of God's grace. First, God does all the work. Then He gives His work to us as a gift. Saul the persecutor doesn't deserve to have the hand of fellowship extended to him. Saul the destroyer of the church doesn't expect to be embraced by the people he was seeking to harm. Saul the enemy who raised havoc (Acts 9:21) doesn't know why he now is received as Brother Saul. It is a surprising, shocking gift—unanticipated, unwarranted.

Paul will later explain what it's like to be a sworn enemy of God, yet receive grace:

Even though I was once a blasphemer and a persecutor and a violent man, I was shown mercy. . . . The grace of our Lord was poured out on me abundantly, along with the faith and love that are in Christ Jesus. Here is a trustworthy saying that deserves full acceptance: Christ Jesus came into the world to save sinners—of whom

---

14. John Piper, *Future Grace* (Sisters, Ore.: Multnomah Books, 1995), 74.

I am the worst. But for that very reason I was shown mercy so that in me, the worst of sinners, Christ Jesus might display his unlimited patience as an example for those who would believe on him and receive eternal life (1 Timothy 1:13–16).

You see, at just the right time, when we were still powerless, Christ died for the ungodly. Very rarely will anyone die for a righteous man, though for a good man someone might possibly dare to die. But God demonstrates his own love for us in this: While we were still sinners, Christ died for us. Since we have now been justified by his blood, how much more shall we be saved from God's wrath through him! For if, when we were God's enemies, we were reconciled to him through the death of his Son, how much more, having been reconciled, shall we be saved through his life! (Romans 5:6–10).

We were by nature objects of wrath. But because of his great love for us, God, who is rich in mercy, made us alive with Christ even when we were dead in transgressions—it is by grace you have been saved (Ephesians 2:3–5).

Although I am less than the least of all God's people, this grace was given me: to preach to the Gentiles the unsearchable riches of Christ (3:8).

Saul's eyesight is restored. He is given food, and his strength returns. He is baptized as a believer in Jesus. At once, he begins telling his story. In the synagogue in Damascus and to all who will listen, Saul declares that Jesus of Nazareth is indeed the Christ (Acts 9:18–22). Saul has become Brother Saul, but he is not yet the apostle Paul. That journey takes many years.

### A VISIT FROM AN OLD FRIEND

For three years Saul wanders between Damascus and the Arabian desert (Galatians 1:17). There is a quick trip to Jerusalem to become acquainted with Peter and meet James, the brother of Jesus (Galatians 1:18). Barnabas, who has befriended Saul, introduces him—retelling his story and assuring Peter that Saul is safe to welcome (Acts 9:26, 27). With threats on his life increasing (Acts 9:29), Saul receives a heavenly command to flee (Acts 22:18, 21). The believers in Jerusalem secretly transport him from the city to the port of Caesarea Maritima and put him on a ship sailing to his home in Tarsus of Cilicia (Acts 9:30). Then Saul disappears for a decade.

These quiet years in the life of Saul are shrouded to us. We know nothing about what projects occupy his time, what pursuits he follows, or what he meditates upon. Is this when he learns to be a tentmaker (Acts 18:3)? Is he preaching in his local church (Galatians 1:23)? Does he write letters to his new friends in Damascus? Does he study the Scriptures to become "wise for salvation" (2 Timothy 3:15)? Does he build up new churches in the surrounding area? Could this be where Saul learns to say, "We do not lose heart" (2 Corinthians 4:1) and "I have learned to be content whatever the circumstances" (Philippians 4:11) and "he who began a good work in you will carry it on to completion" (1:6)? Is this the time when perseverance teaches him "we are hard pressed on every side, but not crushed; perplexed, but not in despair; persecuted, but not abandoned; struck down, but not destroyed" (2 Corinthians 4:8, 9)?

Or does he question his own experience: *What really happened on that road? What did the Voice really say? Why was it so easy to change directions?* Does he wonder why Peter and James don't call him and ask for help or offer him a position in the church headquarters or suggest that he write an autobiography? We just don't know. The Bible record is silent.

One day, there is a knock on the door of Saul's home. It's an old friend, Barnabas. The two haven't seen each other for ten years. ("You haven't changed a bit!" "A little less hair on top of the head." "How's everybody in Jerusalem?" "Whatever happened to . . .?")

Saul invites Barnabas in, but Barnabas is too excited to eat. "I've been looking for you," the man from Jerusalem says to the one-time persecutor. "I want to tell you about this little church I've discovered."

The story begins to unfold. The believers had been fleeing from the persecution that began with the stoning of Stephen ("fleeing from you, Saul"). They scattered across the empire—north, south, east, and west. Far to the north of Jerusalem, in the city of Antioch,[15] the Jewish believers are successfully hiding from the authorities, meeting together in the synagogue on the Sabbath and in little groups during the week, quietly telling the story of Jesus to other Jews, most of whom are hearing it for the very first time. Then, somebody comes up with a new idea. No one remembers who it was. But it is the most exciting thing to happen to the followers of Jesus since the Resurrection! ("It's even bigger than your story, Saul!! Wait till you hear this!!!")

"What would happen if we branched out and adopted a new strategy in telling the story of Jesus," this unknown believer in Antioch suggests. "Why don't we start telling the good news to non-Jews—to the other people in the city? Why shouldn't they hear about Jesus, too?"

It's a new thought, a revolutionary idea. It catches on, and it changes the primary nature of the New Testament church. Seems the Gentiles need Jesus in their lives just as much as the Jews do! "The Lord's hand was with them, and a great number of people believed" (Acts 11:21).

"That's where I came in," Barnabas explains to Saul. "The disturbing news of the revolution in Antioch reached the ears of the church in Jerusalem, and they sent me to investigate" (see verse 22).

That first week in Antioch, Barnabas must have sneaked into the church, sat in the back row, and just listened. Certainly, he didn't announce that he was from headquarters and that he was there to investigate the rumors. After a while, however, he can't keep quiet—but not because what's taking place shocks him. Rather, he loves the idea. It makes him glad, and he encourages the believers (verse 23). And then he thinks about the one-time persecutor and his boldness in telling his story and his confidence in meeting new people. "I thought about you, Saul," Barnabas continues. "I want you to come back with me to Antioch and see for yourself."

It doesn't sound like it takes too long to convince Saul to pack his bags. He quickly puts aside whatever he was doing, and within weeks, the two old friends are back in Antioch. For an entire year they meet with the church, teach the people, and encourage the new direction (verse 26). And Saul begins to understand that not only does God do all the work in salvation, not only does He give us His work as a gift, but He also pursues us no matter where we are or what we're doing. Like an old friend knocking unexpectedly at the door, God keeps showing up, calling, pursuing, offering the gift over and over again. God doesn't leave us; we are the ones who run away. God doesn't turn His back on us; we turn our backs on Him. We do the separating. We do the distinguishing. God likes

---

15. The third largest city in the Roman Empire, after Rome and Alexandria.

these people, we reason, but not those people. Saul learns that such reasoning is untrue.

There is neither Jew nor Greek, slave nor free, male nor female, for you are all one in Christ Jesus (Galatians 3:28).

You are no longer foreigners and aliens, but fellow citizens with God's people and members of God's household (Ephesians 2:19). (*The Message* version of this passage says, "You're no longer strangers or outsiders. You *belong here.*")

Through the gospel the Gentiles are heirs together with Israel, members together of one body, and sharers together in the promise in Christ Jesus (3:6).

The body is a unit, though it is made up of many parts; and though all its parts are many, they form one body. So it is with Christ. For we were all baptized by one Spirit into one body—whether Jews or Greeks, slave or free (1 Corinthians 12:12, 13).

Here there is no Greek or Jew, circumcised or uncircumcised, barbarian, Scythian, slave or free, but Christ is all, and is in all (Colossians 3:11).

There is no difference, for all have sinned and fall short of the glory of God, and are justified freely by his grace through the redemption that came by Christ Jesus (Romans 3:22–24).

More and more grace, more and more people, more and more praise! (2 Corinthians 4:15, *The Message*).

It is no accident that believers are first called Christians at Antioch (Acts 11:26). And Saul the persecutor becomes the apostle Paul (Acts 13:9).

## THE CRESCENDO OF GRACE

Now the crescendo of grace comes into full voice. As in the book of Isaiah, Paul paints as many pictures of "God's abundant provision of grace" (Romans 5:17) as he can think of. Grace *reigns* "through righteousness to bring eternal life" (Romans 5:21). Grace *reconciles* us to God through Jesus (2 Corinthians 5:18). Grace *chooses* us (Romans 11:6), *calls* us (Galatians 1:15), *adopts* us (Ephesians 1:5), *redeems* us (Ephesians 1:7), *saves* us (Ephesians 2:5, 8), *rescues* us (Colossians 1:13), *makes us strong* (2 Timothy 2:1), and *qualifies* us "to share in the inheritance of the saints in the kingdom of light" (Colossians 1:12). Never has there been a believer less afraid of grace!

More than any other of his pictures of grace, Paul prefers the picture that grace "justifies" us.[16] From Paul's point of view, "you cannot speak of the gospel without addressing its central aspect, justification."[17] Luther also prefers this picture, calling justification "the ruler and judge over all other Christian doctrines."[18]

---

16. Justification is the act by which God declares that a sinner will be treated with grace instead of how he or she deserves to be treated. "Justification is not a transformation of inherent character; it does not impart righteousness. . . . In justifying the sinner, God acquits him, declares him to be righteous, regards him as righteous, and proceeds to treat him as righteous." (Siegfried H. Horn, *Seventh-day Adventist Bible Dictionary* [Washington, D.C.: Review and Herald, 1960], 616.)

17. James R. White, *The God Who Justifies* (Minneapolis: Bethany House, 2001), 64.

18. Martin Luther, *The Weimar Edition of Luther's Works*, 39, I, 205.

And Calvin says that justification by grace is "the main pillar on which religion rests."[19] "If this is not the center of Christian theology," Eberhard Jüngel asks, "what is?"[20]

With this legal term, Paul describes the judgment scene in which the Judge pronounces sentence on the guilty sinner. "The Judge does not declare the guilty party to be innocent, for that would be untrue. Neither does the Judge make the guilty person innocent by His sentence. Rather, the Judge says, 'You are justified—I will treat you as if you never had committed a crime.' "[21]

All of us are justified exactly the same way, "freely by his grace through the redemption that came by Christ Jesus" (Romans 3:24). We are justified "by faith apart from observing the law" (verse 28; Galatians 3:24). We are justified by Christ's blood (Romans 5:9). We are justified in the name of the Lord Jesus Christ (1 Corinthians 6:11). We are justified by His grace (Titus 3:7).

"And if by grace," Paul reminds us, "then it is no longer by works" (Romans 11:6). "The promise comes by faith,[22] so that it may be by grace" (4:16). "Since we have been justified through faith, we have peace with God through our Lord Jesus Christ" (5:1). "There is now no condemnation for those who are in Christ Jesus" (8:1). God's grace "came by the grace of the one man, Jesus Christ" (5:15). "The law was put in charge to lead us to Christ that we might be justified by faith" (Galatians 3:24).

By grace alone we are justified, counted righteous, because we are justified by Christ alone. If the Christological formula (*by Christ alone*) "excludes our having any other mediator but Jesus Christ, then the exclusive formula of *sola gratia* [by grace alone] guarantees that everything God has done for humanity in, through and for the sake of Jesus Christ is an unconditional divine gift. . . . If justification did not come about *sola gratia*, but occurred at least in part because of my own merits and qualities, then it would not be because of Christ alone. It would have a further cause apart from God. The *sola gratia* formula protects and ensures that of *solus Christus* [by Christ alone]."[23]

Paul can't let it go. "Grace and peace to you," he says at the opening of his letters. "The grace of the Lord Jesus be with you," he repeats at the close. " 'I do not set aside the grace of God,' " he confesses (2:21). "Let your conversation be always full of grace" (Colossians 4:6). "Be strong in the grace that is in Christ Jesus" (2 Timothy 2:1).

Paul would have taken as a personal mark of identification the instruction of Hebrews 12:15: "See to it that no one misses the grace of God."

---

19. John Calvin, *Institutes,* III, xi, 1. Berkouwer insists that the confession of divine justification "defines the preaching of the Church, the existence and progress of the life of faith, the root of human security, and man's perspective of the future." (G. C. Berkouwer, *Faith and Justification* [Grand Rapids, Mich.: Wm. B. Eerdmans Publishing, 1954], 17.) Lutheran theologians today refer to justification as the "touchstone for the Christian faith" and argue that "no teaching may contradict this criterion" but rather that it "constantly serves to orient all the teaching and practice of our churches to Christ." (*The Joint Declaration on the Doctrine of Justification* [Grand Rapids, Mich.: Wm. B. Eerdmans Publishing, 2000], 46, 16.)

20. Eberhard Jüngel, *Justification: The Heart of the Christian Faith* (Edinburgh: T&T Clark, 2001), 26.

21. Stuart Tyner, *Walking on the Edge* (Riverside, Calif.: Hancock Center Publications, 1996), 32.

22. Biblical faith is being fully persuaded that God has the power to do what He promises to do. See Romans 4:21.

23. Jüngel, ibid., 173, 174.

# GRACE IN QUESTION

## CHAPTER 7: THE JUSTIFIED SINNER

Chapter 7 explores Paul's significant contribution to our understanding of God's grace. We see how his life experience shaped his theology, listen to the many ways he described grace, and hear his favorite explanation of grace in his insistence that we are justified by grace alone through faith alone in Jesus Christ alone.

1. Reread the legend of Hephaistos in the opening pages of this chapter. What qualities do you see in Charis, Grace, that might make her a model for how we understand God's grace to us?

2. During your study group this week, ask for a volunteer to be blindfolded for the entire time you're studying together. At the end of the evening, ask the volunteer how the experience helps understand how Paul desperately desired the light. How does admitting to our spiritual "blindness" assist us in receiving grace?

3. Are we called upon to demonstrate grace by accepting others who are different from us? What does your answer mean for you, your study group, your church?

4. "The disciples were called Christians first at Antioch" (Acts 11:26). What do you see taking place in Antioch that warranted the new name? How does the Antioch experience help us understand what Christianity is supposed to be? How does it help us understand what our church should be doing?

5. Read the paragraph (on page 107) that summarizes Paul's pictures of grace. Which pictures do you appreciate the most? Which ones would you like to explore further? Which pictures would you like to add?

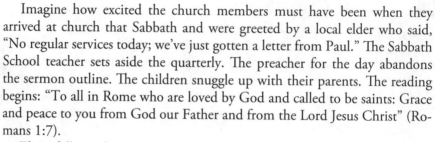

# Grace Notes

## Romans 1–3—The Point of the Sermon

Q. Verses from the early chapters of Romans have been used as stones to throw at specific sinners. How does such a practice violate the Bible's teaching about grace?

Imagine how excited the church members must have been when they arrived at church that Sabbath and were greeted by a local elder who said, "No regular services today; we've just gotten a letter from Paul." The Sabbath School teacher sets aside the quarterly. The preacher for the day abandons the sermon outline. The children snuggle up with their parents. The reading begins: "To all in Rome who are loved by God and called to be saints: Grace and peace to you from God our Father and from the Lord Jesus Christ" (Romans 1:7).

There follow a few words of personal greeting, the expression of how much Paul wants to be with them in Rome, and then this magnificent introduction: "I am not ashamed of the gospel, because it is the power of God for the salvation of everyone who believes: first for the Jew, then for the Gentile. For in the gospel a righteousness from God is revealed, a righteousness that is by faith from first to last, just as it is written: 'The righteous will live by faith' " (verses 16, 17).

Now Paul has their undivided attention. With everyone listening, as Paul knew they would, the reader begins the body of the letter. The change in tone must have surprised them. "The wrath of God is being revealed from heaven against all the godlessness and wickedness of men who suppress the truth by their wickedness" (verse 18).

The church members no doubt squirm a bit in their seats, look at each other with arched eyebrows, and then begin wondering what exactly Paul is trying to drive home. Looking out the windows of the church, the believers can see Rome's pagan citizens walking by, oblivious of the sacred service taking place, on their way to some ordinary—no doubt pagan—activity.

*Of course,* the members of the Roman church must have thought, *that's who Paul is talking about. All those people out there. The pagans. They're the godless ones who suppress the truth.*

"[They] are without excuse" (verse 20). "Their foolish hearts were darkened" (verse 21). "They became fools" (verse 22). "They exchanged the truth of God for a lie" (verse 25). "[They] worshiped and served created things rather than the Creator" (verse 25). "They are sinful, impure, indecent" (see verses 24–27).

Somebody must have shouted, "Preach it, Brother Paul!"

"They have become filled with every kind of wickedness, evil, greed and depravity. They are full of envy, murder, strife, deceit and malice. They are gossips, slanderers, God-haters, insolent, arrogant and boastful; they invent ways of doing evil; they disobey their parents; they are senseless, faithless, heartless, ruthless" (verses 29–31).

"Yes, they are!" a church member says out loud. "Amen," someone else adds. *Now this is a real sermon,* another member thinks. *This is "old-time religion," the way the prophets used to give it to 'em. This is what we need to hear: more judgment against those sinners.*

Then Paul's argument turns abruptly and catches them all by surprise. "You, therefore, have no excuse, you who pass judgment on someone else, for at whatever point you judge the other, you are condemning yourself . . . when you, mere [mortals], pass judgment on them and yet do the same things, do you think you will escape God's judgment? . . . But because of your stubbornness and your unrepentant heart, you are storing up wrath against yourself for the day of God's wrath" (2:1–5).

Now the squirming begins in earnest. This sermon was a whole lot better when it was talking about *them. Why did Paul have to go and spoil everything?*

Suddenly Paul switches gears again. "God 'will give to each person according to what he has done.' To those who by persistence in doing good seek glory, honor and immortality, he will give eternal life. But for those who are self-seeking and who reject the truth and follow evil, there will be wrath and anger" (verses 6–8).

OK, now we understand. Those people out there are bad because they are self-seeking. We are good because we seek God and persistently do good works. Lucky for us, Paul knows us. God will give to each one of us according to the good we have done. We can relax.

But Paul has one more thrust to make to drive his point home. Quoting the Bible, he says, " 'There is no one righteous, not even one; there is no one who understands, no one who seeks God. All have turned away, they have together become worthless; there is no one who does good, not even one' " (3:10–12).

So, if it's not those people out there but all of us, and if it's not their sins but ours as well, and if they don't do good and neither do we, then what's the point of the sermon?

Paul answers. He announces why he's writing the letter. The form of the letter reveals his strategy. To use the early verses of the letter for any other reason is to miss the point totally. This is not about being indecent or arrogant or gossipers or heartless. This is about judgment and grace: *"All* have sinned and fall short of the glory of God, and are justified freely by his grace through the redemption that came by Christ Jesus" (verses 23, 24).

*"Be not deceived by strange doctrines nor by ancient fables."*

—Ignatius, To the Magnesians

*"If we do his will and follow his commandments and love the things he loved,*
*while avoiding every kind of unrighteousness,*
*greed, love of money, slander . . .*
*If we please him in this present world,*
*we will receive the world to come as well."*

—Polycarp, The Letter of Polycarp to the Philippians

*"If the saints sin again, they shall find no salvation."*

—Hermas, The Shepherd

*"The expectation of their reward, according to the doing of each one of them,*
*thou art able to know from their writings."*

—Aristeides, Apology

*"By confession satisfaction is settled,*
*by repentance God is appeased."*

—Tertullian, On Repentance

## CHAPTER 8
# THE UNDEFINED DOCTRINE:
### *The Contradiction of Grace in the Years of Persecution*

AND THEN THE GOSPEL OF GRACE, SO RECENTLY RAISED IN A GLORIOUS crescendo, tragically is reduced to a whisper. For three hundred years, the church becomes preoccupied with other priorities. The essential understanding of what it means to be a Christian changes dramatically.

In the meantime, with a few persistent exceptions, the church virtually forgets the gospel. Administrators concentrate on organizing and managing the expanding membership. Scholars discuss which books are authentic and inspired enough to be included in the canon of the Bible.[1] Theologians debate other doctrinal issues, most of their disputations swirling around the Trinity and the nature of Christ.[2]

But the theological battles are minor skirmishes compared to the most dangerous pressure on the

| TWELVE TIMES OF TROUBLE: PERSECUTION BY ROMAN EMPERORS | |
|---|---|
| NERO | 54–68 |
| DOMITIAN | 81–96 |
| TRAJAN | 98–117 |
| HADRIAN | 117–138 |
| MARCUS ARELIUS | 161–180 |
| SEPTIMUS SEVERUS | 193–211 |
| MAXIMINUS | 235–238 |
| DECIUS | 249–251 |
| VALERIAN | 253–260 |
| AURELIAN | 270–275 |
| DIOCLETIAN | 285–305 |
| GALERIUS | 305–311 |

---

1. Jaroslav Pelikan, *The Christian Tradition: A History of the Development of Doctrine, Volume 1, The Emergence of the Catholic Tradition, 100-600* (Chicago: The University of Chicago Press, 1971), 112.

2. For example, at the end of the first century, Cerinthus proposes that Jesus was the *human* son of Joseph and Mary but "more righteous, prudent, and wise than other men." Marcion teaches that Jesus was not what He appeared to be—"flesh and yet not flesh, man and yet not man; likewise God and yet not God." Later, Noetus preaches that "Christ was the Father Himself." Paul of Samasota, bishop of Antioch from around 260 to 268, separates Jesus and the Word; the Word was from above, while Jesus was a "man from here." And Arius, the influential missionary who died in 335, insists that "there was a time when the Son was not." To the credit of the young church (and thanks, certainly, to the guidance of the Holy Spirit), each challenge is met head on and settled in behalf of the full divinity *and* the full humanity of God's only begotten Son.

early Christians, who are mostly untouched by, even unaware of the doctrinal arguments taking place among their leaders. The primary challenge is more basic. It is survival. Persecution threatens the church's very existence.

### THE PERSECUTION BEGINS

You remember that the persecution of the newborn Christian community begins with the jailing and flogging of Peter and the other apostles (Acts 5:17–42) and then escalates under the violent zeal of Saul of Tarsus, who sets out "to destroy the church" (8:3). Following the stoning of Stephen (chapter 7), Christians are dragged from their homes, thrown into prison, and scattered throughout Judea and Samaria (verses 1–3). James the brother of John is arrested and executed (12:2). According to Eusebius of Caesarea, the early church historian, John is plunged into boiling oil, Peter is crucified, and Paul is beheaded.

Jesus has predicted such treatment. "His eye discerned the fierce, wasting tempests that were to beat upon His followers,"[3] and lovingly He encourages them, " 'Blessed are you when people insult you, persecute you and falsely say all kinds of evil against you because of me' " (Matthew 5:11). " 'Do not be afraid of what you are about to suffer,' " He says to the churches through John. " 'Be faithful, even to the point of death, and I will give you the crown of life' " (Revelation 2:10).

Paul takes up the theme with the Christians living in Rome, in the eye of the storm. "Who shall separate us from the love of Christ?" he asks. "Shall trouble or hardship or persecution or famine or nakedness or danger or sword? As it is written: 'For your sake we face death all day long; we are considered as sheep to be slaughtered' " (Romans 8:35, 36). To the believers at Corinth, Paul expresses the same assurance: "We are hard pressed on every side, but not crushed; perplexed, but not in despair; persecuted, but not abandoned; struck down, but not destroyed" (2 Corinthians 4:8, 9).

Christianity isn't destroyed. However, in the next three centuries Christians are struck down with a diabolic ferocity wherever they speak the name of their Master. In sporadic, violent outbursts, localized at first but eventually empire-wide, the citizens of the heavenly kingdom (Philippians 3:20) suffer in the kingdoms of earth the ravages of unrestrained terror, carried out by people numbed by increasingly barbaric killings.

The pressure is severe. "It is beyond the power of pen," write church members from Gaul, "to state with exactitude the greatness of the affliction here, the mighty rage of the heathen against the saints."[4] The Christians of North Africa are "butchered."[5] "Everyone cowered with fear," says Eusebius about the Decian persecution of A.D. 250 and 251.[6] "No refinement of cruelty was spared."[7] Tertullian reports that if the Tiber River rises too high, or the Nile doesn't rise high enough, or if there is famine or plague in the land, the cry goes up at once: "The Christians to the lion!"[8]

Early in these times of trouble, during the reign of Domitian (81–96), the Christians

---

3. Ellen G. White, *The Great Controversy* (Mountain View, Calif.: Pacific Press®, 1950), 39.

4. *Letter of the Churches,* in Eusebius, *Ecclesiastical History,* 1.4.

5. Tertullian, *Apology,* 37.5.

6. Eusebius, *Ecclesiastical History,* 4.9.

7. Henry Chadwick, *The Early Church* (New York: Penguin Books, 1993), 29.

8. Tertullian, *Apology,* 40.2. Tertullian adds, with a dash of gallows humor, "What, all of them to one lion?"

are defined primarily by their refusal to bow to the state religion. The emperor insists on being addressed by his subjects as "God" and "Lord," and the Roman government charges Christians who refuse to refer to him in these terms with being "unbelievers"[9] and "atheists."[10] Later, during the great persecution of Diocletian ("the most severe persecution which Christianity had yet experienced"[11]), the accusation is that Christians are "disloyal" to the empire[12] and "enemies of the divine religion."[13] Tacitus, the Roman historian (c. 58–c. 116), calls Christians "criminals" who deserve "extreme" punishment.[14] A letter from a Roman lawyer, from the beginning of the third century, refers to Christians as "a gang of desperadoes," "a rabble of impious conspirators," and "a secret tribe that lurks in darkness and shuns the light."[15]

## PERSECUTED FOR THE NAME

At least as early as A.D. 112, during Emperor Trajan's reign, Christians are accused, arrested, interrogated, and sentenced for no other reason than that of *being* a Christian.

"This is the course I have taken with those who were accused before me," writes Pliny, the governor of Bithynia in Asia Minor to the emperor. "I asked them whether they were Christians, and if they confessed, I asked them a second and third time."[16] When a Christian named Ptolemy is imprisoned around A.D. 160, a Roman centurion questions him on this

## AND WHAT ARE YOU?

"Are you a Christian?" the prefect Rusticus asked. It's the year 165. A group of accused Christians is being questioned in Rome by a government official.

Justin answered, "Yes, I am a Christian."

"And you, Charitan, are you also a Christian?"

"I am a Christian, by God's command," replied Charitan.

"What do you say, Charito?"

Charito said, "I am a Christian by God's gift."

Rusticus said to Euelpistus, "And what are you?"

Euelpistus, a slave of Caesar, answered, "I also am a Christian, freed by Christ and share by the grace of Christ in the same hope."

Rusticus addressed Hierax. "Are you also a Christian?"

"Yes," Hierax said, "I am a Christian, for I worship and adore the same God. . . ."

The prefect Rusticus said to Liberian, "And what do you say? Are you a Christian? Are you an unbeliever like the rest?"

Liberian said, "I also am a Christian."

The prefect announced his sentence: "Let those who will not sacrifice to the gods and yield to the command of the emperor be scourged and led away to be beheaded in accordance with the laws."

—*Acta Sancti Justini et sociorum,* IV, V.

---

9. *Acta Sancti Justini et sociorum.*

10. Justin, *Apology,* 1.6.

11. Kenneth Scott Latourette, *A History of Christianity, Vol. 1: Beginnings to 1500* (San Francisco: HarperSanFrancisco, 1953), 90.

12. *Corpus Inscriptionum Latinarum,* 3.12132.

13. Laetantius, *On the Deaths of the Persecutors,* 2.8.

14. Tacitus, *Annals,* 15.44.8.

15. Minucius Felix, *Octavius,* 8.3, 4.

16. Pliny, *Letters,* 10.96.3.

## HOW CAN I BLASPHEME MY KING?

On a Sabbath morning late in February, probably in 156 or 155, the bishop of the Christian church in Smyrna, an elderly and saintly man of prayer named Polycarp, is led roughly to the Roman stadium under threat of execution. Just outside the stadium, the chief constable of the city meets Polycarp and urges him to save himself.

"What harm is there in saying, 'Caesar is Lord'?" the constable demands.

Polycarp's response is steadfast: "I do not intend to do what you advise me."

Inside the stadium, the crowd learns of the arrest of the Christian bishop of their city and roars with bloodthirsty anticipation. The "father of the Christians," as the people of Smyrna referred to him, is driven into the stadium to stand before Statius Quadratus, the proconsul. Again, Polycarp is urged to renounce his faith.

"Change your mind," the proconsul orders. "Swear by Caesar, curse Christ, and I will release you."

Without wavering, Polycarp replies, "Eighty-six years have I served Him, and He has done me no wrong: how then can I blaspheme my King who has saved me?"

"Polycarp has confessed himself to be a Christian," the proconsul's herald announces.

The crowd demands, and is given, the bishop's life.

The letter that tells the story of Polycarp's ordeal is the earliest extant account we have of the death of a martyr. In describing Polycarp's courage, the account remarks, "His face was filled with grace, so that not only did he not collapse in fright at the things which were said to him, but on the contrary the proconsul was astonished."

*sole* point: whether or not he is a Christian. No other accusation is necessary.[17]

"We are hated for our name," complains Athenagorus of Athens to Marcus Aurelius in a letter from 177. "You allow us to be harassed, plundered and persecuted, the multitude making war upon us for our name alone."[18]

The practice continues throughout the years of terror, and saying yes to the accusation generally results in the ultimate sacrifice. "I am a Christian," confesses Cyprian of Carthage in his trial during the reign of Valerian, "when the anti-Christian storm broke out afresh and with redoubled fury."[19] The confession leads to Cyprian's martyrdom on September 14, 258.[20]

If the prosecutors sense a weakening of resolve, or if the accused deny being Christians or say that in the past they had belonged to the Christian community but no longer, they are tested to prove the change in status: The Christians are asked to recite a pagan prayer to the Roman gods, to offer wine and incense to a statue of the emperor, and to curse Christ.[21] If accused individuals hold firm to their confession of Christianity, they are threatened with capital punishment.[22] If they persist, the authorities order their execution. Imagine facing such terror on a daily basis.

Twice now, I've traveled to a remote forest in northern Italy and stood in a shallow cave in which two hundred Waldensian believers perished at the hands of persecutors. Each time, the experience has had a profound effect on me. Just standing in a place of such dedica-

---

17. Justin, *Apology*, 2.2.
18. Athenagoras, *Legatio pro Christianis*, 1, 2.
19. Latourette, ibid., 1:88.
20. Cyprian, *Corpus Scriptorum Ecclesiaticorum Lainorum*, 3.1.
21. *The Martyrdom of Polycarp*, 9.3.
22. Pliny, *Epistles* 10.96.

tion is inspiring. Listening to the story of the valor of people who "had been slain because of the word of God and the testimony they had maintained" (Revelation 6:9) helps one realize how incredibly precious our faith really is. Like the Waldensians, little else mattered to the members of the primitive church once they caught the glory of belonging to Christ.

Tertullian puts it like this: "We want no curious disputation after possessing Christ Jesus, no inquisition after receiving the gospel! When we believe, we desire no further belief. For this is our first article of faith, that there is nothing which we ought to believe besides."[23]

FOCUSING ON THE MERIT OF OUR OWN BEHAVIOR

Unfortunately, however, in the threatening climate of accusation and persecution, when we're asked to put our Christianity out in the open for everyone to see, it's often easy for us to lose our focus on what is central to and important about the Christian experience—on what our faith is really all about. In the first three centuries of the early church, just such a loss of focus takes place. The church fails to see the danger coming, and an ancient heresy is reintroduced to the church—a consuming, corrupting perspective that, to this day, drives us in a perilous direction. In response to the pressure of the constant charges of seditious and immoral behavior, Christians begin to define and distinguish their Christianity not by what Jesus did for them, not by the finished work of grace in their behalf, not by the assurance of life eternal on the basis of the merits of Jesus, but rather *by the nobility and merit of their own behavior.*

At first, it is an innocent and even understandable shift. We are not rebels or anarchists, the Christians insist in the imperial courtrooms, but hard-working, loyal citizens—the kind of people you could wish all Roman citizens were: "by our works also to be found good citizens and keepers of the commandments."[24] "They have the commandments of the Lord Jesus Christ Himself engraven on their hearts," writes Aristeides in his *Apology* from around A.D.150. "They commit neither adultery nor fornication; nor do they bear false witness, they do not deny a deposit, nor covet other men's goods: they honor father and mother, and love their neighbors: they give right judgments; and they do not worship idols in the form of man. They do not unto others that which they would not have done unto themselves. They comfort such as wrong them, and make friends of them: they labor to do good to their enemies."[25] "They obey the established laws," echoes the *Epistle to Diognetus,* "and in their own lives they surpass the laws."[26]

Initially, the persecuted express the *spiritual* reasons that motivate their endurance. They speak in terms of "encouraging the brethren,"[27] "truly learning discipleship,"[28] becoming "imitators of the Lord,"[29] and giving an example that "resembles the gospel story."[30] The martyrs of Lyons and Vienne in 177 glory in the knowledge that "the grace of God was our

---

23. Tertullian, *De Praescriptione Haereticorum,* 7.
24. Justin, *Apology,* 39.
25. Aristeides, *Apology,* 31.
26. *Epistle to Diognetus,* 32.
27. *Letter of the Churches,* in Eusebius, *Ecclesiastical History,* 1.42.
28. Ignatius, *To the Romans,* 5.
29. Eusebius, *Ecclesiastical History,* 2.2–4.
30. *The Martyrdom of Polycarp,* 1.1.

captain."[31] Justin recognizes that those who give their lives rather than abandon their Master are witnessing to unbelievers, leading them "by patience and gentleness, from shame and the love of evil."[32]

But we begin to hear the other motivation, the corrupting perspective, in the middle of the second century. The believers who write about the martyrs begin to magnify the merit of their actions with words about "the blessed martyrs" *"attaining* salvation," and about how they are, in a single moment, *"purchasing* eternal life."[33] Aristeides says that the conduct of the martyrs was in "the expectation of their recompense of reward, *according to the doing* of each one of them."[34] Justin indicates that the good works and the commandment-keeping of the Christians goes beyond a simple desire to be good citizens; indeed, it was *"so that we may be saved* with an everlasting salvation."[35] The great nineteenth-century historian of the church, Philip Schaff, concludes, "They sought the martyr's crown that they might merit heaven."[36]

Thomas Torrance speaks with admiration of these early Christians "in their noble fight against evil." Yet he argues that the theologians harnessed their faith "to the basic urge for self-justification."[37] "Repentance was treated as an eternal principle of self-amendment before God, and reckoned as an adequate means for securing pardon and mercy."[38] Gradually, Christians begin to view the finished work of Jesus for salvation as not quite yet finished.

## CATEGORIES OF SIN AND SINNERS

In this digression to a works orientation, *categories* of sin begin to appear, accompanied by *degrees* of repentance. "For quite minor sins," William Placher reports, "an individual could pray and repent in private. But by the third century those who had committed more substantial sins were supposed to request admission to the order of penitents."[39]

In addition, the persecuted also begin to classify themselves. "It was through persecution," Robin Lane Fox informs us in his comprehensive survey, *Pagans and Christians,* "that *first-class* Christians" came to be thought of as more spiritual, closer to God.[40] Martyrs, of course, would be the most spiritual. (How could one be more spiritual than to die for Jesus?) After the second century, martyrdom is taken as a "higher grade of Christian virtue," capable, notice this, of *"securing an entrance into heaven."* According to church authorities, "the rewards of a virgin were sixty times greater than an ordinary Christian's, but a martyr's were a hundred times greater, the highest of all."[41]

Some Christians actually began to court martyrdom, believing that their death at the

---

31. *Letter of the Churches,* 1.6.

32. Justin, *Apology,* 1.16.

33. *The Martyrdom of Polycarp,* 2.3.

34. Aristeides, *Apology,* 16.3.

35. Justin, *Apology,* 1.65.

36. Philip Schaff, *History of the Christian Church* (Grand Rapids, Mich.: Wm. B. Eerdmans Publishing, 1910), 2:77.

37. Thomas F. Torrance, *The Doctrine of Grace in the Apostolic Fathers* (Grand Rapids, Mich.: Wm. B. Eerdmans, 1960), 134.

38. Ibid., 135.

39. William C. Placher, *A History of Christian Theology* (Philadelphia: The Westminster Press, 1983), 132.

40. Robin Lane Fox, *Pagans and Christians* (New York: Alfred A. Knopf, Inc., 1986), 450.

41. Ibid., 419.

hands of the Romans will erase any sins they have committed.[42] The remembered words of a martyr (not of Jesus, but *of a martyr*) can bestow effective absolution from all shortcomings, even the most mortal of sins. The blood of the martyrs, kept and preserved by believers, is credited with extraordinary potency and healing powers. "Your blood," says Tertullian about the martyrs, "is the key to Paradise."

Below the martyrs in terms of importance are the "confessors"—those whose confession of Jesus resulted in the death penalty, but who, in the interval between sentencing and execution, continue to preach from prison. Church members wait on them, seek their dispensation ("open visas to escape from hell"[43]), and ask *them* to grant forgiveness.

A FAILURE TO GRASP THE SIGNIFICANCE

And what happens to the appreciation of God's grace and the proclamation of the gospel during this time of definition by behavior? The same thing that happens in every age, including our own, whenever people shift their focus from Jesus, where it should be, to themselves.

Jaroslav Pelikan, the thorough historian of Christian doctrine, observes that "the saving work of Christ remained dogmatically undefined" by the church fathers.[44] No compelling statements about grace show up on the early lists of fundamental beliefs, much less, a full presentation of this "greatest and most regal work of God."[45] Pelikan adds that whenever a discussion of grace *was* attempted, it, frankly, "was not very profound."[46] At best, Pelikan charges, this "one great truth around which all other truths cluster"[47] received a "superficial exposition."[48] At worst, there was a "failure to grasp" the significance of the death of Christ.[49]

Grace does not become a "focal point of explicit theological reflection," the Roman Catholic historical theologian Stephen Duffy accurately observes, "until the time of Augustine."[50] Alister McGrath, a prolific English theologian, agrees, pointing out that during these dark centuries, the doctrinal exposition of the saving grace of God is "inchoate and ill-defined" and characterized by "inexactitude and naiveté."[51] Others suggest a more passive dynamic, noticing that Paul's theme of justification just seems "to fade away."[52]

42. Latourette, 1:86.

43. Fox, 458.

44. Pelikan, 141.

45. Clement of Alexandria, *Paedagogus*, 1.12.100.1.

46. Pelikan, 29.

47. White, *Gospel Workers* (Washington, D.C.: Review and Herald, 1948), 315.

48. Pelikan, 145.

49. Torrance, 137: "The Gospel of Christianity was so astounding," Torrance continues, "just because it taught a doctrine of justification by grace alone. . . . The theology [of the Apostolic Fathers] represents a corrosion of the faith both from the side of Judaism and from the side of Hellenism, because the basic significance of grace was not grasped. That is seen very clearly in their attitude to all the main doctrines of the N.T. Gospel. It was not that they were opposed to them, but that they did not grasp them properly."

50. Stephen J. Duffy, *The Dynamics of Grace: Perspectives in Theological Anthropology* (Collegeville, Minn.: The Liturgical Press, 1993), 17, 31.

51. Alister E. McGrath, *Iustitia Dei, A History of the Christian Doctrine of Justification: The Beginnings to the Reformation* (Cambridge: Cambridge University Press, 1986), 23.

52. Robert B. Eno, "Some Patristic Views on the Relationship of Faith and Works in Justification," in *Justification by Faith, Lutherans and Catholics in Dialogue VII*, H. George Anderson, T. Austin Murphy, and Joseph A. Burgess, eds., (Minneapolis: Augsburg Publishing House, 1985), 111.

Consequently, the church greets departures from the full biblical gospel of grace with an uneven response. Sometimes the response is swift and severe. At other times, incidents of doctrinal deviation are ignored.

For example, Gnosticism included the distinct, works-oriented teaching that *truly spiritual* believers don't need salvation, which is part of the reason why Gnostics are declared heretics. Yet when Irenaeus says that God's grace is only for the "righteous and holy, and those who have kept His commandments,"[53] the church fails to contradict him.

When Marcion teaches that "salvation will be the attainment only of those souls which had learned his doctrine,"[54] he is charged with blasphemy and driven from the church. But when Ignatius places qualifications on the unconditional grace of God, when he equates the reception of grace with leaving the "ancient observances" of Judaism, including keeping the Sabbath,[55] the church remains silent.

Origen describes classes of beings arrayed throughout eternity "in a definite order proportionate to the degree and excellence of their merits,"[56] and he is vehemently opposed. But when the eloquent Tertullian teaches that "temporal mortifications would *discharge eternal punishments*"; that confession is "a demeanor calculated to *move mercy*"; that by repentance God is *appeased,* and *satisfaction* is settled, the church acquiesces. When, in trying to explain how God's grace operates, Tertullian creates the theological formula, *reddens unicuique quod suum est*—giving to each his *due,* the church *adopts* his works orientation.

## THE STORM BATTERS THE CHURCH

As the storm of self-justifying fury batters the church, "some of the Christians stood firm, declaring that they could make no compromise." Others, unfortunately, "were in favor of yielding or modifying some features of their faith." In this way, "unsound doctrines" are incorporated into the faith and worship of the church, and "a union was formed between Christianity and paganism."[57]

Traditionally, we have understood this union as having been formed by the rise of idolatry within the church, by the acceptance of the doctrine of the immortality of the soul, and by the growing reverence for the first day of the week. But if it is true that at the foundation of every pagan religion is the principle that we can save ourselves by our own works,[58] then the union also was formed by the prevailing works orientation—making it appropriate to characterize these centuries as a "pagan period" during which, like their pagan neighbors, Christians tried to barter with God for salvation.[59]

From the center of the church's reliance on human merit, God must find a convincing voice that is not afraid of grace.

---

53. Irenaeus, 1.2, 3.

54. Irenaeus, 1.25.2.

55. Ignatius, *To the Magnesians,* 8.1, 2; 9.1.

56. Origen, *De Principiis,* 1.6.3.

57. White, *The Desire of Ages* (Mountain View, Calif.: Pacific Press®, 1940), 35.

58. Ibid., 35.

59. "No sooner do we believe that God loves us than there is an impulse to believe that He does so, not because He is Love, but because we are intrinsically lovable. The Pagans obeyed this impulse unabashed; a good man was 'dear to the gods' because he was good." (C. S. Lewis, *The Four Loves* [New York: Harcourt Brace Jovanovich, 1960], 180.)

# GRACE IN QUESTION

## CHAPTER 8: THE UNDEFINED DOCTRINE

Unfortunately, following the crescendo of grace in the writings of Paul, the topic of how we are saved slides off the radar screen of the early church. Chapter 8 investigates the causes of that absence of emphasis on grace and charts the storm of self-justifying fury that battered the infant church.

1. How can good things like organizing a church, studying the Bible, and clarifying doctrine possibly contribute to our forgetting the gospel? How can we keep such a tragedy from taking place?

2. Read 2 Corinthians 4:8, 9 again: "We are hard pressed on every side, but not crushed; perplexed, but not in despair; persecuted, but not abandoned; struck down, but not destroyed." In what way are we Christians today hard pressed, perplexed, persecuted, and struck down? What assures you that you are not crushed, not in despair, not abandoned, and not destroyed?

3. Discuss the differences between responding to God's grace by living a life of obedience to God's commands and obeying in order to be saved.

4. Create a chart with a circle in the middle and fifteen or twenty circles clustered around it. Label the center circle "Grace" (the "one great truth around which all other truths cluster"). Label the other circles with the names of other doctrines. How can we best remember this absolute principle of understanding the purpose of doctrine?

5. When the fury of the self-justifying storm batters your Christian experience, how are you saved from the storm?

# GRACE NOTES
## REVELATION 3—THE KEY TO THE PALACE

Q. How did the early Christians lose their focus on Jesus and His enduring grace?

Q. How would the counsel of Revelation 3 have helped them maintain their grace orientation?

In the early days of Roman persecution, the apostle John, in exile on the Isle of Patmos, writes a letter to the young Christian church in the city of Philadelphia in Asia Minor (Revelation 3:7–13). The church members there are fading under the persecution. They have only a "little strength" left (verse 8) but are enduring patiently (verse 10). Realizing that "the hour of trial that is going to come upon the whole world" (verse 10) would greatly affect them, the Holy Spirit directs John to write a letter of encouragement (verse 13).

The greeting section of the letter, which points to Jesus as the Source and Inspiration for the message, contains words that sound cryptic to our ears: " 'To the angel of the church in Philadelphia write: These are the words of him who is holy and true, who holds the key of David. What he opens no one can shut, and what he shuts no one can open' " (verse 7).

To the church members in Philadelphia, however, these words wouldn't have sounded cryptic at all. The picture would have been a familiar one, embedded deep within their culture and heritage. More than eight hundred years earlier, in the middle of a group of prophecies against the nations that surround Israel, the prophet Isaiah pauses and turns his gaze inward. With the city in shambles and facing imminent destruction, with the people of Jerusalem tearing down houses to rebuild the wall that was supposed to protect the houses, Isaiah addresses the followers of God: "The defenses of Judah are stripped away. And you looked in that day to the weapons in the Palace of the Forest; you saw that the City of David had many breaches in its defenses; you stored up water in the Lower Pool. You counted the buildings in Jerusalem and tore down houses to strengthen the wall. You built a reservoir between the two walls for the water of the Old Pool, but you did not look to the One who made it, or have regard for the One who planned it long ago" (Isaiah 22:8–11).

In those days, there was a mighty man named Shebna who had been given the important job of steward of the palace (verse 15). But instead of building up the fortifications of Jerusalem, instead of seeing to the protection of others, Shebna was busy accumulating wealth and creating for himself a magnificent final resting place, chiseled out of rock on a high place overlooking the city (verses 16, 18). God calls Shebna " '[a] disgrace to [his] master's house' " (verse 18), instructs that he be deposed from his office (verse 19), and directs that he be replaced by a man named Eliakim, the son of Hilkiah (verse 20). Through the prophet, God tells Shebna, " 'I will clothe him [Eliakim] with your robe and fasten your sash around him and hand your authority over to him' " (verse 21). And then God explains the most important part of the job of palace steward: " 'I will place on his shoulder the key to the house of David; what he opens no one can shut, and what he shuts no one can open' " (verse 22).

Eliakim was to have the key that opened all the doors in the palace, the master key. He was the final authority as to who got in and who didn't. Only he could open all the doors. Only he could keep them shut.

So, when John the revelator spoke to the people in the church of Philadelphia about Jesus as the One who " 'holds the key of David' " (Revelation 3:7), they would have recognized that the One who is "holy and true" is the same One who spoke these words, also recorded by their friend John: " 'Do not let your hearts be troubled. Trust in God; trust also in me. In my Father's house are many rooms; if it were not so, I would have told you. I am going there to prepare a place for you. And if I go and prepare a place for you. . . . I will come back and take you to be with me that you also may be where I am' " (John 14:1–3). " 'I am coming soon. Hold on to what you have, so that no one will take your crown. Him who overcomes I will make a pillar in the temple of my God. Never again will he leave it. I will write on him the name of my God and the name of the city of my God, the new Jerusalem, which is coming down out of heaven from my God; and I will also write on him my new name' " (Revelation 3:11, 12).

Jesus holds the key that unlocks the palace of heaven. You and I don't have the key. We can't get in. Only Jesus can open the door. Jesus is the final authority as to who gets in. We don't make that decision. Only He does. And what He opens, no one can shut.

Salvation is by grace alone because Jesus alone holds the key.

*"The great sweetness of the grace of our Lord Jesus Christ
ever continues its fragrance."*
—AUGUSTINE, SELECT LETTERS


*"In Augustine Western Christianity
finds its most influential shaper of the doctrine of grace."*
—STEPHEN DUFFY, THE DYNAMICS OF GRACE


*"Augustine made grace virtually the central theme
of Western theology."*
—HANS KÜNG, GREAT CHRISTIAN THINKERS


*"Although he may not have been the greatest of Latin writers,
he was almost certainly the greatest man who ever wrote Latin."*
—JAROSLAV PELIKAN, THE CHRISTIAN TRADITION


*"Augustine sincerely experienced his memories
as drenched in God's grace."*
—GARRY WILLS, SAINT AUGUSTINE

# THE PERFECT CHURCH:

*The Rediscovery of Grace in the Battles of Augustine*

IN THE YEAR 284, DIOCLETIAN BECOMES THE EMPEROR OF ROME. AN ABLE soldier and administrator, Diocletian sets about at once to reorganize the empire. He names an old fellow soldier, Maximian, as regent in the west and gives him the joint title of Augustus. A few years later, in a further attempt to strengthen the military and its defense of his empire, Diocletian designates two Caesars—one on the Rhine frontier, and the other, Galerius, on the Danube.

Diocletian and Galerius had grown up together in the army. The two old friends are life-long worshippers of the pagan gods and firm supporters of emperor worship. At the time, the Christian church is growing rapidly, and its growth seems to Diocletian and Galerius to threaten Rome. In quick succession the emperor issues three edicts of persecution against Christianity. "Churches were ordered destroyed, sacred books confiscated, clergy imprisoned and forced to sacrifice by torture. In 304 a fourth edict required all Christians to offer sacrifices. It was a time of fearful persecution."[1]

During these years of persecution, the soldiers of Emperor Diocletian adopt a clever tactic. They would knock at the door of suspected Christians and make unmistakable threats: "Give to us the sacred Christian books you possess," the soldiers demand. "We will throw the books into a bonfire and destroy them, but we'll leave you alone. But withhold the books or tell us you have none, and we will search your house. If during the search we find the books we're looking for, we will cast them into the fire and then destroy you along with them."

The threatened Christians are given minutes to retreat into their homes and make the life-or-death decision. Many of them refuse to hand over the books and walk back to face the soldiers—and imminent martyrdom. Many others decide it is better to stay alive, and they hand over the books. The Latin word for "handing over" is *traditore,* and those who took this road were considered by some in the church as having apostatized, as having become *traditores*—traitors.[2]

---

1. Williston Walker, *A History of the Christian Church* (New York: Charles Scribner's Sons, 1959), 100.

2. Jaroslav Pelikan, *The Christian Tradition, A History of the Development of Doctrine, Volume 1, The Emergence of the Catholic Tradition (100–600)* (Chicago: The University of Chicago Press, 1971), 311, 312.

Consider the need for grace from the perspective of one who has been overcome.

General Douglas MacArthur's promise, "I shall return," "seemed a promise of magic" to those defending the Philippine Islands during the Second World War. MacArthur left Lieutenant General Jonathan Wainwright in command of the Northern Luzon Force, defending the Bataan Peninsula and Corregidor Island. MacArthur's last command to Wainwright was, "You've got to hold."

But Wainwright's forces were overwhelmed by superior forces in some of the most bitter and desperate combat in world military history. The soldiers suffered from malaria. "The water was contaminated. Men ate roots, leaves and monkey meat. The Filipino troops, wearing helmets fashioned from coconuts, grew gaunter and gaunter. At night the Japanese murdered sleep with firecrackers, shell fire, and obscene taunts shouted through megaphones."

Wainwright surrendered on May 6, 1942. "A terrible silence fell over Corregidor. White flags were raised from every flagstaff that was still standing. The next day the prisoners began the brutal Death March—the long trek northward in which between seven thousand and ten thousand died of disease, starvation, sadistic beatings, and outright execution."

Three years and several months passed. At the end of August 1945, General Wainwright, only four days earlier liberated from a prisoner-of-war camp, was taken to MacArthur's temporary headquarters. Now "a ghastly spectacle," Wainwright considered himself a failure and expected to be reprimanded for losing the battle and giving up to the enemy.

In MacArthur's words: "He was haggard and aged. He walked with difficulty and

After Diocletian and the decisive Battle of the Mulvian Bridge (October 28, 312), Constantine becomes emperor, and the persecution ceases. In the course of a few years, Christianity goes from being outlawed in the Roman Empire, to being tolerated, and then to being fully accepted (through what we refer to as the Edict of Milan, early in the year 313).

### THE COMMUNION OF PERFECT SAINTS

The Christians who had handed over their books to the soldiers of the empire continue as church members. In 311, with the persecution coming to an end, a man by the name of Caecilianus becomes the bishop of Carthage in North Africa. His ordination to the office is administered by Felix of Aptunga, one of the *traditores* who had surrendered copies of the books to the Roman soldiers. Some church members consider Felix to be lapsed, to have become a "collaborator," a "betrayer." They regard his act of ordaining Caecilianus to be a shameful compromise "between the ideal holiness of the church and the actual quality of its members."[3] The situation causes a split among the members of the church at Carthage—a split that becomes a schism in the young church.

Believing that the only church that was a true church was "one in which the 'communion of saints' was a communion of genuine, perfect saints,"[4] a portion of the church membership choose a different man, Majorinus, to be their bishop, and the choice is confirmed at a meeting of north African bishops who agree (pure "sons of the martyrs" the bishops were called). Majorinus and the Numidian bishops teach

---

3. Peter Brown, *Augustine of Hippo* (Berkeley, Calif.: University of California Press, 1967), 213. "Peter Brown has written the most informed and most sensitive biography of Augustine." (Hans Küng, *Great Christian Thinkers* [New York: Continuum, 1996], 81.)

4. Pelikan, 309.

that those who had given up their books are no longer worthy of being church members, that the clergy who had lapsed are no longer holy enough to be clergy, and that those who were ordained or baptized by these lapsed clergy have received an invalid sacrament: "He who receives faith from the faithless, receives not faith but guilt."[5]

In 316, Donatus succeeds Majorinus as bishop. By now the split is so deep and Donatus such a powerful spokesperson for their position (he came to be known as Donatus the Great), that the schismatics take his name, calling themselves *Donatists*. The fractured North African church becomes the subject of two church councils called by Constantine, but the division only grows wider. The "counter-church" "rose up in every town and locality as a rival to the church Catholic, altar being set against altar in every neighbourhood."[6]

The Roman world soon sees the pitiful sight of Christians persecuting other Christians. Elderly people in one church are beaten by people in the other church. Worshippers are barred from entering their places of worship. Churches are broken into, altars smashed,[7] and the houses of opponents are burned. "The Donatist enthusiasts carried clubs called 'Israels'; they would 'purify' Catholic basilicas with coats of whitewash; they would destroy the altars of others."[8] The most violent among

with the help of a cane. His eyes were sunken and there were pits in his cheeks. His hair was snow white and his skin looked like old shoe leather. He made a brave effort to smile as I took him in my arms, but when he tried to talk his voice wouldn't come. For three years he had imagined himself in disgrace for having surrendered Corregidor. He believed he would never again be given an active command.... His voice wavered and he burst into tears," a whipped man, suffering torments of shame through those years of humiliation.

Two days later, on September 2, 1945, Wainwright occupied a position of honor on the deck of the battleship *Missouri* in Tokyo Bay, standing next to MacArthur as the supreme commander accepted the surrender of the enemy. Wainwright, the soldier who had been defeated, was promoted. He succeeded MacArthur as commander of the American and Filipino forces.
—Adapted from William Manchester, *American Caesar.*

the Donatists call themselves the "Lord's athletes." Their enemies call them "hut people." Their chant, *"Laus Deo"* ("God be praised"), becomes a war cry.[9]

Church historian Kenneth Scott Latourette refers to the Donatists as one of "the strict elements of the Church."[10] Van der Meer

5. Augustine (quoting an opponent), *Against the Letters of Petilian,* 4.8.
6. F. van der Meer, *Augustine the Bishop,* Brian Battershaw and G. R. Lamb, trans. (London: Sheed and Ward, 1961), 80. My copy of this comprehensive biography of Augustine is a prized possession, given to me by my neighbor and friend Iris Landa just after the death of her husband, Paul. Paul was a long-time professor at La Sierra University and an enthusiastic church historian. Many times he would drop into my office at La Sierra, comment on the latest grace books on my shelves, and begin a delightful conversation on the nature of grace and the history of the doctrine of salvation.
7. Augustine, *Letters,* 29.12.
8. Brown, 219.
9. Garry Wills, *Saint Augustine* (New York: Lipper/Viking, 1999), 75.
10. Kenneth Scott Latourette, *A History of Christianity, Volume I: to AD 1500* (New York: HarperCollins Publishers, 1953), 139.

characterizes the "troubling minority" as "protesting" and "conservative."[11] The encyclopedic Will Durant refers to the movement as "bands of revolutionaries, at once Christian and communist," a "theological aberration."[12]

The Donatists, however, thought of themselves as the holy among the impious, the cleansed among the polluted, the pure among the defiled—and they contrast themselves not to the pagan world around them but to others within the Christian church. No sinner can be a part of a perfect church, the Donatists claim, and they are the ones who can point out the sinners. They are the ones to do the "pruning," the weeding out of the unworthy. The Donatist church "had kept itself pure from a single, unspeakable crime," Peter Brown reminds us,[13] from the one sin of becoming *traditores* during the persecutions of Diocletian. Their "innocence," their ritual purity, their meritorious suffering, they now propose, are all God's methods of preserving His chosen people. God will listen to their prayers alone.

## The croaking North African frogs

In the spring of 391,[14] eighty years after the Donatist controversy began, a man named Augustine arrives in the city of Hippo in what today is Algeria. Augustine is thirty-six, but in the world of Christianity, he is still a child. Baptized in Milan only four years earlier, the enduring influence of his Christian mother silenced re-

cently by death, not yet ordained as the pastor he soon would be, Augustine has come to Hippo seeking solitude, not public life.

But the tension in North Africa between the mother church and the Donatists is raging, and Augustine is immediately drawn in. The noisy sounds from the Donatist celebrations in their nearby basilica can easily be heard in the church to which Augustine has come to study and teach and establish his second monastery.[15] "The clouds proclaim with thunder that the Church is rising everywhere in the world," he writes in the midst of his study of the Psalms, "while these frogs sit in their marsh and croak—We are the only Christians!"[16]

Not that these tensions are new to Augustine. He has been on the edge of the storms of Donatism most of his life. Here in this new place and new service he had hoped to avoid the controversies completely or at least to have the strength to endure them.[17] But he has underestimated the Donatist influence in his own congregation. In a very short time he realizes he will have to meet the self-exalted theology head on.

Augustine enters the battle with three distinct perspectives.

## 1. In need of salvation

First of all, Augustine has a clear realization of his own weaknesses and shortcomings. He knows he is a sinner and that he needs salva-

---

11. Van der Meer, 80.

12. Will Durant, *The Age of Faith* (New York: Simon and Schuster, 1950), 47, 48.

13. Brown, 218.

14. Following Peter Brown's precise chronological tables in *Augustine of Hippo.*

15. Augustine, *Letters,* 29.11 (written in 395 to his friend Alypius, bishop of Tagaste).

16. Augustine, *Psalms,* 95.11.

17. Augustine, *Letters,* 21.2. Written early in 391 to Valerius, who was the bishop at Hippo when Augustine arrived. In speaking of the "great hazards" of his new occupation, Augustine said, "It is not that I have observed some new breakers or storms unknown to me by previous observation or report or reading or meditation, but that I completely miscalculated my ability and strength to avoid them or endure them."

tion. "There is much in my life and conduct that I deplore," he writes in 392.[18] Recalling the moment of his conversion, he says that his words had been, "Why not now? Why not an end to my impure life in this very hour?" Quoting Psalm 5, Augustine cries out, "Do not be mindful of our old iniquities," which he later personalizes as the biting cares of place-seeking, the desire for gain, the wallowing in self-indulgence, the scratching of the itch of lust. Then, from Psalm 115, "You have broken my chains; I will sacrifice to you the offering of praise."[19]

His acceptance of a position of leadership in the church in Hippo, "my subordinate post" he calls it,[20] brings with it an even greater sense of his own need. "I was compelled," he apologizes to Bishop Valerius, whom he has been ordained to assist, "to assume the second place at the helm, although I did not know how to hold an oar." Then, explaining his reluctance, he continues: "Now that I at last recognize my weak points, it is my duty to investigate all the remedies to be found in His Scriptures and to see that prayer and study procure for my soul adequate strength for such dangerous tasks. . . . Do you really love the Church which you want me to serve with this poor equipment?" I have "so many deficiencies," Augustine goes on, "that it would be easier for me to enumerate the things I have acquired than those I want to acquire."[21]

In contrast to Augustine, it is often the case that those who find the least comfort in grace, those who argue against it most vehemently, those who most fear grace, are those who place the lowest estimate on the power of sin in their own lives. The sins of others are much more disagreeable than our own, we somehow reason—missing the reality that the doctrine of grace *begins* with a realization of our universal need for God's grace and our absolute inability to provide salvation for ourselves.

## 2. NO HIERARCHY OF SINS

Second, as he enters the battle against Donatism, Augustine already knows that there is no biblical *hierarchy* of sins; all of us have sinned (Romans 3:23), and all sin separates us from our heavenly Parent. One sin is not more *sinful* than another sin.

In 392, Augustine writes to Bishop Aurelius of Carthage complaining about the church's seeming uneven discipline of certain behaviors—what he refers to as Paul's "three classes of vice from which has sprung an incalculable crop of sins"—orgies and drunkenness, sexual immorality and debauchery, and dissension and jealousy (Romans 13:13). Why single out just one of these sets of vices, Augustine asks. One of them "the church punishes most severely; the other two appear to be quite tolerable." Augustine sees the situation as "disgraceful."[22]

Nor does Augustine believe that all Donatists are pure and without sin simply because they avoided becoming *traditores*. In a letter written in 396, Augustine tells the story of a young man who had been rebuked by his bishop for repeatedly "thrashing" his mother, an older woman "crippled with age and a lonely widow." Upset at the bishop's rebuke,

---

18. Augustine, *Letters,* 22, 9.
19. Augustine, *Confessions,* 8.12.28; 9.1.1.
20. Augustine, *Letters,* 22.1.
21. Ibid., 21.1, 3, 4.
22. Ibid., 22.2, 3, 7.

## AUGUSTINE'S DEVELOPMENTAL THEOLOGY

There are those who object to Augustine. Some believe his theology is just plain wrong. They quote passages that obviously differ from orthodoxy. Others find his work confusing, with too many opinions voiced on too many subjects.

Augustine probably wouldn't have disagreed. Instead, he would have confessed: "I now think an error what I had previously thought to be the truth." —*Acta Contra Fortunatum Manichaeum,* I.

### Staggering quantity

Augustine's mind *did* change as he wrote and preached over a period of about forty years. Garry Wills calls the quantity of his work staggering—"his own incomplete review of his books numbered ninety-three. There are, besides, almost three hundred of his letters and over four hundred sermons, out of the estimated eight thousand that he preached." —*Saint Augustine,* (New York: Lipper/Viking, 1999), xii.

Jaroslav Pelikan points out that "any theologian who would have written either the *Confessions* or the *City of God* or *On the Trinity* would have to be counted a major figure in intellectual history. Augustine wrote them all, and vastly more." —*The Christian Tradition* (Chicago: The University of Chicago Press, 1971), 1:292.

### Contradictions and transitions

The sheer quantity of his work and the fact that he wrote over such a long period as he publicly fought the battles of the young church also make it true that he can be quoted on most of the sides of any particular issue. "So massive was Augustine's literary output that one can almost literally find anything there that one wants to find. . . . Augustine's writings contain many apparent contradictions. His thinking on many theological subjects developed and changed over time, so that it is important to notice transitions within his thought. . . . Augustine's theology is not so much inconsistent as it is developmental." —Roger E. Olson, *The Story of Christian Theology* (Downer's Grove, Ill.: InterVarsity Press, 1999), 260, 261.

Even Augustine's most bitter opponents would turn to him for the foundational arguments for their beliefs. "Pelagius will even quote from Augustine's book 'On Free Will' in support of his own views. So, paradoxically, the great opponent of Augustine's old age had been inspired by those treatises of the young philosopher, in which Augustine had defended the freedom of the will against a Manichaean determinism." —Peter Brown, *Augustine of Hippo* (Berkeley, Calif.: University of California Press, 1967), 148.

"Such was the authority of the Augustinian view of nature and grace that even those who relapsed into Pelagian forms of teaching had to do so in Augustine's terms. The Reformation of the sixteenth century has repeatedly, and to some degree accurately, been interpreted as a movement in which the anti-Pelagian doctrines of Augustine about the necessity of grace were used to attack the anti-Donatist doctrines of Augustine about the mediation of grace." —Pelikan, 1:331.

### Rooted in experience

Wouldn't the more significant objection be to someone whose youthful opinions *never* changed? Isn't it true of all of us that we grow in our understandings, especially of the deep issues, the spiritual explanations, our theology? One church historian put it simply: "As he aged, he modified some earlier views." (E. Glenn Hinson, *The Early Church* [Nashville, Tenn.: Abingdon, 1996], 331.) Couldn't this—*shouldn't this*—be said of all growing Christians? Might not Paul's thoughts in 1 Corinthians 13:11 be correctly applied here: "When I was a child, I talked like a child, I thought like a child, I reasoned like a child. When I became a man, I put childish ways behind me"?

Augustine's "theology, though buttressed by the Scriptures, philosophy, and ecclesiastical tradition, was so largely rooted in his own experience as to render his story more than usually the interpretation of the man." —Williston Walker, *A History of the Christian Church* (New York: Charles Scribner's Sons, 1959), 160.

"It is easy to dismiss such works as immature. But we do this partly because Augustine himself matured so quickly; and, in following Augustine, we have left his early works behind." —Brown, 120.

The challenge to applying Augustine successfully is to be sure we accurately are representing him by quoting what he said in his later, more mature statements on a subject.

the young man left the church and converted to Donatism. He received baptism "while still in his frenzy, and is arrayed in the white vestments of a candidate for baptism while still raging for his mother's blood." Augustine would have disliked this situation in any case, but, in particular, he hates the "snarling and brawling" done "in the name of religion."[23]

### 3. THE SWEETNESS OF GRACE

And finally, the new pastor at Hippo brings to the battle with the Donatists a dawning realization of the goodness of God's grace. From before the days of his conversion, Augustine has been learning that grace offers something to sinners that isn't offered anywhere else.

In Milan, he listens as Bishop Ambrose preaches "the sound doctrine of salvation."[24] He studies Paul's insistence that only God's grace through Jesus "will deliver [us] from this body of death" (Romans 7:24, NKJV).[25] He sees God's grace shining in the lives of others.[26] He feels it in his own life: "The heart is aroused in the love of Your mercy and the sweetness of Your grace," he reflects.[27] When his mother dies in 387, he writes these words: "Her debts have been forgiven by Him to whom no one can repay the price which He, who owed nothing, paid on our behalf."[28]

The battles between Augustine and the Donatists rage for more than a decade.[29] In spite of the unnecessary excesses of the authoritarian

---

23. Ibid., 34.2, 3; 29.2.
24. Augustine, *Confessions,* 5.13.23.
25. Ibid., 3.21.27.
26. Ibid., 8.1.1.
27. Ibid., 10.3.3.
28. Ibid., 9.13.36.

29. I don't know if Ellen White ever studied Augustine's battles with the Donatists. But in her chapter on the Communion service, "In Remembrance of Me," in *The Desire of Ages,* she takes a decidedly anti-Donatist position: "When we suppose one to be in error and sin, we are not to divorce ourselves from him. By no careless separation are we to leave him a prey to temptation, or drive him upon Satan's battleground. This is not Christ's method. It was *because* the disciples were

church against its schismatic children (as well as the unfortunate justification for such violence in the name of orthodoxy that the medieval church would find in these early battles), the church learns for the time being that it "is not what is done by the bishop or priest" that is decisive in the life of the believers, "but what is done by God in Christ."[30] It is Augustine's preaching far more than any other single influence that patiently teaches the church this lesson, doing "more than ten brigades of police could have done to maintain order."[31] We can say with confidence that the Christian church today is not Donatist because of Augustine. Instead of thinking of our church as a country club for perfect saints, we see it as a community of justified sinners, saved by grace alone, forgiven, accepted, and learning how to respond to God's persistent love.

In an essay titled "Visible Grace: the Church as God's Embodied Presence," Philip Kenneson suggests that while God's grace is made clear to us in many different manifestations, "one of the most scandalous ways in which God has promised to be present is in and through the church . . . the all-too-sinful church with which we are all well acquainted." Kenneson continues: "What the church offers the world is something it has first received only by God's prior gracious initiative. As a result, the church's identity and mission as a mediator of God's presence remains inextricably tied to its identity as a recipient of God's self-gift;"[32] as the "herald of God's grace."[33]

G. K. Chesterton reminds us that the great lesson of the classic story "Beauty and the Beast" is "that a thing must be loved *before* it is lovable."[34] Robert Capon insists that the church "is a community of merely human beings"[35] that has been entrusted with the proclamation of the astonishingly good news of salvation. Paul puts it like this: "God demonstrates his love for us in this: While we were still sinners, Christ died for us" (Romans 5:8).

erring and faulty that He washed their feet." She then concludes the thought with an even stronger statement, which, had she published it fifteen hundred years earlier, at the end of the fourth century instead of in 1898, would have been collected in the writings against the Donatists: "None should exclude themselves from the Communion because some who are unworthy may be present. . . . Hearts and hands that are unworthy may even administer the ordinance, yet Christ is there to minister to His children. All who come *with their faith fixed upon Him* will be greatly blessed." ([Mountain View, Calif.: Pacific Press®, 1940], 655, 656, emphasis supplied.)

30. Hans Küng, *Christianity* (New York: Continuum, 1996), 291.

31. Van der Meer, 92.

32. Philip Kenneson, "Visible Grace: the Church as God's Embodied Presence," *Grace Upon Grace,* Robert Johnston, Gregory Jones, and Jonathan Wilson, eds. (Nashville: Abingdon Press, 1999), 173.

33. Ibid., 177.

34. G. K. Chesterton, *Orthodoxy* (New York: Dodd, Mead & Co., 1908).

35. Robert Farrar Capon, *The Astonished Heart* (Grand Rapids, Mich.: Wm. B. Eerdmans Publishing Company, 1996), 2.

# GRACE IN QUESTION

## CHAPTER 9: THE PERFECT CHURCH

Finally, in the late fourth century, a devout pastor and informed writer brings the focus of the church back to where it needs to be—in the process, making grace once again the central focus of Western theology. This chapter introduces the first great challenge in Augustine's battle with those who would diminish the importance of God's grace.

1. Have you ever felt like a traitor to your Christian faith? Ever felt defeated, like General Jonathan Wainwright felt? (See the sidebar "Grace for the Defeated" on pages 126, 127.) Why is grace so precious to us in moments of failure and defeat?

2. Is your local church a communion of "genuine, perfect saints"? Do any of the following pictures represent your understanding of what a church is all about? What other pictures would you like to add?
   a. an exclusive society accepting only those people who have the right qualifications.
   b. a fortress protecting us from the dangers of our society.
   c. a hospital in which hurting people find healing.
   d. a volunteer fire department that assists people in putting out fires.

3. If a Donatist-type group were alive and well today in your community, what do you think would be the one sin people would have avoided to join the group?

4. Has your theology, like Augustine's, developed over the years? Do you agree that this should be said of all growing Christians? (See the sidebar "Augustine's Developmental Theology" on pages 130, 131.)

5. Watch scenes from Disney's animated *Beauty and the Beast* that highlight Chesterton's point "that a thing must be loved *before* it is lovable."

# Grace Notes
## Colossians 1–3—The Clothes of the Chosen

Q. What does grace offer to sinners that isn't offered anywhere else?

Q. How might Augustine have utilized the book of Colossians in his battles with the Donatists?

The church members at Colossae had an enviable reputation: "We have heard of your faith in Christ Jesus and of the love you have for all the saints" (Colossians 1:4). Paul has been listening to Epaphras, a fellow minister (verse 7), and has heard about the actions of this Christlike little church.

Where does that kind of faith and love come from? It springs, Paul says, "from the hope that is stored up for you in heaven and that you have already heard about in the word of truth, the gospel that has come to you" (verses 5, 6).

From the day they first heard that gospel and "understood God's grace in all its truth" (verse 6), they have been living lives worthy of the Lord and pleasing Him in every way; "bearing fruit in every good work, growing in the knowledge of God, being strengthened with all power according to his glorious might so that you may have great endurance and patience" (verses 10, 11).

Paul carefully chronicles the growth. There is no mistaking his language. Before the "every good work" comes the "stored up" hope.

The Father . . . has qualified you to share in the inheritance of the saints in the kingdom of light. For He has rescued us from the dominion of darkness and brought us into the kingdom of the Son he loves, in whom we have redemption, the forgiveness of sins (verses 12–14).

Once you were alienated from God and were enemies in your minds because of your evil behavior. But now he has reconciled you by Christ's physical body through death to present you holy in his sight, without blemish and free from accusation (verses 21, 22).

Just as you received Christ Jesus as Lord, continue to live in him, rooted and built up in him, strengthened in the faith as you were taught, and overflowing with thankfulness (2:6, 7).

You have been given fullness in Christ (verse 10).

When you were dead in your sins and in the uncircumcision of your sinful nature, God made you alive with Christ. He forgave us all our sins (verse 13).

Since, then, you have been raised with Christ, set your hearts on things above, where Christ is seated at the right hand of God (3:1).

But there is always more growing to do. None of us has arrived at that perfect similarity to the character of Christ. None of us has come to the place where we have no more overcoming ahead of us. So Paul continues. He is confident he now can raise the subject of growth because his friends in Colossae are rooted and grounded in grace. They have been qualified. Rescued. Redeemed. Forgiven. Reconciled. They have been raised from spiritual death by Christ, given new life. Now, *now,* in their fullness in Christ, in their resurrected state, in their new life, *from within grace,* they continue to grow, setting their hearts on things above.

Put to death, *therefore,* whatever belongs to your earthly nature (verse 5, emphasis supplied here and in the verses that follow).

*But now* you must rid yourselves of all such things as these: anger, rage, malice, slander, and filthy language (verse 8).

Do not lie to each other, *since you have taken off your old self* with its practices *and have put on the new self,* which is being renewed in knowledge in the image of its Creator (verses 9, 10).

*Here* there is no Greek or Jew, circumcised or uncircumcised, barbarian, Scythian, slave or free, but Christ is all, and is in all (verse 11).

Let the peace of Christ rule in your hearts, *since as members of one body you were called to peace* (verse 15).

Paul pulls it all together with a beautiful picture of the clothes that the chosen wear. *"Therefore, as God's chosen people, holy and dearly loved,* clothe yourselves with compassion, kindness, humility, gentleness and patience. Bear with each other and forgive whatever grievances you may have against one another. Forgive *as the Lord forgave you.* And over all these virtues put on love, which binds them all together in perfect unity" (verses 12–14, emphasis supplied).

The "holy and dearly loved" wear clothes of compassion. Kindness, humility, gentleness, and patience look natural on the people who realize God has chosen them. Try to wear the clothes on your own, before you accept God's grace, and they become "filthy rags" (Isaiah 64:6).

*"Here I am as a result of your goodness."*
—Augustine, *Confessions*


*"Augustine held the essence of the gospel to be*
*the justification of the ungodly."*
—Alister McGrath, *Iustitia Dei*


*"Augustine was convinced that God's grace is not acquired;*
*grace is given."*
—Hans Küng, *Great Christian Thinkers*


*"Every new stage of his development is inaugurated by*
*a renewed and deepened study of Scripture."*
—Jaroslav Pelikan, *The Christian Tradition*


*"Pelagius gave an answer for the few, the strong:*
*Augustine for the many, the weak."*
—Garry Wills, *Saint Augustine*

## CHAPTER 10
# THE SECOND BATTLE:
### *The Refuge of Grace in the Challenge of Pelagius*

T HE HEROIC *TRUE STORY* BEHIND ONE OF HISTORY'S GREATEST LEGENDS
explodes onto the screen!" trumpeted the marketing department of
Touchstone Films early in 2004. "Prepare for more thrills, more adven-
ture and more intensity."

The Jerry Bruckheimer-Antoine Fuqua "demystified version" of King Arthur and
the Knights of the Round Table made a fascinating addition to the well-known
story. Early in the tale, set in the fifth century, a British monk by the name of Pelagius inspires a young Arthur with talk of peace, leadership, and shared responsibility.
Fifteen years later, Arthur still glows as he tells of his respect for Pelagius in a conversation with Bishop Germanius, an emissary from Rome. Germanius has arrived
in a hostile Britain on the eve of the empire's collapse in that cold and rainy outpost.
The Saxons are invading from the north. The Woads (British rebels who hate the
Romans) are lurking in the forests. Arthur is about to return to Rome, where he
believes Pelagius is alive and well.

"The teachings of Pelagius on free will and equality have been a great influence,"
Arthur says. "There is no destiny, only free will."

In fact, the monk Pelagius is a real character—much more real actually, than the
elusive Arthur. His story did take place early in the fifth century, although probably
not in time to have known even an early Arthur. Unlike Arthur and Guinevere,
Lancelot and Galahad, Merlin and Excalibur, we can follow Pelagius's actual history
through his influential teachings, which were among the most powerful in the life of
the early Christian church.

From Britain, Pelagius did go to Rome, did teach about free will, and did attract a considerable following. But then he ran into Augustine, the feisty pastor of
the church in Hippo in North Africa. We learn the most about the monk who is
sometimes referred to as "the enemy of the grace of God"[1] in his debates with the

---

1. Robert B. Eno, "Some Patristic Views on the Relationship of Faith and Works in Justification,"
*Justification by Faith, Lutherans and Catholics in Dialogue VII,* H. George Anderson, T. Austin Murphy,
and Joseph A. Burgess, eds. (Minneapolis: Augsburg Publishing House, 1985), 117.

"doctor of grace." As the Donatist controversy was coming to an end for Augustine (see chapter 9), a second great battle was just beginning. It's a battle we're still fighting in your church and mine all these years later.

## THE BARBARIANS INVADE ROME

By 400, the Roman Empire is disintegrating, and Rome, the great city once known as the capital of the world, is in decline. The population of the empire has reached seventy million, but only a handful, less than 10 percent, is actually Italian. The vast majority wait with thinly veiled anticipation and yet with fear for the Roman collapse. The once mighty Roman army is made up now almost entirely of foreign recruits—mercenaries willing to fight Rome's battles for a share in Rome's wealth. And the battles are many! During the last few decades of the fourth century, control of the northern and eastern borders of the empire has become increasingly difficult as Germanic tribes push incessantly into the territory, taking valuable farmland and occupying the eastern cities, waiting for another wave of incursions to begin.

The Huns have been the chief menace for a while, and they will return in a few years with a horrific new leader named Attila. The Vandals have swept across the empire and are settling in Spain. Now it is the Gothic tribes who threaten—those from the western reaches of their homeland, the Visigoths; and, from the remote eastern regions, the powerful Ostrogoths.

The Romans consider these invading people to be *barbarians*. They apply this term to anyone who lives outside the Roman Empire, anyone who speaks a language other than Latin, anyone who is born into what the Romans consider an inferior culture. At the beginning of the fifth century, the barbarian invaders all

look alike to the citizens of Rome: The men are tall and bearded, they are all blonde and blue eyed, and they dress funny, refusing the dignified tunics and delicate sandals preferred by the Roman people in favor of rough trousers and heavy shoes. There is extreme prejudice and oppressive discrimination against the unwelcome aliens. Corrupt dealing to swindle the uneducated is virtually a matter of policy.

The barbarian confederation is really just a loose collection of competitive, warring tribes rather than a unified nation with a strong central leadership. Consequently, at times, groups of barbarians turn to Rome for protection against other groups of barbarians. Around 370, Visigoth factions under a leader named Fritigern are fighting other Visigoths led by Athanaric. The forces of Fritigern are being beaten badly, and Fritigern appeals to Rome for help. In return for Rome's coming to their rescue, he enlists his men as soldiers in the Roman auxiliary forces. By 392, the successor to the Visigoth leadership, Alaric, is in command of more than twenty thousand of these *foederatae*—troops recruited from tribes federated with the empire.

For a few years, Alaric directs his soldiers at the forefront of the empire's struggles. Alaric has been trained for these responsibilities by the principal general of the Roman army, a superior military leader, Flavius Stilicho. But when Emperor Theodosius dies in 395, Alaric rebels and forms his own army, taking the Visigoth forces with him. In fierce battles, the Roman army prevails. But Alaric repeatedly slips through Rome's clutches and escapes. A few years of relative quiet ensue. Then, in 408, Alaric reappears with an even larger army, threatening the empire once again. Stilicho goes to the boy emperor, Honorius, in Ravenna, and appeals for gold and silver to buy off Alaric. The senate is belligerent. They refuse the request and turn on their general, accusing him of trying to build his own power base against Honorius and of plotting a coup to place his own son on the throne. On the 22nd of August, 408, Stilicho is assassinated.

Now, with the most effective military leader of the age out of the way and with the political leadership of the empire quarreling with each other in Ravenna, Alaric turns his sight on Rome. With his Visigoth troops, he begins a long siege of the eternal city. Belatedly, the senate attempts to bribe Alaric with the gold and silver Stilicho had requested.[2] But all deals fall through. On the 24th of August, 410, someone inside Rome opens the Salaria Gate, and Alaric and his hungry, angry Visigoth army pour into the city. Three days of murderous, destructive rampaging takes place. Thousands perish. The "sack of Rome," just a few years earlier an unthinkable occurrence, causes a shock wave that reverberates with chilling consequence across the vast reaches of the empire. The city of Rome had been untouched by the violence and carnage of war for almost seven hundred years.

In Bethlehem, a stunned Jerome weeps bitterly at the news: "My voice sticks in my throat; and, as I dictate, sobs choke my utterance," he says.[3] Augustine retreats to his study in North Africa and begins work on his masterpiece, *The City of God*, with words about the great city's fall and the ragings of "the bloodthirsty barbarians."[4] Others believe that with the end of the world structure, the end of the world itself is near and Christ is about to return.[5]

## WHO WAS TO BLAME?

Among the Romans who flee the ancient capital to escape the Visigoth sack is a remnant of the pagan populace. These people had continued to hold to their religious ways in spite of the spread and official acceptance of Christianity and the antipagan laws that forbade their practices and festivals. For these displaced citizens, holdovers from a once powerful and exclusive religious-political alliance, the end of civilization as they knew it at the hands of an uncultured, violent mob is obviously the result of replacing the worship of the old pagan gods with the worship of Jesus of Nazareth. The gods have betrayed the Romans because the Romans have abandoned the gods.

Interestingly, to add to the pagan argument, the barbarians mostly are Christians. In the middle of the fourth century (from around 340 to somewhere in the 380s) a missionary named Ufilas had worked among the Gothic people and had translated the Bible into their language (in the process, providing them for the first time with an alphabet). Like Valens, the emperor at the time, Ufilas was an Arian, believing that Jesus was human but not divine. In spite of this fundamental difference in doctrine, the Goths withheld their most venomous violence from the Christians in Rome. Most of the survivors of the sack, Christians and pagans, were those who found refuge in the Christian catacombs and churches. "To their very threshold the bloodthirsty enemy raged," Augustine reflects. "There his murderous fury owned a limit. There in its sacred places, as they

2. The bribe consisted of five thousand pounds of gold, thirty thousand pounds of silver, four thousand silken tunics, three thousand scarlet-dyed hides, and three thousand pounds of pepper.

3. Jerome, Letter 127 (To Principia).

4. Augustine, *The City of God*, 1.1.

5. Garry Wills, *Saint Augustine* (New York: Penguin Putnam, Inc., 1999), 114. "Rome had, for men of that time, seemed the organizing principle of all human history. Rome gone, what sense was to be made of the world?"

fled from the enemy's steel, those very Romans were spared by the barbarians through their respect for Christ."[6]

### THE FREEDOM TO CHOOSE

Pelagius is among those who flee the horrors of the Gothic invasion. For years the British monk has been preaching to packed churches in Rome. He advocated a variation of the Christian message, emphasizing not the good news of what Christ has accomplished for us but instead the basic good nature of human beings and the freedom of their will to choose to do good.[7] If God commands us to do good and not sin, Pelagius reasons, then we must have the inherent capacity to do what God commands. If the capacity is a natural part of God's good creation, then we must be able to choose not to sin without the assistance of grace or any other spiritual force or persuasion.[8]

"Be ye therefore perfect," Pelagius concludes, quoting his favorite New Testament passage "even as your Father which is in heaven is perfect" (Matthew 5:48, KJV). Since perfection is possible for humans, Pelagius insists, it is obligatory. For him, this "becoming perfect" is a "coming of age," like children who, upon being released "from dependence on the *pater familias* could at last go out into the world as mature, free individuals, able to uphold in heroic deeds the good name of their illustrious ancestry."[9]

For all who had stumbled into sin or who had sinned willfully or knowingly, the setting free is through baptism and by the work of Christ alone.[10] No question about where justification comes from. But sin isn't inevitable, Pelagius asserts, and those who haven't sinned don't need to be justified. So a salvation *not based on grace* must be available for those who have lived a life of victory, keeping the commandments of God perfectly.

In this victorious state, new Christians aren't dependent on the power or the grace of the Father, don't need to beg God for His grace or His forgiveness, and are capable of exerting their own will power to accomplish the commanded good behavior—becoming in the process *worthy* of salvation.[11] The power of the

---

6. Augustine, ibid.

7. "Originally created good by God," Peter Brown summarizes the position of Pelagius, "the powers of human nature had, admittedly, been constricted by the weight of past habits and by the corruption of society. But such constriction was purely superficial. The 'remission of sins' in baptism, could mean for the Christian, the immediate recovery of a full freedom of action, that had merely been kept in abeyance by ignorance and convention." (*Augustine of Hippo* [Berkeley, Calif.: University of California Press, 1967], 365.)

8. Followers of Pelagius tended to be among the wealthier class of Rome's citizens, and the force of the Pelagian message drove them to remarkable acts of generosity. One young couple liquidated their entire land holdings in order to give the money to the poor. Others became patrons of Pelagius, providing for his welfare in Rome and wherever he traveled, enthusiastically supporting his disciples as far away to the north as Britain and to the south in Sicily and Rhodes, circulating his letters and pamphlets, and sending what amounted to missionaries to establish Pelagian "cells."

9. Brown, 352.

10. "No man between Paul and Luther so emphasized justification by faith alone." (Williston Walker, *A History of the Christian Church* (New York: Charles Scribner's Sons, 1959], 168.)

11. The Pelagians anticipated the objection "If you go all the way with grace, what will happen to obedience and commandment keeping?" They argued, "If the process of a person's salvation, from beginning to fulfillment, is entirely and solely dependent on grace, then all grounds for striving to live in conformity to God, for striving to order oneself and one's love to God, appear to be undercut." (See Rebecca Harden Weaver, *Divine Grace and Human Agency* [Macon, Ga.: Mercer University Press, 1996], 8.)

human will can break the bondage of sin, Pelagius teaches.[12] The resultant state of sinless perfection will produce a church of "absolute certainty through absolute obedience," a people "without spot or blemish," a good example for those who live in what is still an evil world.

Peter Brown points out that no matter how biblical or Christian Pelagius attempted to sound, his theology "rested firmly on a bedrock of the old ethical ideals of paganism."[13]

THE BATTLE BEGINS

After Rome falls to the Goths, Pelagius and many followers move to the south. They stop in North Africa, at Augustine's town of Hippo, but the bishop is away on business and doesn't return while Pelagius is there, although the two pastors do exchange polite letters. The group finally moves on to the east, to Jerusalem. There, the Pelagian writings on sin, free will, and grace turn the Holy Land into a cauldron of controversy.

When, in 415, Augustine finally reads Pelagius's work *On Nature,* he realizes he can no longer stay quiet about this new theological challenge. Augustine answers Pelagius by writing *On Nature and Grace,* and the battle is joined.

The local bishops in Palestine realize they too must respond. By the end of the year, December 20, 415, they convene a synod in Diospolis (present day Lydda) to hear Pelagius and to be able to ask him pointed questions about his teachings. Pelagius is brilliant! He distances himself from certain of his disciples who have taken his beliefs to extreme; he explains difficult passages in his own works that

have seemed to make him heretical; and he dismisses his accusers, including Augustine and Jerome, as ambiguous, conspiring enemies with personal grudges to resolve. The bishops buy the entire package.

Then, in a deliberate maneuver, Pelagius himself transcribes the proceedings of the synod, completely spinning the results in his direction. He has been given a "clean slate," he writes. His opinions are "approved" by these holy men of the Holy Land. The synod has resulted in an "exoneration" of his teaching and a "declaring orthodox" of his belief. Supporters of Pelagius quickly disseminate the summary. Augustine himself receives a copy, with no note of greeting or explanation attached.

The opponents of Pelagius, led by Augustine, immediately go into high gear. In two hastily called councils (both in North Africa—one in Carthage, the other in Milevis), three hundred African bishops agree *unanimously* that the synod in Diospolis has made a mistake. Then, fearing that well-placed supporters of Pelagius, especially those in Rome,[14] might bring about an even deeper acceptance of Pelagius's teachings, the Africans send a collection of documents to Innocent I, the bishop of Rome. The collection includes two cautiously worded, biblically based condemnations of Pelagian ideas, one from each of the African councils; an explanatory letter from Augustine; a marked copy of Pelagius's work *On Nature*; and a personal letter of appeal to Pelagius himself. All of the documents have been carefully crafted to show that acceptance of Pelagius's theology would mean big trouble ahead for the church.

12. C. FitzSimons Allison, *The Cruelty of Heresy* (Harrisburg, Penn.: Morehouse Publishing, 1994), 125.

13. Brown, 367.

14. In Rome, church authorities, led by Rome's bishop, had moved quickly to fill the power vacuum created by the fall of Rome and the moving on of the Goths. The church remains virtually the last power structure in the city.

Innocent, "a man of great ability and commanding character,"[15] responds just as the Africans hoped he would. If such ideas against grace really exist, he writes on January 27, 417, of course he will condemn them. To judge for himself, Innocent summons Pelagius to Rome.

Before Pelagius arrives, however, Innocent dies (March 12, 417). Within a week, a new bishop has been elected—an easterner named Zosimus, who has very different feelings about the synod in the Holy Land and about the African bishops and the others who are opposing Pelagius.

Zosimus is impressed by the letters he receives from Pelagius and by the stirring defense of Pelagian ideas offered by his follower Caelestius. In mid-September, he warmly welcomes Pelagius to Rome.[16] Then he writes to the Africans, "If only you had been present, my beloved brethren. How deeply each one of us was moved! Hardly anyone present could refrain from tears at the thought that persons of such genuine faith could have been slandered."[17]

The bishop of Rome characterizes Augustine's opinion as "hairsplitting" leading only to "these pointless debates." He also criticizes the councils that have condemned Pelagius. They were "over-hasty," he says, based on "unscrupulous witnesses." The accused have cleared themselves, Zosimus concludes, reversing Innocent's decision. And riots break out in Rome, orthodox Christians fighting Pelagian Christians.

Persuasive letters begin to fly from the pen of Augustine, warning various officials and influential church members of "the new heresy hostile to the grace of Christ."[18] One of the appeals goes directly to Emperor Honorius in Ravenna. Honorius acts quickly. On April 30, 418, he issues an edict calling Pelagius a "disturber of the faith." The emperor expels Pelagius from Rome and rules that anyone, *anyone,* who speaks in his behalf is to be brought before the authorities. Zosimus doesn't relish a quarrel with the emperor. He retreats fully and condemns Pelagius.

While the battle isn't over yet, its outcome has been decided. We hear no more of Pelagius and presume that he died before 420. Caelestius leaves Rome and eventually finds an able ally in Julian of Eclanum, a young man who will skillfully and persistently contend with Augustine for the rest of Augustine's life. The third general council of the church meets in Ephesus in June of 431. This council once and for all accepts Augustine's position and refutes Pelagianism. However, by this time, Augustine has been in his grave for almost ten months. He died on August 28, 430, at the age of seventy-six, during the Vandals' siege of Hippo.

PELAGIUS IS STILL AMONG US

I mentioned that the battle with Pelagian thought is one we're still fighting in our churches. Less than a week after I began working on this chapter, a visitor to one of our church's Bible studies interrupted a com-

---

15. J. N. D. Kelly, *The Oxford Dictionary of Popes* (Oxford: Oxford University Press, 1986), 37. Kelly points out that Innocent "seized every opportunity of asserting the primacy of the Roman see, making more substantial claims for the papacy than his predecessors. As a result he not only proved one of the outstanding popes of the early centuries, but has sometimes been saluted as 'the first pope.' "

16. Brown, 359.

17. Zosimus, Letter, "Postquam," 1.

18. Augustine, *Letters,* 178.1.

ment I was making and stated that, in order to be perfectly just, God must base salvation not on grace but on our obedience, our overcoming, our cooperation with the Holy Spirit. She quoted a few well-chosen Bible verses to bolster her argument: "Thou shalt not kill. Thou shalt not commit adultery. Thou shalt not steal" (Exodus 20:13–15, KJV). "Overcome evil with good" (Romans 12:21). "The only thing that counts is faith expressing itself through love" (Galatians 5:6). "I will show you my faith by what I do" (James 2:18). "Here are they that keep the commandments of God" (Revelation 14:12, KJV).

"It would be unfair for salvation to be only a gift," she continued. "If salvation were given equally to all, it would negate any difference between Christian behavior and non-Christian behavior, between those who obey God and those who ignore Him, between those who keep the Commandments—every one of them—and those who don't."

In discussions about salvation, this objection is voiced frequently. It issues, Philip Yancey observes, from our "inbuilt resistance to grace"[19]—a resistance that exhibits itself in a "nervous moralism and ceaseless attempts to placate an angry God."[20] "Gifts are a problem to us," Debbie Vance writes in an *Adventist Review* article titled "The Trouble With Grace." "We are disciples of the make-your-own-way, the pull-your-own-weight. We are capable, self-reliant, high-achieving. And we are guilty. We believe, deep down, that we don't deserve anything we haven't worked, suffered, or paid for."[21]

I requested a clarification from the woman. "Why demand that salvation be *unequal?*" I asked. "What makes you afraid of grace?"

"I don't think I'm afraid," she answered, "unless it's a fear that grace is unfair. If I get to heaven and have to live next door to someone who didn't even try, I'm going to be pretty frustrated. I work really hard at being a good Christian. I just want to be given what I deserve, nothing more."

"If salvation were based on our behavior," I pressed, "would it be possible for someone to get to heaven without grace, without Jesus?"

"Of course not," she answered quickly.

"Not even possible?"

She thought a moment. "Maybe it's possible. Maybe if you had really strong will power."

"Ever heard of Pelagius?" I asked.

Well, she hadn't. And I didn't think she needed to hear about him right then. But without knowing him, she actually wanted the same thing he wanted. Pelagius wanted a world in which good would be done regularly, in which people would rather do good than not do good. Pelagius wanted us all to be like his friends who sold their possessions and gave to the poor. King Arthur wanted people to live in peace. This woman wanted people to try. It's what we all want, isn't it?

By the way, it's what the Bible wants, too. Striving to be Christlike is what Christians are supposed to do. "Let this mind be in you which was also in Christ Jesus" (Philippians 2:5, NKJV). "Let the word of Christ dwell in you richly" (Colossians 3:16).

The Pelagian road begins its detour at the very point where we connect our desire for good with our hope for eternal life; where we attempt to create salvation without unmerited,

---

19. Philip Yancey, *What's So Amazing About Grace?* (Grand Rapids, Mich.: Zondervan, 1997), 45.

20. Timothy George, *Theology of the Reformers* (Nashville: Broadman Press, 1988), 30.

21. Deborah Anfenson-Vance, "The Trouble With Grace," *Adventist Review*, January 7, 1988, 15, 16.

undeserved grace. "They pursued it not by faith but as if it were by works" (Romans 9:32). "It does not, therefore, depend on man's desire or effort, but on God's mercy" (verse 16) "[He] has saved us and called us to a holy life—not because of anything we have done but because of his own purpose and grace" (2 Timothy 1:9). "He who began a good work in you will carry it on to completion" (Philippians 1:6).

Any and every attempt to secure salvation without grace, like the doctrine of Pelagius, minimizes the condition for standing in the presence of a perfect, holy God (1 Samuel 6:20; Psalm 24:3, 4). It contradicts the Bible's insistence that *all of us* have sinned (Romans 3:23). It denies the Bible's conclusion that *all of us* need a Savior (Romans 3:24; 5:6–10). It fails the gospel requirement that what God does for us must be good news (Luke 2:10; Acts 5:42).

Salvation by willpower doesn't work. Never has. Never will.

---

# GRACE IN QUESTION
## CHAPTER 10: THE SECOND BATTLE

Augustine's fight for the primacy of grace in the theology of the church lasts his entire life. Chapter 10 describes the battle that occupied his attention during the last years of his life, the battle against the Pelagians, who believed there must be a salvation without grace.

1. What is the condition for standing in the presence of a perfect, holy God? Read Ellen White's *Steps to Christ,* page 62, the entire page.

2. Look up the word *perfect* in a dictionary and discuss its meaning. Does *perfect* mean one must stop being imperfect? Does it mean being 99.9 percent without flaws? What's a perfect grade-point average? What about a perfect batting average? Draw some spiritual conclusions.

3. Consider Peter Brown's comment about "the bedrock of the old ethical ideals of paganism" (page 141). If this comment refers to any attempt to become worthy of salvation by our own good behavior, how and where has this "pagan ethic" become part of the Christian tradition? What can we do to eliminate "paganism" from our own spiritual experience?

4. Discuss the proper place in our Christian life for "overcoming evil with good," for "faith expressing itself through love," for "keeping the commandments." What happens if we pursue these good things "not by faith but as if it were by works"? What might happen if we forget that "he who began a good work in you will carry it on to completion"?

5. Why doesn't God reward us with heaven according to what we *deserve?*

# GRACE NOTES
## 1 SAMUEL 6—THE CART OF THE PHILISTINES

It was a bad idea from the very beginning.

The Israelite army, camped at a place called Ebenezer, is engaged in a battle against the Philistines (1 Samuel 4:1). The first day has gone poorly for the Hebrews, who have lost thousands of their soldiers (verse 2). The "elders of Israel" think the answer is to bring the ark of the covenant from Shiloh and take it into battle on the next day (verse 3). Hophni and Phinehas, Eli's sons, carry the ark to Ebenezer, which emboldens the Philistines and leads to one of the worst days the army of Israel would ever experience. Thirty thousand soldiers are lost. Hophni and Phinehas are killed. And the ark of the covenant is captured (verses 10, 11).

The defeat is compounded when the news reaches Eli the priest, now ninety-eight years old, blind, and overweight. When the messenger gets to the part about the ark, Eli falls backward off his chair, breaks his neck, and dies (verse 18).

Now, for seven months (6:1), " 'the ark of the god of Israel,' " as the Philistines called it (5:7), is paraded through the Philistine cities. In Ashdod, Gath, and Ekron, "the Lord's hand was heavy upon the people" (verse 6). The Philistines are thrown into "a great panic" as people begin to die from a disease (verses 9, 11). "So they called together all the rulers of the Philistines and said, 'Send the ark of the god of Israel away; let it go back to its own place, or it will kill us and our people' " (verse 11).

The rulers place the problem before a meeting of the Philistine priests and diviners. They ask,

> "What shall we do with the ark of the Lord? . . ."
>
> They answered, "If you return the ark of the god of Israel, do not send it away empty, but by all means send a guilt offering to him. Then you will be healed, and you will know why his hand has not been lifted from you."
>
> The Philistines asked, "What guilt offering should we send to him?" They replied, "Five gold tumors and five gold rats, according to the number of the Philistine rulers, because the same plague has struck both you and your rulers.
>
> "Make models of the tumors and of the rats that are destroying the country, and pay honor to Israel's god. Perhaps he will lift his hand from you and your gods and your land. . . .
>
> "Now then, get a new cart ready, with two cows that have calved and have never been yoked. Hitch the cows to the cart, but take their calves away and pen them up.

Q. What has been frightening to you about standing in the presence of a perfect, holy God?

Q. In what ways does God's grace, His treating us as if we were blameless and holy, help us to stand?

"Take the ark of the LORD and put it on the cart, and in a chest beside it put the gold objects you are sending back to him as a guilt offering. Send it on its way, but keep watching it. If it goes up to its own territory, toward Beth Shemesh, then the LORD has brought this great disaster on us. But if it does not, then we will know that it was not his hand that struck us and that it happened to us by chance" (6:2–9).

The rulers of the Philistines do exactly what their priests told them to do. And when the cows are hitched to the cart, they go "straight up toward Beth Shemesh, keeping on the road and lowing all the way; they did not turn to the right or to the left" (verse 12).

In Beth Shemesh, people working in a field see the ark and are overjoyed. They drop their harvesting tools, run to the Philistine cart, take the ark out, and place it on top of a big rock at the edge of the field (verse 15). Then they chop up the wood of the cart, sacrifice the cows, and offer them as a burnt offering, thanking the Lord for the return of the ark (verse 14).

But then the people of Beth Shemesh do something really stupid. Seventy people gather around the ark, and against specific, well-known instructions, *they open it and look inside* (verse 19)! Immediately, the seventy people die.

The remaining citizens of the village of Beth Shemesh look at each other and ask the burning question: " 'Who can stand in the presence of the LORD, this holy God?' " (verse 20).

Why is it that the people of earth tremble in the presence of holiness (Psalm 114:7)? It is God's righteousness that makes Him holy (Isaiah 5:16). His name is holy (1 Chronicles 29:16). His throne is holy (Psalm 47:8). His temple is holy (79:1). The ground where He appears is holy (Exodus 3:5). His Sabbath is holy (Deuteronomy 5:12; Ezekiel 20:20).

By contrast, our guilt separates us from Him: " 'O LORD, God of Israel, you are righteous! We are left this day as a remnant. Here we are before you in our guilt, though because of it not one of us can stand in your presence' " (Ezra 9:15). Our rebellion and sin make it impossible for us even to serve the holy God (Joshua 24:19).

But here comes the amazing welcome of grace: "May he strengthen your hearts so that you will be blameless and holy in the presence of our God and Father when our Lord Jesus comes with all his holy ones" (1 Thessalonians 3:13). In the grace of Christ, in His blameless and holy righteousness, we who are unholy are treated as if we were holy in the presence of the holy God.

Many years after the Philistines returned the ark of the covenant to Beth Shemesh, King David attempts to bring the ark to Jerusalem. Following the example of the Philistines, the priests place it on a cart drawn by oxen. This first attempt to move the ark ends in disaster.

Three months later, King David prepares for a second attempt at bringing the ark all the way to its new home in Jerusalem. First, however, he compares the previous attempt and God's original instructions. His study reveals a serious flaw in how the priests and Levites had transported it. Calling them together, David says, " 'It was because you, the Levites, did not bring it up the first time that the LORD our God broke out in anger against us. We did not inquire of him about how to do it in the prescribed way.' So the priests and Levites consecrated themselves in order to bring up the ark of the LORD, the God of Israel. And the Levites carried the ark of God with the poles on their shoulders, as Moses had commanded in accordance with the word of the LORD" (1 Chronicles 15:13–15).

God had already prescribed the proper method of moving the ark. He had asked for direct contact between the Levites and the ark; they were to carry it on their shoulders, with nothing in between them and God. It was *the Philistines* who had decided to move the presence of the holy God on a new cart drawn by cows.

The Philistine cart represents all our efforts to be holy or to become holy in any way other than the way the holy God already has determined. He "has saved us and called us to a holy life—not because of anything we have done but because of his own purpose and grace. This grace was given us in Christ Jesus before the beginning of time" (2 Timothy 1:9).

" 'In your unfailing love you will lead the people you have redeemed. In your strength you will guide them to your holy dwelling' " (Exodus 15:13). "He provided redemption for his people; he ordained his covenant forever—holy and awesome is his name" (Psalm 111:9).

*"The religion of the Bible is a religion of grace,*
*and without grace there could be no gospel and no salvation."*
—Kenneth Kinghorn, *The Gospel of Grace*


*"Grace is not grace if there are any ifs, ands or buts about it.*
*Grace is unconditional.*
*There is no salvation based on works."*
—Carl Braaten, *Justification*


*"A man whose hands are full of parcels can't receive a gift."*
—C. S. Lewis, *Letters to an American Lady*


*"I do not seek to understand so that I may believe;*
*but I believe so that I may understand."*
—Anselm, *Proslogion*


*"Each generation is converted by the saint*
*who contradicts it most."*
—G. K. Chesterton, *Saint Thomas Aquinas*

# CHAPTER 11
# THE SCHOLASTIC DANCE:
## *The Purchase of Grace in the Middle Ages*

ANTHONY WAS A RICH, YOUNG MAN BORN IN EGYPT LATE IN THE THIRD century. His wealth came from the property he inherited when his parents died before he was twenty. His good health provided him with such a strong constitution that he is said to have lived to be 106 years old! But it wasn't his wealth or his health that characterized his early life. Anthony felt tormented by demons.

One day Anthony heard a sermon about the conversation between Jesus and another rich, young man: " 'If you would be perfect,' " Jesus said in the story recorded in Matthew 19, " 'go and sell what you possess and give to the poor, and you will have treasure in heaven.' " Anthony took the story personally. He sold all his possessions, left home, and eventually went to live as a hermit in the desert. There he spent the rest of his life praying, fasting, and practicing the strictest self-denial—hoping to overcome his demons by drawing near to God.

People began to talk about Anthony the Hermit. They would go to the desert just to watch him. Some determined to imitate his lifestyle and joined him in the desert. Many of these followers lived alone as did Anthony, but others lived in groups. Early in the fourth century, one of these groups formed a community in which the members lived and ate together, were assigned work, had similar dress, regular hours of meditation, and common worship habits. They called their community a *monastery.* Soon similar communities, called *convents,* were established for women as well.

By the time of Charlemagne in the ninth century, there were monasteries around the world, and competing monastic orders—Benedictines, Dominicans, Franciscans, Augustinians, etc. Each monastic group held a slightly different view on how to obtain eternal salvation—as well as how to get through life successfully (including how monks should wear their hair: shaved from the front of their heads back to an imaginary line connecting the ears, as the Celtic monks did, or shaved "on the top of their heads, leaving a thin circle of hair all round the head just above the temples, in memory of Christ's crown of thorns,"[1] as the clergy in Italy did).

---

1. Robert Lacey, *Great Tales From English History* (New York: Little, Brown and Company, 2003), 42. In 664, at the synod held at the Abbey of Whitby the "tonsure" question was settled in favor of the haircuts of the southern monks.

Much good came from the monasteries. Early evangelists such as the influential sixth-century Irish monk Columba (521–597) used their monasteries as a base for missionary activity. The monasteries also can be credited with much of the copying, preservation, and illumination of the Scriptures that took place. Exquisite examples of these activities still astound and inspire us, such as the Book of Kells[2] and the Lindisfarne Gospels from the "new Iona," founded off the northeastern coast of England by Aidan, a monk from Iona, around 634 or 635.[3]

The monasteries were also places where the medieval commitment to learning held strong. From the time of the Venerable Bede in the late seventh and early eighth centuries, the educational work of the monastic schools grew, until, in France in the eleventh century, the commitment to intellectual growth had become a movement we know as Scholasticism. The "Schoolmen" led the theological discussions of the day. Lanfranc, a noted teacher who died in 1089, was the prior of a monastery in Normandy before becoming the Archbishop of Canterbury (1070–1089) under William the Conqueror.

Anselm (1033–1109), who studied at the same monastery where Lanfranc taught, succeeded Lanfranc as prior and again, in Canterbury, as the Archbishop. Called by many "the father of Scholasticism," Anselm set about to prove the truths of theology. Church historians usually speak of Anselm only in superlatives: He was "without doubt the greatest theologian of his time," comments Justo Gonzalez.[4] Anselm's

### THE EARLY MISSIONARIES OF IONA

In 563, accompanied by twelve followers, an Irish monk named Columba sailed from Ireland in a frail coracle of wicker and hides. They sailed until, from the top of a small hill on the mostly deserted island of Iona in the Hebrides, they were assured their beloved land was out of sight. As a gesture of commitment, they buried the boat on the beach. Then they took possession of the island and founded a monastery.

Columba was a simple man, "direct, determined, brave . . . alight with faith and devotion," James Charles Roy describes him in his book, *Islands of Storm*. ([Chester Springs, Penn.: Dufour Editions, Inc., 1991], 146.) "Certainly he had a genius for training and inspiring missionaries," observed Scott Peck following a quick pilgrimage to Iona. "By the time he died thirty-five years later most of Scotland had become Christian." (*In Search of Stones: A Pilgrimage of Faith, Reason, and Discovery* [New York: Hyperion, 1995], 206.) The monastery had become "the lamp of Christ whose flame lighted pagan Europe." (F. Marian McNeill, *Iona, A History of the Island* [London and Glasgow: Blackie & Sons, 1920], 14.)

In *The Great Controversy* (Nampa, Idaho: Pacific Press®, 1950), Ellen White says it like this: "From Ireland came the pious Columba and his co-laborers, who, gathering about them the scattered believers on the lonely island of Iona, made this the center of their missionary labors. . . . A school was established at Iona, from which missionaries went out, not only to Scotland and England, but to Germany, Switzerland, and even Italy." (Page 62.)

---

2. The Book of Kells is a lavishly illustrated and ornamented calfskin (vellum) manuscript that contains transcriptions of Matthew, Mark, Luke, and John. The book, completed around 800, was created by monks from Iona. It now resides in the Library of Trinity College in Dublin.

3. Williston Walker, *A History of the Christian Church* (New York: Charles Scribner's Sons, 1959), 180.

4. Justo Gonzales, *A History of Christian Thought, Volume 2, From Augustine to the Eve of the Reformation,* rev. ed. (Nashville: Abingdon, 1987), 167.

most influential contribution to Christian theology was his discussion of the atonement in his book *Cur Deus homo (Why God Became Man)*. Picking up where Tertullian had left off almost nine hundred years earlier (see chapter 8), Anselm proposed "the satisfaction theory of the atonement," stating that Christ's death on the cross "satisfied" the justice of God.[5] This theory replaced the church's "ransom theory," which had held sway for more than five hundred years.[6]

Peter Abelard (1079–1142), the most influential teacher of the next generation, was one of the great geniuses of Christian theology. He openly disagreed with Anselm's doctrine of satisfaction and emphasized God's love more than God's wrath. Abelard taught that the incarnation and death of Jesus are the highest expression and clearest communication of God's love. The effect of the Cross, Abelard argued, is toward humanity, not toward God.[7]

At their best, these medieval thinkers—philosophers as much as theologians—attempted to cast religion in the best possible intellectual light. They appealed to reason at every turn. They marshaled arguments logically. They relentlessly explored the implications of ideas. And they insisted that the Christian gospel is rational. Dietrich Bonhoeffer expressed his feeling that the mission of monasticism "was to preserve in the Church the primitive Christian realization of the costliness of grace."[8]

## THE IONA EXPERIENCE

The tiny island of Iona is approachable today only from Oban in Argyle on the west coast of Scotland by a forty-five-minute ferry boat ride, a drive on the narrow, winding roads of the Island of Mull, and then a ferry again over the last thousand yards of the frigid, wind-whipped water of St. Ronan's Bay. A quick walk through the village (no cars permitted) brings one to stunning eighth- and ninth-century stone crosses and to the remains of an abbey founded about 1200 by Benedictine monks.

Unlike Scott Peck, who found his visit to Iona "disappointing" and the island lacking in "the quality of holiness we'd anticipated," my experiences on the island have been magical, aided by sudden bursts of sunshine warming the chilly ocean breezes, by the quiet of the peaceful landscape, by the realization of the holy mission that began there, and by the best chocolate-orange ice cream bar I've ever tasted! The "holy island" has hosted such travelers as Sir Walter Scott, William Wordsworth, Joseph Turner, Felix Mendelssohn, and Samuel Johnson, who wrote, "That man is little to be envied . . . whose piety would not grow warmer among the ruins of Iona."

5. "The theory says that Christ paid a debt that all humanity owes God because of disobedience. God's justice demands payment of a satisfaction or else the order of the universe would be disrupted. The needed satisfaction is like a debt to God's honor that humanity must repay, but humanity is incapable of repaying it without suffering complete loss in hell. God in his mercy provides a perfect substitutionary sacrifice that satisfies his own honor and preserves the moral order of the universe." (Roger E. Olson, *The Story of Christian Theology* [Downer's Grove, Ill.: InterVarsity Press, 1999], 324.)

6. Around 600, Pope Gregory the Great explained the ransom theory in its clearest detail. The theory proposes that God the Father offers Christ's death on the cross in exchange for the right to save humans. Satan, according to the theory, was tricked into thinking he could keep Christ in the tomb forever and so accepted the ransom.

7. Abelard's theory has been called "the moral influence" or "moral example" theory. "According to Abelard, what humanity needs is a new motive for action, not a compensation paid to God on its behalf." (Olson, 328.) Captivated by the parable of the prodigal son, Abelard saw the Cross as God's running toward humanity, demonstrating His loving heart.

8. Dietrich Bonhoeffer, *The Cost of Discipleship* (New York: Collier Books, 1963), 50.

> ### "THE DUNCE WAS RIGHT"
>
> Chesterton tells of one good-natured student who "pitied Thomas so much as to try to help him with his lessons, going over the elements of logic like an alphabet in a horn-book.
>
> "The dunce [Thomas] thanked him with pathetic politeness; and the philanthropist went on swimmingly, till he came to a passage about which he was himself a little doubtful; about which, in point of fact, he was wrong. Whereupon the dunce, with every appearance of embarrassment and disturbance, pointed out a possible solution which happened to be right.
>
> "The benevolent student was left staring, as at a monster, at this mysterious lump of ignorance and intelligence; and strange whispers began to run round the schools."
>
> —*Saint Thomas Aquinas* (New York: Doubleday, 1956), 48.

## STRIVING FOR SALVATION

But we have to say as well that the monasteries and convents attracted a group of men and women who were drawn to the strictest of lifestyles and to a religious understanding that insisted that too much talk about God's grace tends to make people spiritually lazy. By their austerities and self-denial, by going without food or sleep for weeks, by not bathing or even washing their feet, by living with insects and rats or on a column in the heat of the desert, these people had come to believe that they were striving heroically for their salvation.

The primary austerity, interestingly, was celibacy. Jerome, who lived in a cave in Bethlehem while he translated the Bible into Latin, liked to point out that Adam and Eve were married, but only *after* they sinned. Peter was married, the monastics admitted, but *before* he met Jesus. Anyway, they reasoned, Jesus loved John, who had not married, more than He loved Peter, who had!

You can readily see how this sidetrack of ascetic behavior was at odds with the Bible's insistence that no human works contribute to salvation. John Cassian, in the early fifth century, taught that both God's grace *and* human efforts play a necessary role in salvation. "People can move toward salvation without grace," Cassian said. However, the Synod of Orange, which convened in 529, tried to hold the line: "Undeserved grace," the council insisted, "precedes meritorious works."[9]

The debate then turned to the question of how we receive this undeserved grace. The medieval conclusion emphasizes the sacraments—including baptism, the Lord's Supper, and marriage—as the "means of grace" for believers. If the *matter* of the sacrament is correct (the water in the baptistry, for example) and if the *form* of administering the sacrament is correct ("I baptize you in the name of the Father," etc.), then, and only then, does grace flow from God to the believer. Grace still originates with God, but we have to do something before He offers that grace to us.

More than this, medieval religious leaders add to the list of sacraments the notion of *penance.* Christ's atonement, they teach, takes care of the forgiveness necessary for all our sins up to the time we are baptized. After that time, however, we have to atone for our own sins by being truly sorry for what we did (called *contrition*), by telling our priest about it (*confession*),[10] by paying the penalties the church determines

---

9. William Placher, *A History of Christian Theology* (Philadelphia: The Westminster Press, 1983), 126.

10. "The Fourth Lateran Council, in 1215, required confession to the priest at least once a year." (Walker, 249.)

will satisfy our offenses against God (*satisfaction*), and finally, by having the priest, acting as God's agent, declare our forgiveness (*absolution*). Without this entire process, no guilty sinner could be assured of salvation.

## THE WISDOM OF A DUMB OX

Somewhere around 1225, in an old castle in a small Italian town halfway between Rome and Naples, the count of Aquino and his wife have another son, their seventh. The family names him Thomas, but, apparently because he is quite round and moves slowly and doesn't seem to be too bright, the unflattering nickname that sticks is "the dumb ox." He is possessed by a "dullness," G. K. Chesterton says of Thomas, and is "conspicuous by his tall and bulky figure, and completely failing or refusing to be conspicuous for anything else."[11]

While he is still a teenager, Thomas decides to become a monk and chooses to join the Dominican order, which is also known as the Order of Preachers. Thomas's parents are hostile to the Dominicans and want him instead to become a Benedictine. When Thomas joins the Dominicans anyway, his brothers break into the monastery, kidnap him, and for a year imprison him in one of the family's castles to try to persuade him to change his mind.

Ultimately, Thomas escapes his imprisonment ("It is probably not a fable that it was his sisters who engineered his escape"[12]), goes back to the Dominicans, and ends up—this "dumb ox"—becoming one of the most important religious thinkers of the Middle Ages. We know him as Thomas Aquinas, the great-

### JUSTIFICATION AND SANCTIFICATION

According to Francis Schaeffer, "the only difference" between justification and sanctification "is that one is once for all and the other is moment by moment" (*True Spirituality* [Wheaton, Ill.: Tyndale House, 1971], 79.) Actually, that is *not* the only difference. It is not even the *major* difference.

The major difference is that justification is about salvation and sanctification is not about salvation. Justification is about God's grace forgiving us and accepting us and making us a member of His family. Sanctification is about growing up in the family, learning how to live a life of praise, and overcoming the temptations that so easily entice us to the pigsties.

But "even if we are overcome by the enemy" (Ellen G. White, *Steps to Christ* [Nampa, Idaho: Pacific Press®, 1956], 64), even when our *sanctification* is not proceeding as nicely as it should, we are not thrown out of the family, disinherited, or abandoned—*because* our justification is sure!

est of the scholastic theologians—"the crown jewel of scholasticism."[13] With just a handful of other theologians, Aquinas sets the church's theological course for ages to come.

Regarding grace, Aquinas follows the lead of John Cassian and others and pushes the church door wide open for the influence of both grace and works on our salvation.[14] Aquinas teaches that the primary purpose of God's grace is to perfect human nature. God's grace

---

11. G. K. Chesterton, *Saint Thomas Aquinas* (New York: Doubleday, 1956), 48.

12. Ibid., 51.

13. Olson, 330.

14. "It is clear that Thomas's changing views on the nature and divisions of grace are complex and difficult to follow." (Alister E. McGrath, *Iustitia Dei, A History of the Christian Doctrine of Justification: The Beginnings to the Reformation* [Cambridge: Cambridge University Press, 1986], 107.) "Aquinas finds full room for the two dominating conceptions

works on us, Aquinas says, until He makes us perfect, righteous beings. Justification is about being made just, he writes, and grace is "the divine help by which God moves us to do and to will what is good."[15] Aquinas takes God's act of declaring that He will treat us just as if we had never sinned—the act that we usually refer to as "justification"—and marries it to the acts of God throughout our lives that help us overcome temptation and grow more and more like Jesus—what we call "sanctification." He says, "When a human mind undergoes justification, it must both abandon sin and approach justice by a movement of the free will."[16]

Aquinas concludes that *salvation* is a combination of both justification and sanctification. It's a *process* that takes a lifetime. We won't know our place in eternity for certain until the day we wake up in heaven and God says to us, "Welcome home!"

LIVING WITH NO ASSURANCE

Imagine if you accepted Aquinas's theology today and you entered every day not knowing if your salvation was sure. Imagine driving to work or school hoping that you've confessed all your sins and really were forgiven, just in case you have an accident and your life ends. Imagine beginning to take part in a Communion service in your church one Sabbath and suddenly being filled with fear that a sinful thought has entered your mind in the last few moments and that now you are unworthy of eating the bread and drinking the wine. Imagine having to reinterpret the parable of the prodigal son to make the welcoming parent run down the hill and say, "It's about time

you came home after all I've done for you. Be careful not to make any mistakes or I'll throw you out of the family again as quickly as you can say 'pigsty.' "

Imagine having to ignore one Scripture passage after another—passages like Romans 5:8: "God demonstrates his own love for us in this: While we were still *sinners,* Christ died for us" (emphasis supplied here and in the following texts). And 2 Corinthians 5:19: "God was reconciling the world to himself in Christ, *not counting [our] sins against [us].*" And Ephesians 2:4, 5: "God, who is rich in mercy, made us alive with Christ *even when we were dead in transgressions*—it is by grace you have been saved."

Since the church accepted Thomas's teaching, it is no wonder that it also began to emphasize the painful, eternal flames of hell. If nothing else was going to work, the church might as well try to scare us into being holy. No wonder the church began to teach that sinners could *purchase* a remission of a portion of the penalties for their sins with a generous gift to a monastery or a church. Or by participating in a crusade against the infidels. Or by taking a pilgrimage to a sacred place or at a special time. Or by paying for a bridge or a road that helped people get to church.

As I was growing up in the little churches on the central California coast, as I was reacting to camp meeting sermons as if they might be the last sermons preached before Jesus returned, and as I was trying to pass the tests in my academy Bible classes and college religion classes, the theology I was hearing was Thomistic—from Thomas Aquinas, straight out of the

---

of mediaeval piety—grace and merit." (Williston Walker, *A History of the Christian Church* [New York: Charles Scribner's Sons, 1959], 247.)

15. Thomas Aquinas, *Summa Theologica,* Q. 111, Art. 2. McGrath speaks of Thomas's "mature discussion of the nature and divisions of grace." (McGrath, 106.)

16. Aquinas, Q. 113, Art. 5.

Middle Ages. Until I discovered the everlasting gospel of God's unrelenting, uncompromising grace just a few years ago, I too was motivated by the flames of hell, by what I could do to remit a portion of the penalties for my sins, and by the constant fear that I wasn't good enough to make it to heaven.

And then the gospel began to teach me that salvation *is not about* avoiding hell but about living forever in the presence of Jesus, our Redeemer. The good news *is not about* what we do to avoid the wages of sin, but about what Jesus did to demonstrate God's endless love so that " 'whoever believes *in him,* shall not perish but have eternal life' " (John 3:16). Christianity *is not about* being afraid of grace, afraid of the offer that "guarantees" eternal life (see Ephesians 1:3–14), but about trusting that God has the power to do what He promises to do (Romans 4:21). When Jesus says, " 'Do not let your hearts be troubled. . . . I am going there to prepare a place for you. And if I go and prepare a place for you, I will come back and take you to be with me' " (John 14:1–3), He really means it!

Not only can we not make God love us more than He already does by not getting married or living on a pile of dirt or existing with insects in the heat of the desert, we can't do it by praying or keeping the Sabbath or paying our tithe or singing with the praise team either. The robe of Christ's righteousness, "woven in the loom of heaven, has in it *not one thread of human devising.*" [17]

What we do in response to the grace God has freely given us is entirely another story, and a very important one. There is plenty of counsel in the Bible about praying and keeping the Sabbath and paying our tithe and about how to treat the people we love and how to treat our enemies—*but it's not the story of how we receive salvation!* We should rejoice and be thankful that there are people among us who are gifted in the areas of responding to God with Sabbath keeping and praying and treating other people with love, and we should invite them at every occasion possible to instruct us out of their giftedness. But we must never allow them to tell us that they are instructing us about *salvation.* They are not! They're telling another story, the one about sanctification.

ANGELS DANCING IN THE DARK AGES

After the Middle Ages, people who were excited about new discoveries and increasing knowledge began to refer to the period we've been looking at in this chapter as the "Dark Ages." No one who lived earlier was as bright as they were, they seemed to believe. One of those discussions suggested that the medieval theologians and philosophers apparently had nothing better to do than to sit around and discuss silly matters of absolutely no consequence whatsoever. And someone, hundreds of years after the fact, characterized those discussions as revolving around how many angels could dance on the head of a pin.

Actually, historians never have been able to find the "dancing on the head of a pin" conversation, although Aquinas comes close when he discusses whether or not angels have bodies, and if they do, how much space those bodies occupy. The charge originally was meant as a nasty comment about people who aren't as smart as we are, and it even ended up in a little ditty called "A Nursery Rhyme of Scholasticism," which went like this:

William of Occam, oh, where have you been?
"I've been out dancing on the head of
a pin."

---

17. Ellen G. White, *Christ's Object Lessons* (Hagerstown, Md.: Review and Herald, 1941), 311.

What do you conclude, now your task
is complete?
"It's fine for the angels, but hard on
the feet."

I find the historical development away from grace a fascinating subject to study. But frankly, it's much more important for us to discuss how *we* respond today to the biblical gospel of grace and its encouraging message for our lives. So think for just a moment now about the gospel as if *it* were the pin—the sharp point of theology that is capable of supporting all our rejoicing and all our celebrating of what God has done to make eternal life a reality for you and me. Then the real question becomes not how many *angels* can dance on the head of a pin—on the point of the gospel—but how many *Adventists* can dance on the head of the gospel pin?

I realize that for most of us traditional Adventists, the question is itself a bit problematic. But speaking in a spiritual sense, the Bible frequently connects the gospel with the rejoicing of dancing (as in Psalm 30:11, "You turned my wailing into dancing; you removed my sackcloth and clothed me with joy"; and Jeremiah 31:3, 4, " 'I have loved you with an everlasting love; I have drawn you with loving-kindness . . . take up your tambourines and go out to dance with the joyful' ").

The good news of the everlasting gospel is that salvation is not about what you and I do or don't do. It's not about what we eat or drink, what we wear or don't wear, how we treat the people we love or how we treat our enemies. Those concerns are the *result* of the gospel. The gospel is about God's grace (Acts 20:24). The gospel is about salvation (Ephesians 1:13). And salvation is about what *Jesus* has done for you and me: Christ is "the source of eternal salvation" (Hebrews 5:9). " 'Salvation belongs

to our God, who sits on the throne, and to the Lamb' " (Revelation 7:10). Salvation "is in Christ Jesus" (2 Timothy 2:10).

Listen to Isaiah's description of God's thoughts: " 'My righteousness draws near speedily, my salvation is on the way, and my arm will bring justice to the nations. The islands will look to me and wait in hope for my arm. Lift up your eyes to the heavens, look at the earth beneath; the heavens will vanish like smoke, the earth will wear out like a garment and its inhabitants die like flies. But my salvation will last forever, my righteousness will never fail' " (Isaiah 51:5, 6). "In that day they will say, 'Surely this is our God; we trusted in him, and he saved us. This is the LORD, we trusted in him; let us rejoice and be glad in his salvation' " (25:9).

THE SALVATION EQUATION

For the last couple of years, Virginia Orr, a delightful friend of mine in our church, has been questioning me about grace. Virginia grew up in a traditional, conservative Adventist family in which dear people with good intentions placed most of the emphasis not on Jesus and what He has done but on *her* obedience and *her* good behavior and *her* overcoming. Grace, as you can imagine, is a relatively new concept in Virginia's life, and she is full of questions. At one point, Virginia gave me a book to read, and with her typically thought-provoking, humorous turn of phrase, she inscribed it with these words: "To Stuart, who by his works is teaching me about grace." On another occasion, in the middle of a small-group study on salvation, Virginia threw her hands up and declared, "I'm going back to being saved by works; it's so much easier!"

As usual, Virginia was right. *It is easier* to have our eternal destiny determined by how we measure up to a fixed standard. It's what we seem to want to do. It offers an equation for getting into heaven that, throughout history, hundreds of thousands of strong-willed people have been convinced they could manage all by themselves. The ancient pagans pursued paradise with just such a motivation. The Hebrew people adopted the equation in spite of consistent prophetic testimony to the contrary. The Donatists talked themselves into believing they already had it accomplished. The Pelagians argued that if it should be done, it could be done. Anthony and his followers thought they could fulfill the requirements on a pile of dirt in the desert. Aquinas and his fellow teachers reasoned that it should be part of church doctrine. Many of us grew up in the Adventist Church struggling under the weight of the legalistic burden, biting the bullet and trying our hardest, believing we should "Just do it!" (the Nike heresy).

Now we know better. Here's the Bible's simple salvation equation: "All have sinned and fall short of the glory of God, and are justified freely by his grace" (Romans 3:23, 24). "You who are trying to be justified by law have been alienated from Christ; you have fallen away from grace" (Galatians 5:4).

---

# GRACE IN QUESTION
## CHAPTER 11: THE SCHOLASTIC DANCE

In the thousand years between Augustine and the Reformation, there was further confusion concerning the doctrine of grace as the medieval theologians defined, analyzed, explained, and processed the topic. By the end of this period in the history of grace, believers were desperate for clear teaching on the topic.

1. Talk about the good things accomplished by the monasteries—evangelism, preserving and copying the Scriptures, the emphasis on education. What is taking place in your local church to further these worthy goals? What more would you like to see done?

2. Ask everyone in your group to bring a picture of a "holy place" in their lives, a place where they feel they have communed with God. Are there common elements in each of the places? Why is this an easy assignment for some but more difficult for others?

3. What happens to our spiritual experience when things like the tonsure question take over our focus? (See pages 149, 150, including footnote 1.) What have been "tonsure questions" in your life? How did you get past such peripheral emphases?

4. Read the description of how Thomas Aquinas felt about grace (from the last paragraph on page 153 through the end of that section). Why would Protestants have a problem with a definition of justification that suggests that salvation is all about our being *made* righteous or just? What are the big differences between being *made* righteous and being *treated* as righteous? (Chapter 12, on the Reformation, will explore this question further.)

5. When the Bible tells us to "take up [our] tambourines and go out to dance with the joyful," what "tambourine" do you take up? How do you celebrate God's gift of grace?

# GRACE NOTES

## EXODUS 3—THE ANGEL OF THE LORD

Q. In what ways might the medieval discussion about angels have led people away from grace?

Q. What do we learn about God and grace from the Bible's stories about the angel of the Lord?

It is *"an* angel of the Lord" who finds the shepherds in the hills near Bethlehem and tells them about the birth of Jesus (Luke 2:9, emphasis supplied here and in the following verses). But it is *"the* angel of the LORD" who finds Hagar near a spring in the desert and tells her about the birth of Ishmael (Genesis 16:7–11).

It is *"an* angel of the Lord" who opens the doors of the prison cell in Jerusalem and leads Peter out of jail (Acts 12:2–9). But it is *"the* angel of the LORD" who stands in the road to stop Balaam and his donkey (Numbers 22:31).

It is *"an* angel of the Lord" who comes from heaven to the tomb of Jesus, rolls back the stone, and sits on it (Matthew 28:2). But it is *"the* angel of the LORD" who comes and sits under the oak near the winepress where Gideon was hiding from the Midianites (Judges 6:11).

Is there a difference between *"an* angel of the Lord" and *"the* angel of the Lord"? Apparently there *is* a difference, and the difference is huge!

Twice, John the revelator tries to worship *an* angel of the Lord who had brought a message to him. "I fell at his feet to worship him. But he said to me, 'Do not do it! I am a fellow servant with you.' " " 'Worship God!' " (Revelation 19:10; 22:9). But when Manoah and his wife realize they have seen *the* angel of the Lord, they say, " 'We have seen God!' " (Judges 13:20–22).

Hosea tells us that the angel with whom Jacob wrestled was God (Hosea 12:3)—the Lord God Almighty (verse 5). Jacob agrees: " 'I saw God face to face,' " he says in awe (Genesis 32:30). Gideon calls his angel visitor "LORD"— *Elohim* (Judges 6:18, 23). Zechariah reports the angel's words to Joshua, the high priest: " 'I have taken away your sin' " (Zechariah 3:4).

Moses' experience at the burning bush teaches us more about the angel of the Lord:

> The angel of the LORD appeared to him in flames of fire from within a bush. Moses saw that though the bush was on fire it did not burn up. So Moses thought, "I will go over and see this strange sight— why the bush does not burn up." When the LORD saw that he had gone over to look, God called to him from within the bush, "Moses! Moses!" And Moses said, "Here I am." "Do not come any closer," God said. "Take off your sandals, for the place where you are standing is holy ground." Then He said, "I am the God of your father, the God of Abraham, the God of Isaac and the God of Jacob." At this, Moses hid his face, because he was afraid to look at God. The LORD said, "I have indeed seen the misery of my people in Egypt. I have heard them

crying out because of their slave drivers, and I am concerned about their suffering. So I have come down to rescue them from the hand of the Egyptians and to bring them up out of that land into a good and spacious land, a land flowing with milk and honey" (Exodus 3:2–8).

*The* angel of the Lord is none other than God Himself! And here's what we learn about God from the appearances of *the* angel of the Lord.

We learn that God initiates contact with us. He shows up unbeckoned over and over: to Hagar, Abraham, Jacob, Moses, Balaam, Gideon, and Elijah. Sometimes God appears to us physically. Sometimes that physical appearing is calculated to attract our attention. ("I will go over and see this strange sight—why the bush does not burn up.") We learn that God's appearance makes the places of our lives holy because He is there. We learn that we stand properly before this holy God when there is nothing between us. ("Take off your sandals.") When we pay attention, we find out that God knows our names. ("Moses! Moses!") He sees His people. He hears us. He's concerned about us. It is God who rescues us. It is God who takes us to the Promised Land.

The angel of the Lord also teaches us that it's OK to ask God questions and that God answers:

> But Moses said to God, "Who am I, that I should go to Pharaoh and bring the Israelites out of Egypt?" And God said, "I will be with you. And this will be the sign to you that it is I who have sent you: When you have brought the people out of Egypt, you will worship God on this mountain." Moses said to God, "Suppose I go to the Israelites and say to them, 'The God of your fathers has sent me to you,' and they ask me, 'What is his name?' Then what shall I tell them?" God said to Moses, "I AM WHO I AM. This is what you are to say to the Israelites: 'I AM has sent me to you.' " God also said to Moses, "Say to the Israelites, 'The LORD, the God of your fathers—the God of Abraham, the God of Isaac and the God of Jacob—has sent me to you.' This is my name forever, the name by which I am to be remembered from generation to generation" (verses 11–15).

The angel of the Lord promises to be with us. He gives our lives direction. He calms our fears. He delights in revealing Himself to us. He is the God whom all generations worship. For the people who live by faith, who accept that God has the power to do what He promises to do (Romans 4:21), the angel of the Lord is the fulfillment of that promise, the revelation of the God of grace.

In all their distress he too was distressed, and the angel of his presence saved them. In his love and mercy he redeemed them; he lifted them up and carried them all the days of old (Isaiah 63:9).

*"Sinners are lovely because they are loved;*
*they are not loved because they are lovely."*
—Martin Luther

*"Luther's doctrine of justification fell like a bombshell*
*on the theological landscape of medieval Catholicism."*
—Timothy George, *Theology of the Reformers*

*"The clarion call of the Reformation was salvation by grace alone."*
—Scott Hoezee, *The Riddle of Grace*

*"People cannot do and need not do anything*
*to earn or add to Christ's work.*
*It was Sola Gratia, grace only."*
—Francis Schaeffer, *How Should We Then Live?*

*"Our works cannot reconcile us with God*
*or obtain grace for us."*
—The Augsburg Confession (1530)

# Chapter 12
# THE TRUE TREASURE:
## *The Priority of Grace in the Reformation*

ON A WEDNESDAY MORNING IN THE SECOND WEEK OF APRIL 1521, THE acclaimed German artist Albrecht Dürer stands in the Vyd Chapel of the parish church of St. John the Baptist in Ghent in Flanders.[1] Dürer is there not to pray or to confess his sins but to see something he has never seen before, something so "stupendous," to use his word, that it will remain burned in his memory for the rest of his life. There are, of course, no cameras to record the scene. There are no reporters taking notes of the occasion. We must rely on a hard-to-find entry in Dürer's diary and on an obscure painting of the moment, painted three hundred years after the fact, in 1820, by Pieter Frans der Noter and Felix de Vigne.

The painting places Dürer (easy to recognize with his long, flowing hair) and five others in front of the object the great artist has traveled to see. Hanging on the wall of the cathedral is a massive altarpiece known as *The Adoration of the Mystic Lamb*, completed in 1432 by the master Flemish artist Jan van Eyck.[2] No less an authority than Thomas Hovig, former director of the Metropolitan Museum of Art in New York City, has called the twelve panels that make up the front of the painting "the single finest work ever created in all of western civilization."[3] In restrained,

---

1. The city of Ghent is in present day Belgium. The Vyd Chapel is named for the wealthy donors who paid for the artwork in the chapel, Jodocus Vyd and Elizabeth Borluut. Since 1540, the cathedral has been known as St. Bavo's.

2. An altarpiece is a devotional work of art, painted or sculpted, many containing multiple scenes, hinged together and placed on or above the altar in a Christian church. The Ghent altarpiece stands over ten feet high and is sixteen feet long.

3. Art is so personal, I'm not really sure such a thing can be said. However, Hovig makes a strong case in justifying his personal choice: "The painting is world famous for its monumental conception and for the consummate, almost microscopic care with which every detail has been rendered. No other work comes close in its intense portrayal of materials. Everything, from the hundreds of jewels and pearls to the hairs on the fleece of the Mystic Lamb, seems to have been painted with a single-hair brush. The colors of crimson, azure, soft emerald, gold, and silver look as if they had been distilled from melted down gems. The truly wondrous thing is that van Eyck's zeal for details did not diminish the overall grandeur or the powerful feelings of spirituality, devotion, and piety." (*Art for Dummies* [Foster City, Calif.: IDG Books Worldwide, 1990], text with color plates following page 22.)

reverent tones, Dürer comments that the picture "is a very splendid, deeply studied painting, extremely good."[4]

In the lower center panel, van Eyck placed fourteen worshipping angels surrounding an engraved, red altar on which a wounded yet regal lamb stands purposefully, gazing directly back at the viewers of the painting. The inscription, in Latin, reads, "Behold the Lamb of God who takes away the sin of the world." *The Ludion Guide to the Ghent Altarpiece* assures us, "The meaning is clear to anyone familiar with Christian symbolism." The Lamb is Jesus, and the overarching theme of van Eyck's altarpiece is "humanity's salvation through Christ."[5]

### EXPOUNDING THE GOSPEL CLEARLY

On Sunday, April 17, 1521, several days after Dürer viewed the magnificent altarpiece, Martin Luther arrives in the German city of Worms (pronounced "Vorms"). Summoned on March 6 by Emperor Charles V to appear before the assembly to renounce or reaffirm his views, Luther has traveled with the imperial guarantee of safe travel. No sooner does he arrive before his accusers than they confront him with a collection of his own writings and ask, "Are these books yours?"

Luther stares back at Aleander, the papal nuncio.[6]

"Do you still believe the errors that these words teach?"

Luther asks for one day to think about his answer, and the request is granted.

"In the candlelight of the next evening," at six o'clock, Monday, April 18, Luther "calmly stood his ground."[7] Diarmaid MacCulloch, professor of history at Oxford, calls Luther's reply to this challenge "the turning point on which his life depended."[8] Here is the moment when Luther becomes "both a potent political factor and a *fait accompli,*" reports historian Heiko Oberman[9]—the day in which the church concludes once and for all that he is an irredeemable heretic.

"Unless I am convicted by Scripture and plain reason," Luther says, "my conscience is captive to the Word of God. I cannot and will not recant." Then, according to tradition, these famous words: "Here I stand. I can do no other. God help me. Amen." By the time the assembly concludes a month later, Luther, already excommunicated, has been declared an outlaw.

On Tuesday, April 26, Luther leaves Worms to return to Wittenberg. He plans to take several weeks to make the journey, stopping along the way to preach. But on May 4, near Eisenach, in the same Thuringian forest in which Luther had picked berries as a child, the bodyguard appointed by the emperor to assure safe-conduct suddenly reins in his horse, announces to Luther that he won't be needed any longer, and gallops away. Immediately, ten horsemen appear, dressed in the full armor of knights. With crossbows drawn, the knights

---

4. Albrecht Dürer, *Diary of His Journey to the Netherlands*.

5. Peter Schmidt, *The Ghent Altarpiece* (Ghent-Amsterdam: Ludion, 2001), 12.

6. Patrick Collinson, *The Reformation* (New York: Modern Library, 2004), 63.

7. Martin Marty, *Martin Luther* (New York: A Lipper/Viking Book, 2004), 68.

8. Diarmaid MacCulloch, *The Reformation, A History* (New York: Viking, 2003), 127. Critics say about MacCulloch's book, "One would be hard put to imagine a more detailed, even-handed, clearly written account." The book is "widely considered to be the authoritative account of the Reformation."

9. Heiko Augustinus Oberman, *The Dawn of the Reformation* (Edinburgh: T & T Clark, 1986), 44.

surround Luther, blindfold him, and take him away to Wartburg Castle.

In Flanders a few days later (May 17), Albrecht Dürer notes in his diary that tidings had just come to him "that Martin Luther had been so treacherously taken prisoner." After repeating the story of the kidnapping, Dürer writes that the knights have "carried off the pious man, who had been betrayed; a man enlightened by the Holy Ghost, a follower of Christ and of the true Christian faith, and whether he lives yet or whether they have put him to death, I know not." Then, in the diary, Dürer begins a prayer: "O God, if Luther be dead, who will henceforth expound the Holy Gospel so clearly to us!"

Actually, in the immediate centuries before Luther and Dürer, the "Holy Gospel" has not been expounded very much at all. Once again the church has lost sight of what should have been its central focus. Entangled in constant controversies, overdefined to the most confusing detail, relegated to the periphery, the theme of God's grace has disappeared as surely as the outlaw professor in the Thuringian forest. In fact, while it certainly is true that Luther's rediscovery of God's grace provided the spark that lit the Reformation fire, it also is accurate to say that "the firewood for the Reformation was piled up long before Luther."[10]

The firewood came in three dimensions.

## THE HUNGER FOR THE BIBLE

The first dimension, one without which the Reformation might never have taken place, is the people's hunger for the Bible. Most of the Bible reading taking place at the time is occurring in the monastic schools, where educated teachers, skilled in Latin (which few people, by now, speak), interpret God's Word primarily within the framework of existing church dogma. The courageous Waldensians of the Alpine valleys of southern France, Switzerland, and northern Italy have been translating the New Testament into the vernacular book by book. But their precious, handwritten copies are rare.

In England, John Wyclif (c. 1330–1384) works with determination to put an English Bible into the hands of the English people, and he sends out preachers, Lollards, to take the gospel to the common folk. Yet, coupled with Wyclif's loudly proclaimed ecclesiastical and doctrinal differences with the church, the Bible preaching rouses opposition. In a synod in 1382, called by the Archbishop of Canterbury, twenty-four of Wyclif's opinions are condemned, his teaching position at Oxford is cancelled, and the Lollards are arrested and imprisoned.

As the life of "the Morning Star of the Reformation" is ending in England, the exaltation of the Bible is just beginning in Bohemia, a territory roughly equivalent to today's Czech Republic. In Prague, the admired teacher and priest Jan Hus (c. 1373–July 6, 1415) is winning wide support through the fiery weekly sermons he's delivering at Bethlehem Chapel, not in Latin but in the common language of the people.[11] Two groups, both responding to the preaching of Hus, both calling themselves Hussites, both arguing that the Bible must be the determining factor, come to different conclusions about the biblical values believers

---

10. Hans Küng, *Justification* (New York: Nelson, 1964), 9.

11. If you visit Prague today, don't fail to see the Jan Hus monument in the Old Town Square, dedicated exactly five hundred years after Hus was burned at the stake in Constance. Also spend some time at the *Betlemska kaple* (Bethlehem Chapel), which the *Fodor's Guide* calls "the most revered of all Hussite churches in Prague."

should hold.[12] Church authorities feel threatened by this consuming interest in the Bible. They warn that the preaching must stop. Then they impose harsh punishments. Hus and many of his followers are burned at the stake.

But the interest in the Bible deepens. Italian Lorenzo Valla (c. 1406–1457) lays a foundation for New Testament studies with a 1444 publication in which he holds Bible translations to the high standard of classical Latin. In the same year, Swiss artist Konrad Witz (c. 1400–1446) becomes the first Western painter to depict a scene from the Bible in a *local* setting. His large painting *The Miraculous Draft of Fishes* shows Jesus and the disciples, not on the Sea of Galilee, but on Lake Geneva, with Mount Blanc and the cliffs of the Salieve in the background.[13]

The movable-type printing press of Johannes Gutenberg (c. 1400–1468) makes its debut around 1455 with a huge edition of the entire Bible, and suddenly, hundreds of copies of the Bible become available. In Germany, Johann Reuchlin (1455–1522) publishes a Hebrew grammar and lexicon in 1506 to support a better understanding of the Old Testament, "unlocking the treasures of the Hebrew language to Christian students."[14] Valla's early investigations into the textual challenges of the Vulgate translation spur Erasmus (c. 1466–

1536) to publish in Basel, Switzerland, his influential Greek edition of the New Testament (1516).

The desire to read the Bible is growing, and with it the possibility of personal encounters with the dynamic Bible experience of salvation by grace alone. There is more than enough firewood here for Martin Luther! Contrary to what Dürer feared, Luther has not been killed but been "kidnapped" by friends to protect him from his enemies. Disguised as a knight (*Junker Georg*, "Knight George," they call him), Luther spends a secluded ten months in Wartburg Castle translating the New Testament into German.[15]

## THE CRY FOR CHURCH REFORM

The second dimension of pre-Reformation firewood can be found in the widespread cry for someone to somehow reform the embarrassing state of the church.

The cry begins in protest against the local clergy. "Historians have no difficulty in drawing up an indictment of the evils of the unreformed church," says the *Oxford Illustrated History of Christianity,* especially the church's "priestly professional personnel."[16] Harvard history professor Steven Ozment, in his book *Protestants: the Birth of a Revolution,* examines the "clergy's growing immorality

---

12. The *Utraquists* forbade the forbidden, and the *Taborites* repudiated what was not recommended. Both groups based their beliefs on the Bible and demanded free preaching of the gospel. Frequently there was fierce fighting between the two groups, but often they fought side by side against those trying to crush them. From about 1453, a union grew of Utraquists, Taborites, and Waldensians, which eventually formed the spiritual ancestry of the Moravians.

13. Witz's painting is still on display in the Museum of Art and History in Geneva.

14. Williston Walker, *A History of the Christian Church* (New York: Charles Scribner's Sons, 1959), 293.

15. "The most lasting fruit of this period of enforced retirement was his translation of the New Testament, begun in December, 1521, and published in September of the following year. . . . Luther's work was idiomatic and readable. It largely determined the form of speech that should mark future German literature, wrought and polished by a master of popular expression. Few services greater than this translation have ever been rendered to the development of the religious life of a nation." (Walker, 311.)

16. *The Oxford Illustrated History of Christianity,* John McManners, ed. (Oxford: Oxford University Press, 1990), 246.

## REYNARD THE FOX

Reynard the Fox was the celebrated main character of the medieval folk tales increasingly popular in Europe after the twelfth century. The satirical stories were a safe way for the peasants to criticize and show their contempt for the upper classes, the church, and the clergy.

In the following story fragment, Reynard has been summoned by the king to answer accusations by the other animals. If Reynard represents the church, how were the people feeling about the church? What "evil deeds" do you think the people were talking about?

"I am very sorry for the evil deeds that I have done," said Reynard to Gray the Badger. "I have done many evil things against all the beasts that live, but especially against my uncle, Bruin the Bear, and against Tibert the Cat. I have killed poor Chanticleer's children. I have even talked against the king and his good queen. Now I am weary of my sins. I promise to change my ways."

Hardly had the fox finished speaking when they came near a house where there were many geese and chickens beside the road. Reynard kept edging closer, until at length he made a dive for a fat rooster, but the rooster got away, although he lost some of his feathers.

"Come, come, uncle," cried Gray, "I thought that you had promised to be good and to do no more evil. Is this the way you keep your word?"

"I beg your pardon, my dear nephew; I forgot myself, but I ask you to forgive me," replied Reynard.

When at length they drew near the king's castle, Reynard thought of all the wicked things he had done and began to fear for his life. But he put on a brave face and walked among his enemies as boldly as if he had never done an evil thing. When he came before the throne of the king, he said: "Heaven grant your majesty glory and honor. Your highness, there was never a king who had a truer servant than I have been to you."

The king cut Reynard short and said: "Stop your talking, traitor. I know what lies you can tell. You need not think that by soft words you can make me believe that black is white."

Then all the animals that Reynard had injured cried out against him and said, "Let him be put to death, O king!" But the king decided that Reynard should have a fair trial. Each beast and bird whom Reynard had injured told his story.

When at length Reynard was allowed to answer them, he spoke cunningly and managed to lay the blame upon someone else. But in the end Reynard was judged to be guilty and ordered to be hanged.

Do you think Reynard was hanged? Oh no! He was far too cunning for that. Just how he made the king think that he was his best friend and how Reynard brought his enemies into disgrace is another long story.

and pastoral negligence" and the emergence of a laity who refuse to listen any longer to "a clergy they often found to be their intellectual and moral inferiors."[17] In the middle of the sixteenth-century in an English parish, a Jay Leno–like "Jay Walk" survey found that "168 out of 311 country clergy were unable to repeat the Ten Commandments and some could not say who composed the Lord's Prayer."[18]

17. Steven Ozment, *Protestants: The Birth of a Revolution* (New York: Doubleday, 1991), 236.
18. McManners, ibid.

But the dissatisfaction doesn't stop with local clergy. The complaints go all the way to the head of the church, to the pope himself.

In a papal election early in the fourteenth century, the College of Cardinals[19] takes almost a year of "bitter debate and intrigue"[20] to elect a new pope. The man they choose has a long history of special favor with the French court.[21] In 1309, he moves the headquarters of the church to Avignon, in France, from where he and the next six popes, all Frenchmen, rule the church, yielding repeatedly to the influence of the French kings. In 1377, the last of the French popes returns to Rome.

When the next conclave convenes, rioting breaks out in the streets of Rome as Romans demand that a Roman become pope. Fearing for their lives, the cardinals elect an Italian.[22] But they soon discover that this new pope has a furious temper, which he turns on the cardinals, subjecting them to "violent abuse and uncontrollable tirades."[23] Within two months, the cardinals are convinced that the pope is deranged. At a secret meeting on August 2, 1378, the cardinals declare his election invalid because of the threats of violence, and they ask him to abdicate. When he refuses, the cardinals depose him and elect a new pope in his place.[24]

Suddenly, there are two popes, both claiming to be the leader of the church; each excommunicating the other, nominating their own cardinals, and threatening war upon the other's supporters. This becomes "the greatest crisis in the history of the papacy."[25] Europe is "pained and scandalized; the papacy sank enormously in popular regard."[26] No wonder that "all the world called for a reform."[27]

In 1409, before the "Great Schism" is over, a church council meets in Pisa. Both popes are deposed on charges of being "schismatics, heretics, and perjurers," and a third man elected to the papacy.[28] This only worsens the situation—now there are three popes instead of two. Finally, in November 1417, the Council of Constance asserts its interests as superior to the pope's, declares the papacy to be a constitutional monarchy instead of an absolute one, and elects one man to succeed the three.[29] John XXIII and Benedict XIII are deposed (John as an "unworthy pontiff"), and Gregory XII abdicates.

The spectacle of the schism, coupled with the openly immoral character of several of the

---

19. The *College of Cardinals* meets at the death of a pope in a *conclave* to elect the next pope or *pontiff*. By at least the early fifth century, the terms *bishop of Rome* and *pope* had become interchangeable. The office itself is known as the *papacy*, or, in Roman Catholic writings, the *primacy of Peter*. The practice of changing one's name upon election began in 532, when an aged man named Mercurius, perhaps thinking that the name of the pagan god Mercury was inappropriate for the leader of the Christian church, decided upon his election as pope to be called instead John.

20. J. N. D. Kelly, *The Oxford Dictionary of Popes* (Oxford: Oxford University Press, 1986), 212.

21. Bertrand de Got, archbishop of Bordeaux, who becomes Clement V; pope, June 5, 1305–April 20, 1314.

22. Bartolomeo Prignano, archbishop of Bari, who became Urban VI; pope, April 8, 1378–October 15, 1389.

23. Kelly, 227.

24. Cardinal Robert of Geneva, Clement VII; antipope, September 20, 1378–September 16, 1394.

25. Francis A. Burkle-Young, *Passing the Keys* (Lanham, Md.: Madison Books, 1999), xxi.

26. Walker, 267.

27. Hans Küng, *Christianity* (New York: Continuum Publishing, 1996), 465.

28. The Council of Pisa was attended by twenty-four cardinals, four patriarchs, eighty archbishops, a hundred bishops, a hundred abbots, and many others. "Well over 200 prelates signed the document, including all of the cardinals." (Michael Walsh, *The Conclave* [Norwich, Norfolk, UK: Canterbury Press, 2003], 103.)

29. Cardinal Oddo Colonna became Pope Martin V, and reigned November 11, 1417–February 20, 1431. The Council of Constance also condemned Jan Hus as a heretic.

### THE IMPORTANCE OF GRACE TO PROTESTANTISM

"Periodically in the Church this prodigious news of free salvation becomes indistinct because of the very efforts the Church makes in exhorting us to obey, to be virtuous and to do good works, so that little by little these appear to be the condition for salvation. . . . Yet periodically, also, the Church is renewed by those who discover afresh the free gift of God and cry it out. . . .

"Such a one was Luther. Nothing illustrates better this periodic oscillation of outlook than the history of Protestantism. Luther discovered afresh in his turn that salvation is not earned, but is a gift of God, free and offered in advance to the sinner, and that it is sufficient to accept it by faith. From his cry of relief, the Reformation was born, like an explosion, at a time when the Church was insisting on works, merits and indulgences, all of which laid the cost of salvation upon men's own souls." —Paul Tournier, *Guilt and Grace* (New York: Harper & Row, 1962), 194.

"The clarion call of the Reformation was salvation by grace alone." —Scott Hoezee, *The Riddle of Grace* (Grand Rapids, Mich.: Wm. B. Eerdmans Publishing, 1996), 54.

"The center about which all the petals clustered was the affirmation of the forgiveness of sins through the utterly unmerited grace of God made possible by the cross of Christ." —Roland H. Bainton, *Here I Stand: A Life of Martin Luther* (Nashville: Abingdon Press, 1950), 51.

"The doctrine of justification for Luther was the fundamental and central dogma of Christianity. It is the all-summarizing Word of the gospel. In relation to this doctrine we cannot yield an inch. It is a justification that distinguishes Christianity from all other religions." —Carl E. Braaten, *Justification, The Article by Which the Church Stands or Falls* (Minneapolis: Fortress Press, 1990), 23.

"Protestantism was born out of the struggle for the doctrine of justification by faith alone. For Luther this was not simply one doctrine among others, but 'the summary of all Christian doctrine.' " —Timothy George, *Theology of the Reformers* (Nashville: Broadman Press, 1988), 62.

"*Grace* is the most important word in the Protestant vocabulary." —Robert McAfee Brown, *The Spirit of Protestantism* (New York: Oxford University Press, 1961), 53.

"It is my firm conviction that 'Protestant' means absolutely, positively nothing unless the one wearing the term believes, breathes, lives, and loves the uncompromised, offensive-to-the-natural-man message of justification by God's free grace by faith in Jesus Christ alone." —James R. White, *The God Who Justifies* (Minneapolis: Bethany House, 2001), 26.

"The Protestant principle emphasizes the infinite distance between God and man. It emphasizes man's finitude, his subjection to death, but above all, this estrangement from his true being and his bondage to demonic forces—forces of self-destruction.

"Man's inability to liberate himself from this bondage has led the Reformers to the doctrine of a reunion with God in which God alone acts and man only receives. Such receiving, of course, is not possible in an attitude of passivity, but it demands the highest courage, namely the courage to accept the paradox that 'the sinner is justified,' that it is man in anxiety, guilt, and despair who is the object of God's unconditional acceptance." —Paul Tillich, *Theology of Culture* (London: Oxford University Press, 1959), 68.

next popes,[30] makes the medieval papacy an easy target. "The great gulf between the biblical image of the shepherd guiding the flock toward the heavenly city and the series of Renaissance popes who exploited the flock for their own advancement in the earthly city" is more than most Christians can bear.[31] "The papacy had become secularized, the pope one more Renaissance princeling among many others."[32]

### THE DISCOURAGING DOCTRINE OF SALVATION

But there is firewood much more inflammable than the wicked ways of the shepherds in Rome. The larger cause of the Reformation is the discouraging conclusion of the medieval doctrine of salvation.

"Religion in the later Middle Ages was obsessed with the doctrine of justification by works."[33] All the talk is of merit: how it can be earned, how it is deposited in the bank account of the church, and how eternal life will be granted if the account grows large enough. There is, of course, always more work that needs to be done, more merit to be gained, more performing, more obeying.

In his discussion of the causes of the Reformation, Catholic church historian Father John Jay Hughes concludes that ultimately it is the "jungle growth of religiosity" in the late

Middle Ages (which he defines as pilgrimages, relics, indulgences, and endowed Masses), acts that are "designed to guarantee personal salvation," that "obscured the truth."[34]

"There was a commerce in grace," observes Garry Wills, "which was conceived of as a quantifiable item. Venial sins lowered the level in the tank. Mortal sin drained it totally. Occasions of grace filled the tank back up. People were encouraged to go to confession frequently, even for minor sins, since more grace was poured in each time.

"Grace became a private possession (or deprivation)," Wills continues. "Prayers were said to boost the private supply of grace. Saying the rosary earned an indulgence of specified days spared in purgatory (if the rosary was a properly blessed one). Indulgences could be earned by going to certain churches on certain feasts (some would pop in and out repeatedly to rack up a larger number). The clergy manned a hydraulic system pumping grace back into souls, or measuring its flow to this or that good cause."[35]

In this rampant works orientation, church authorities not only teach people to fear grace, they also threaten them with expulsion from the church—and ultimately from an eternal home in heaven—for any interest in or support for or leniency toward those who preach the gospel.

---

30. Historians use words such as *ruthless, violent, vengeful, grasping,* and *licentious* to describe the popes of this period. Simony (the purchase of church office) and nepotism (favoritism shown or patronage granted to relatives) are standard operating procedure within the Vatican of the time. The pope known as the Spanish Bull, Alexander VI (Rodrigo de Borja y Borja; Borgia in Italian) may have been the most carnal pope in the entire history of the papacy. Rebuked in 1460 by Pius II for his immorality, Borgia fathered six children before his election and two more afterward. He was fondest of the children born to his aristocratic mistress Vannozza Catanei, including the brutal Cesare, whom he made bishop at eighteen and cardinal a year later; and Lucretia, whose name became synonymous with an influence of vulgarity and wanton amorality on the princes of the church.

31. Carter Lindberg, *The European Reformations* (Oxford: Blackwell Publishers, 1996), 53.

32. Walsh, 111.

33. Alister E. McGrath, "Do We Still Need the Reformation?" *Christianity Today,* December 12, 1994, 28–33.

34. John Jay Hughes, *Pontiffs: Popes Who Shaped History* (Huntington, Ind.: Our Sunday Visitor Publishing, 1994), 123, 124, 133.

35. Garry Wills, *Papal Sin* (New York: Doubleday, 2000), 173.

The Reformers face a frightening choice. "While the Reformation began as a protest against the abuses of the system of indulgences rampant in the Church, it rapidly became a theoretical critique of the Church's perceived theology of grace. Such a critique had many consequences for other areas of theology and for Church practice, so that in the end the Reformers saw themselves as having no alternative than to start from scratch and form their own Churches established on a renewed theology of grace."[36]

Theologian Alister McGrath summarizes the primary characteristics of the Protestant doctrine of justification by grace alone that distinguish it from the commonly held doctrine.[37]

1. Justification, in Protestant terms, is the *declaration* that the believer is righteous—in contrast to the Catholic understanding, which insists that justification is a process by which sinners are *made* righteous. The Protestant view involves a change in a sinner's *status* rather than his or her *nature*.

2. Protestants make a deliberate and systematic distinction between *justification* (the external act by which God declares the sinner to be righteous) and *sanctification* (the internal process of renewal or regeneration within humans).

3. Protestants define justifying righteousness as the righteousness *of Christ*, alien and external to humans, and imputed to them.

As Martin Luther begins to get those three distinctions clear, he moves into action. On October 31, 1517, with Johann Tetzel selling indulgences nearby and with the biggest day of the year for meritorious worshipping of relics approaching, Luther posts his famous ninety-five theses on the door of the Wittenberg Castle church.[38] In the middle of that document, Luther announces the central importance of the gospel of grace. "At the heart of the church doctrine that came out of Luther's Reformation was the axiom he enunciated in 1517: 'The true treasure of the church is the most holy gospel of the glory and grace of God.' "[39]

The Reformation has begun.

## THE MYSTIC LAMB

Not long ago, after completing a camp meeting assignment in the Netherlands, I spent a few days with good friends Arthur and Anita van Zanten and their girls, who live in the middle of Holland. For about three years we had been talking about my dream to follow in the footsteps of Albrecht Dürer and see van Eyck's *The Adoration of the Mystic Lamb*. Yet each time we had been together something else came up—usually my schedule and the need to hurry home. Anita had been telling me for months before this trip that this time I could borrow their car, drive into Belgium, find Ghent, and visit the cathedral with its treasure.

However, when they picked me up at the campground, Arthur and Anita announced that I would *not* be borrowing their car because Arthur was going to Ghent with me to see the magnificent altarpiece. As you can imagine, I

---

36. Neil Ormerod, *Grace and Disgrace: A Theology of Self-Esteem, Society, and History* (Newtown, NSW: E. J. Dwyer, 1992), 129.

37. Alister E. McGrath, *Iustitia Dei, A History of the Christian Doctrine of Justification: From 1500 to the Present Day* (Cambridge: Cambridge University Press, 1986).

38. "It was as if in the sixty years since its invention the printing press had been treading water, waiting for this moment." (Patrick Collinson, *The Reformation* [New York: Modern Library, 2004], 63.)

39. Jaroslav Pelikan, *The Christian Tradition, Vol. 4: Reformation of Church and Dogma (1300–1700)* (Chicago, Ill.: The University of Chicago Press, 1984), 128.

hardly slept that night, realizing that the very next day a dream of mine would come true.

On Monday morning, Anita and I went to the lovely Kröller-Müller Museum outside Otterlo in De Hoge Veluwe National Park. I was stunned by the rich private collection, which has been growing since 1907 and which included works by Manet, Monet, Renoir, Seurat, Cezanne, Modigliani, and especially Vincent van Gogh. I counted fifty-five van Gogh paintings—only part of their superb collection—hanging on the walls of the distinctive countryside museum! I must admit, however, that my mind was on another painting; one three hours away, one that had been created 450 years before van Gogh's last works. The morning moved slowly. I thought the afternoon would never come.

At noon, Arthur left the hospital where he is the chief physician for the intensive care unit, and met us for lunch. Then we jumped into his car and began the journey south through Holland and Belgium, all the way to a convenient parking place just outside the cathedral of St. Bavo in Ghent. As we parked, I glanced at my watch and was horrified to realize that the chapel that housed the altarpiece would close in less than ten minutes! We hurried in the door, got our bearings, and rushed up the aisle. But when we approached the chapel, the man who had been selling tickets had already closed his moneybox and was walking away. I ran to him and stopped him.

"I'm sorry we're late," I said fearfully and out of breath. "The traffic . . . And we didn't know how to get here . . . And we made a wrong turn . . . And I've come all the way from California . . ."

The man with the closed moneybox looked back at me with a rather bored, blank expression. Then he said, "Just go in."

"What about a ticket?" I asked.

"Ah, don't worry about it. I've already closed the box. Enjoy the painting."

To this day, the thought of that moment and the unexpected gift makes me emotional.

Arthur and I walked into the chapel, and there it was! None of the guidebooks, not even Thomas Hovig, had done it justice or prepared me for the glory. The size, the colors, the textures, the composition, the exalted theme, the beauty and power of the message—it was overwhelming.

Several guidebooks had warned us not to be disappointed if the crowd was so large that the guards would have to usher us in and out in just a couple of minutes. But when we entered, there were only four other people in the chapel, and they were leaving. Arthur stayed for a few moments and then left to visit the gift shop. Suddenly, I was all alone with the Mystic Lamb! For twenty miraculous minutes, until long after closing time, no one else was in the room.

When Arthur returned, he handed me a poster of the altarpiece he had purchased in the gift shop. "Something to remember this moment by," he said with a smile. Today, the poster is framed and hangs over the desk in my study, just above the computer screen. I have only to stop the work I'm doing, lift my head from the monitor, and look at the Mystic Lamb gazing directly into my eyes.

Above the Lamb, in the top center panel is a regal Being sitting on a throne, making a gesture of blessing. Much debate has swirled about whether the figure represents Jesus, the triumphant King of kings, returning to earth to claim all those He has redeemed or whether we are gazing at God the Father, high and lifted up, surveying the fruit of the labors of His only begotten Son, the gift of His own beneficent grace.

I'm convinced that van Eyck wanted us to see Jesus in the central figure. The tapestry draping the throne offers a hint. But there also is one unmistakable clue. To the right of the central figure sits John the Baptist, who, in the tradition of the artistic depiction of saints, is recognizable by his "attribute"—the quality included in paintings that identifies the subject.[40] John's chief attribute is his finger pointing to Jesus. John is saying, " 'Behold! The Lamb of God who takes away the sin of the world!' " (John 1:29, NKJV). In the Ghent altarpiece, John is pointing to the central figure.

John's attribute epitomizes the Christian message: "Behold! The Lamb of God!" It is the theme of Pauline preaching and the purpose of the New Testament church. It is the heart and goal of the Reformation that began with Martin Luther and continued with all the Reformers who followed him. It is the everlasting gospel we have been commissioned to share worldwide. When it comes to the doctrine of salvation, stop whatever work you're doing and look into the eyes of Jesus.

## GRACE IN QUESTION
### CHAPTER 12: THE TRUE TREASURE

The Reformers discovered afresh the exhilarating good news that our salvation is based on the grace of God, not on our merits or our good works. This chapter considers the causes of the Reformation and what grace means to Protestants.

1. Who are the people who have "expounded the Holy Gospel" clearly to you, as Luther did for Albrecht Dürer? Think about where you've learned about grace and the gospel, and share with your study group just one person who has influenced you.

2. How do you feel about the Reformers and others who literally gave their lives so that the Bible could be translated into the common languages? What is so powerful about the Bible? Why do you think the church leaders were so opposed? What do we do today that demonstrates how we value the Bible?

3. After 1444, when Konrad Witz painted Jesus on Lake Geneva, the world of art followed Witz's lead and depicted Bible stories in local settings. This approach was standard for centuries—until our time. Today, it is unusual to see Christ in a contemporary setting, and we almost never find a painting that puts Him in contemporary clothing. Do you think we've gained or lost by not having the incarnation principle in our art?

4. Obviously, the medieval church was not the first nor the last religious organization to be troubled by the immorality of some leaders. Your local church may even have been hurt by the same problem. How can church members prevent such lapses from destroying their own Christian experience?

5. Discuss the artistic term *attribute* (see footnote 40 on this page). By what attribute would you like others to know you?

---

40. "Each saint is vividly characterized by elements to help identify him or her, such as costumes, objects, positions, or animals. . . . This 'identifying code' of the saints, which was common from popular works to the most sophisticated masterpieces, had been defined by devotion and art during the course of a millennium. It remained substantially unchanged from the Middle Ages on, a common language for all of Europe, without social or intellectual distinctions." (Rosa Giorgi, *Saints in Art* [Los Angeles: Getty Publications, 2003], 8.)

# GRACE NOTES
## REVELATION 5–7—THE BEAST OF REVELATION

Q. How did the Reformation help us to listen to John's invitation to "Behold the Lamb of God"?

Q. What benefits are there in beholding the Lamb in the book of Revelation?

There are beasts in the book of Revelation that can cause grown-ups to have nightmares. There are frightening locusts, for example, that appear in the smoke that comes up from the shaft of the Abyss, rising like a gigantic furnace to darken the sun and sky (Revelation 9:1, 2). "The locusts looked like horses prepared for battle. On their heads they wore something like crowns of gold, and their faces resembled human faces. Their hair was like women's hair, and their teeth were like lions' teeth. They had breastplates like breastplates of iron, and the sound of their wings was like the thundering of many horses and chariots rushing into battle. They had tails and stings like scorpions, and in their tails they had power to torment people for five months" (verses 7–10). The agony of their sting is so horrific that it makes people wish they were dead (verse 6). The locust king is an angel of the Abyss with a Hebrew name, Abaddon, and a Greek name, Apollyon (verse 11).

There are three slimy frogs, evil spirits, that come out of the mouths of a dragon, a beast, and a false prophet (16:13). "They are spirits of demons performing miraculous signs, and they go out to the kings of the whole world, to gather them for the battle on the great day of God Almighty . . . to the place that in Hebrew is called Armageddon" (verses 14–16).

There is a composite beast that rises out of the sea, speaking "proud words and blasphemies" and strutting his authority for a short time (13:5). "He had ten horns and seven heads, with ten crowns on his horns, and on each head a blasphemous name. The beast I saw resembled a leopard, but had feet like those of a bear and a mouth like that of a lion. The dragon gave the beast his power and his throne and great authority. One of the heads of the beast seemed to have had a fatal wound, but the fatal wound had been healed. The whole world was astonished and followed the beast" (verses 1–3).

Another beast in Revelation, one with the power of life and death (verse 15), rises out of the earth, speaking like a dragon (verse 11). "He performed great and miraculous signs, even causing fire to come down from heaven to earth in full view of men. . . . He deceived the inhabitants of the earth. . . . He also forced everyone, small and great, rich and poor, free and slave, to receive a mark on his right hand or on his forehead, so that no one could buy or sell unless he had the mark, which is the name of the beast or the number of his name" (verses 13–17).

And there in the background, watching over all the minions, is the mother of all beasts, the great dragon, the "ancient serpent called the devil, or Satan, who leads the whole world astray" (12:9).

It's a scary lot. Enough beasts to cast the most frightening horror story of all time.

But there's another beast in Revelation. One that ends all horror and puts a stop to all nightmares. One that conquers all those thundering, slimy creatures with their big talk and tormenting stings. This is a beast unlike all the rest.

It appears in the center of the throne of God (5:6), surrounded by worshipful beings (verse 14). This beast inspires choirs to sing new songs (verse 9), harpists to play their harps (14:2), and heavenly beings to light golden censers full of incense (5:8). This beast breaks the seals to open scrolls that reveal the will of God (verse 7), writes His name on His followers' foreheads (14:1; 3:12), and leads His people like a shepherd to " 'springs of living water' " (7:17), where they will never again go hungry, never again be thirsty, never again be overcome by the scorching heat (verse 16).

It's a Lamb. A Lamb worthy of receiving worship because it was slain, and with its blood has "purchased" people from every tribe and language and people and nation (5:9).

> Then I looked and heard the voice of many angels, numbering thousands upon thousands, and ten thousand times ten thousand. They encircled the throne and the living creatures and the elders. In a loud voice they sang: "Worthy is the Lamb, who was slain, to receive power and wealth and wisdom and strength and honor and glory and praise!"

> Then I heard every creature in heaven and on earth and under the earth and on the sea, and all that is in them, singing: "To him who sits on the throne and to the Lamb be praise and honor and glory and power, for ever and ever!" (verses 11–13).

> After this I looked and there before me was a great multitude that no one could count, from every nation, tribe, people and language, standing before the throne and in front of the Lamb. They were wearing white robes and were holding palm branches in their hands. And they cried out in a loud voice: "Salvation belongs to our God, who sits on the throne, and to the Lamb" (7:9, 10).

The Lamb is Jesus, the only beast of the book of Revelation worthy of worship. The only beast whose life extends beyond the history of this earth. All the scary creatures are going to pass away, but the Lamb goes on "for ever and ever."

And we'll be there to sing the praises, saved by grace through faith in the Lamb. Salvation belongs to Him.

" 'Behold! The Lamb of God who takes away the sin of the world!' " (John 1:29, NKJV).

*"It is here that the real focus of the Reformation controversies is to be found."*

—ALISTER MCGRATH, *CHRISTIANITY TODAY*

*"The Council of Trent marked the birth of the modern Catholic Church."*

—JUSTO GONZÁLEZ, *THE STORY OF CHRISTIANITY*

*"At the heart of Catholic particularity is the assertion that justification necessarily involves sanctification."*

—STEPHEN DUFFY, *THE DYNAMICS OF GRACE*

*"The Jesuits insisted absolutely on the necessity of good works for justification and salvation."*

—LEWIS SPITZ, *THE PROTESTANT REFORMATION*

*"The bishops rejected Luther's claim that justification comes from grace alone. Human efforts matter too."*

—WILLIAM PLACHER, *A HISTORY OF CHRISTIAN THEOLOGY*

## CHAPTER 13
# THE BOUNDARY STONES:
### *The Reaction to Grace in the Council of Trent*

C ARDINAL GIOVANNI MARIA DEL MONTE[1] STANDS UP IN THE FRONT OF the cathedral and clears his throat. "On this, the thirteenth day of December in the year of our Lord fifteen-forty-five," the papal representative begins, addressing the delegates, "does it please you, for the praise and glory of the holy and undivided Trinity; for the advance and exaltation of the Christian faith and religion; for the extirpation of heresies; for the peace and unity of the Church; for the reform of the clergy and Christian people; for the suppression and destruction of the enemies of the Christian name; to decree and declare that the holy and general Council of Trent begins and has begun?"

Thirty-five dignitaries of the church, forty-two theologians, an assortment of political appointees, and a few other consultants respond as one: "It pleases us."

Del Monte continues. Since it is almost Christmas, he says, and since the festivities of the closing and opening of the year are about to take place, "does it please you that the next session be held on the seventh of January in the year of our Lord fifteen-forty-six?"

"It pleases us," the delegates answer.

With that brief exchange, the first session of what soon would be recognized as the most important church council yet held in the long history of the Catholic Church begins and ends.[2] A little less than a month later, when the delegates get together again in the dead of the northern Italian winter, the eradication of heresies is in the forefront of their thinking.[3] The suppression and destruction of their

---

1. Giovanni Maria Ciocchi del Monte (1487–1555), within a short time after the opening of the Council of Trent, is elected pope and reigns for just over five years (February 1550–March 1555) as Julius III.

2. "After the conclusion of Trent in 1563, with the content and agenda of Catholicism now redefined . . ." (*The Oxford Illustrated History of Christianity,* John McManners, ed. [Oxford: Oxford University Press, 1990], 242.) "Trent defined with final authority what Catholics must believe." (Roger E. Olson, *The Story of Christian Theology* [Downers Grove, Ill.: InterVarsity Press, 1999], 445.)

3. As the Catholic Church watched the Reformation advance in what they considered "doctrinal deviation," they thought of Paul's warning of the rise of "savage wolves" bringing "heresies" to the church

enemies has become the motivating goal of the council.

## THE ENEMIES AND THEIR HERESIES

Who were these "enemies" who must be suppressed and destroyed for "the peace and unity" of the church? Certainly, the Swiss Reformers are on the list. The feisty Zwingli (1484–1531) is now dead, killed in a battle with one of Switzerland's Catholic cantons. But bold Guillaume Farel (1489–1565), systematic John Calvin (1509–1564), and gentle Theodore Beza (1519–1605) are very much alive. So is the hero of the Scottish Reformation, John Knox (c. 1505–1572), who is just beginning his work in St. Andrews. Enemy number one would have been Martin Luther, whose death occurs February 18, 1546, not quite six weeks after the council opens its debate on justification.

In fact, it would be accurate to say that, without naming them, Trent sets itself against all the Protestant Reformers. Church historians are united in this understanding of Trent's purpose: Trent is "Catholicism's official response to the Reformation," Alister McGrath asserts.[4] Hubert Jedin calls the doctrinal statements of the Council of Trent "boundary stones" that help establish the identity of the Catholic Church in the face of Protestantism.[5] According to Steven Duffy, the "principal intent" of the council "was to frame a Catholic consensus on justification over against the Reformers' challenge."[6] Elizabeth Dreyer agrees: The Council's "primary aim," she writes, "was to establish clearly the church's teaching against that of the reformers."[7] Through the council, observes Kenneth Latourette, "the Roman Catholic Church put its house in order and girded itself for combat with the Protestants."[8] Hans Küng says it this way: The Reformation "challenged the council, accelerated it and was its permanent opponent." And then Küng adds, "How else are we to understand the fact that every doctrinal statement of Trent has an anathema against the Reformers? What the Reformers did not dispute was not discussed at all."[9] "Whatever the Protestants attacked now became official and final doctrine of the Catholic Church."[10] "The Roman Catholic Church reacted to the Reformation with a series of definitions of the principal doctrines in controversy."[11]

The Reformation "heresies" that demanded "extirpation" are not so much the cry to change the church structure, nor the preference for

(Acts 20:29), and they welcomed "the opportunity that such 'heresies' provided for clarifying orthodoxy. In the process of defining Catholic particularity, doctrinal emphases that had previously been able to coexist as parts of a comprehensive (or undifferentiated) Catholic tradition now became the themes of opposing and mutually exclusive systems." (Jaroslav Pelikan, *The Christian Tradition, Vol. 4: Reformation of Church and Dogma (1300–1700)* [Chicago: The University of Chicago Press, 1984], 245.)

4. Alister E. McGrath, "Do We Still Need the Reformation?" *Christianity Today,* December 12, 1994, 31.

5. Hubert Jedin, *Crisis and Closure of the Council of Trent,* N. D. Smith, trans. (London: Sheed & Ward, 1967), 160.

6. Stephen J. Duffy, *The Dynamics of Grace* (Collegeville, Minn.: The Liturgical Press, 1993), 227.

7. Elizabeth Dreyer, *Manifestations of Grace* (Collegeville, Minn.: The Liturgical Press, 1990), 149.

8. Kenneth Scott Latourette, *A History of Christianity, Volume 1: Beginnings to 1500* (San Francisco: HarperSanFrancisco, 1953), 871.

9. Hans Küng, *Christianity* (New York: Continuum, 1996), 483, 484.

10. Justo L. Gonzalez, *A History of Christian Thought, Volume III,* rev. ed. (Nashville: Abingdon, 1975), 246.

11. Pelikan, 274.

"the Bible alone," nor even the quarrel with papal authority. These protests certainly rankled devout Catholics, but even they admitted the need for reform. The major theological battleground is the doctrine of how humans are saved.[12] There are just two doctrinal possibilities: We are saved by grace alone through faith alone in Jesus Christ alone, as the Reformers insist, or, as the leaders of the church maintain, we are saved by a combination of what Christ has done for us and what we accomplish over our lifetime.

Again, there is a wide agreement among church historians about this issue being the cause of the Reformation and the focus of Trent. "In the teaching of the medieval church [the Protestant reformers] exposed what seemed to them to be a pernicious compromise between divine grace and human achievement."[13] "When the Reformation came, the providence of God raised Martin Luther to restore the gospel of pure, costly grace," says Dietrich Bonhoeffer.[14] "Luther's primary concern was theological and pastoral: reaffirming the gratuitous nature of justification in the face of religious practices that suggested that it must be earned."[15] "Luther himself regarded the Reformation as having begun over, and to have chiefly concerned, the correct under-standing of the Christian doctrine of justification."[16] Here, in the doctrine of salvation by grace alone, was "the principal point of difference with the Protestants."[17] "The central issue of the Reform was that of grace."[18]

## THE BOUNDARY STONES ARE SET

The delegates clearly understood their task: They must nail down the Catholic doctrine of salvation before any more Protestant inroads can be made with all this "by grace alone" business—"attempting a definition of the Catholic consensus on justification in the face of the Protestant challenge,"[19] "the definition of Catholic dogma in relation to the perceived errors of Protestantism."[20]

They get to work immediately. First, the delegates set an agenda for themselves of answering the questions about justification that the Reformers have raised:

1. What is justification? What do we mean when we say that a person is justified?
2. What are the causes of justification? What is God's role and what is ours?
3. What does it mean to say that one is "justified by faith"?
4. What role do human works and the sacraments play before, during, and after justification?

---

12. "The priority of his [Luther's] soteriology [how we are saved] over his ecclesiology [how the church is administered] is particularly evident in his remarkable statement of 1535, to the effect that he will concede the Pope his authority if the latter concedes the free justification of sinners in Christ." (Alister E. McGrath, *Iustitia Dei, A History of the Christian Doctrine of Justification: From 1500 to the Present Day* [Cambridge: Cambridge University Press, 1986], 10.)

13. Brian A. Gerrish, *Grace & Gratitude: The Eucharistic Theology of John Calvin* (Minneapolis: Fortress Press, 1993), 90.

14. Dietrich Bonhoeffer, *The Cost of Discipleship* (New York: Collier Books, 1963), 50.

15. John Jay Hughes, *Pontiffs: Popes Who Shaped History* (Huntington, Ind.: Our Sunday Visitor, 1994), 139.

16. Alister E. McGrath, *Luther's Theology of the Cross* (Oxford: Blackwell Publishers, 1985), 22.

17. Pelikan, 280.

18. Neil Ormerod, *Grace and Disgrace: A Theology of Self-Esteem, Society, and History* (Newtown, NSW: E. J. Dwyer, 1992), 129.

19. McGrath, *Iustitia Dei,* 63.

20. Ibid., 54.

## THE DEBATED NUANCES OF GRACE

Medieval theologians tended to define grace by the effect it produces in our lives. Since there are many effects of grace, some experts thought they should identify each of them.

For example, the experts at Trent discussed the differences between *gratia praeveniens* (prevenient grace) and *gratia susequens* (subsequent grace). "Prevenient grace" is God's grace that comes before anything else, calling sinners to Himself and turning the human will to Him. "Subsequent grace" is any grace that God gives after prevenient grace.

The theologians also differentiated between *gratia operans* (operative grace) and *gratia cooperans* (cooperative grace). In the *formal* setting, they would have declared, "operative grace" makes a human acceptable to God and "cooperative grace" makes our deeds acceptable to God. In the *effective* realm, "operative grace" makes our will desire to do good, but it takes "cooperative grace" to actualize our good will in good deeds.

The debaters at Trent also spent time trying to distinguish between *gratia gratis data*— actual grace, external divine assistance; and *gratis gratum faciens*—sanctifying grace, a supernatural habit in humans.

Think about these detailed nuances of grace the next time you raise your voice to sing "Amazing grace, how sweet the sound!"

5. What precedes, accompanies, and follows justification?
6. What supports the Catholic teaching on justification?

"Though not everything was included here," Justo Gonzalez observes, "a useful starting point had been provided."[21]

Building a consensus on this crucial matter, however, was not going to be an easy task. Among the debaters at Trent are theologically trained experts from across the broad spectrum of Catholic thought. Some seem almost to agree with the Reformers. Others refuse to countenance any statement whatsoever that the Protestants made: Cardinal Reginald Pole from England is reported to have remarked, "Luther has said so, therefore it is false."[22] The Franciscans are in the majority at the council but don't agree on any one understanding, with older Franciscans holding a slightly different view from younger Franciscans. Thomist scholars—those who hold to the teachings of Thomas Aquinas, mostly Dominicans—advocate positions widely held in the Catholic circles of the day. Augustinians and Jesuits differ. The followers of Augustine stress the necessity of what they call "a double justification." The Jesuits insist that good works are absolutely necessary in order to be justified and saved.[23] "The debates over this Somme-like battleground were painful and long drawn out."[24]

---

21. Gonzalez, 241.

22. Hans Küng, *Justification* (London: Burns and Oates, 1957), 100.

23. This was the Jesuits' first church council. The Society had received incorporation in 1540 from Pope Pius III, and from that day forward, they "became what probably was the most potent single influence in a Catholicism now reformed, renewed, propagandist and vehemently anti-Protestant." The Jesuits were represented at Trent by Diego Lainez (1512–1565), "an unbending conservative" who "enjoyed the status of papal theologian. His views on justification carried considerable weight." (Bernard M. G. Reardon, *Religious Thought in the Reformation*, 2nd ed. [London: Longman, 1995], 278.)

24. Diarmaid MacCulloch, *The Reformation: A History* (New York: Viking, 2004), 228. The Somme is a river in northern France, in the valley of which were fought major battles of World War I and World War II.

Throughout the long summer months and into the autumn, one draft after another of their statement on justification is proposed, debated, and rejected. Words and phrases are clarified or amended, ratified or revised. Reports of the proceedings include descriptions of intense discussions of divergent definitions articulating the finest points of difference. Occasional general dissatisfaction erupts over a proposed draft. Controversy and compromise are commonplace. "No other decree of this council, and few decrees of any council before or since, received such meticulous care." [25]

It takes the delegates almost a year of serious deliberations to hammer out an agreement. On January 13, 1547, the council finally issues its Decree on Justification, a document of such importance that it has been called "without any doubt the heart of the theological work of the council." [26]

## THE COUNCIL'S DECREE ON JUSTIFICATION

The introduction to the decree utilizes frank words: "Since there is being disseminated at this time, not without the loss of many souls and grievous detriment to the unity of the Church, a certain erroneous doctrine concerning justification . . ." The opening concludes by "strictly forbidding that anyone henceforth presumes to believe, preach or teach otherwise than is defined and declared in the present decree." There simply is no question for the document's framers—Christians either accept this version of how we are saved or else!

From the other side of the controversy, salvation by grace alone meets a much different reception. Beginning with Luther himself, the experience of being saved by the grace of

---

### THE OPEN GATES OF PARADISE

"I had hated that phrase 'the righteousness of God' which, according to the use and custom of all the doctors, I had been taught to understand philosophically, in the sense of the formal or active righteousness (as they termed it), by which God is righteous, and punished unrighteous sinners.

"Although I lived an irreproachable life as a monk, I felt that I was a sinner with an uneasy conscience before God; nor was I able to believe that I had pleased Him with my satisfaction. I did not love—in fact, I hated—that righteous God who punished sinners. . . .

"At last, God being merciful, as I meditated day and night, . . . I began to understand that 'righteousness of God' as that by which the righteous lives by the gift of God, namely by faith, and this sentence, 'the righteousness of God is revealed,' to refer to a passive righteousness, by which the merciful God justifies us by faith, as it is written, 'The righteous lives by faith.'

"This immediately made me feel as though I had been born again, and as though I had entered through open gates into paradise itself. From that moment, the whole face of scripture appeared to me in a different light."

—From Luther's own introduction, in 1545, to *The Works of Dr. Martin Luther* (*Kritische Gesamtausgabe*), 54.185.12–186.21.

---

God and not by our own merits or attempts at being righteous is far from a "grievous detriment." It is a fulfilling revelation, akin to having the gates of paradise thrown open. While the point certainly can be overdrawn, Patrick Collinson's history of the Reformation

---

25. Pelikan, 281.
26. Owen Chadwick, *The Reformation* (Baltimore: Penguin Books, 1964), 274, 275.

BY GRACE THROUGH FAITH

"This doctrine of justification is sometimes expressed in the abbreviated form: we are justified by faith. However, a major distortion of the doctrine occurs if it is taken to mean that faith is the human act by which we merit justification. God's act of justification is a free gift and is in no way dependent upon us although it calls for our response. Thus a more adequate brief statement of the doctrine is that we are justified by grace through faith. We cannot merit justification even by our act of faith. Faith is simply the appropriate response of trust and acceptance of God's unconditional affirmation of us." —Daniel Migliore, *Faith Seeking Understanding* (Grand Rapids, Mich.: Wm. B. Eerdmans Publishing, 1991), 175.

"One can never be justified on the basis of his own faith. Through all of salvation the only base is the finished work of Jesus Christ on the cross in history. Faith is the empty hand, the instrument by which we accept God's free gift. Faith is simply believing God. It is not a leap in the dark. It is ceasing to call God a liar, and believing him. Justification is only on the basis of the finished work of Christ. Faith is the instrument by which we accept that finished work." —Francis Schaeffer, *True Spirituality* (Wheaton, Ill.: Tyndale House Publishers, 1971), 78.

"One is looking around for something to insinuate into the relationship between grace and sin, and the vilest form of this interposition is that one makes a merit of one's believing or a virtue of one's faith. . . . The publican may be the greatest pharisee of them all by exchanging the humility of his faith for the justifying grace of God." —Carl E. Braaten, *Justification* (Minneapolis: Fortress Press, 1990), 24.

"Faith is not our Savior. It earns nothing." —Ellen G. White, *The Desire of Ages* (Nampa, Idaho: Pacific Press®, 1940), 175.

contends that the doctrine of salvation by grace infused Christians with a new and lasting joy, affecting *all the areas of their lives,* even restoring the dignity of marriage and placing the affectionate family in the center of the community.[27] Luther reads the theological developments in a way opposite to how they are read at the council. Trent, he thinks, is "angry with God."[28]

But at Trent in 1547, the full focus is on justification. Faced with the explosion of the Protestant acceptance of salvation by grace alone, the theologians of Trent refuse to bend. Historian Owen Chadwick summarizes the decree with these words: "Confronted by the doctrine of justification by faith alone, they declared that faith alone was not sufficient for justification."[29]

The decree devotes sixteen chapters to a point-by-point exposition of the Catholic teaching before proceeding to condemn thirty-three specific Reformation opinions. The chapters state the teaching of Trent in positive form. The canons that follow the chapters express those teachings in negative form. Here is where Trent most "sharply criticizes the Protestant position."[30]

But the decree begins benignly. Chapter 1 declares that all have sinned. Chapter 2 repeats the mystery of the advent of Jesus as the Redeemer for the entire world. Chapter 5 confesses that "we need the grace of God." The chapters quote Bible support for each position they take.

---

27. Patrick Collinson, *The Reformation: A History* (New York: The Modern Library, 2004), 178–181.

28. Martin Marty, *Martin Luther* (New York: A Lipper/Viking Book, 2004), 186.

29. Owen Chadwick, 274.

30. Anthony A. Hoekema, *Saved by Grace* (Grand Rapids, Mich.: Wm. B. Eerdmans Publishing Company, 1989), 164.

## THE FIRST DIFFERENCE: SOMETHING ELSE COMES FIRST

The glaring differences between the Catholic and Protestant interpretations of salvation begin to show up in chapter 3. A theme is introduced that carries throughout the entire document.

While grace comes from God alone, and while it is grace that justifies us, the chapter affirms, we will never receive the benefit of grace, we will never be justified until we have been "born again in Christ." There is something on our part, something we must do, that comes before justification, before we become "worthy" candidates for grace. Translation to "the state of grace" takes place only through "the sacrament of baptism" chapters 4 and 7 add. Sinners "may be disposed through [God's] quickening and helping grace to convert themselves to their own justification by freely assenting to and cooperating with that grace" (chapter 5). Canon 7 invites the believer to strive more earnestly "to dispose himself for grace."

Justification takes place only when we have been "aroused to consider the mercy of God"; only when we begin to love God "as the fountain of all justice, and on that account are moved against sin by a certain hatred and detestation" (chapter 6); only when we "keep the commandments of God"; only when faith, hope, and charity are infused within us "at the same time" as the remission of sins (chapter 7). After all, and here Trent quotes James 2:17, "faith . . . [without works] is dead" and of no profit. Why else would Jesus say to His followers, Trent asks, "If thou wilt enter into life, keep the commandments" (Matthew 19:17, KJV)? Chapter 8 summarizes: "The uninterrupted unanimity of the Catholic Church has held and expressed that we are therefore said to be justified by faith, because *faith* is the beginning of human salvation, the foundation and root of all justification."

According to Canon 4, if anyone says that a human's free will, "moved and aroused by God, in no way cooperates toward disposing and preparing itself to obtain the grace of justification," let him be anathema ("cursed," "reviled," "shunned"). "If anyone says that the sinner is justified by faith alone," Canon 9 warns, "meaning that nothing else is required to cooperate in order to obtain the grace of justification, and that it is not in any way necessary that he be prepared and disposed by the action of his own will, let him be anathema."

## THE SECOND DIFFERENCE: THE DEFINITION OF JUSTIFICATION

Chapter 3 is also the place where we are introduced to the Catholic definition of justification.

The Reformers define justification as an act of God that declares that sinners will be treated as if they are righteous. "In justifying the sinner God acquits him, declares him to be righteous, regards him as righteous, and proceeds to treat him as righteous."[31]

In contrast, Trent's Decree on Justification tells us that justified sinners are "made just." Justification "is not only a remission of sins but also the sanctification and renewal of the inward man through the voluntary reception of the grace and gifts whereby an unjust man becomes just" (chapter 7). "Not only are we reputed," the chapter continues, but we truly "are just." In fact, chapter 10 explains, "through the observance of the commandments of God

---

31. "Justification," in Siegfried H. Horn, *Seventh-day Adventist Bible Dictionary* (Hagerstown, Md.: Review and Herald, 1960), 616. See the discussion of justification in chapter 7, pages 80, 81.

and of the church, faith cooperating with good works," we receive "an increase" in our justification, a "further justification."

"If anyone says that the justice received is not preserved and also not increased before God through good works, but that those works are merely the fruits and signs of justification obtained, but not the cause of its increase, let him be anathema" (Canon 24).

From the Catholic perspective, "justification is at once acquittal and a making righteous in the full ethical sense," explains Stephen Duffy, a Roman Catholic professor of systematic and historical theology at Loyola University in New Orleans. Justification "embraces both relational and behavioral renewal, all due to a single formal cause."[32] In the *New Catholic People's Encyclopedia* we find the following definition: "Justification means the process by which man is saved from his state of sin and reborn in Christ through sanctifying grace, a process which makes him just or right in the sight of God."[33] *The Catechism of the Catholic Church* states, "Justification includes the remission of sins, sanctification, and the renewal of the inner man."[34] "In Roman Catholic theology according to Trent, justification is thought of primarily as an infusion of grace which results in a change in man's spiritual and moral nature, rather than as a declarative act, in which God imputes the righteousness of Christ to the believer."[35]

You see the fundamental differences between the Reformation and the Catholic definitions. For Protestants, justification is an event; for Catholics, it is a process. ("Luther had focused on an instant of justification, in which God saved sinners by pure grace. Trent pictured justification as a process in which divine grace and human efforts cooperate at every step and not only lead God to count us as justified but also begin to transform us so that we more nearly deserve that status."[36]) The Reformers carefully and deliberately separate justification and sanctification. ("Justification is an act of God's reckoning; sanctification is an act of God's transforming."[37]) Catholics combine the two dynamics into one and call it justification. Protestants call *sanctification* "the work of a lifetime"; Catholics refer to the same life-long endeavor as *justification.*

THE THIRD DIFFERENCE: THE ASSURANCE OF SALVATION

The third major difference between the Council of Trent's Decree on Justification and the Reformation understanding of grace has to do with the assurance of our salvation.

"Chapter 9 contests the view commonly attributed to Luther that faith brings with it an infallible certitude of one's own justification"[38] and flatly denies "the possibility of absolute certitude concerning the state of grace, perseverance, or salvation," calling such certainty

---

32. Duffy, 241.

33. Published by the Catholic Press in Chicago, 1973.

34. *The Catechism of the Catholic Church* (New York: Doubleday, 1995), Section 2019, page 544. This edition of the *Catechism,* for two years after its release as the best-selling book in the world, carries an introduction by Pope John Paul II and the imprimatur of Joseph Cardinal Ratzinger, now Pope Benedict XVI. The article on justification, grace, and merit, pages 535–545, is liberally footnoted with references to the Council of Trent.

35. Anthony A. Hoekema, 163.

36. William C. Placher, *A History of Christian Theology* (Philadelphia: The Westminster Press, 1983), 204.

37. John Piper, *Future Grace* (Sisters, Ore.: Multnomah Books, 1995), 26.

38. Avery Dulles, *The Assurance of Things Hoped For* (Oxford: Oxford University Press, 1994).

"presumption."[39] "It must not be said that sins are forgiven or have been forgiven," the chapter flatly states, "although among heretics and schismatics this vain and ungodly confidence may be and in our troubled times indeed is found and preached with untiring fury against the Catholic Church." "No one can know with certainty," the chapter concludes, "that he has obtained the grace of God."

The Reformers believed that, because we have Christ, we have eternal life (1 John 5:12). A biblical understanding of salvation by grace alone through faith alone in Jesus Christ alone brings with it "the assurance of the believer's acceptance. It brings the joy of being reunited with God *now*. No matter how sinful one's past life, God pardons all sins, and we are no longer under the condemnation and curse of the law. Redemption has become a reality: 'In Him we have redemption through His blood, the forgiveness of sins, according to the riches of His grace' (Eph. 1:7)."[40] "We have the assurance of salvation now and in the judgment."[41]

## THE SOURCE OF OUR THEOLOGY

The Council of Trent's Decree on Justification was published more than 450 years ago, solidifying the deep division between Roman Catholicism and Protestantism that remains firmly in place today. That division is not just a cultural one; it is based on fundamental doctrinal differences, none more essential than the different understandings of how we are saved.

Looking at all those years, with all the theological developments and denominational movements that have taken place, where do you find the source of your belief system?

On paper, there is no question for Seventh-day Adventists: Our doctrines are direct descendants of the Protestant Reformation. We believe that God is the Originator of all good impulses, that it is His grace that awakens our desire for grace, that our faith is also His gift to us. We are convinced that we can do absolutely nothing to affect our standing in God's grace, that He loves us with an unconditional, unfailing love. We know that we begin from our justification and grow in grace from there and that our growth is a matter of our sanctification, not our justification. We are assured that ten million years from now we will be in heaven, singing praises to the Lamb.

But where are we *experientially*? I'm sure it's the same in your church as it is in ours. Most Adventist young people, as well as their older brothers and sisters, their parents and grandparents, continue to worry that grace will undermine our commitment to God's law, continue to be reluctant to express a full assurance of salvation. These are fears that arise from the theology of the Council of Trent, not from the Reformation. It is high time for us to agree to reclaim our Reformation roots in our lives as well as on paper.

---

39. Duffy, 242.

40. *Seventh-day Adventists Believe . . .*, 2nd ed. (Silver Spring, Md.: General Conference Ministerial Association, 2005), 138.

41. Seventh-day Adventist Fundamental Belief #10, "The Experience of Salvation."

## GRACE IN QUESTION

### CHAPTER 13: THE BOUNDARY STONES

Chapter 13 brings us to a pivotal historical experience that not only helps us better understand the doctrine of grace but also helps us discover the true force of the Protestant Reformation. We look in on the theologians gathered in northern Italy to discuss the Reformers' insistence on justification by grace alone and to examine their fears that the Reformation will undermine the church.

1. Read the first part of the chapter and then discuss how the Council of Trent helps clarify what the purpose of the Reformation was and what was the Reformers' chief "heresy."

2. Do you ever feel that we cross the line from having a healthy interest in a topic to having an obsession about it? How do you know when you've crossed the line? Does the hair-splitting over "kinds of grace" fall into this category? (See the sidebar on page 178.) How can we keep our interest in grace from becoming an obsession? What's different about grace that permits us to fill our entire field of vision with the unending love of Jesus?

3. Ask someone to read aloud Martin Luther's experience as recorded in the sidebar on page 179. Share times when theological breakthroughs made you feel like you "had entered through open gates into paradise."

4. Draw or color a picture of a situation in which someone is exhibiting faith. What does your drawing reveal about your theology?

5. What could take place in your church to "reclaim our Reformation roots" in our experiences as well as on paper? Make specific plans for a weekend this year in which your entire church family explores the Reformation together.

# GRACE NOTES
## 1 JOHN 5—THE ASSURANCE OF SALVATION

The Old Testament people of God do not approve of lying. They obey the Ten Commandments: " 'You shall not give false testimony' " (Deuteronomy 5:20). They rely on criminal laws that require multiple witnesses: "No one shall be put to death on the testimony of only one witness" (17:6). They establish truth by eyewitness testimony:

> One witness is not enough to convict a man accused of any crime or offense he may have committed. A matter must be established by the testimony of two or three witnesses.
>
> If a malicious witness takes the stand to accuse a man of a crime, the two men involved in the dispute must stand in the presence of the LORD before the priests and the judges who are in office at the time. The judges must make a thorough investigation, and if the witness proves to be a liar, giving false testimony against his brother, then do to him as he intended to do to his brother. You must purge the evil from among you. The rest of the people will hear of this and be afraid, and never again will such an evil thing be done among you (19:15–20).

Isaiah speaks of those who deprive the innocent of justice by their false testimony, classifying them among the ruthless, the mockers, and all who have an eye for evil (Isaiah 29:20, 21). "Like a club or a sword or a sharp arrow," the people repeat to each other, "is the man who gives false testimony against his neighbor" (Proverbs 25:18).

On this subject, the New Testament people of God agree with their Old Testament brothers and sisters. Matthew includes the old counsel about multiple testimony (Matthew 18:15, 16). Mark tells the story about those who gave false testimony against Jesus (Mark 14:55–59). Luke tells of Jesus repeating the commandment against false testimony (Luke 18:20). John records Christ's conversation with Nicodemus, including, "I tell you the truth, we speak of what we know, and we testify to what we have seen, but still you people do not accept our testimony" (John 3:11).

Then John takes the discussion to a higher level. His argument is interesting. He restates the principle: We accept human testimony, he says (1 John 5:9). When he tells the believers, "Demetrius is well spoken of by everyone," he expects them to believe him because "you know that our testimony is true" (3 John 12). When John the Baptist says, " 'I saw the Spirit come down from heaven as a dove and remain on him' " (John 1:32), we believe his testimony. When the Samaritan woman tells the people of her town what Jesus had

Q. Restate the differences between the theology of grace of the Reformers and the position on justification of the theologians of Trent.

Q. How does "God's testimony" about grace give us the assurance of eternal salvation?

revealed to her, many of them believe in Jesus because of the woman's testimony (John 4:39).

If we accept human testimony, John continues, shouldn't we pay attention when God testifies? "God's testimony is greater because it is the testimony of God," John argues (1 John 5:9). And just what is the testimony of God? It is His testimony about His Son, Jesus (verses 9, 10): "God has given us eternal life, and this life is in His Son. He who has the Son has life; he who does not have the Son of God does not have life. I write these things to you who believe in the name of the Son of God so that you may know that you have eternal life" (verses 11–13).

God's testimony is to the truth about grace, the truth about His giving us eternal life. God's testimony is the truth about how our eternal life is totally bound up in Jesus. Anyone who has Jesus has life. That is what God's testimony about His Son is all about. That is the truth we are to believe "so that you may know that you have eternal life."

More than any other Bible writer, John connects the words of God and God's testimony about the gift of Jesus giving us eternal life: "The word of God and the testimony of Jesus Christ" (Revelation 1:2); "The word of God and the testimony of Jesus" (verse 9); "God's commandments" and "the testimony of Jesus" (12:17). When John listens to the angel telling of the " ' "wedding supper of the Lamb" ' " (19:9) and the "fine linen, bright and clean" that has been given to us to wear (verse 8), the angel assures John, " 'These are the true words of God' " (verse 9). Then the angel adds this observation: " 'The testimony of Jesus is the spirit of prophecy' " (verse 10).

If we are going to speak "the true words of God," if we are going to speak with the same spirit that animates all Bible prophecy, we must give our testimony about Jesus and tell the truth about grace, the truth about God giving us eternal life through His Son and only through His Son.

" 'Those who bear testimony to Jesus are inspired like the prophets' " (verse 10, NEB). "(This witness to Jesus inspires all prophecy.)" (Phillips). "The essence of prophecy is to give a clear witness for Jesus" (NLT).

A section of *The Adoration of the Mystic Lamb* (1432), by Flemish artist Jan van Eyck. Around the altar in the lower panel, van Eyck painted in golden letters, "Behold the Lamb of God, who takes away the sin of the world." On the right above, John the Baptist points to Jesus, portrayed as King of kings (see chapter 12, pages 161 and 162, and 169–171).

*"Periodically an old epoch ends, and a new one begins."*

—LeRoy Edwin Froom, *Movement of Destiny*

*"There is religion for you, it is free as the mountain brook,*
*it is plenteous as the dew on mount Hermon,*
*it is as rich as the fruits in autumn,*
*there is 'enough and to spare,' it is ever green as the foliage in the spring."*

—William Miller, *To the Believers in the Second Advent*

*"The people were roused, and began to inquire the way of salvation."*

—Ellen G. White, *The Great Controversy*

*"Had the Scriptures failed? Was there no reward of saints?*
*Was there to be no judgment day? Was the Bible false?"*

—Arthur Spalding, *Origin and History of Seventh-day Adventists*

*"The second advent and God's grace*
*are the last two assurances of Scripture to a waiting church."*

—Harry Lowe, *Redeeming Grace*

## CHAPTER 14
# THE GREAT DISAPPOINTMENT:
### *The Opposition to Grace in the American Frontier*

ON THE WEEKEND OF OCTO-
BER 22, 1994, exactly 150
years after that remarkable
occurrence at the beginning
of the Seventh-day Adventist story that
we call "the Great Disappointment," I
was attending a youth ministry training
conference in Mount Vernon, Ohio. The
speaker was so excited about connecting
us to that historic Adventist event that he
began his Friday night sermon, October
21, with these words: "Do you realize
that if this group were living in northeastern America 150 years ago in 1844 what
we'd be getting ready for tomorrow?"

Someone in the back of the auditorium,
just as eager to make the historic connection, shouted out, "We'd be getting ready
for the Great Disappointment!"

Well, that wasn't exactly what the
speaker was looking for! He chuckled,
waited for the laughter to subside, and
then tried to recapture our focus by starting again and talking about the Second
Coming, the real reason for all the hopeful expectations in 1844.

In that distant autumn, in the little
towns of New England, the brisk breezes
already are blowing, the colorful leaves already are falling, and people already are

---

ON THE SECOND ADVENT

From a letter from William Miller to Joshua V.
Himes, August 17, 1826:

Come, blessed Savior! nor let time delay
The sacred morn of that expected day,
When all the happy throng, the heavenly band,
Descending from above, "the spirit land;"
When the seventh trump its solemn blast shall sound,
And Gabriel's voice shall shake the solid ground.
Then sleeping myriads from their graves shall rise,
And meet their Savior in those nether skies;
While those who yet remain, by men oppressed,
Will feel a sudden change and join the bless'd;
Where, in one chorus joined, the song be raised,
To God, the Father, Son,—"Ancient of days."

When the Sun of righteousness shall rise
With healing wings, and grace on grace distil,
And cleanse the church on Zion's holy hill;
Where sin no more controls, nor death by sin,
But justified and glorified with him:
No need of sun or moon, for he's our light;
No changing seasons there, nor gloomy night;
No parting there of friends, nor farewells given,
But gathered all in one from earth and heaven.
On this my faith is fixed, my hope is raised—
To him the glory, and his name the praise.
Then, while I stay in this unfriendly state,
Lord, give me grace, and patiently I'll wait.

gathering their winter's supply of firewood. But Sunday after Sunday throughout Maine and New York, Vermont, and Massachusetts, one particular minister has something other than winter on his mind. For ten years he has been preaching about just one subject. His name is William Miller (1782–1849), and he believes that Jesus is about to come again.

People from many churches join him: Methodists, Baptists, Congregationalists, Presbyterians, Lutherans. "Their denominational barriers were hurled to the ground; conflicting creeds were shivered to atoms; the unscriptural hope of a temporal millennium was abandoned, false views of the second advent were corrected, pride and conformity to the world were swept away; wrongs were made right; hearts were united in the sweetest fellowship, and love and joy reigned supreme. If this doctrine did this for the few who did receive it, it would have done the same for all if all had received it."[1]

Great camp meetings take place, with thousands of people attending, studying their Bibles day and night to find out all they can about Christ's second coming. They search for answers to their questions. They reread familiar passages, like the ones in Matthew 24. They ponder mysterious verses, like the ones in the books of Daniel and the Revelation. Every text is turned inside out. Every commentary examined. Every possible interpretation explored.

Finally, in a series of explanations that seem at the time to be reasonable and accurate, Miller pinpoints not only the year he believes Jesus will return but the exact month and day as well: October 22, 1844.

So, the summer of 1844 ends with great expectations for the believers in the soon advent of Jesus. The days of September fly by. Millerite Adventists can hardly contain their enthusiastic longing for Christ's return. The calendar announces October 1, 1844, and the believers feel an inescapable conviction that before this month ends they will be in heaven.

Just three more weeks of earth's dreary days. Then two weeks to go. One week left. The day after tomorrow. October 22 finally arrives, and dawn finds little groups of believers gathered together in farmhouses and on hillsides, praying together, singing songs of the Second Coming, and claiming the promises of salvation. It is a wondrous time. A time of freedom. Hours of joy.

Then the day passes, and Jesus doesn't return.

It's hard for us to imagine the depths of the despair that overwhelms them. The bitterness. The humiliation. The dejection. The disappointment. Instead of soaring through the heavens, they have to trudge through muddy streets and jeering crowds. Instead of entering heavenly mansions, they have to return to their cold, little homes. Instead of kneeling with the angels before Jesus, they must get down on their knees and beg to get their old jobs back. Instead of eating fruit from the tree of life, they dig potatoes out of the hard ground. Winter is approaching quickly. They will have to shovel snow from their doorsteps. The nights will be long and dark and bitterly cold.

For the rest of their lives those Adventists refer to this time in the bleakest of terms. They call it the Great Disappointment.[2]

### THE FULLNESS OF TIME

Now let me digress for just a moment to ask a few questions about timing.

---

1. Ellen G. White, *The Great Controversy* (Nampa, Idaho: Pacific Press®, 1950), 379, 380.
2. Adapted from Stuart Tyner, *Walking On the Edge* (Riverside, Calif.: Hancock Center Publications, 1996), 21–23.

A familiar verse in Galatians 4:4 tells us that Christ's *first* coming took place in "the fullness of time" (NKJV), a phrase we generally apply literally. Before we continue with an analysis of the Great Disappointment, let's consider "the fullness of time" and see if there's any assistance there in understanding what happened on October 22, 1844. And more importantly to this study, let's see if there are any connections between the Great Disappointment and the opportunity to obey the command to take the everlasting gospel of God's amazing grace to every nation, kindred, tongue, and people.

Should we apply this concept of "fullness" just to the Incarnation, to the one-and-only-time-in-the-history-of-the-universe event to which Galatians 4:4 clearly is referring? Should we restrict our understanding of "fullness" only to that moment in the sweep of the Roman Empire when the confluence of need and opportunity create the exact right time for Jesus to come to earth?

Or, on the other hand, is it possible that the "fullness of time" might be a divinely appointed strategy, a carefully considered yet *common* method of operating with people on planet Earth in which God sees and hears (Exodus 3:7) and determines that the time is ripe for a significant change, a new direction, a fresh epoch in human history? Of course, we can't know for certain, but the concept is an intriguing one to consider as historical pattern as well as in reference to the Incarnation.

For example, might an approach that uses the "fullness of time strategy" apply to the Flood? Might the Godhead have seen how great human wickedness had become that *every* inclination of human hearts was *only* evil *all* the time (Genesis 6:5) and have determined that a "fullness" had been reached? When God's heart was "filled with pain," had the fullness of antediluvian time come?

Could we apply such a strategy to the timing of the Exodus, when Egypt had reached its zenith of power and influence, and the ancient Hebrews were at their lowest point, fully dependent and agonizingly weak? Did that moment bring with it a fullness of time in which the Hebrew people's only hope of salvation was through trusting in Yahweh alone? Did the Exodus moment create an opening early in the Old Testament record for the central truth of grace to be experienced?

Might we make an application of "fullness" to the return of the captives from exile in Babylon? Or to the Gentiles' readiness to hear the gospel from Paul and Barnabas and Silas (see chapter 7)? Or to sixth-century Britain's readiness to hear God's call from the isolated monastery on the Isle of Iona (see chapter 11)? Or to the German people's readiness in the sixteenth century to listen to the monk from Wittenberg (see chapter 12)?

If we apply "the fullness of time" to *a pattern* of divine/human interaction, even if we don't fully understand the concept or completely comprehend its application, then it is only a small step through an immense open door to approach an exploration of what might have made nineteenth-century America the right place and the right time for the birth of a new group of seekers after the heart of God. It may not be so surprising that in the autumn of 1844, this people was born in the disappointment of making a very public mistake in their interpretation of the Bible. It may not be so farfetched to discover that, once again in the flow of human history, a confluence of need and opportunity had created an explosive opening for the everlasting gospel of grace.

But if we accept the premise and make the application, we must be prepared for the possibility that the exploration may take us to places we didn't expect to go.

THE AMERICAN FRONTIER IN THE EARLY
NINETEENTH CENTURY

Think about the place and the time. The nation's infancy of exploration, colonization, and independence is over. Now, with the turn of the century and the beginning of the 1800s, the new American republic is experiencing its adolescent growth spurt. The American people are "feeling their oats." The Marshall Court (1801–1835) is increasing the power of the federal government. The Louisiana Purchase of 1803 immensely increases the nation's territory. Advances in transportation (the Erie Canal, the steamship, railroads) make it easier for people to move west. The War of 1812, another conflict with England, deepens the notion of invincibility among the young Americans and creates a new national hero—the next Washington—in Andrew Jackson. By the time Jackson assumes the presidency in 1829, the Monroe Doctrine has become a cherished part of the American landscape, declaring that no European power is welcome in "our hemisphere," putting into law the notion of Manifest Destiny, which has been active in American opinion since early in the century.[3]

In 1823, the U.S. Supreme Court rules that the "right of occupancy" of the Native Americans is not as essential as the U.S. Government's "right of discovery." With this ruling in place, it is an easy progression to the Indian Removal Act of 1830,[4] making more room for a flood of European immigrants: the tired, the poor, the huddled masses yearning to breathe free.[5]

But the legal right to remove the Native Americans to make room for more Europeans does not directly translate into a universal welcoming party for the Irish, Polish, Italian, German, and Scandinavian newcomers. The "Americans" aren't too crazy about these other ethnic groups either. However, between 1828 and 1844, a half million immigrants become citizens. By the late 1840s, two hundred thousand immigrants are showing up every year from "the old country," eager for a new beginning in this God-given land of opportunity.

And so many of them are Roman Catholics! In 1807, there are seventy thousand Catholics in America when only a few years earlier they had been welcome only in Maryland. By 1830, there are five hundred thousand. And by 1860, the number swells to more than three million. Instead of embracing the diversity or attempting to understand the fundamental differences, religious Americans act out of fear and build up barriers. Anti-Catholic riots take place in Massachusetts and Pennsylvania in the 1830s and 1840s. Secret societies are formed (such as the Secret Order of the Star-Spangled Banner, organized in 1849) to oppose further immigration of Catholics and the "popery" that follows them everywhere. The American Party, commonly referred to as the "Know-Nothings" because they vow to know no Catholicism in American politics, actually fields a presidential candidate in the 1850s.

So we have this explosive combination of forces: (1) multiple legal rulings dividing "us" old settlers from "them," the natives who were

---

3. Manifest Destiny was the nineteenth-century belief that God had given the United States not only the right but also the duty to expand throughout the North American continent.

4. In 1820, 120,000 Native Americans lived east of the Mississippi. By 1844, less than one quarter of them remained.

5. From "The New Colossus," the celebrated poem of Emma Lazarus (1849–1887), engraved on a plaque on the Statue of Liberty.

here first but who don't share in our "God-given" destiny; (2) a growing discomfort between "us" citizens of the United States and "them," the recent Europeans who keep coming to "our" shores; (3) the open spaces of the new territories in the west inviting the masses crowded in the cities of the east; and, (4) the transportation technology to make our expansion dreams come true.

Add to these factors a "Great Awakening" of religious fervor.[6] There is a new emphasis on translating the Bible,[7] a sudden interest in missionary activity, and an explosive growth in the churches.[8] Deeply felt social issues—the abolition of slavery, equal rights for women, heightened standards of temperance, utopian ideals, and universal education—combine with a widespread interest in spiritual revival. Put them all together and you have all the dynamic forces you need to open up a discussion in America about what the heart and soul and center of personal Bible religion is all about.

Think of the discussion one could have had about the overwhelming difference the gospel of grace makes in human existence. Consider the spiritual peace that could have come to the experiences of these work-oriented souls if they had just heard Jesus say, " 'Come to me, all you who are weary and burdened, and I will give you rest' " (Matthew 11:28). Imagine what might have happened if the United States had been turned to a faith in which all who have fallen short of the glory of God come to Jesus for salvation instead of trying to earn it by their own labor.

AN OPENING FOR THE GOSPEL

Charles Finney could have been the first to seize the opportunity.

On the first day of July 1824, in Adams, New York, Charles Finney (1792–1875), a tall, recently converted man in his early thirties, preaches his first sermon as an ordained Presbyterian minister. He is a student of law, a cello player, an expert horseman, an accurate marksman who loves to hunt, and a man with a passionate fondness for music and Shakespeare.[9] But it is Finney's work as a preacher and revivalist that establishes his reputation as one of the foremost religious leaders of the nineteenth century. In the book *131 Christians Everyone Should Know,* the editors of *Christian History Magazine* place Finney alongside evangelists such as George Whitefield, Dwight L. Moody, and Billy Sunday, and say that Finney "inspired thousands of preachers."[10] Dr. Michael Horton tells us that the Billy Graham Center gives a place of honor to Finney, that Jerry Falwell calls Finney "one of my heroes," and that Finney's legacy lives on in the Vineyard

---

6. Among the American colonists in the 1730s and 1740s, a religious movement arose that historians refer to as America's first Great Awakening, led largely by Jonathan Edwards (1703–1758) in Massachusetts (you remember his most famous sermon, "Sinners in the Hands of an Angry God"), and George Whitefield (1714–1770), the famous Methodist preacher from England who visited and preached in most of the colonies and became known as "the lightning rod of the Great Awakening." A Second Great Awakening followed in the early 1800s, reviving interest in religion and inspiring a wave of social activism. The preaching of evangelists and revivalists during this time emphasized the personal conversion experience.

7. In 1800, the Bible was available in 71 languages and dialects; by 1830, 86 more had been added; and by the time J. N. Andrews became the first Adventist missionary (1874), the number had grown to 273.

8. Between 1800 and 1860, the largest Protestant denominations in America grew by 1,300 percent.

9. From G. Frederick Wright's Memorial Lecture, given in Oberlin, Ohio, March 21, 1891.

10. Mark Galli and Ted Olson, *131 Christians Everyone Should Know* (Nashville, Tenn.: Broadman & Holman, 2000), 69.

FINNEY ON JUSTIFICATION

From *Finney's Lectures on Systematic Theology* (1851)
Lecture LVI. "Justification."

II.3. "For sinners to be forensically pronounced just is impossible and absurd."

III.2. "The doctrine of imputed righteousness, or that Christ's obedience to the law was accounted as our obedience, is founded on a most false and nonsensical assumption. Christ's righteousness could do no more than justify himself. It can never be imputed to us."

III.4.d. "It certainly cannot be true that God accepts and justifies the sinner in his sins. . . . The Bible everywhere conditionates justification upon sanctification."

Movement, the Promise Keepers, televangelism, and the Church Growth Movement.[11]

In 1825, Finney is preaching to the settlers of upstate New York. Under the force of his sermons, revivals "break out" in the villages of Jefferson and St. Lawrence counties. Between 1827 and 1832, Finney's revivals sweep New York, Philadelphia, and Boston. In 1832, Finney turns to pastoring, leading the congregations of two churches in New York City. In 1837, he moves to Oberlin, Ohio, where he pastors and at the same time teaches theology at the Oberlin Collegiate Institute. He serves as president of the Institute from 1851 until 1866.

Finney is so committed to baptizing new believers that he turns revivalism into a virtual science. Stressing the importance of emotion in religion, he creates new evangelistic techniques ("new measures" they are called by supporters; "revivalistic gimmicks" by detractors) to "provoke" conversions and "shock, scare, badger and persuade the hearers into a change of will."[12] The techniques include placing newspaper ads for the revival meetings, conducting "protracted meetings" that are held each night for two or three weeks, singing hymns addressed to the stages that mark the spiritual journey (much like we have sung "Just As I Am" at the close of an evangelistic sermon), naming specific sinners and their sins during public prayers from the pulpit, and introducing "the anxious bench"— a precursor to our "altar call"—in which the preacher invites sinners to come to the front of the tent or auditorium to receive Jesus.[13] Thousands respond and are baptized.

In fact, Finney's dedication to evangelism is so strong that he becomes convinced that issues of "doctrinal precision" could actually hinder the spread of frontier Christianity and the salvation of souls. "His love of souls overruled all difficulty on nice questions of theological difference," one biographer writes.[14]

---

11. Dr. Michael S. Horton is professor of apologetics and theology at Westminster Theological Seminary in California and editor of *A Confessing Theology for Postmodern Times* (Wheaton, Ill.: Crossway Books, 2000). This quotation is taken from a Horton article titled "The Disturbing Legacy of Charles Finney," *Issues, Etc. Journal,* vol. 2, no. 4 (Summer 1997).

12. From Donald Scott's essay, "Evangelicalism, Revivalism, and the Second Great Awakening," *The 19th Century* (City University of New York, the National Humanities Center, October 2000).

13. "Finney changed the emphasis of evangelical revival from God-prompted to human-sponsored." (Wendy Murray Zoba, *Evangelical Christianity* [New York: Doubleday, 2005], 54.)

14. Keith J. Hardman, *Charles Grandison Finney: Revivalist and Reformer* (Grand Rapids, Mich.: Baker and Syracuse University Press, 1987), 25.

Finney and his supporters announce their willingness to accept "a certain amount of error" as long as baptisms are taking place and the church is being built.

In particular, Finney develops a new view of justification. "With pronounced emphasis," says American church historian E. Brooks Holifield, Finney "qualified the doctrine of justification by making it conditional on obedience to the law."[15] He preaches of four "unalterable conditions," all of which must be present and active for salvation to be granted: (1) faith in Christ; (2) repentance, which he refers to as a "total outward reformation" (one of Finney's most popular sermons is an 1831 presentation titled "Sinners Bound to Change Their Own Hearts"); (3) "present sanctification," a "full consecration to God," and "perfection in holiness"; and (4) "perseverance in faith and obedience." For Finney, the gospel is pardon for sinners who sin no more. "The penitent soul remains justified," he insists, "no longer than this full-hearted consecration continues."

Later, Finney writes: "Neither is the atonement, nor anything in the mediatorial work of Christ, the foundation of our justification."[16] He tells people to present *their righteousness* to God. The Reformers insisted we are saved by the faithfulness of Christ; Finney teaches that we are saved by *our own faithfulness*. "God had no right to justify the sinful," Finney preaches; "God could justify only the obedient."[17] Michael Horton summarizes: "Finney embraced a works-righteousness that exceeded the Counter-Reformation position."[18] Finney is "passionate in his disagreement with the learning and heritage of the reformers. He dismissed their return to Scripture and Christ-centered grace."[19]

Finney's works-orientation goes over well with the hearty frontier do-it-yourselfers.[20] Americans thought of themselves as the creators of a new Garden of Eden. Citizens carved their own success out of the resistant frontier. National redemption will follow from collective efforts toward social improvement. In the same way, Finney teaches, individuals can achieve their own eternal salvation by their stubborn obedience, their willful overcoming, and their persistent good works.

The reception from Finney's denomination, however, is far from enthusiastic. In 1834, the Presbyterian General Assembly publishes an "Act and Testimony" proposed by "Old School" theologians to deal with the division in the church that Finney and other "New School" teachers and preachers caused. The document states that its purpose is "to endeavour to exclude from her communion those who disturb her peace,

---

15. E. Brooks Holifield, *Theology in America: Christian Thought from the Age of the Puritans to the Civil War* (New Haven, Conn.: Yale University Press, 2003), 365.

16. In an article for the Alberta Reformation Fellowship titled, "Charles Finney's Doctrine of Justification," David Linden quotes this Finney remark and then states, "I would nominate that as the most wicked thing I have read in Charles Finney."

17. Holifield, ibid.

18. Michael Horton, "Charles Finney vs. the Westminster Confession," the Alliance of Confessing Evangelicals (copyright 1995).

19. Linden, ibid.

20. "Finney's gospel message grew out of a much higher estimation of natural human capacity in the process of salvation." (Mark A. Noll, *America's God: from Jonathan Edwards to Abraham Lincoln* [Oxford: Oxford University Press, 2002], 296.)

corrupt her testimony, and subvert her established forms." It describes the teachings of the new school as having propelled the church into a "solemn crisis," with "alarming errors," "perversion of our doctrinal formularies," the "corruption of [the Presbyterian Church's] peculiar testimony," and with fatal "Arminian and Pelagian heresies."[21]

The document specifically charges the New School with denying that humans need Christ or His atonement for their salvation and asserting instead that humans can exert their own regeneration and that the concept of an imputed righteousness is "a novelty, and nonsense." In conclusion, the document states that its framers "cling to the Church's venerable ramparts, because they afford a sure defense of those precious, though despised, doctrines of grace, the pure transmission of which has been entrusted as a sacred duty to the Church."

Others agreed, believing that "Finney had degraded, even cheapened, the gospel by suggesting that redemption, after all was said and done, was largely a human prerogative."[22] Presbyterian seminary professor Charles Hodge (1797–1878) writes, "The Bible teaches that we are all sinners, and that, being sinners, we have lost the favor of God and are unable to affect our own redemption."[23]

So, here in the middle of nineteenth-century America, we have this political-social-cultural readiness to hear the gospel ("an environment primed for theological productivity," is the way Mark Noll characterizes it[24]), perhaps even a "fullness of time." The readiness is met first by a commanding, controversial, religious revival cautioning its followers to be afraid of grace, preaching the ability and obligation of humans to save themselves by their own efforts, obedience, and faithfulness.

Is there another response to the readiness? We wait with anxious breath to hear how believers in the Second Advent will translate their assurance of salvation into a message for the world.

### With eyes fixed on Jesus

Two months after the Great Disappointment, on a cold December morning, five young women are having worship together on the second floor of a country house in South Portland, Maine.[25] While the women are praying, one of them, Ellen Harmon, feels overpowered by the Holy Spirit. "I was wrapped in a vision of God's glory," she later recalls, "and I seemed to be rising higher and higher, far above the dark world."[26]

Ellen sees the discouraged Second Advent believers walking along a path that leads to heaven. Behind the travelers is a light, identified as the events they had just experienced. Ahead of them, at the end of the path, is the New Jerusalem, the heavenly city where they will enter eternity. Whenever the believers become disheartened, Jesus encourages them by

---

21. Dutch pastor and professor of theology Jacobus Arminius (1560–1609) opposed Calvin and emphasized the believer's free will. On Pelagian heresies, see chapter 10.

22. Kenneth J. Collins, *The Evangelical Moment: The Promise of an American Religion* (Grand Rapids, Mich.: Baker Academic, 2005), 31.

23. Charles Hodge, *The Way of Life,* 1841 ed. (New York: Paulist Press, 1987), 233.

24. Noll, 294.

25. Arthur L. White, *Ellen G. White: The Early Years, Volume 1, 1827–1862* (Hagerstown, Md.: Review and Herald, 1985), 55.

26. Ellen G. White, *Early Writings* (Hagerstown, Md.: Review and Herald, 1945), 13.

raising His right arm. A glorious light shines on the pathway, and the people shout, "Hallelujah!"

Later, Ellen shares her understanding of the vision: "If they kept their eyes fixed on Jesus, who was just before them, leading them to the city, they were safe."[27] For the next seventy years, Ellen's message stays the same: *Keep your eyes on Jesus!*

"Do not allow your minds to be diverted from the all-important theme of the righteousness of Christ," she reminds us many years later.[28] In 1864, she writes, "It is a good thing that the heart be established with grace. This is the ground of our steadfastness."[29] And later: "The church, endowed with the righteousness of Christ, is His depositary, in which the riches of His mercy, His grace, and His love, are to appear in full and final display."[30]

Unfortunately, however, somewhere early in the story we stop listening to the voice of the gospel. In five "Sabbath Conferences" held in 1848 and then in almost twenty more meetings held until December 1850, the early leaders hammer out the important statements that would distinguish this new body of believers. But Adventist historians long have recognized that the resultant list of "leading doctrines," published in the *Review and Herald* in 1854,

miss the point entirely of what should have been the central feature of our faith.

Here is how LeRoy Froom, in his book *Movement of Destiny,* states the situation: "The conspicuous feature in this tabulation is that there was omission of all reference to salvation through Christ and Christ alone. That paramount truth which was definitely believed was evidently taken for granted by James White, editor, and the supporting publishing committee of three: J. N. Andrews, R. F. Cottrell, and Uriah Smith. . . . This omission was characteristic of practically all of our leading writers of the time and in fact for three decades thereafter. Our literature of the day so attests."[31]

Norval Pease agrees. "Early periodicals and books reveal a meager amount of material in this field. Most of the attention was given to such subjects as the law of God, the Sabbath, the prophecies, and conditional immortality. The masthead of the *Review* from August 15 to December 19, 1854, listed the 'Leading Doctrines Taught by the *Review*.' This list included no mention of justification, righteousness, or any related topic. For many years, the volumes of the *Review* disclose practically no discussions on justification by faith."[32]

Adventist ministers stuck to preaching about the "distinctive truths" and failed to present the gospel of grace.[33] "The vital, life-

---

27. Ellen G. White, *The Day-Star,* January 24, 1846.

28. Ellen G. White, *Review and Herald,* April 5, 1892.

29. Ellen G. White, *Testimonies for the Church* (Nampa, Idaho: Pacific Press®, 1948), 1:438.

30. Ellen G. White, *The Desire of Ages* (Nampa, Idaho: Pacific Press®, 1940), 680.

31. LeRoy Edwin Froom, *Movement of Destiny* (Hagerstown, Md.: Review and Herald, 1971), 89, 90.

32. Norval F. Pease, *By Faith Alone* (Nampa, Idaho: Pacific Press®, 1962), 109. In the late 1940s, Norval Pease was the pastor of the same church where I am one of the pastors today, before becoming president of La Sierra College from 1954–1960.

33. "Many of [the ministers] were drawn into discussions and debates involving the law of God and other vital Bible truths. Imperceptibly, not a few of those who engaged in such discussions became self-reliant, and there developed in their hearts a spirit of sureness, self-dependence, and argumentativeness. In time this bore unwholesome fruit." (The board of trustees of the Ellen White Estate, Washington, D.C., May 10, 1962. In the "Historical Foreword" to *Testimonies to Ministers* [Nampa, Idaho: Pacific Press®, 1962], xviii.)

giving doctrines of the gospel and the cross of Christ conversion, justification, sanctification, righteousness by faith were taken for granted," writes A. V. Olson.[34]

Even Arthur Spalding, the consistently generous chronicler of the early Adventists, refers to this time with a hint of wishing-it-were-otherwise in his voice: "Nor is it to be understood that these pioneers grasped completely all the truths now held by the denomination. Knowledge of truth is progressive, and only they who grow in that knowledge are living Christians. Some of the truths hereafter stated categorically were years in developing fully."[35]

Surely October 22, 1844, was a great disappointment to those who had longed for Jesus to return, trusted their eternal standing to His grace alone, waited to sing, " 'This is the LORD, we trusted in him; let us rejoice and be glad in his salvation' " (Isaiah 25:9). Just as surely, how greatly disappointing it must have been for heaven to have to wait another forty years to hear the gospel from the American believers in the Second Advent.

---

34. A. V. Olson, *Through Crisis to Victory, 1888–1901* (Hagerstown, Md.: Review and Herald, 1966), 10.

35. Arthur W. Spalding, *Origin and History of Seventh-day Adventists* (Hagerstown, Md.: Review and Herald, 1961), 1:235.

# GRACE IN QUESTION

## CHAPTER 14: THE GREAT DISAPPOINTMENT

Chapter 14 examines that fascinating occurrence in the early history of Adventism that we call the Great Disappointment. We explore the culture of America in the early nineteenth century and find the forces that created a readiness to hear the gospel. We celebrate the dynamics that brought new believers together but wonder why we failed to seize the opportunity fully.

1. Describe one or two disappointments you have experienced in your life—not big tragedies, but times when something you wished for didn't happen or when something you hoped wouldn't happen actually did. Are there any similarities in the disappointments members of your group describe? How do these memories help us understand the disappointment of 1844?

2. Reread William Miller's poem about the Second Coming on page 189. Look at the last line. How does grace help us wait patiently?

3. Ask study group members who have children to talk about times when they knew the kids were ready for a new experience. How did they know, for example, when the children were ready to walk? What clues told them when the time had come to leave them alone in a Sabbath School class? Or to send them off to elementary school? Or to get baptized? Apply these experiences to the notion of "the fullness of time" on page 191.

4. How do you think American history might have been different "if the United States had been turned to a faith in which all who have fallen short of the glory of God came to Jesus for salvation, instead of trying to earn it by their own labor" (page 193)?

5. Spend time together exploring how your church, including its teachings and its programming, helps you to "keep your eyes on Jesus" (see page 197).

# GRACE NOTES
## ACTS 4—THE COMMUNITY OF FAITH

Q. How do you
see the "riches
of God's grace"
appearing in full
and final display
in your church?

Q. How does
grace help us
manage the ten-
sions in today's
communities of
faith?

The events covered in the last part of Acts 4 occur very early in the careers of the apostles. But already Peter and John could have described the way the Christian community successfully and effectively ministers to others. They might have defined Christian ministry as the challenge of managing the tensions between positive yet conflicting ministry opportunities.

For example, there are tensions between the big, public opportunities in which thousands hear the message spoken with clarity, power, and disturbing force (Acts 2:37–41) and the private opportunities when one person, even one of insignificant quality in the eyes of the self-important, is touched, healed, and changed (3:1–9).

There are potential conflicts between the opportunity to perform acts of kindness, which takes time (2:44–47), and the opportunity to proclaim Jesus with conviction, to make the teachings of our faith believable, which takes study and preparation, immersion in the Source of our conviction, and concentration on both its story and its connection to our story (3:12–26).

There are tensions between the opportunity to be good citizens, obeying the rules and laws of human authority; and the opportunity to allow the enthusiastic testimony of what you have seen and heard, regardless of the consequences (4:19, 20).

There are tensions between the opportunity to express one's thoughts in the most exalted tones, like the unified prayer of the believers in this passage, with its uplifting thoughts of the Creator of the universe, the Sovereign Lord; of the Holy Spirit, the Agent of inspiration; and of Jesus, the Anointed One (verses 24–26); and the opportunity of returning to the practical, of suggesting an immediate course of action if someone is hungry, if someone is in need (verses 32–35).

Like all Christians, we have been commanded to be in the world, to know the people to whom we minister, to understand their needs and challenges, to speak to them through the color and cadence of their culture (2 Corinthians 1:12). Yet we have been cautioned not to be of the world, to know the differences between who we are and who the world is, to understand the underlying causes of human need, to speak of transcending values, and to focus on eternal realities (1 John 2:15, 16). "We fix our eyes not on what is seen," Paul says to the congregation at Corinth, "but on what is unseen. For what is seen is temporary, but what is unseen is eternal" (2 Corinthians 4:18).

Acts 4:32 tells us "all the believers were one in heart and mind." Successful and effective ministry is the managing of the tensions between the conflicting demands of both the heart (in this nonmedical metaphor, the source of our emotions) and the mind (the seat of our intelligence). On a daily basis, ministry opportunities include contact and conversation with many whose hearts are despairing and whose minds are anxious (to use the words of Deuteronomy 28:65). The psalmist identifies human hearts and minds as "cunning" (Psalm 64:6). Isaiah calls our hearts "rebellious" (see Isaiah 46:8). But our passage contains this one ambiguous yet intriguing little phrase that points the way to the managing of the tension between heart and mind. Acts 4:33 says, "Much grace was upon them all."

All the tasks of ministry in the community of faith would be more acceptable, more achievable, if we would remember that *our* place in the kingdom, our gifts for ministry, and our opportunities to minister are not self-generated. They are not a reward for our goodness. They are not a payment in return for our merits. Rather, they are another unmistakable evidence of the undying love, the stubborn grace, the unquenchable, favorable disposition of a steadfast, tender, and compassionate God. And so we cry with the psalmist, "Test me, O LORD, and try me, examine my heart and my mind" (Psalm 26:2). Give us " 'wholehearted devotion and . . . a willing mind' " (1 Chronicles 28:9).

Five of us pastors from the La Sierra church went to South Africa to preach at the camp meeting in the Transvaal Conference. We arrived at camp fresh from a sobering visit to Robben Island off Capetown, where Nelson Mandela had been imprisoned for twenty-seven years—our introduction into the local history of separation and oppression. At the camp meeting we became immersed in conversations with dear people who were dealing with the church's insistence on integration: people who were hurting because of the pain of what felt to them like rejection and even betrayal, and people who were hurting because the community was taking so long in becoming fully Christian.

Two things happened that kept our eyes fixed on what we had come to South Africa to do, which was to preach about the undying grace of God. One was the way people kept coming up to Pastor Devo, a young South African, exclaiming how he had grown up, matured, and become such a fine young man—married now, with plans for a family. The community of faith had been watching and was proud of and encouraged by what they saw. And the second thing was the way people, especially young women, kept coming up to Pastor Chris, thanking her for her sermons and her insight—but more than that, for the shining example of what a committed Christian could become in God's purpose and strength. The tension was there again—this time between how much growth each of us has yet to experience and how motivating is the example of one whose life already is resting in the hands of God.

Our prayers must be for the expansion of the tensions of ministry in each of our communities of faith as well as for the continuance of the sanctified energy necessary for the successful and effective managing of the tensions.

"With great power the apostles continued to testify to the resurrection of the Lord Jesus, and much grace was upon them all" (Acts 4:33). It can be our experience as well, in all of today's tension-filled communities of faith.

*"Some power had cut the cable
that anchored the church to the Eternal Rock,
and its members were drifting away to sea without chart or compass.
What situation could be more alarming than this?"*
—ARTHUR DANIELLS, *CHRIST OUR RIGHTEOUSNESS*

*"Righteousness by faith
was not new light when it was preached in Minneapolis.
It was neglected light."*
—A. V. OLSON, *THROUGH CRISIS TO VICTORY*

*"God has rescued these truths from the companionship of error."*
—ELLEN G. WHITE, SERMON AT MINNEAPOLIS, OCTOBER 21, 1888

*"The heart of the Advent message is Christ and Him crucified."*
—QUESTIONS ON DOCTRINE

*"Have Adventists really learned the lessons of 1888,
or are we merely perpetuating the experience?"*
—GEORGE KNIGHT, *ANGRY SAINTS*

CHAPTER 15

# THE CALIFORNIA CONSPIRACY:
## *The Recovery of Grace in the Debates of 1888*

ARTHUR SPALDING CALLS THE YEARS RIGHT AFTER THE GREAT DISAPPOINT-MENT "a period of chaos" and says the believers "were a shipwrecked remnant, clinging to the spars of their disintegrated hope."[1] Attempting to explain the Disappointment and, at the same time, find the center of theological focus for those who remained, the young Adventists try out one strange theory after another.

Some keep setting new dates for the Second Coming: 1845, 1846, 1849, 1850, and on.[2] Early in 1851, Joseph Bates convinces himself that the symbolism of the Old Testament sanctuary service holds a secret the believers have missed. Bates sees the seven times the priest had to sprinkle blood on the altar, "the seven spots" he calls them, as a prophetic period of seven years that it would take for the High Priest to cleanse the sanctuary. Based on that "prophecy," combined with his belief in the heavenly sanctuary, Bates determines that Jesus will return in the fall of that year, 1851. Later, Bates confesses his error.

Others determine that the problem had not been with the timing but with the behavior of the people. A few interpret Jesus' words in Matthew 18:3 (" 'Unless you change and become like little children . . .' ") as being meant *literally.* They begin imitating babies, crawling around on all fours inside their homes and outside as well. Others teach that 1844 had ushered in the millennium of the "antitypical Sabbath," and that, in such a time, it would be a sin to work. Instead, they sit around and discuss theology. Some turn to shouting and rolling around in church to demonstrate their advanced holiness.

Later, Ellen White tells about the many "non-essential, fanciful theories" church leaders had to deal with—theories by which "the enemy strives to eclipse the great truths for this time." "Some have advocated the theory that believers should pray with their eyes open. Others teach that, because those who ministered anciently in

---

1. Arthur W. Spalding, *Origin and History of Seventh-day Adventists* (Hagerstown, Md.: Review and Herald, 1961), 136.

2. William Miller himself hung on for a few years after the Disappointment, then died on December 20, 1849.

sacred office were required, upon entering the sanctuary, to remove their sandals and wash their feet, believers now should remove their shoes when entering the house of worship. Still others refer to the sixth commandment, and declare that even the insects that torment human beings should not be killed. And some have put forth the theory that the redeemed will not have gray hair—as if this were a matter of any importance."[3]

THE ALBANY CONFERENCE

On April 29, 1845, sixty-one delegates from churches and Adventist societies meet in Albany, New York, in what became known as the Albany Conference, with William Miller presiding and Joshua V. Himes as secretary. Just six months after the Disappointment, already there are new doctrines competing for the attention and approval of the believers. In particular, the conference dealt with four troubling questions, all suggested by proponents: (1) Does Bible prophecy require a literal return of the Jews to Palestine before Jesus can return? (2) What happens to people after they die—are they conscious or unconscious in death?[4] (3) What should they do about those agitating for the observance of the seventh-day Sabbath when most believers consider the Sabbath a Jewish fable? (4) And had God shut the door of opportunity for repentance in 1844, and would it remain closed forever?

The leaders of the conference are divided on several of the subjects. Joseph Bates accepts the Sabbath only a week before the meeting in Albany begins. "The heralding of the Sabbath now became Bates's special burden and mission."[5] Himes convinces Miller that they had been mistaken on the shut-door theory. Josiah Litch joins them and says, "We erred and ran off our track."[6] Others refuse to give an inch. Joseph Turner meets Ellen Harmon in a meeting in Portland, Maine, and tries to hypnotize her into agreeing with his position. It doesn't work! Pastor S. S. Snow begins calling himself "Elijah, the Prophet," ending up "in wildest fanaticism and complete separation from his Adventist brethren."[7] The leaders begin to realize that the doctrines "were not detached, independent, unrelated points of truth. Rather, they together constitute the base of a coordinated *system* of truth."[8]

PROBLEMATIC PASSAGES ABOUT THE LAW

Another issue that troubles the early Adventists is their understanding of biblical law. As the Sabbath of the fourth commandment begins to hold an increasingly significant place in the thinking of the believers, they become more concerned about answering objections to the keeping of the law.

On the positive side are all those Bible passages that uphold and praise the law: "The law of the LORD is perfect" (Psalm 19:7). "I long for your salvation, O LORD, and your law is my delight" (119:174). "The law is holy, and the commandment is holy, righteous and good" (Romans 7:12). " 'Do not think that I have come to abolish the Law or the Prophets;

3. Ellen G. White, *Gospel Workers* (Hagerstown, Md.: Review and Herald, 1948), 313.

4. "At that time probably three fourths of Adventists believed in the conscious state of the dead, but the opposite doctrine was gaining." (Spalding, 154.)

5. LeRoy Edwin Froom, *Movement of Destiny* (Hagerstown, Md.: Review and Herald, 1971), 81.

6. Josiah Litch, *The Morning Watch*, April 24, 1845.

7. Spalding, 162.

8. Froom, 87.

I have not come to abolish them but to fulfill them' " (Matthew 5:17).

But then there are those problematic passages: " 'Unless your righteousness surpasses that of the Pharisees and the teachers of the law, you will certainly not enter the kingdom of heaven' " (verse 20). " 'Woe to you, teachers of the law and Pharisees, you hypocrites! You are like whitewashed tombs, which look beautiful on the outside but on the inside are full of dead men's bones and everything unclean' " (23:27). "You are not under law, but under grace" (Romans 6:14). "[God] forgave us all our sins, having canceled the written code, with its regulations, that was against us and that stood opposed to us; he took it away, nailing it to the cross" (Colossians 2:13, 14).

And, especially, the book of Galatians seems to challenge the Sabbatarian position: "By observing the law no one will be justified" (2:16). " 'I do not set aside the grace of God, for if righteousness could be gained through the law, Christ died for nothing!' " (verse 21). "All who rely on observing the law are under a curse" (3:10). "The law was put in charge to lead us to Christ that we might be justified by faith. Now that faith has come, we are no longer under the supervision of the law" (verses 24, 25).

## INTERPRETING THE PASSAGES

Throughout the late 1840s and early 1850s, the position of the Advent believers (including Joseph Bates, Uriah Smith, James White, and J. N. Andrews) is that the law in the book of Galatians is the *moral law,* the Ten Commandments. The position is argued strongly in J. H. Waggoner's 1854 book, *The Law of God: An Examination of the Testimony of Both Testaments.*

But in 1856, Stephen Pierce writes that the law in Galatians is the *ceremonial law,* and Pierce's position becomes the position of the Seventh-day Adventist denomination for the next thirty years. In 1876, evangelist Dudley Canright states the position again in his book *Two Laws.*

In the 1880s, Alonzo Jones and E. J. Waggoner (the son of J. H. Waggoner), challenge the church's position. Both men are teachers at Healdsburg College in northern California and editors of *The Signs of the Times.* In a series of nine articles (July 8–September 2, 1886), Waggoner takes the stance that the law in Galatians is the moral law, the Ten Commandments. Even the commandments are meant to lead us to Christ, Waggoner writes.

The change of interpretation is opposed from church headquarters in Battle Creek, especially by Uriah Smith, the editor of the *Review and Herald,* and George Butler, the president of the General Conference. "For 30 years our position has held that the law in Galatians has been the Ceremonial Law," the leaders argue. "To change that interpretation now would undermine our commitment to the Sabbath, by agreeing that the Fourth Commandment had been nailed to the Cross." In fact, "Butler regarded the 'new' interpretation as a threat to the very heart of Adventist theology," which he believed to be "the continuing sacredness of the seventh-day Sabbath embedded in the moral law."[9] (A. V. Olson points out, "as the result of the constant emphasis upon the law and the Sabbath in lectures, sermons, and debates, Adventist preachers became known as legalists, and were accused of believing in salvation through works rather than through faith in Christ's work for them. It was a common charge that the Adventists did not really believe in Christ and His work of grace."[10])

---

9. George R. Knight, *From 1888 to Apostasy* (Hagerstown, Md.: Review and Herald, 1987), 24.
10. A. V. Olson, *Through Crisis to Victory, 1888–1901* (Hagerstown, Md.: Review and Herald, 1966), 11.

Smith and Butler also contend that interpreting the law as the moral law would overthrow confidence in the testimonies of Ellen White. The two leaders remember a letter she wrote in the 1850s to J. H. Waggoner in which they say she insisted that the law in Galatians is *not* the moral law.

Butler presses his point of view. In 1886, he visits Healdsburg College, trying to persuade Jones and Waggoner to change their minds. He enlists Ellen White's help in a series of letters to her. And he publishes a book he calls *Law in the Book of Galatians*. He sends the book to every delegate to the General Conference session in Battle Creek and submits it to a theological committee, which splits in its conclusions, five to four.

At this time, Dudley Canright again becomes part of the discussion. One of the denomination's most effective evangelists, Canright grasps Waggoner's points.[11] Unfortunately, he concludes that if the church had been wrong on the point of the law in Galatians, it may have been wrong on other points as well. He asks the General Conference to drop his membership, a request that is granted on February 17, 1887. The General Conference president writes in the *Review*, "Canright thought we were exalting the law above Christ." Two years later, in 1889, Canright produces a scathing critique of the church titled *Seventh-day Adventism Renounced*. He was never able to "adjust his law-oriented theology to account for the truth of the gospel of salvation by grace through faith," George Knight

explains. "He saw no option but to throw over the law and join the gospel-oriented Baptists. Subsequently he would become the Adventists' most formidable opponent."[12]

Waggoner also responds to Butler's opposition, writing a book he calls *Gospel in the Book of Galatians*. Before the book is published, however, Ellen White writes to Waggoner and Jones from Basel, Switzerland. In a letter dated February 18, 1887, she says much that seems to agree with the two teachers. There is a danger, she writes, "of our ministers dwelling too much on doctrines, preaching altogether too many discourses on argumentative subjects when their own souls need practical godliness. . . . The wonders of redemption are dwelt upon altogether too lightly. We need these matters presented more fully and continuously in our discourses and in our papers. We need our own hearts to be deeply stirred with these deep and saving truths. There is danger of keeping the discourses and the articles in the paper like Cain's offering, Christless."[13]

But she also reproves Jones and Waggoner for the public nature of their debate with Smith and Butler. Then she adds that she had been looking for the 1850s letter to J. H. Waggoner and can't find it. She remembers telling him that his position was incorrect, she says, but she can't remember what was incorrect about it. It might even have been, she continues, that she had been counseling him against the public nature of the controversy.

Someone forwards the letter to George Butler and when he reads it, he sees it as a

---

11. Canright had worked in California with E. J. Waggoner's father, J. H. Waggoner. In the summer of 1875, the two evangelists held meetings together in Gilroy and Hollister, before Canright was called to the East Coast by the General Conference. See Harold O. McCumber, *The Advent Message in the Golden West* (Nampa, Idaho: Pacific Press®, 1968), 114, 115.

12. George R. Knight, *Angry Saints* (Hagerstown, Md.: Review and Herald, 1989), 27.

13. White, *Counsels to Writers and Editors* (Nashville: Southern Publishing, 1946), 75–82.

confirmation of his position. Within weeks he uses the letter, apparently without permission, in an editorial in the *Review*. Now Ellen White writes quickly to him. In a letter dated April 5, 1887, her question to Butler basically is "What in the world were you thinking?!!" She repeats the same cautions about public debate and then instructs that, in consideration of fairness, Waggoner would have to be given the opportunity to present his views publicly. "Don't be afraid or too proud to yield," she concludes. "We want the truth as it is in Jesus."

On August 28, Butler announces in the *Review* that the Ministerial Institute at the General Conference session to be held in Minneapolis in October 1888 will consider the topic of the law in Galatians. Presentations will explain both sides of the issue.

As you can imagine, the months before the session are busy with "trial runs" of the presentations. In California, Jones and Waggoner are invited to camp meetings and workers meetings. S. N. Haskell, president of the California Conference, attends the meetings.

As the General Conference session approaches, one California pastor, William Healy, writes to the leaders of the denomination that Jones and Waggoner are hatching a "California conspiracy." Healy reports that the two theologians are working on a secret, sinister scheme to overthrow traditional Seventh-day Adventist theology.

In Battle Creek, Butler becomes physically ill. Quickly he reprints his 1886 book for the 1888 delegates and then sends a telegram to all delegates in which he urges, "Stand by the old landmarks."

However, Butler's biggest effort by far is an almost forty-page-long letter to Ellen White. In it, he accuses her of betraying him. He asks her to endorse the "true" view, which, of course, is his. "It would be quite a shock to me," Butler

## WAGGONER ON RIGHTEOUSNESS

From E. J. Waggoner's presentations at the 1888 General Conference, edited and published in 1890 as *Christ and His Righteousness* (Oakland, Calif.: Pacific Press®, 1890).

"For one to be judged 'a doer of the law' it would be necessary that he had kept the law in its fullest measure every moment of his life. If he had come short of this, he could not be said to have done the law."

"What a deplorable condition! We must have the righteousness of the law or we cannot enter heaven, and yet the law has no righteousness for one of us. It will not yield to our most persistent and energetic efforts the smallest portion of that holiness without which no man can see the Lord."

"Since the best efforts of a sinful man have not the least effect toward producing righteousness, it is evident that the only way it can come to him is as a gift. That righteousness is a gift is plainly stated by Paul in Rom. 5:17: 'For if by one man's offense death reigned by one; much more they which receive abundance of grace and of the gift of righteousness shall reign in life by One, Jesus Christ.'"

"Surely, this is a profitable exchange for the sinner, and it is no loss to God, for He is infinite in holiness, and the supply can never be diminished."

"What of the declaration that He 'will by no means clear the guilty'? That is perfectly in keeping with His long-suffering, abundant goodness. He does something which is far better: *He removes the guilt*, so that the one formerly guilty does not need to be cleared, he is justified, and counted as though he never had sinned."

"It is not for our goodness that He loves us, but because of our need."

adds, that "after studying the question so long and having it seem so clear to me, if it should be shown to you the position I held was wrong."

Ellen never responds. On October 1, 1888, just before the session, Butler condemns her silence, blames her for his broken health, and threatens her, telling her to come up with "the proper interpretation" or lose his support of her work.

As Ellen and her son arrive at the session, she turns to Willie and says, "We're in for it." Willie claims to know nothing about the controversy. I was "innocent as a goose" he says. He further states that he didn't even know "my friends at BC [Battle Creek] were talking about us."[14]

### THE MINISTERIAL INSTITUTE

Butler doesn't show up at Minneapolis. His health is gone, and he announces that he will be retiring. R. M. Kilgore, president of the Illinois Conference, appeals to the delegates not to decide the issue. It is "cowardly" to discuss the topic without the General Conference president, Kilgore offers. Ellen White, sitting nearby, notes, "Kilgore's position is not of God."

Jones and Uriah Smith begin the session with a debate on the ten horns of Daniel 7. The Minneapolis *Journal* remarks that the Adventists tackle difficult theological problems "with about the same industry that an earnest man would assail a cord of wood."[15] Smith, the editor of the *Review and Herald,* the author of the book *Thoughts on Daniel and the Revelation,* and the champion of the church's traditional interpretation on the subject, takes some of his initial time to complain that they are even discussing the topic. He considers it

"evil" and "utterly unnecessary" to be talking about another interpretation, and assures the listeners he knows nothing about this "new" truth. Jones responds by saying, "Elder Smith has told you he does not know anything about this matter. I do. And I don't want you to blame me for what he does not know." Ellen, still sitting nearby, responds, "Not so sharp, Brother Jones. Not so sharp!"

When it is Waggoner's turn, he states that the purpose of the law is to point out our sin and show us that we need a Savior. It is the *moral* law, he says, that does this. Indeed, that is the intention of the moral law—to lead us to Christ so "that we might be justified by faith" (Galatians 3:24). Waggoner and Jones establish that "no one can enter the kingdom of God without being clad in the spotless robe of Christ's righteousness. This robe can neither be purchased with silver and gold nor earned by good works. This message was a clarion call to make Christ and His righteousness the center of all our living and our preaching. It placed special emphasis on righteousness by faith as a real personal experience rather than a mere theory."[16]

Speaking about the experience a few years later, Jones recalls how some in Minneapolis had rejected the message, while others had accepted it with all their hearts. "People had worn out their souls almost, trying to manufacture a sufficient degree of righteousness to stand through the time of trouble, and meet the Saviour in peace when He comes; but they had not accomplished it. These were so glad to find out that God had already manufactured a robe of righteousness and offered it as a free gift to every one that would take it, that would answer now, and in the time of the plagues,

---

14. Willie C. White, *Letter to Dan Jones,* April 8, 1890.
15. Minneapolis *Journal,* October 19, 1888.
16. A. V. Olson, 35.

and in the time of judgment, and to all eternity, that they received it gladly just as God gave it, and heartily thanked the Lord for it."[17]

On October 7, 1895, Elder A. O. Tait writes a letter to Willie White, in which he remembers: "I found that doctrine just the food that my poor soul needed there at Minneapolis, and I was converted at that meeting, and have been rejoicing in the light of it ever since."

On the other hand, J. H. Morrison, president of the Iowa Conference, protests that Adventists always have believed in justification by faith and that the subject is being "overstressed." Morrison is fearful that the law might lose its important place in Seventh-day Adventist theology.

Members of the board of trustees of the Ellen G. White Estate, writing about the Minneapolis meetings in the "Historical Foreword" to the book *Testimonies to Ministers and Gospel Workers* (1962), report on the differences in the way the message was received: "To many, the message of righteousness by faith struck home, and there was a response of heart and soul which led to victorious experience in personal Christian living. There were others who identified themselves with certain cautious and conservative leaders from Battle Creek who saw what they thought were perils in some of the teachings presented. When the Conference came to a close, these men had failed to gain the blessing God had in store for them."[18]

Ellen White recalls the meeting like this:

The Lord in His great mercy sent a most precious message to His people through Elders Waggoner and Jones. This message was to bring more prominently before the world the uplifted Saviour, the sacrifice for the sins of the whole world. It presented justification through faith in the Surety.[19]

The present message, justification by faith, is a message from God.[20]

You will meet with those who will say, "you are too much excited over the matter. You are too much in earnest. You should not be reaching for the righteousness of Christ, and making so much of that. You should preach the law." As a people we have preached the law until we are as dry as the hills of Gilboa, that had neither dew nor rain. We must preach Christ in the law, and there will be sap and nourishment in the preaching that will be as food to the famishing flock of God. We must not trust in our own merits at all, but in the merits of Jesus of Nazareth.[21]

## LEARNING FROM 1888

The issues of 1888 continue to be with us. Even the question of whether the church received or rejected the message remains a matter of debate. Nevertheless, the message of Christ's righteousness, the everlasting gospel of God's saving grace, was placed so firmly in a central position that no one can ever again discuss Adventist theology without referring to this cardinal, fundamental feature of our faith.

Minneapolis also reminds us that the real issue in Christianity is not which law it is in the book of Galatians. Of course, we don't accept the notion that we need no longer honor

17. A. T. Jones, *General Conference Bulletin*, February 13, 1893, 243, 244.
18. See *Testimonies to Ministers and Gospel Workers* (Nampa, Idaho: Pacific Press®, 1962), xxiii–xxxvi.
19. Ellen G. White, *Letter 57*, 1895.
20. Ellen G. White, *Review and Herald*, September 3, 1889.
21. Ellen G. White, *Review and Herald*, March 11, 1890.

the Ten Commandments or that obedience to God's law has been nailed to the cross of Christ. But the essential purpose of Galatians is not to define the differences between moral and ceremonial law. The essential purpose of Galatians is to establish beyond question *the ground of our justification*. On this issue, Galatians is crystal clear. No one is justified by observing the law (whatever law it is), but by faith in Jesus Christ (2:16). Clearly, no one is justified before God by the law (whatever law) because the righteous live by faith (3:11). Those who are trying to be justified by law (either the ceremonial or the moral law) have been alienated from Christ; they have fallen away from grace. (5:4).

Christ is the end of the law (whatever law! any law!) *for righteousness* (Romans 10:4). Once we see Jesus face to face, we easily give up all the law-keeping we do to try to merit heaven, all law-keeping for justification, all law-keeping to make God love us more. " 'If righteousness could be gained through the law, Christ died for nothing!' " (Galatians 2:21). How could it possibly be clearer than that?

No wonder we Adventists don't need to be afraid of grace. We understand that the law has led us to Jesus (Galatians 3:24), where we are justified, saved, redeemed, ransomed, and brought back to life. And not by anything we have done, not even by our obedience to God's perfect law, but by grace alone, through faith alone, in Jesus Christ alone.

# GRACE IN QUESTION
## CHAPTER 15: THE CALIFORNIA CONSPIRACY

The fledgling group of Advent believers attempted to recover from the Great Disappointment by throwing themselves into the development of a group of doctrines that would characterize their new church. The passages concerning law in the book of Galatians gave them particular trouble and ultimately had to be dealt with at the General Conference session of 1888. The debates of '88 placed Christ and His righteousness in the center of Adventist belief.

1. Have you ever been exposed to strange ideas about the conditions people must meet to get to heaven, like the ones Ellen White speaks of on pages 203, 204? What were those conditions? How does knowing that we're saved by grace alone help us meet such beliefs?

2. Talk about laws you're glad are in effect—what laws are you happy to obey? Traffic laws? Personal property laws?

3. Discuss what it means to present Christian topics in a "Christless" manner. What turns a Christless presentation into a Christ-centered one?

4. What's the proper way for Christians to relate to people who disagree with their theology—especially with those who refuse to accept the grace of God?

5. Read again the passages from Galatians listed on this page. Are you convinced that we can do nothing to merit heaven, to justify ourselves, or to make God love us more than He already does?

# GRACE NOTES
## ACTS 13; 14—THE GODS OF GALATIA

On Paul and Barnabas's first journey to open up the doors of faith to new believers (Acts 14:26, 27), they travel into the large Roman province of Galatia (13:14). In the Galatian cities, the apostles encounter three distinct religious groups. It's probably not too strong to say that these encounters shaped their ministry.

The first encounter is with Jews and non-Jews who warm to the good news about Jesus. This gospel preaching already had begun to characterize the young Christian church:

> Day after day, in the temple courts and from house to house, they never stopped teaching and proclaiming the good news that Jesus is the Christ (Acts 5:42).

> Then Philip began with that very passage of Scripture and told him the good news about Jesus (8:35).

> Then Peter began to speak: . . . "You know the message God sent to the people of Israel, telling the good news of peace through Jesus Christ, who is Lord of all" (10:34, 36).

> Men from Cyprus and Cyrene, went to Antioch and began to speak to Greeks also, telling them the good news about the Lord Jesus (11:20).

Now, Paul and Barnabas strengthen this infant preaching tradition throughout Galatia. On a Sabbath morning in the synagogue in Pisidian Antioch (13:14–16), Paul summarizes his sermon with these words: " 'We tell you the good news' " (verse 32). In the countryside around Lystra and Derbe, "they continued to preach the good news" (14:6, 7). In Lystra, Paul announces, " 'We are bringing you good news' " (verse 15). In Derbe, "they preached the good news in that city" (verse 21).

When the congregations in the synagogues are dismissed, "many of the Jews and devout converts to Judaism followed Paul and Barnabas, who talked with them and urged them to continue in the grace of God" (13:43). On some Sabbaths, "almost the whole city gathered to hear the word of the Lord" (verse 44). The Gentiles who believe are especially glad about the good news, and the gospel is honored (verse 48). The message of salvation by grace alone through faith in Jesus "spread like wildfire all through the region" (verse 49, *The Message*).

Q. What were the two perspectives that caused conflict in Minneapolis?

Q. Which three religious groups are contending for attention in this encounter in Galatia?

The second encounter with religious groups comes in Lystra, where a man with crippled feet, who had been "lame from birth and had never walked" (14:8), is healed. The people of Lystra watch the man jump up and begin walking (verse 10), and they conclude that Paul and Barnabas must be gods. Soon the people are joined by priests from just outside of the city, where they serve in a temple that is dedicated to Zeus, the supreme god of the Greek pantheon.

Across the Aegean Sea, on the far side of Greece, stands another temple to Zeus, a Doric-style temple at Olympia that contains a statue of Zeus that is one of the seven wonders of the ancient world. When Paul is in Galatia, the huge statue, created by the brilliant Athenian sculptor Pheidias, is already five hundred years old. The statue sits on a base that is about twenty feet wide and three feet high. The statue itself is forty feet high—equivalent to a modern four-story building. A Greek named Pausanias describes the statue: "On his head is a sculpted wreath of olive sprays. In his right hand he holds a figure of Victory made from ivory and gold. . . . In his left hand, he holds a scepter inlaid with every kind of metal, with an eagle perched on the scepter. His sandals are made of gold, as is his robe. His garments are carved with animals and with lilies. The throne is decorated with gold, precious stones, ebony, and ivory."

So sure of their gods are these priests of Zeus in Galatia that the only explanation they can imagine for the healing of the crippled man is that the gods had " 'come down to us in human form' " (verse 11). To the site of the healing, they bring bulls and wreaths for the crowd to sacrifice to Paul and Barnabas. They proclaim that Barnabas is none other than Zeus himself, and that Paul, apparently the more talkative one, is Hermes, the great messenger of the gods (verse 12).

Paul tries to explain that the two of them are " 'only men, human like you' " (verse 15). But not even these public denials seem to dissuade the crowd (verse 18). The good news for these people is that Zeus has honored them because of some exemplary behavior on their part, some action worthy of the smile of the gods.

Paul and Barnabas encounter a third religious group in Galatia. It's not a new group to them; they've done battle with them before. Paul will later refer to them as "the circumcision group" (Galatians 2:12), "perverters of the gospel" (see 1:7), "false brothers" (2:4), "hypocrites" (see verse 13), and "agitators" (5:12). These men, who came from Jerusalem, from James, insist that God judges "by external appearance" (2:6) and demand that, before the Gentiles can be counted as Christians won by the grace of Christ, they first have to obey the laws that all good Jews respect. Paul claims that these Jews are "not acting in line with the truth of the gospel" (verse 14).

In his epistle to the Galatians, Paul tells of speaking directly to Peter and the other "Judaizers" who had made a god of the law. We know, Paul says, " 'that a man is not justified by observing the law, but by faith in Jesus Christ. So we, too, have put our faith in Christ Jesus that we may be justified by faith in Christ and not by observing the law, because by observing the law no one will be justified' " (verse 16). "You who are trying to be justified by law have been alienated from Christ; you have fallen away from grace" (5:4).

The same three religious groups remain in the church today. One group seems to be in alignment with the great gods of the secular world—the gods who demand certain behaviors from us before they respond or pay attention. We work hard for them.

Another group makes considerable religious-sounding fervor, demanding that we must be known primarily as law keepers, who, if we do well enough in our law-keeping, will win the approval of God and merit His favor.

And finally, there are those who acknowledge their sinfulness (" ' "God, have mercy on me, a sinner" ' " [Luke 18:13].), who admit to their weakness (" 'My grace is sufficient for you, for my power is made perfect in weakness' " [2 Corinthians 12:9].), and who eagerly accept the gospel—the good news that Jesus is the Christ, the One who saves us by His grace alone.

*"There is not one in one hundred who understands for himself
the Bible truth on this subject."*
—ELLEN G. WHITE, *REVIEW AND HERALD*, SEPTEMBER 3, 1889

*"No longer must he strive to find some worthiness in himself,
some meritorious deed by which to gain the favor of God."*
—ELLEN G. WHITE, *SIGNS OF THE TIMES*, JULY 4, 1892

*"The sweetest melodies that come from God through human lips—
justification by faith, and the righteousness of Christ."*
—ELLEN G. WHITE, *REVIEW AND HERALD*, APRIL 4, 1893

*"By His words Christ communicated knowledge of the very highest order,
telling [humans] what they must do to be saved."*
—ELLEN G. WHITE, *GENERAL CONFERENCE BULLETIN*, APRIL 1, 1899

*"Our churches are dying for the want of teaching
on the subject of the righteousness of Christ."*
—ELLEN G. WHITE, *GOSPEL WORKERS*

## CHAPTER 16
# THE CENTRAL TRUTH:
### *The Annotation of Grace in the Writings of Ellen White*

LMOST TEN YEARS AGO, I BEGAN NOTICING, AND SOON AFTERWARDS collecting, anything a bit unusual that had to do with grace. I had become immersed in the doctrinal study of grace, but, frequently, in the midst of all that study, I would bump up against grace in unexpected places: strange book titles, curious quotations, and out of the ordinary objects. They all brought smiles to my face, and I decided to hang on to all of them.

*Grace Is Not a Blue-Eyed Blond,* written in 1968 while Grace Kelly was Princess Grace of Monaco, was a gift "to the Stuart Tyner Grace Library" from my long-time friend Chris Blake. It really is a book about the doctrine of grace.[1] *Saving Grace* is not about the doctrine of grace. It's a Julie Garwood romance novel.[2] *Days of Grace* isn't about the doctrine either. It's the encouraging autobiography of legendary tennis star Arthur Ashe.[3] Walter Wangerin's *Miz Lil and the Chronicles of Grace* is about a pastor at the Grace Lutheran Church on Gum Street.[4] Hank Ketchum's *Dennis the Menace: Prayers and Graces* is a cute little collection of bedtime and mealtime prayers.[5] I'm still not sure how to categorize Neal Cassady's *Grace Beats Karma: Letters from Prison, 1958–1960,* but I'm pretty sure it wasn't meant to be doctrinal.[6] Then, of course, there are all those books about *Graceland,* at least one of them subtitled *The Living Legacy of Elvis.* That's not about the doctrine of salvation either! I've heard about but haven't located yet a treasury of sports writing by women writers called *A Kind of Grace.* Can't wait to read that one.

The pages of the *Los Angeles Times* are good places to find curious grace quotations. "Come hear the silence," the newspaper invites before a week of Ravi Shankar

1. R. Lofton Hudson, *Grace Is Not a Blue-Eyed Blond* (Waco, Tex.: Word Books, 1968).

2. Julie Garwood, *Saving Grace* (New York: Pocket Books, 1993).

3. Arthur Ashe, *Days of Grace* (New York: Alfred A. Knopf, 1993).

4. Walter Wangerin, Jr., *Miz Lil and the Chronicles of Grace* (New York: HarperCollins Publishers, 1988).

5. Hank Ketchum, *Dennis the Menace: Prayers and Graces* (Louisville, Ky.: Westminster John Knox Press, 1993).

6. Neal Cassady, *Grace Beats Karma: Letters from Prison, 1958–60* (New York: Blast Books, 1993).

## DEAD MAN WALKING

What do you think movie critic Richard Schickel means by the following comment in his review of the movie *Dead Man Walking*? "How hard it is to achieve even modest states of *grace* in this world. How patiently we must work to achieve them." —*Time,* January 8, 1996, page 69, emphasis supplied.

Does he mean the same thing that Sister Helen Prejean means when she writes in her book *Dead Man Walking* that while eating his last meal, convicted killer Patrick Sonnier seemed "to have found some space, some *grace,* some kind of lagoon in the present moment, even though close by are white, crashing rapids"? —Helen Prejean, *Dead Man Walking* (New York: Vintage Books, 1993), 205, emphasis supplied.

Do you think either of them means the same thing that Hebrews 4:16 means when it says, "Let us then approach the throne of *grace* with confidence, so that we may receive mercy and find *grace* to help us in our time of need"? (Emphasis supplied.)

In the sports section, a Seattle government official is quoted answering a question about the possible move of the Seattle Seahawks football team to Los Angeles: "There can be no *grace* in breaking the faith of the community that has supported the Seahawks for all these years."

Of course, you can find the confusing quotes everywhere. On the Oprah Winfrey show, Barbara Walters remembers Johnny Carson as "a man with more *grace.*" When Bob Dole retires from the Senate, he credits the *grace* of God for permitting him to walk again after a battlefield injury. At the Republican National Convention, Colin Powell refers to the United States as "a country that exists by the *grace* of a divine Providence." Golfer Sally Krueger hits a seven-iron during a Pebble Beach Pro-Am tournament, and the ESPN commentator remarks, "Isn't that a picture of *grace?*" Photographer Tom Kelley says of Marilyn Monroe that she was "*graceful* as an otter." Richard Nixon resigns from the presidency and leaves Washington, D.C., with these words: "May God's *grace* be with you in all the days ahead."

I took a picture in Manhattan of a bagel shop called New Grace; they advertised "free delivery"! I have an Arizona Diamondback jersey, number 17, hanging in my closet, a Christmas present from my daughter-in-law Jennifer. The name on the back of the jersey? "Grace"—for Mark Grace, the Diamondback's first baseman for a couple of seasons.

ELLEN WHITE'S FOUR USAGES OF GRACE

Ellen White refers to grace in at least 12,858 separate places.[7] Not that she uses the word 12,858 times. The number, taken from a White Estate document, enumerates the different places in all of Ellen White's different

sitar concerts in the Santa Monica Civic Auditorium, "Seven blissful evenings of *grace* and celebration." In a section about "Hot Tickets" for the Orange County Performing Arts Center, the paper praises jazz legend Dave Brubeck for "continuing to push the musical envelope with daring, soaring *grace.*" Also in the entertainment section, an ad for a TV miniseries includes the sentence: "Witness a powerful family's fall from *grace* and their season in purgatory." In a news story about the rescue of two people during a flood in Yuba City, the paper quotes a rescue worker who says, "By the *grace* of God they were great swimmers."

---

7. I have seen another listing where the number is even larger. But this is the number I was given when I started reading everything she wrote about grace, and these are the quotations I'm using for research for this chapter.

letters, books, chapters, and pages where she writes about grace—twelve thousand eight hundred and fifty eight separate places! In almost every one of those places, she uses the word itself more than once. Before I die, I intend to read every single reference, but that's not something you do quickly, and right now I'm at just a little over three thousand. I've got a long way to go! As is true of all those references to grace in the pages of the *Los Angeles Times,* so with the 12,858 Ellen White passages: To determine the exact intent and meaning of each reference, one needs to know the context. Without the context, things can get confusing, and one can end up with the entirely wrong idea.

In many places, the word *grace* appears in a Bible passage that Ellen White is quoting. For example, she quotes John 1:14: " 'The Word was made flesh, and dwelt among us, and we beheld His glory, the glory as of the only begotten of the Father, full of grace and truth.' "[8] She quotes 2 Corinthians 13:14 on page 52 of the same book: " 'The grace of the Lord Jesus Christ, and the love of God, and the communion of the Holy Ghost, be with you all.' " Here are a couple more such quotations: " 'By grace are you saved through faith; and that not of yourselves; it is the gift of God; not of works, lest any one should boast. Ephesians 2:8.' "[9] " ' "Neither count I my life dear unto myself, so that I might finish my course with joy, and the ministry, which I have received of the Lord Jesus, to testify to the gospel of the grace of God." Acts 20:24.' "[10]

Sometimes Ellen White uses *grace* in the same way we use the term when we say that a beautiful older woman has aged with grace, or a proper English gentleman treats people with grace. "Cultivate cheerfulness," she says in *Medical Ministry,* "for this is an excellent grace."[11] In *Counsels on Health* she says, "Humility is a precious grace, peculiarly pleasing to God."[12] In an article in the *Review and Herald* in 1881, she refers to "the grace of meekness."[13] In another place, she calls attention to "the grace of true politeness."[14] In *Child Guidance* she points out that reverence is "another precious grace that should be carefully cherished."[15]

If we wanted to make a point about God's redeeming grace—about His everlasting, unquenchable love that declares us to be justified and decides to treat us just as if we'd never sinned—we wouldn't impose that understanding of grace into a sentence about grace being cheerfulness, or humility, or meekness, would we? In these references, Ellen White is not talking about salvation or justification or forgiveness. She's talking about the beauty and attractiveness of Christlike character qualities.

JUSTIFYING GRACE

Often, when Ellen White does want to talk about grace in terms of salvation or justification or forgiveness, she identifies grace with

8. Ellen G. White, *The Faith I Live By* (Washington, D.C.: Review and Herald, 1958), 17.

9. White, *Review and Herald,* January 29, 1895.

10. White, *The Acts of the Apostles* (Mountain View, Calif.: Pacific Press®, 1911), 393.

11. White, *Medical Ministry* (Mountain View, Calif.: Pacific Press®, 1963), 213.

12. White, *Counsels on Health* (Mountain View, Calif.: Pacific Press®, 1923), 590.

13. White, *Review and Herald,* January 25, 1881.

14. White, *Conflict and Courage* (Washington, D. C.: Review and Herald, 1970), 352.

15. White, *Child Guidance* (Nashville: Southern Publishing Association, 1954), 80.

unmistakable clarity. We are *"justified by His grace."* [16] "The gospel of Christ is from beginning to end the gospel of *saving grace."* [17] "Full and free is the gift of *saving grace."* [18] "The idea of doing anything to merit *the grace of pardon* is fallacy from beginning to end." [19] "The disciples proclaimed the message of *redeeming grace."* [20] "By the grace of Christ we are *saved."* [21] "God's *pardoning grace* . . ." [22] "God's *forgiving grace* . . ." [23]

How could she possibly be clearer than when she points out that we can do *nothing* to merit saving grace or to earn our way to heaven? Look closely at these comments:

Grace is an attribute of God exercised toward undeserving human beings. We did not seek for it, but it was sent in search of us. God rejoices to bestow His grace upon us, not because we are worthy, but because we are so utterly unworthy. Our only claim to His mercy is our great need. [24]

We owe everything to God's free grace. Grace in the covenant ordained our adoption. Grace in the Saviour effected our redemption, our regeneration, and our exaltation to heirship with Christ. Not because we first loved him, did God love us; but "while we were yet sinners," Christ died for us, making full and abundant provision for our redemption. Although by our disobedience we have merited God's displeasure and condemnation, yet he has not forsaken us, leaving us to grapple with the power of the enemy. [25]

Christ came to ransom and redeem us. We cannot purchase anything from God. It is only by grace, the free gift of God in Christ, that we are saved. [26]

Let the subject be made distinct and plain that it is not possible to effect anything in our standing before God or in the gift of God to us through creature merit. Should faith and works purchase the gift of salvation for anyone, then the Creator is under obligation to the creature. Here is an opportunity for falsehood to be accepted as truth. If any man can merit salvation by anything he may do, then he is in the same position as the Catholic to do penance for his sins. Salvation, then, is partly of debt, that may be earned as wages. If man cannot, by any of his good works, merit salvation, then it must be wholly of grace, received by man as a sinner because he receives and believes in Jesus. It is wholly a free gift. Justification by faith is placed beyond controversy. And all this controversy is ended, as soon

---

16. White, *Signs of the Times,* September 5, 1892, emphasis supplied.

17. White, *Evangelism* (Washington, D.C.: Review and Herald, 1946), 552, emphasis supplied.

18. White, *God's Amazing Grace* (Washington, D.C.: Review and Herald, 1973), 179, emphasis supplied.

19. White, *Faith and Works* (Nashville: Southern Publishing, 1979), 24, emphasis supplied.

20. White, *God's Amazing Grace,* 218, emphasis supplied.

21. White, *Review and Herald,* July 25, 1899, emphasis supplied.

22. White, *Christ's Object Lessons* (Washington, D.C.: Review and Herald, 1941), 251, emphasis supplied.

23. White, *Reflecting Christ* (Washington, D.C.: Review and Herald, 1985), 78, emphasis supplied.

24. White, *The Ministry of Healing* (Mountain View, Calif.: Pacific Press®, 1909), 161.

25. White, *Review and Herald,* October 15, 1908.

26. White, *That I May Know Him* (Washington, D.C.: Review and Herald, 1964), 83.

as the matter is settled that the merits of fallen man in his good works can never procure eternal life for him.[27]

We must learn in the school of Christ. Nothing but His righteousness can entitle us to one of the blessings of the covenant of grace. We have long desired and tried to obtain these blessings but have not received them because we have cherished the idea that we could do something to make ourselves worthy of them. We have not looked away from ourselves, believing that Jesus is a living Saviour.[28]

Since we can be saved only through the grace of God, which is a free gift, why is it that man will, to his own hurt, lift himself up in pride and take glory to himself for his supposed good works? The divine favor, the grace of God bestowed upon us through Jesus Christ, is too precious to be given in exchange for any supposed meritorious work on the part of finite, erring man. Man has nothing in himself. The most exalted talent does not originate from man, but is the endowment of his Creator, and can purchase nothing from God. Gold and silver cannot buy the favor of God; for the wealth of the world is the intrusted talent of the Lord. Let no one think that costly offerings to benevolent enterprises will elevate him in the sight of God, or purchase for him the favor of Heaven, or procure for him a place in the mansions which Jesus has gone to prepare

for those who love him. The precious blood of Christ is wholly efficacious.[29]

Christ has made the way by dying our sacrifice, by living our example, by becoming our great high priest. He declares, "I am the way, the truth, and the life." If by any efforts of our own we could advance one step toward the ladder, the words of Christ would not be true.[30]

What more could she say to make it clear? Salvation through Christ alone "is wholly a free gift," "wholly of grace," "wholly efficacious," "not because we are worthy." "It is only by grace."

Yet some people still are not sure about Ellen White's stance on grace. Many think grace is too general, not "peculiar" enough, not really Adventist. Not enough of the distinctive-three-angels'-messages-commandment-keeping-truth for the last days. But listen to this:

The message of the gospel of His grace was to be given to the church in clear and distinct lines, that the world should no longer say that Seventh-day Adventists talk the law, the law, but do not teach or believe Christ.[31]

Of all professing Christians, Seventh-day Adventists should be foremost in uplifting Christ before the world. The proclamation of the third angel's message calls for the presentation of the Sabbath truth. This truth, with others included in

27. White, *Faith and Works,* 19, 20.
28. White, *Faith and Works,* 36.
29. White, *Review and Herald,* January 29, 1895.
30. White, *Review and Herald,* November 4, 1890.
31. White, *Testimonies to Ministers and Gospel Workers* (Mountain View, Calif.: Pacific Press®, 1923), 92.

the message, is to be proclaimed; but the great center of attraction, Christ Jesus, must not be left out. It is at the cross of Christ that mercy and truth meet together, and righteousness and peace kiss each other. The sinner must be led to look to Calvary; with the simple faith of a little child he must trust in the merits of the Saviour, accepting His righteousness, believing in His mercy.[32]

Christ and His righteousness—let this be our platform, the very life of our faith.[33]

In immediate connection with the scenes of the great day of God, the Lord by the prophet Joel has promised a special manifestation of His Spirit. Joel 2:28. This prophecy received a partial fulfillment in the outpouring of the Spirit on the day of Pentecost; but it will reach its full accomplishment in the manifestation of divine grace which will attend the closing work of the gospel.[34]

This message [in Minneapolis in 1888] was to bring more prominently before the world the uplifted Saviour, the sacrifice for the sins of the whole world. It presented justification through faith in the Surety; it invited the people to receive the righteousness of Christ, which is made manifest in obedience to all the commandments of God. Many had lost sight of Jesus. They needed to have their eyes directed to His divine person, His merits, and His changeless love for the human family. All power is given into His hands, that He may dispense rich gifts unto [humans], imparting the priceless gift of His own righteousness to the helpless human agent. This is the message that God commanded to be given to the world. It is the third angel's message, which is to be proclaimed with a loud voice, and attended with the outpouring of His Spirit in a large measure.[35]

The danger has been presented to me again and again of entertaining, as a people, false ideas of justification by faith. I have been shown for years that Satan would work in a special manner

---

32. White, *Gospel Workers* (Washington, D.C.: Review and Herald, 1948), 156, 157.
33. White, *Review and Herald,* August 31, 1905.
34. White, *The Faith I Live By* (Washington, D.C.: Review and Herald, 1958), 292.
35. White, *Testimonies to Ministers and Gospel Workers* (Mountain View, Calif.: Pacific Press®, 1923), 91.

to confuse the mind on this point. The law of God has been largely dwelt upon and has been presented to congregations, almost as destitute of the knowledge of Jesus Christ and His relation to the law as was the offering of Cain. I have been shown that many have been kept from the faith because of the mixed, confused ideas of salvation, because the ministers have worked in a wrong manner to reach hearts. The point that has been urged upon my mind for years is the imputed righteousness of Christ. I have wondered that this matter was not made the subject of discourses in our churches throughout the land, when the matter has been kept so constantly urged upon me, and I have made it the subject of nearly every discourse and talk that I have given to the people.[36]

Contrary to what so many have thought, Ellen White was not afraid of grace!

SANCTIFYING GRACE

If it's so clear, how could there ever be a problem? What's behind "all this controversy" she talks about? Why are so many of us so sure she preaches only salvation by works?

The first "problem" is that Ellen White not only talks about the grace that saves and justifies, but she also talks about the grace that transforms and sanctifies. *Justifying grace* is God's act of forgiving sinners and declaring that they will be treated just as if they never had sinned. *Sanctifying grace* is God's power working in our lives to change and mold us into His image. (See chapters 12 and 13 for the background of this distinction in the Reformation.) Since being saved and becoming more like Jesus *both* are essential topics to growing Christians, it is fortunate for us that Ellen White addresses both subjects. (See chapter 17.)

Sometimes when she talks about *sanctifying grace*, she identifies it with the same forceful clarity she uses when she talks about *justifying grace*. "The heart is *sanctified by grace*," she says.[37] "The *transforming power of grace*," she calls it;[38] "the subduing, *transforming power of His grace*";[39] "the *grace that will enable us to overcome.*"[40] "The *grace of Christ purifies* while it pardons."[41] "It is His *grace that gives [us] power to obey* the laws of God."[42]

Our problem occurs when Ellen White doesn't identify which type of grace she's talking about. Sometimes she speaks of grace without giving any adjectives to help us understand what her topic really is. If we think she's referencing *justifying grace* when she's really talking about *sanctifying grace*, we can totally misinterpret her comments.

Here are a couple of examples. The compilation *God's Amazing Grace* contains a quotation in which Ellen White says: "It is only by the grace of God, combined with the most earnest efforts on our part, that we can gain the victory."[43] That's a simple enough concept

---

36. White, *Faith and Works,* 18.

37. White, *Review and Herald,* October 8, 1895, emphasis supplied.

38. White, *Conflict and Courage* (Washington, D.C.: Review and Herald, 1970), 316, emphasis supplied.

39. White, *Testimonies for the Church* (Mountain View, Calif.: Pacific Press®, 1948), 4:625, emphasis supplied.

40. White, *Manuscript Releases* (Silver Spring, Md.: E. G. White Estate, 1990), 5:254, emphasis supplied.

41. White, *That I May Know Him* (Washington, D.C.: Review and Herald, 1964), 336.

42. White, *God's Amazing Grace,* 103.

43. Ibid., 341.

if you understand her to be speaking of *sanctifying grace.* Of course we cooperate with God in the sanctification process. We repent of the things we do that damage our relationship with Christ. We determine to overcome. We give our lives to Him. We ask for His strength on a daily basis. We rejoice that He has given us the victory.

But look at the problem if we decide she is speaking about *justifying grace!* Suddenly we make her contradict all those times she insists that we can do nothing to be justified: "If by any efforts of our own we could advance one step toward the ladder, the words of Christ would not be true." We *do not* combine our "most earnest efforts" with the gift of grace to produce *justification.* Either she is speaking of *sanctification,* becoming like Christ, or we must conclude that she can't make up her mind on the subject and so resorts to talking out of both sides of her mouth.

Here's another example: "The Christian must put forth strenuous exertions, and God will unite divine grace with his human effort."[44] Again, problems arise only if we make her say, "God will unite *justifying grace* with human effort." If we agree she is speaking of *sanctifying grace,* we allow her to stay consistent instead of making her contradict her own position.

This approach resolves much of the tension, eradicates contradictions, and makes it easy to accept statements like this one from *God's Amazing Grace:* "His grace is given to work in us to will and to do, but never as a substitute for our effort. Our souls are to be aroused to cooperate."[45] Of course! No problem at all! She's talking about *sanctification.*

## The second challenge

There's another reality that many construe as a problem. Ellen White writes so much over such a long period that sometimes, with the passing of time, she modifies positions she held early on.[46] Woodrow Whidden's book *Ellen White on Salvation* sums up her growth in the subject of salvation like this: "The four years immediately following Minneapolis was the period of full maturity. It was full maturity in the sense of greater clarity of expression and marked emphasis."[47]

Some people will be unhappy with the suggestion that Ellen White's understanding *grew,* that she knew grace better as the days went by, that anyone called and used by God might *mature* in their comprehension or expression. But according to the way we Adventists view the doctrine of inspiration (and it's a position to which Ellen White made a significant contribution), God doesn't call someone to labor for Him—not even the writers of the Bible—and then reveal to them the totality of His character and will all at once, leaving nothing for them to learn.

Of the Bible, Ellen White herself wrote: "Written in different ages, by men who differed widely in rank and occupation, and in mental and spiritual endowments, the books of the Bible present a wide contrast in style, as well as a diversity in the nature of the subjects unfolded. Different forms of expression

---

44. White, *Review and Herald,* October 30, 1888.

45. White, *God's Amazing Grace,* 111.

46. Woodrow W. Whidden II claims she wrote "more than 25 million words in books, magazine articles, letters and unpublished manuscripts." (*Ellen White on Salvation* [Hagerstown, Md.: Review and Herald, 1995], 9.)

47. Ibid., 114.

are employed by different writers; often the same truth is more strikingly presented by one than by another."[48] And, "the Scriptures were given to [us], not in a continuous chain of unbroken utterances, but piece by piece through successive generations, as God in His providence saw a fitting opportunity to impress [humans] at sundry times and divers places."[49]

In December 1844, Ellen White, then just seventeen years old, begins to listen to the voice of God in a new way, and to repeat what He said for the counsel and guidance of the Advent people. The biographical information available at the Ellen G. White Estate (www.whiteestate.org) tells the story. Following the Great Disappointment and her initial vision in December 1844, Ellen "traveled with friends and relatives from place to place to relate [it] to the scattered companies of Adventists," giving them encouragement and urging them not to give up hope in the return of Jesus.

It isn't until April 1847 that she and her husband, James, begin to understand the importance of the seventh-day Sabbath. Eleven years pass before she experiences what we call her "great controversy vision." Instruction on healthful living doesn't come until the middle of 1863. Clarity on the gospel of grace deepens with the preaching of Jones and Waggoner at the General Conference session in Minneapolis in 1888,[50] more than forty years after she first accepted the call to work for God.

Like Paul in his first letter to the Corinthians,[51] and like Augustine early in the fifth century,[52] Ellen White readily speaks of her personal growth.

I do not claim infallibility, or even perfection of Christian character. I am not free from mistakes and errors in my life. Had I followed my Saviour more closely, I should not have to mourn so much my un-likeness to His dear image.[53]

We are not perfect. We may err and do and say things that may not be all right, but we hope no one will be injured in any way by our sayings or doings. We are trying to humbly follow in the footprints of our dear Saviour. We need His Spirit and His grace every hour, or we shall make blunders and shall do harm.[54]

We have many lessons to learn, and many, many to unlearn. God and heaven alone are infallible. Those who think that they will never have to give up a cherished view, never have occasion to change an opinion, will be disappointed. As long as we hold to our own ideas and opinions with determined persistency, we cannot have the unity for which Christ prayed.[55]

48. White, *The Great Controversy* (Mountain View, Calif.: Pacific Press®, 1950), vi.
49. White, *Selected Messages* (Washington, D.C.: Review and Herald, 1958), 1:19, 20.
50. See chapter 15, "The California Conspiracy."
51. "When I was a child, I talked like a child, I thought like a child, I reasoned like a child. When I became a man, I put childish ways behind me" (1 Corinthians 13:11).
52. Augustine said, "I now think an error what I had previously thought to be the truth." See the discussion of Augustine's "developmental theology" in the sidebar in chapter 9, pages 130, 131.
53. White, *Letter 27,* 1876, to James White.
54. White, *Letter 18,* 1879, to Willie White.
55. White, *Review and Herald,* July 26, 1892.

Regarding the testimonies, nothing is ignored; nothing is cast aside; but time and place must be considered.[56]

Recently I spent several hours in my office with an intense gentleman who has put a great distance between himself and the Seventh-day Adventist Church, in which he had spent most of his life. His journey has led him away from our understanding of the Second Coming, away from the Sabbath, away from church membership, and into a convinced expectation of an immediate rapture of the righteous. As I listened carefully to his theory, I began to hear a recurring theme. "What has made you so angry at Ellen White?" I asked him, interrupting his presentation.

The story that followed was long and bitter. It centered on a narrow, legalistic, Ellen White–quoting grandmother. She raised her little boy, this man's father, in a strict, demanding, unsatisfying works orientation. The boy left home and the church at the earliest opportunity. Much later, after his own children were grown, he experienced a sudden stroke. Paralysis was followed by a rapid deterioration, and he died "never experiencing the joy of grace." Through his tears, the boy's son in my office blamed it all on Ellen White. "She led us astray on the gospel," he accused, "and my father won't be in heaven because of her."

It is a sad, unfortunate story—one that's repeated far too many times. Many miss out on the joy of salvation by grace alone because they have concluded that Ellen White promotes instead a salvation by grace plus works. Many others, assuming the same thing about her and knowing that such a course is contrary to the gospel, refuse to listen to anything she says.

If you ever find yourself confused by something Ellen White says, please don't give up. Determine the context—"the time and place." Realize that sometimes it's just the nuances in the metaphors that seem to be in conflict. Look closely. Don't decide to throw out *everything* she says simply because you're puzzled by *something* she says. If you think you hear a works orientation from her, don't overlook her grace orientation. Keep studying. Don't leave. Don't quit believing in the doctrine of salvation by grace alone. Remember her counsel, given right after the disappointment of October 1844.[57] It's just as applicable for us today as it was all those years ago.

"If they kept their eyes fixed on Jesus," she insisted, "they were safe."

---

56. White, *Selected Messages,* 1:57.
57. White, *The Day-Star,* January 24, 1846.

# GRACE IN QUESTION
## CHAPTER 16: THE CENTRAL TRUTH

In chapter 16, we consider a great volume of inspirational literature: the more than five thousand periodical articles and forty books that make up the writings of Ellen White, who was born on November 26, 1827, and died on July 16, 1915, at the age of eighty-seven. Sometimes Ellen's words on the topic of grace are stunningly clear. Sometimes they appear contradictory and confusing. Here we examine four ways she uses the word *grace* and explore how misunderstanding the context of what she says can be problematic.

1. Look for confusing statements about grace in ads, news broadcasts, and your local newspaper. Bring the collection to your study group, read each statement, and discuss whether and how the statements lead people away from the biblical meaning of grace.

2. Distinguish between *justifying grace* and *sanctifying grace*.

3. How are Seventh-day Adventists uniquely prepared to present the everlasting gospel of God's saving grace? What other emphases in our belief system contribute to a full presentation of what grace can mean in the lives of the believers?

4. Print out a dozen or so pages with the name of one doctrine on each page. Print another page that says "Grace." Place the Grace page in the center of the floor, and surround it with the pages representing the other doctrines. Discuss the relationship of each doctrine to the central one. See the sidebar "The One Great Central Truth" on page 220.

5. Share experiences—your own, ones from your family, or ones with which you are acquainted—in which a quarrel with Ellen White led someone to stop being an Adventist. How does the counsel to keep our eyes on Jesus work as a preventative medicine for such an experience?

# GRACE NOTES
## EXODUS 32; 33—THE PECULIARITY OF GOD'S PEOPLE

Q. What objections to grace have you heard from people who want us to be God's "peculiar people"?

Q. What should distinguish God's followers from all the other people on planet Earth?

"Grace is too general," some people object. "Everybody believes in grace. We're supposed to be a 'peculiar people' " (from the King James rendering of 1 Peter 2:9).

What is it that distinguishes the followers of God from all the other people on earth? How "peculiar" are God's people supposed to be?

There's an interesting answer in a familiar story in the book of Exodus. Moses has been on Mount Sinai for over a month, communing with God face to face and receiving from God's hand the Ten Commandments. The Israelites in the plain around the mountain begin to wonder if they will ever see Moses again. They go to Aaron, tell him they're tired of waiting for " 'this fellow Moses' " (Exodus 32:1), and ask him to fashion for them a visible representation of God like the ones the Egyptians took so much delight in worshiping (hippos, cows, birds, jackals, etc.).

Aaron goes to considerable work to fulfill the people's request. He takes up a collection of gold for the project, creates a mold in the shape of a calf, builds a huge fire and melts the gold, pours the gold into the mold, and then, after the casting has cooled and hardened, he chisels off the rough edges until the idol looks just the way he wants it to look (verse 4). When Aaron has completed it, he presents it to the people and invites them all to a great celebration of their golden calf.

On the next day, the people start dancing around the idol and shouting, " ' "These are [the] gods . . . who brought [us] out of Egypt" ' " (verses 6, 8). Then, up on the top of Mount Sinai, the conversation between God and Moses takes an unexpected detour. God leans in to Moses and quietly commands him to leave the mountain. " 'Your people,' " He says matter-of-factly, " 'whom you brought up out of Egypt, have become corrupt' " (verse 7).

The Bible doesn't record the thoughts of Moses at that moment, but surely he thought God had made a mistake. "I thought they were *Your* people," Moses may have wanted to respond, "and that *You* brought them out of Egypt. When did they get to be *my* people?"

Had Moses asked that question, God would have answered him like this: "When they began worshiping that golden calf, they turned from Me to you and your brother. Now, you deal with them, because I'm so angry I might do something I really don't want to do" (see verses 8–10).

A lengthy interlude follows this moment in the conversation. Moses storms into camp, breaks the Ten Commandment tablets in his anger (verse 19), and deals severely with the idolaters. Then he turns to his brother. The exchange between the two of them is one of the funniest passages in the Bible, as well as being for me an evidence of the Bible's authenticity (see verse 21ff). Nobody would make up a story like this. It *has* to be real!

Moses asks, "What did they do to you that would make you do such a thing?"

Aaron replies, "Don't be mad at me! You know how evil the people are. They just gave me the gold, I threw it into the fire, and out came this calf!"

By the time Moses gets back to the top of Mount Sinai, God has made some definite plans. Here's what He tells Moses: "You and the people you brought out of Egypt are going to pack up and leave this place and head for the Promised Land. I promised I'd drive out the inhabitants ahead of you, and I'm sending an angel to go ahead of you and do just that. But I'm not going to take the trip with you. For your safety, just go with the angel" (see 33:1–3).

Moses' answer is genuine and heartfelt. " 'If your Presence does not go with us, do not send us up from here,' " he pleads (verse 15). Then follows this insightful observation: " 'What else will distinguish me and your people from all the other people on the face of the earth?' " (verse 16).

Here is Moses' insight. It's not the size of our encampment that makes us God's "peculiar" people. It's not the strength of our leaders. It's not our wealth, not the amount of gold we give to our projects, not the force of our army, not the number of people we win to our side, not the size of our educational system, not the span of our medical work—all those things we frequently use to tell people who we are. What distinguishes us from all the other people on the face of the earth is not even that we have been handed the tablets of stone bearing the Ten Commandments. What distinguishes us is God's presence among us.

We either flee from the presence of God and try to make it on our own (Revelation 20:11) or we embrace His grace and run to Him who is able to keep us from falling and to present us before God's glorious presence "without fault and with great joy" (Jude 24).

*"Spiritual transformation is essential,
not optional, for Christ-followers."*
—John Ortberg, Grace: An Invitation to a Way of Life

*"To live in grace a life of peace and virtue
and forbearance with others . . ."*
—James Joyce, A Portrait of the Artist as a Young Man

*"It is the confidence that God has pardoned us
that enables believers to grow in grace."*
—John Cobb, Jr., Grace & Responsibility

*"Unconditional grace is the glorious foundation
of all else in the Christian life."*
—John Piper, Future Grace

*"To be a child of God means to be constantly receiving grace."*
—Ellen G. White, Review and Herald, January 8, 1895

# THE CANCELED DEBT:
## *The Motivation of Grace in a Life of Obedience*

**M**Y WORKSHOP SESSION AT A MINISTRIES CONVENTION HAD JUST BEGUN when, out of the corner of my right eye, I caught a glimpse of a tape recorder.[1] It was just a little silver mini-recorder, clutched in the hand of a middle-aged man whose suit was as serious as the frown on his face. From its place on the front row of the room, the tape recorder followed my movements back and forth as the gentleman made sure he captured every word I said.

I wasn't bothered by the recorder. In fact, I was flattered. I took it as a compliment. *I must be saying something memorable,* I thought, trying not to lose my focus. So I continued to talk about my assigned topic, attempting to make it clear that the fundamental core of all we Adventists are and do and believe is the everlasting gospel of God's unrelenting, saving grace—the one "great truth around which all other truths cluster."[2]

But as soon as the session concluded, the man on the front row revealed the real purpose of his recording. He jumped to his feet and, interrupting someone who was asking a question, began shouting at me. "You have a hidden agenda," he said at the top of his voice. "You are trying to destroy the standards of the Seventh-day Adventist Church, and"—here he paused and brandished the little silver tape recorder—"I have the proof right here in my hand!"

Some compliment! I thought he was finding inspiration in the discussion of the wonder of God's enduring love. Instead, like Paul's imaginary questioner in Romans 3:31, he was hearing only a nullifying—a making void of the law through faith.

### DOES GRACE WEAKEN CHRISTIAN COMMITMENT?

Is it possible to celebrate the freedom of grace without making law-oriented people nervous? Can we discuss the need for Christians to grow without making

---

1. Much of this chapter originally appeared in the *Journal of Adventist Education,* October/November 1998. The issue was coordinated for the General Conference Department of Education by Dr. Ed Boyatt, who was at the time superintendent of education for the Oregon Conference. Ed now chairs the department of administration and leadership in the School of Education, La Sierra University. He and his wife, Teri, are active members and inspirational leaders in our church at La Sierra, and dear friends.

2. Ellen G. White, *Gospel Workers* (Washington, D.C.: Review and Herald, 1948), 315.

grace-oriented people angry? Can we establish a grace orientation in our lives, our homes and classrooms and churches, and still share the insights that build Christian character? Can these two fundamental emphases of Christianity—a central appreciation for everything God has done for us in Jesus and a consistent call to become more and more Christlike—coexist successfully? Or does one emphasis necessarily undermine the other? If we focus on and teach our children to appreciate the fullness of God's grace, are we, by that very focus, destroying their determination to obey? On the other hand, if we concentrate on obedience and teach our children to obey, are we running the terrible risk of damaging total trust in God's grace?

If you listen to the concerns of many in our church family today, you can easily conclude that the gospel of God's saving grace inevitably *weakens* Christian commitment and leads to the abandonment of Christian ideals.

"Doesn't the research indicate that the higher your grace orientation, the lower your standards?" one church leader asked me recently, incorrectly interpreting a finding of the *Valuegenesis* research.

"Grace lessens one's commitment to obedience," another pastor insisted, protesting something I said in a sermon.

"Don't we confuse our children," a parent queried, "by saying that God loves them unconditionally and then telling them they better be good?"

Not long ago I received by email an impassioned review of a book that one Adventist Book Center (ABC) manager had decided to carry in his store. The book was about another Sabbath-keeping denomination that had "suddenly discovered grace," which was the reason, the reviewer concluded, its church members had quit keeping the seventh-day Sabbath, abandoned their high standards, and started eating lobster! The concern of the ABC manager was unmistakable: Take this as a warning, all you who preach grace—the Sabbath is about to mean less to you, and your diet is about to change.

## THE FOUNDATION OF ALL OUR SPIRITUAL GROWTH

You come to a totally different conclusion when you see the way Ellen White writes about the connection between forgiving grace and the transformation of the human heart:

- *"Nothing* but the grace of God can convict and convert the heart."[3]
- "It is the grace of Christ *alone,* through faith that can make us holy."[4]
- "The gospel of His grace *alone* can cure the evils that curse society."[5]
- "God's grace *alone* can work a reformation."[6]
- "It is the matchless grace of God *alone* that will triumph over the rebellion of the heart."[7]
- "It is His grace that gives man power to obey the laws of God. It is this that enables

---

3. White, *Testimonies for the Church* (Mountain View, Calif.: Pacific Press®, 1948), 4:552, 553, emphasis supplied.

4. White, *Steps to Christ* (Mountain View, Calif.: Pacific Press®, 1956), 60, emphasis supplied.

5. White, *Mind, Character and Personality* (Nashville: Southern Publishing, 1971), 1:66, emphasis supplied.

6. White, *Testimonies for the Church,* 4:378, emphasis supplied.

7. White, ibid, 3:321, emphasis supplied.

him to break the bondage of evil habit."[8]
- "His matchless grace *alone* can save our feet from falling."[9]

Other writers agree. In his book *The Transforming Power of Grace,* Thomas Oden explains, "Grace is presupposed in every serious call to repentance, faith, new birth, and holy living."[10] In the middle of *In the Grip of Grace,* Max Lucado says, "Where the grace of God is embraced, forgiveness flourishes. The longer we walk in the garden, the more likely we are to smell like flowers. The more we immerse ourselves in grace, the more likely we are to give grace."[11] Spurgeon calls this dynamic the "free-grace road to obedience."[12]

"Law keeping is the *result* of salvation by grace, not the precursor to it, not the maintainer of it," Scott Hoezee states in his book *The Riddle of Grace: Applying Grace to the Christian Life.* "True disciples keep the Law not in a quid-pro-quo attempt to get something in return but simply as a natural, gracious, lovely result of God's saving activity in Christ. Once you are a citizen in God's kingdom by God's grace, you quite naturally act distinctively."[13]

A CHANGE IN STATUS

The first year I was in college, the Republican National Convention took place in Daly City, California, just south of San Francisco, in a building known as The Cow Palace. Four of us freshmen students from a political science class at nearby Pacific Union College drove to the Bay area to see if we could get in on the political fun. Though I didn't realize it, something was about to happen that later would help me understand the operation of grace.

After being refused entrance by one authority after another (police, security guards, ticket-takers, ushers), we were discouraged and about to go home. We stood on the outside, watching all the people going into the building, knowing we weren't going to be able to join them. But just then we were caught up in the middle of a crowd demonstrating for one of the candidates for the presidency. Shoved along like twigs of driftwood in the surge of the tides, we were pushed past a chain-link barrier, through a checkpoint for examining credentials, and by a phalanx of whistle-blowing, club-wielding police officers who were determined to keep nondelegates out of the arena. Somehow, we got in.

Even inside the building, however, we were barred from the great hall where all the action was taking place. Occasionally we caught a glimpse of hundreds of delegates sitting beneath broadcast booths from which seasoned television reporters were commenting on the procedures. Even though we thought we looked like all the rest of the delegates, however, just when we thought we were about to get into the inner arena, a guard would approach us, ask for our credentials, and when we couldn't produce any, would turn us away.

8. White, *The Ministry of Healing* (Mountain View, Calif.: Pacific Press®, 1909), 115, emphasis supplied.

9. White, quoted in *The Seventh-day Adventist Bible Commentary,* Francis D. Nichol, ed. (Washington, D.C.: Review and Herald, 1957), 6:1109, emphasis supplied.

10. Thomas Oden, *The Transforming Power of Grace* (Nashville: Abingdon Press, 1993), 24.

11. Max Lucado, *In the Grip of Grace* (Dallas: Word Publishing, 1996), 107.

12. Charles Spurgeon, *Grace & Power* (New Kensington, Penn.: Whitaker House, 2000), 207.

13. Scott Hoezee, *The Riddle of Grace: Applying Grace to the Christian Life* (Grand Rapids, Mich.: Wm. B. Eerdmans Publishing Company, 1996), 35, 36.

Then something happened that changed my status, and consequently, altered my behavior.

I was standing on the outskirts of a small circle of delegates who had gathered in the hallway to discuss strategies for winning in November. As I eavesdropped on their conversation, hoping to pick up a quotable tidbit or two, I heard something drop on the floor. I reached down, picked up the dropped item, and offered it to the people standing in front of me. They politely declined my offer; they didn't think they had dropped anything. I glanced at what I had picked up and only then realized that I had in my hand *a delegate's badge*. Embossed on the badge was the name of a delegate: "Corely Thompson, Missouri."

It suddenly occurred to me that I was in possession of something that had the power to change my fortunes. I looked more closely at the treasure. Then, without the natural compulsions that might have prevented such a brazen decision (I was only a freshman in college, remember), I pinned the badge to the front of my coat, turned, and walked toward the arena.

As I approached the short hallway that separated me from the convention, I noticed two guards checking the credentials of everyone walking toward them. I took a deep breath, tried to put a confident, Republican look on my face, and strolled up to the guards. One of them looked at my badge, gave me a slight, positive nod, and moved out of the way so I could walk in. And a moment later, I was inside!

I spent the rest of the day listening to the speeches, observing the dignitaries, raising my hand in support of proposals with which I agreed, and voting against anything I didn't like. As long as I kept the badge pinned to my jacket, I enjoyed the full benefits of an actual delegate. As Stuart Tyner, young Democrat student from Angwin, I was relegated to the outside of the arena. But as Corley Thompson, Republican delegate from Missouri, I was accepted. The badge changed the way the authorities related to me. I was still a Democrat. I hadn't changed political parties. But suddenly I was given a new name and a new status and was treated just as if I had always been a Republican. What's more, my new status changed my behavior. ("I once was maligned, but now I'm GOP!")

## GRACE PRECEDES BEHAVIOR

Paul Tillich summarizes the theology of such a situation succinctly: "Being precedes action," he explains.[14] First you are; then you do. Grace precedes behavior.

However you say it, the reality is clear: It is God's saving grace *and nothing else* that gives us a new name and a new status. And that's what transforms our behavior! It is grace that makes us desire grace. It is grace that makes us want to grow in Jesus (2 Peter 3:18). It is the fact that we have been justified by grace alone that makes us interested in being sanctified.

Whatever biblical picture we choose, the cause and the effect are always the same:

- *It is because we have been given the victory* that we pursue the enemy (1 Samuel 17:50–52).
- *It is because we are not condemned* that we go and sin no more (John 8:11).
- *It is because we have seen the Light* that we refuse to walk in darkness (verse 12).

---

14. Paul Tillich, *Morality and Beyond* (Louisville, Ky.: Westminster John Knox Press, 1963), 14.

WELCOME HOME

A girl I know named Sally decided to run away from home when she was fifteen years old. Her mom and dad hadn't gotten along for years, but recently the fighting had become worse. The last straw was when Dad started smoking, aggravating her mom's allergies.

"I'm not coming back," Sally announced on her way out the door. But life as a runaway was incredibly difficult. In order to survive, Sally started running with a group of people none of us would have chosen for her. Soon a multitude of bad habits had overcome her. After six months on the street, with her health broken, Sally's resolve was gone. She got on a bus for the short trip back to the town where she had grown up.

When Sally's mother answered the knock at the back door and saw Sally standing there, she didn't hesitate at all. She threw her arms around Sally, almost carried her into the house, and started talking about how good it was to have her home again. Dad had left shortly after Sally had, and the last few months had been peaceful.

A couple of hours later, Sally was sitting on the bed in her old upstairs bedroom. Mom stopped by the room and announced she was on her way to the grocery store. "Is there anything I can get you?" she asked.

Without a thought, Sally said she had started smoking and needed a new carton of cigarettes. Mom smiled and left for the store, and then it hit Sally: the allergies! Surely this would test Mom's welcome-home attitude. Better not unpack her suitcase yet.

Mom returned from the store an hour or so later, carried the groceries in from the car, and began putting things away. Sally listened as Mom worked in the kitchen and then started up the steps toward the bedroom. Then she walked into the room with a sweet smile on her face and laid a new carton of cigarettes on Sally's bed.

Sally told me that the desire to smoke left her at that very moment, and she's never smoked since. Mom's gracious action shook the smoking desire completely out of her.

I'm not sure I would have had the strength to do the same thing Sally's mom did. But I do know this: It was *grace* that broke the bondage of Sally's bad habits. It is God's kindness that leads us to repentance (Romans 2:4).

- *It is because we were bought with a price* that we desire to honor God (1 Corinthians 6:20).
- *It is because we have been reconciled* that we continue in our faith (Colossians 1:19–23).
- *It is because our debt has been canceled* that we behave properly (Luke 7:43).

The principle is universal, even when stated in the negative: " 'He who has been forgiven little loves little' " (Luke 7:47).

WHAT IT MEANS TO GROW IN GRACE

Do we really want to become more and more like Jesus? If that is true, we can approach success in our efforts in *only one way:* We must grow *in grace*. It is only when grace is in the driver's seat, when grace is central, that we obey and overcome in the way we want to obey and overcome. And only then does character building produce the results we want.

Do you remember or have you heard about the film Adventists used to show during the first few nights of stop smoking seminars? *One in 20,000* was a well-made docudrama about the physical consequences of smoking. In full, living color, viewers participated in the surgical removal of a cancerous lung from a life-long smoker. From the first sharp incisions of the scalpel to the final sutures at the end of the operation, we saw it all. I remember that when the lights came on after that film, *nobody* rushed out of the building to light up. Instead, they went straight to the trashcans to deposit their half-used packs of cigarettes, and they did it with the sincere intention never to smoke again. The surgeon's scalpel had scared the smoke right out of them. Character building had begun in earnest!

However, fear doesn't provide lasting motivation. A picture of a cancerous lung isn't strong enough to tear a powerful addiction from a smoker's body. Even with the graphic reminder of the disastrous physical consequences of their intemperance still throbbing in their memories, many of those well-intentioned smokers went back to their habit. Smoking, like bad habits in general, is best overcome from within the security of God's all-encompassing grace. That's one of the reasons why the dear people at the Alcoholics Anonymous and Narcotics Anonymous meetings take their first step toward recovery by admitting that there has to be a power stronger than themselves.

Let's examine four principles of graceful and effective obeying and character building. While we're doing so, let's see if we can talk about God's grace and the transformation of our characters *at the same time* without frightening anyone across the broad spectrum of Adventism.

*Principle #1: Start With Jesus.* Here's the way Jesus Himself states the principle: " 'As I am lifted up from the earth, I will attract every-one to me' " (John 12:32, *The Message*). The more we talk about Jesus, the more we sing about His amazing grace, the more we model our ministry after His, the more we will be attracted to Jesus. The more we learn about Jesus the more we will appreciate the gospel of God's grace (Acts 20:24)—the good news of God's full acceptance of us in Jesus (Acts 15:8–11), His continuing faithfulness (Psalm 100:3–5), and His loving kindness (Titus 3:3–7). And the more we are attracted to the beauty of the character of Jesus, the more we will desire to be changed into His likeness. Paul states the principle concisely and unequivocally: "God's kindness leads you toward repentance" (Romans 2:4). "Those who seek to correct others should present the attractions of Jesus," Ellen White counsels us. "Talk about Christ, and when the heart is converted, everything that is out of harmony with the Word of God will drop off."[15]

Too often, however, many of us begin with a desire to correct an objectionable trait of character—our own or someone else's. We work on the flaw until we get it right, and then we decide that, as reborn Christians, we are "safe to save," or at least to come to Jesus now—which is, of course, *exactly backwards* from the way we ought to be doing it. Perhaps we even try to "grace it up" a bit by adding a question like "what would Jesus do?" to our discussion, or by asking how to find grace in a specific standard or value.

However, it's not enough to ask where we find grace in a particular topic. Grace is not a minor subset of a standard or a character-building activity or a last-minute addendum to our instruction. Grace is the "great truth around which all other truths cluster. In order to be rightly understood and appreciated, ev-

---

15. White, *Signs of the Times,* July 1, 1889.

ery truth in the Word of God"—including the truth about how important it is for our characters to glorify our Father in heaven (Matthew 5:16)—"must be studied in the light that streams from the cross of Calvary."[16] It is grace that gives meaning and purpose to character building, not character building that illuminates grace. Come to Jesus first.

*Principle #2: Separate spiritual growth from entrance requirements for heaven.* Don't turn the exciting possibilities of becoming more and more like Jesus into a discouraging process that holds the threat of not making it into heaven. The Bible Belt bumper-sticker sermon "Turn or Burn" is not the message we're trying to convey here.

Students at Adventist schools seem to have a difficult time separating even the most common regulations of an educational institution from entrance requirements for heaven. If a church school makes a rule, they mistakenly reason, then the appropriate behavior must get you into heaven. Not long ago I talked to two young men who had been expelled from an academy for refusing to stop wearing their baseball caps backwards. As they shared their experience with me, it became clear that, while they knew they had been unnecessarily stubborn, they were confused as to why *God* cared about how they wore their caps. That's actually what they thought—that *God* apparently had declared that wearing a baseball cap with the bill pointing forward was more *Christian* than wearing the cap with the bill aimed another direction! They didn't understand that this was simply a local application of a noninspired, nonsacred dress code agreed upon by a majority of a particular faculty group—and that there was nothing at all spiritual about it. The boys felt that if they didn't conform to *God's* regulation, the

---

### CHILDREN UNDERSTAND GROWTH

Use illustrations from nature to demonstrate to your children the importance of growing.

- Take a walk in the woods. Call attention to the differences between the magnificent giant sequoia trees and the little stumps that at some time stopped growing.
- Plant a few vegetables in a window box and keep track of the daily growth.
- Talk about puppies and kittens, ducklings and lion cubs.
- Watch a fuzzy caterpillar turn into a delicate work of art.
- Take a picture of your children in front of barren winter trees and then put them in the picture again when the spring foliage is shouting new birth and growth from every branch and twig.

For more examples of growing in grace, see Stuart Tyner, *The Colors of Grace in Our Homes* (published by the Pacific Union Conference Church Resource Center and AdventSource, 1996).

---

church didn't want them, and they wouldn't be in heaven. No wonder they were confused!

We need to be as clear on this point as we possibly can be. We grow in Jesus because we are His children, never in order to become His children (1 John 3:1). We behave with propriety so that people will glorify God (Matthew 5:16), not so that we can convince God to like us. We need to develop our characters so that we can honor God, not so that we can earn our way into heaven. It is grace that inspires us to grow, not growth that purchases grace or favor.

---

16. White, *Gospel Workers*, 315.

"Discipleship," Dietrich Bonhoeffer reminds us, "is merely the life that springs from grace."[17]

*Principle #3: Keep growing.* Growing in Jesus is indeed the work of a lifetime. We all start at different points. We all grow at different rates. And we all need to keep growing. *None* of us has a character that is perfectly Christlike. In fact, the closer any of us come to Jesus, "the more faulty you will appear in your own eyes; for your vision will be clearer, and your imperfections will be seen in broad and distinct contrast to His perfect nature."[18]

But the fact that we need to keep growing is not to be an occasion for discouragement. "Do not draw back in despair," Ellen White pleads. "We shall often have to bow down and weep at the feet of Jesus because of our shortcomings and mistakes, but we are not to be discouraged. Even if we are overcome by the enemy, we are not cast off, not forsaken and rejected of God."[19] We are encouraged to find both the desire to keep growing and the grace that keeps us committed to growth within the family of faith.

We see in the lives of the people of the Bible the ever-present necessity of growth. Abraham learns that God has the power to keep His promises. David realizes he needs to repent. Jonah finds out how important it is to follow God's directions. The prodigal son returns to his father. Mary discovers the power of forgiveness. Martha learns to sit at Jesus' feet. Peter struggles with commitment. Saul becomes Paul. The "great cloud of witnesses" fills every sacred page.

*Principle #4: Stay in the center.* Finally, don't be surprised when people criticize you for your grace orientation. Because of the extra need to focus on the gospel of grace during another age with a prevailing works orientation, because of the wide variety of interpretations on the subject that make so many of us afraid of grace, and especially because of the legalistic "baggage" many of us bring to the topic, there's a great likelihood that your orientation toward God's grace will not fully be understood or appreciated. When confrontations occur, stay in the center of the debate. Hold to the high calling to be Christlike and to the necessity of proceeding within a grace orientation.

At a distant camp meeting recently, a theology professor said to me, "Isn't it wonderful to teach grace from the Old Testament, where it's so easy to balance grace with the law?" I'm always troubled by a call for "balance" that indicates that *legalism* is at one inappropriate end of the pendulum swing and *grace* is at the other. It's true that when the pendulum swings too far to the right, we end up overemphasizing *our* character, *our* obedience, *our* spirituality, *our* response, and *our* works. And it's equally true that such an emphasis generally ends up producing a dry, unproductive, and unsatisfying experience.

But the other end of the pendulum swing is permissiveness, antinomianism, and lawlessness, *not grace.* In actuality, grace is the *center* position in our faith, the *core* to which both the extremes of legalism and lawlessness need to return. Grace is the "one great *central* truth to be kept ever before the mind in the searching of the Scriptures." Every other truth is invested "with influence and power *corresponding to its relation to this theme.*"[20] Grace is at the *heart* of the church doctrine that came out of the Refor-

---

17. Dietrich Bonhoeffer, *Cost of Discipleship* (New York: Collier Books, 1963), 63.

18. White, *Steps to Christ,* 64.

19. Ibid.

20. White, MS 31, 1890.

mation, "the *central* teaching of the Christian faith,"[21] the center of Adventist theology.

## OUR MOST DESPERATE NEED

I had just concluded a youth ministry training event in a city in the Southwest when a local church youth leader approached me with a negative evaluation of the weekend.

"What didn't you like?" I asked him, hoping for a suggestion to improve the training.

"It was that moment during church when you asked all of us to stand up and clap with the song," he responded. "It was all downhill from there." Actually, his criticism was just the tip of the iceberg. The next few minutes revealed a deep-seated distrust of praise music and a dislike of the general directions he saw youth ministry taking. "Clapping is just the symptom," he said. "I'm teaching my youth that applause has no place in church."

When he paused long enough for me to cut in, I asked him what would happen if the kids in his youth group came across the psalm that invited us to clap our hands and shout unto God with the voice of triumph (Psalm 47:1)? His answer astounded me. "David didn't know everything there is to know about worship," he declared.

Well, in a way, the youth leader was right. None of us knows *everything* about *anything.* Certainly, David wouldn't have claimed omniscience. But the youth leader was setting *himself* up as the final authority on what was right and wrong—even if he had to say the Bible had made a mistake.

There are a lot of other people just like him, people who seem to know exactly what's right and what's wrong—and most often it's *their* understanding and *their* doctrine that's right, and it's *your* understanding that's wrong. Not

> ### CHOOSE
>
> "The single clenched fist lifted and ready,
> Or the open asking hand held out and
> waiting.
> Choose: for we meet by one or the other."
> —Carl Sandburg

even the solid teaching of Scripture can shake their opinion. This is especially true of the way we Adventists have approached the subject of grace. We've been so fearful of losing our identity as keepers of the law, so worried that we might undermine the commitment to obey, so concerned that we might fail to uphold the Sabbath, that we are now used to saying, "Yes, we are saved by grace alone, but . . ." Our members are confused on what we believe about salvation. Sadly, in the pew, the "but" has become more indicative of our doctrine than the "grace."

We see in the Bible "time and time again how God in His grace and for His glory overrules the weakness and sinfulness of His chosen instruments," Professor Iain Duguid reflects in his book *Living in the Grip of Relentless Grace.* "God delights in writing straight with a crooked pencil. He delights in using clay pots in which to store His treasure. The reason for this is simple. His strength is most abundantly seen in our weakness, and His glory is most apparent when He uses the most insignificant people to bring about His wonderful purposes (2 Corinthians 4:7)."[22]

Someday we'll all be changed in a moment, in the twinkling of an eye. Until then, we have two desperate needs: to grow more and more like Jesus, and to accomplish that growth in the security and acceptance of His everlasting grace.

---

21. Alister McGrath, *Luther's Theology of the Cross* (Oxford: Blackwell Publishers, 1985), 8.
22. Iain M. Duguid, *Living in the Grip of Relentless Grace* (Phillipsburg, N.J.: P & R Publishing, 2002), xiv.

# GRACE IN QUESTION

## CHAPTER 17: THE CANCELED DEBT

Chapter 17 looks at objections to our full acceptance of grace: "Doesn't grace lessen one's commitment to obedience?" some ask. "Don't we have to balance our presentation of grace with an emphasis on law?" This chapter presents grace as the central position of our faith, the great motivator of our behavior, and the security in which we grow more and more like Jesus.

1. Think about the standards you hold as a growing Christian. Name several of them— living healthfully, remembering the Sabbath, living in harmony with others, etc. John Piper said, "Unconditional grace is the glorious foundation of all else in the Christian life." How is that statement true for you even of our standards?

2. Ask someone in your study group to role-play a Christian skeptical of grace. Improvise a conversation with this person about the place of grace in the life of an Adventist Christian. Ask the skeptic to argue with everything you bring up. After a short conversation, consider where the "actor" got the material from which to build his or her responses.

3. Read aloud the seven Ellen White statements on pages 230, 231. Read around the circle, perhaps even reading the sentences again and again. If that's all the instruction about grace you ever had, what could you conclude?

4. You must have heard stories like those I've heard that underscore the point that status changes behavior (pages 231, 232). Share some of those stories with each other, and discuss Tillich's statement that "being precedes action."

5. Repeat the four principles of growing in grace. What do each of these principles mean for your life this week?

# GRACE NOTES
## JAMES 2—THE WITNESS OF A LIFETIME

Two men came to church this past Sabbath. It was their first visit.

One of them was dressed up: a suit from Nordstrom's, an impeccable white shirt, a hundred-dollar tie, Italian shoes, and just the right accessories to let us know how much he cared about making a good first impression. The greeters welcomed him warmly. They invited him to sign the guest book. A deacon opened the door into the sanctuary for him and ushered him down toward the front. He wanted to sit on the middle aisle.

The other man arrived at almost the same time. He had on an old pair of Levis, as though he didn't know how we dress up for church around here. No starched shirt. No tie. Old Nikes.

"Can I help you?" one of the greeters asked cautiously. "Are you looking for someone?"

"No," the shabby man answered. "Just thought I'd join you for worship today."

"Well, we're certainly glad you joined us." The response was polite, but cold.

With that, the man let himself into sanctuary, and, noticing how everyone else was dressed, sat down toward the back and off to the side, out of sight, out of the way (see James 2:2, 3).

This story of two worshippers, updated here as if it happened just this past weekend, is how James begins a frank discussion of what happens to our behavior when we're saved by grace. Throughout the years, the discussion has been troublesome, thanks to James's contention that our works play a large part in our salvation. We are faced with three possible explanations: (1) James is wrong and should have deferred to Paul. (2) James is right, and it's Paul who doesn't get it. (3) James is trying to tell us something important that doesn't, in spirit at least, contradict Paul. Let's listen more closely to James in this paraphrase of his argument:

> I know I should just begin preaching politely here about discrimination, but what I really want to do is yell at the greeters, "You are evil! You are insulting. Who made you the judge of whom to welcome and whom to treat with rudeness? You, and rich people like him, are slandering the exalted name of all *Christians*" (see James 2:4–7).

> You quote the Bible right and left, but apparently you've never read the foundational law of biblical Christianity: "Love your neighbor as

Q. What strengthens your commitment to grow spiritually in the security of God's everlasting grace?

Q. In what ways do our lives reveal our theology?

yourself." So, while you pride yourself in being obedient keepers of the Ten Commandments, your prejudice reveals that you're nothing more than a law-breaker. You wouldn't think of not remembering the Sabbath, and you're full of all the "Thou shalt nots," yet you fall all over this one and make yourself guilty of breaking them all (see verses 8–11).

(OK, take a deep breath. Count to ten. Calm yourself.) This is what I'm trying to say: We're all going to face the judgment some day. We have to start talking and acting as though we realize how we're going to be judged. If you want to go to that final trial and shake your fist at the Judge and say, "Sentence me on the basis of how well I've treated nicely dressed people," go ahead. As for me, I intend to ask for mercy and plead to be judged by the law that already has determined that my freedom is a gift, not something I've earned. That way the outcome is sure: Mercy triumphs over judgment (see verses 12, 13).

James doesn't understand why any believer would act any other way. Our actions, he argues, should be in accordance with what we believe! If we believe we are saved by grace alone through faith alone in Jesus Christ alone, then we should fall on God's mercy. If we say that's what we believe but don't act in accordance, we're done for. Our statement of faith isn't going to save us (see verse 14).

James tries to make his point with a simple illustration. "Suppose a church member has fallen on hard times," he says. "Maybe a Gulf Coast hurricane has destroyed his home. [Can you picture what James is talking about?] Suppose you go up to this person and say, 'I'm praying for you. I hope you stay warm tonight and that your next meal is delicious and satisfying,' and that's it! No opening of your home. No twenty-dollar bill for groceries. Not even a brown bag with a fast-food combo. Just 'I'm praying for you . . .' Do you think that's good enough?

*"In the same way,"* James stomps his foot here, "you say you're one of the faithful, you're a Christian (which means you've accepted the gospel's good news of salvation by grace alone), yet your behavior (your lack of action for the hurricane victim) shouts louder. It says, 'Give me judgment without mercy.'

"You want to know what I think about your Christianity?" James asks. "I think it's dead!" (see verses 15–17).

Remember, we separate justification and sanctification for salvation, but we keep them together for witness. I can make my justification clear to you by how I live my life. Even the demons believe in God, James reminds us. But God terrifies them. They're afraid of Him. So, what good is their belief? It's nothing but foolishness to say you believe without allowing that belief to change your life positively (see verses 18–20).

James points to the Bible and says it's full of examples. Abraham. Rahab. We know they were God's friends, he states, by how they responded to Him—by how they lived their lives (see verses 21–25).

Here is the conclusion James reaches: A person of faith is a living illustration of the effectiveness of God's grace (see verse 26). You can see that a person is justified by grace alone by how they live their lives, not just by what doctrine they claim to believe (see verse 24).

*"Every moment, we live by and are saved by God's inexhaustible grace."*

—EDWARD HEPPENSTALL, *PERFECTION*

*"At every point in the story, God takes the initiative."*

—THE RIGHTEOUSNESS BY FAITH CONSULTATION, *ADVENTIST REVIEW*, JULY 31, 1980

*"Seventh-day Adventists must be in the vanguard,*
*foremost proponents, stewards of His matchless, saving grace."*

—CHARLES BRADFORD, *ONLY BY GRACE*

*"There is no such thing as divine grace plus human something."*

—JOHN M. FOWLER, *MINISTRY*, AUGUST 1993

*"Jesus is not one of the pillars of our faith;*
*He is, instead, the foundation of the pillars.*
*Without that foundation, the pillars—*
*no matter how solid, no matter how firm*
*in and of themselves—sit on flimsy sands."*

—JOEL MUSVOSVI,

*ADULT SABBATH SCHOOL BIBLE STUDY GUIDE,*

THIRD QUARTER, 2001

CHAPTER 18

# THE EVERLASTING GOSPEL:
*The Persistence of Grace in Our Fundamental Focus*

THE DOCTRINE OF SALVATION REMINDS ME OF THE OLD HOUSE AT 51 EAST Bay Street in Charleston, South Carolina. One of Charleston's first wealthy German merchants, Caspar Christian Schutt, purchased the lot on which the house stood in 1799, and had the house built over the next three years. He placed his store on the lower level and kept building up until the house reached three stories high. Inside, the house was decorated with exquisite taste, filled with lovely, comfortable furnishings. Outside, covered verandas supported by pillars that reflect the three major orders of classic Greek columns—simple, straight-forward Doric on the lower level; substantial, sturdy Ionic in the middle; and detailed, ornate Corinthian on top—shade enormous south-facing windows from the heat of the afternoon sun.

In the same manner, the gospel doctrine is a complex structure.[1] It's a home in which we find residence, shelter, and security. The community around the house has changed considerably through the years, but the doctrine has stayed the same, furnished and decorated by its Builder, offering comfort and calm to all who choose to come here to live.

On the outside of the house of salvation by grace, the doctrine is supported by biblical passages of monumental significance. There are simple, straightforward, Doriclike passages: " 'I have loved you with an everlasting love' " (Jeremiah 31:3). " 'I forgive you for everything you have done' " (Ezekiel 16:63, New Jerusalem). "It is by grace you have been saved" (Ephesians 2:5).

Then there are those supporting passages that are sturdy and powerful, like the Ionic pillars: " 'Has he not made me an everlasting covenant, arranged and secured in every part? Will he not bring to fruition my salvation and grant me my every desire?' " (2 Samuel 23:5). "[He] has saved us and called us to a holy life—not

---

1. Please be mindful here of the serious limitations of all analogies and take this comparison at face value rather than attempt to extend the similarities too far. I haven't tried to figure out what the vacant lot might represent theologically, or what the date of purchase or the German merchant might stand for. The verandas covering the windows from the hot sun in the south are merely an architectural reality and not meant to be religiously symbolic. For now, just look at the furnishings and the columns.

because of anything we have done but because of his own purpose and grace. This grace was given us in Christ Jesus before the beginning of time" (2 Timothy 1:9).

And like a Corinthian column, some passages on salvation by grace are more detailed and ornate and take a little more time and concentration to appreciate fully: "The [Lord] is compassionate and gracious, slow to anger, abounding in love. He will not always accuse, nor will he harbor his anger forever; he does not treat us as our sins deserve or repay us according to our iniquities" (Psalm 103:8–10). "For if, by the trespass of the one man, death reigned through that one man, how much more will those who receive God's abundant provision of grace and of the gift of righteousness reign in life through the one man, Jesus Christ" (Romans 5:17).

The columns have supported the structure from antiquity to Augustine to the twenty-first century, through persecution and reformation and opposition, at General Conference sessions and in local church study groups. The subject is simple enough to be the foundation for the faith of a child, and complex enough to be the enduring challenge during the lifetime of the most brilliant of theologians. Grace is as original as "in the beginning, God," and as contemporary as this morning's sunrise. It is the relevancy in which we reside, and the assurance we have of inhabiting eternity.

But for some reason, we keep acting as if we are afraid of grace.

## AFTER MINNEAPOLIS

In 1924, at a Ministerial Association Advisory Council held in Des Moines, Iowa, former General Conference president Arthur G. Daniells is asked to arrange for a compilation of the writings of Ellen White on the subject of justification by faith. Members of the council express their worry that, in the thirty-five years since 1888, the treasure presented at Minneapolis already has been buried. "The major portion of our membership today has been raised up since these experiences came to us," Daniells writes. "They are unacquainted with them; but they need the message."[2] Those who attended the 1888 session "have held a firm conviction, and cherished a fond hope, that some day this message would be given great prominence among us."[3]

It hadn't happened. And now, all the major players from Minneapolis are gone. Uriah Smith dies on the way to his office at the *Adventist Review* in 1903. George Butler dies in 1918.

E. J. Waggoner continues as editor of the *Signs of the Times* until 1892, when he moves to England to lead out in the publishing work there. He comes under the influence of John Harvey Kellogg and adopts, among other ideas, "spiritual affinity" views on marriage,[4] which Ellen White later characterizes as "dangerous, misleading fables."[5] After the 1903 General Conference session, Waggoner returns from England and joins the faculty of Emmanuel Missionary College in Berrien Springs, Michi-

---

2. Arthur G. Daniells, *Christ Our Righteousness* (Takoma Park, Md.: The Ministerial Association of Seventh-day Adventists, 1926), 11.

3. Ibid., 35.

4. "That is, that one not rightfully a marriage partner here might be one in the life to come, and this allows a present spiritual union." (A. V. Olson, *Through Crisis to Victory, 1888–1901* [Washington, D.C.: Review and Herald, 1966], 313.)

5. Ellen G. White, *Letter 224,* 1908.

gan, before moving to Battle Creek, where he is reunited with Kellogg. This last move brings him again into disagreement with Ellen White. After a 1906 divorce, Waggoner marries a nurse whom he had met in England. On May 28, 1916, at the age of sixty-one, Waggoner dies in his home of a heart attack.

A. T. Jones becomes the editor of the *Review and Herald,* a member of the General Conference Committee, an evangelist, and a conference president. But conflict with Ellen White and the flattering interest from and persuasive influence of Kellogg leads him slowly away from the church. In mid-1907, church leaders withdraw Jones's ministerial credentials. He is formally disfellowshiped on August 21, 1909. In 1912, he joins the Seventh-day Adventist Reform Movement, but that body disfellowships him in 1914. In 1916, he preaches the funeral sermon for his old friend Waggoner. And on May 12, 1923, while undergoing treatment at Battle Creek Sanitarium, he suffers a cerebral hemorrhage and dies. [6]

Before Ellen White dies in 1915, she does all she can to hold on to Jones and Waggoner. Others, however, use their retreat from the mainstream of Adventism as an opportunity to disavow what they preached clear back in 1888. It proves, these detractors say, "that they had had no message from God" and that "the work they had done was all a mistake."[7] Ellen White strongly disagrees, holding firm to her conviction that the Minneapolis message had been divinely inspired.

Daniells accepts the council's compilation assignment with fervor. In the next few months, he conducts "exhaustive research" through all of Ellen White's writings, feeling the burden of "rescuing these gems from their obscurity."[8] The little book that results from his research, *Christ Our Righteousness,* published in 1926, is a precious study—full of wonder and reverence.

## BECOMING REACQUAINTED WITH MINNEAPOLIS—AGAIN

I first read Daniells's book during the 1970s, when the Adventist Church once again was becoming reacquainted with Minneapolis, in what George Knight calls "Adventism's renewing struggle over Jones, Waggoner, and their contribution to Adventist theology."[9] Morris Venden's preaching at La Sierra about "righteousness by faith" introduced the topic afresh to Adventists, and to many of us, it felt like the beginning of another reformation—one that could have been as significant to Adventism as the Reformation of the sixteenth century had been to Christianity. At the La Sierra church, Venden's sermons were taped, copied, and mailed to interested people all over the country.

My wife, Karen, and I were among those interested people. When the tapes arrived, usually by Thursday's mail, we became excited. It wasn't just our hunger for the good news; we felt like we were receiving illegal contraband—smuggled goods from southern California! We imagined that the mere possession of the proscribed items put us at risk with denominational authorities. At Pacific Union College in northern California, we skipped church

---

6. For a thorough and compelling study of the life of Alonzo T. Jones, see George Knight's excellent *From 1888 to Apostasy* (Hagerstown, Md.: Review and Herald, 1987).

7. White, *Letter 24,* 1892.

8. Daniells, 9.

9. George R. Knight, *Angry Saints* (Hagerstown, Md.: Review and Herald, 1989), 131.

From "The Dynamics of Salvation"

The Righteousness by Faith Consultation

The good news, the gospel, is so utterly different from human modes of thought that it is startling. It is easily distorted or lost or obscured—even by theological debate. Therefore it must be told and retold, probed ever more deeply, heard once and ever anew.

Before we can accept the good news, we must see that we can do nothing to restore ourselves to God. . . . His generosity amazes us. He lavishes salvation; we do nothing to earn it. He is not an angry sovereign, nor a demanding judge. Rather, He pours out liberally, without regard to what we deserve. Our only condition is our need; we have no claim on Him at all.

God's grace always surprises the self-righteous; they cannot comprehend the idea that salvation is really totally free. They cling to some vestige of meritorious human activity, some remnant of their own achievement in which they may find secret satisfaction.

God does not coerce, not even for our best good. He has provided salvation as a gift, but He does not force that gift upon us. He has made reconciliation, but we must agree to be reconciled. The human response to grace centers in faith, and the essence of faith is trust, taking God at His word. . . . There is no merit in faith itself. We are not saved by faith but by grace. The cross alone is our salvation; faith is our personal acceptance of the cross as God's decisive act in our behalf.

These terms—justification, reconciliation, forgiveness, adoption, and sanctification—along with the concepts they entail, all point to our new status as Christians. They tell us how lofty are our privileges and how holy is the name with which we are named.

At every point in the new life, from its beginning to its ultimate glorification, we depend entirely on grace received through faith.

on Sabbath morning and secretly gathered in someone's living room or in an old barn owned by other sympathetic Adventist smugglers.

There were solid reasons why the gospel seemed like such good news. "Many of us grew up with fear," Pastor Dan Smith remembers. "My brothers and I were obsessed with the fear that one unconfessed sin would keep us out of heaven if it was on our records when our name came up. We sinned plenty—but we tried very hard to repent quickly, so that our names could not come up before our records were cleared." Dan would look around at his relatives, "preachers for fifty years, and because I happened to know they weren't perfect yet, I wondered what hope there was for people like me!"[10]

Ultimately, Venden's taped sermons challenging that fear came out in the open. People organized retreats on the subject of righteousness by faith. They invited Venden to repeat his famous sermons, like "The Grasshopper Complex." Madelyn Haldeman, professor of New Testament studies at La Sierra, ably filled in when Venden was unavailable. (One Sabbath morning at a retreat, instead of listening to Madelyn, I was looking out the window, wondering about this new direction that seemed to be sweeping the church. When she noticed my distraction, she said, "Smile! Don't you know Jesus loves you?")

South African pastor Smuts van Rooyen established the theological foundations clearly and with great eloquence. I will never forget the moment when, on a Sabbath afternoon in a classroom in Angwin, Smuts reversed for me the long-accepted understanding on how and

---

10. Dan Smith, *Lord, I Have a Question* (Nampa, Idaho: Pacific Press®, 2004), 107. For the last eleven years, Dan has been the senior pastor at the La Sierra University Church and is responsible for the church's motto: "Grace—Everyone, Everywhere, and Every Time."

why the thief on the cross had been saved. "The thief on the cross is the rule," Smuts insisted, "not the exception." I felt then as though someone had punched me in the stomach. But the revolutionary assertion is exactly right: We are saved by Jesus alone—never, ever, by what we've managed to accomplish.

We studied the book of Romans as we'd never studied it before. We examined Taylor Bunch's writings from the 1920s and 1930s that compared not embracing the 1888 message to ancient Israel's turning away from the Promised Land at Kadesh-Barnea. We resurrected Robert Wieland and Donald Short's privately published 1950 paper "1888 Reexamined" and debated their argument that the church had failed to accept the message Jones and Waggoner brought. We devoured A. V. Olson's 1966 book *Through Crisis to Victory,* and LeRoy Froom's *Movement of Destiny,* published in 1971—both of which presented a different, more positive view of the church's acceptance of the message. It was a pivotal time in our lives.

The denomination also seemed poised to embrace the gospel fully. In "An Open Letter to the Church" in the *Adventist Review* of May 24, 1979, Neal Wilson, the president of the General Conference, announced the church's intention to convene a representative group of scholars and theologians "to survey and study difficult theological issues." The group became known as the Righteousness by Faith Consultation, and its 145 members met in Washington, D.C., October 3 and 4, 1979. At the close of the meeting, an editorial committee of twenty-four members was appointed to prepare for publication the materials growing out of the meeting. This group met February 4–7, 1980, and produced a paper, "The Dynamics of Salvation," that was published in the July 31, 1980, issue of the *Adventist Review* and published again eight years later in the February 1988 issue of *Ministry*.

In six detailed, biblically supported sections, the document sets forth the Seventh-day Adventist belief that salvation is by grace alone through faith alone in Jesus Christ alone. It seeks to combine theological accuracy with clarity and practicality "so that the reader may experience the benefits of salvation and not merely grasp its theory." You can view the entire statement today on the Web site of the Biblical Research Institute (www.adventistbiblicalresearch.org).

But once again, the emphasis on grace came and went. We moved on to other things. The church dealt with more pressing matters: its own rapid growth in third-world countries, challenges to its confidence in Ellen White, organizational issues. I began teaching Bible classes in Adventist academies. The freshmen surveyed the Old Testament, the sophomores studied the New Testament, the juniors concentrated on Bible doctrines, and we worked at preparing the seniors for marriage. Adventist colleges were struggling to keep enrollment up and accreditation challenges down. There just wasn't a lot of time for retreats or stories about Minneapolis and righteousness by faith.

The first faculty meeting I ever attended as a teacher focused on a problem the school was having with kids going to a particular skating rink after school. Some of the faculty said what students did on their own time wasn't our business. Others said the rink's influence was so negative that it spilled over onto our campus. Wanting to bring my recent enthusiasm for grace into this local situation, I made the mistake of offering my opinion. (It was my very first day as a teacher!) In my best, borrowed Morris Venden wisdom, I said, "Remember, sin is in people, not in places." One of the other teachers, a veteran of twenty some years at that school, responded, "That's the dumbest thing I've ever heard!" There was no discussion of grace the rest of that day, and the emphasis faded.

### CONFUSED BY A LACK OF *GRACE*

Twenty years passed. I picked up *Christ Our Righteousness* and read it and appreciated it again. But this time something else struck me as well. I noticed, quite accidentally, how few times Daniells actually had used the word *grace*. Other than in Bible passages or in quoting Ellen White, he scarcely used this compelling biblical word that so richly captures the essence of the gospel.

I began to look through other Adventist publications to see how other Adventist authors treated the subject. What I found surprised and confused me. We Adventists write frequently about "Christ our righteousness," "righteousness by faith," "perfect righteousness," "the Cross," "the good news," and "the gospel"—especially "the everlasting gospel." But we don't seem to like to use the word *grace*.

Here's an example of how difficult it's been for us. The adult Sabbath School lesson quarterly for the first quarter of 1974 was titled, like Daniells's book, "Christ Our Righteousness." In this publication, like nearly all other Sabbath School quarterlies, there are thirteen weekly divisions and ninety-one daily lessons—each division and lesson with a title. In the first quarter of 1974—a quarter, remember, about Christ our righteousness—the word *grace* doesn't appear one single time in all those titles! One hundred and eight Bible passages

are quoted at the beginning of the daily lessons throughout the quarter. Only 2 of those 108 passages contain the word *grace*.[11] How hard would one have to work, I wondered, to compile that many Bible passages on this subject that don't use the word *grace?* And why would one do it?

This 1974 quarterly quotes Ellen White 249 times. Only 19 of the 249 quotations use the word *grace*. (On *one spread, God's law* is referred to 19 times.[12] On another spread, the word *conduct* is used 19 times.) Of the 19 quotations that use the word *grace,* 1 is about "the grace of meekness" and 7 are about the power of God's grace to make us obedient to the law. So, only 11 of the 249—less than 4.5 percent of all the Ellen White quotations in the entire quarterly—actually use the word *grace* to speak about God's saving, justifying, forgiving, unconditional, uncompromising, amazing grace. Why?

Here's another example. One of the most eagerly read books of the 1970s, especially among church members who were responding to the discussion in the church about righteousness by faith, was Douglas Cooper's *Living God's Love.*[13] On page 75 of the book, Cooper uses the phrase "God's love and grace." Other than that single instance, I couldn't find any other usage of the word, even when the author rhapsodizes about "love without an if" and "God's constantly available, ungrudgingly given, total forgiveness extended unhesitatingly to you and me," which are both well-crafted, unambiguous definitions of grace![14]

Dr. Edward Heppenstall was pastor of the La Sierra church, professor of theology at La

---

11. Romans 12:3; Ephesians 2:8, on pages 77, 78 of the quarterly.
12. Pages 104 and 105 of the quarterly.
13. Mountain View, Calif.: Pacific Press®, 1975.
14. Pages 31, 98.

Sierra College, chair of the department of systematic theology at the Theological Seminary at Andrews, professor of theology at Loma Linda University, and the teacher whom most of the pastors I know credit as teaching them about grace. Even he preferred to use the phrase "saving righteousness" when writing his book *Salvation Unlimited*.[15]

On the day I finished reading this book for the first time, I asked a well-known, veteran Adventist theologian, a friend of Heppenstall's, why Heppenstall had such a hard time using the word *grace*. The theologian thought for a moment and answered, "Well, it just sounds so Catholic, doesn't it?"

Is that the problem? Have we been afraid that the language of grace makes us sound Roman Catholic? That we'd be promoting an absolution that would free us to return to our sinning? That a "holy doctrine full of grace" would promote an allegiance to Rome—or at least minimize the differences between us? Can you think of a theological term that sounds *less* Catholic or less about a system of religion that binds you to your own good works?

## THE IMPRECISION OF LANGUAGE

Has there been through all these years a failure to comprehend the significance of the words we use when we talk theology? Perhaps we think our words aren't noteworthy or important enough to choose carefully. A pastor once said to me, "You make too much of words. We're all trying to say the same thing."

Perhaps the pastor was right. Perhaps I shouldn't get so upset when I read in the *Adventist Review* that "the door to grace is repentance."[16] Perhaps the writer is not, after all, trying to subvert grace and place our repentance, our works, in the primary place, coming before grace, causing God to move toward us. Perhaps the writer is, instead, just trying to "say the same thing" using other words, no matter how awkward I consider those words to be.

Perhaps when the *South Pacific Record* carries an article that insists that "keeping God's laws, obedience, and doing the will of God form an integral part of salvation by grace,"[17] I should stay calm. I should smile and think, *The writer's really just saying the same thing we're all trying to say. Don't worry that someone might start believing that salvation is a matter of grace plus what we do. He doesn't really mean that. And specific words really are not that important.*

When an Adventist historian writes in a work about Martin Luther that "faith is a virtue which man uses to acquire grace,"[18] I probably shouldn't scribble in the book words that start out with "What is so frightening about this statement . . ." I probably shouldn't hold on to all those inflammatory thoughts about this being the exact sentiment over which Luther went to war!

---

15. Washington, D.C.: Review and Herald, 1974. Dr. Heppenstall didn't follow this pattern in writing other books or in preaching: "Grace is the eternal and free favor of God, manifested toward the weak, the guilty, and the unworthy. Grace is entirely apart from every supposition of human worth and sinless perfection. Grace belongs where human sinfulness exists. It superabounds over human weakness. Sinners are the only persons with whom grace is at all concerned. Every moment we live by and are saved by God's inexhaustible grace. . . . Salvation by grace means being shaken loose from the folly of implanting our ego at the center with the belief that we must arrive at sinless perfection to be sure of salvation." (Heppenstall, in *Perfection* [Nashville: Southern Publishing Association, 1975], 81, 82.)

16. *Adventist Review,* August 24, 1989.

17. *South Pacific Record,* June 8, 1991.

18. *Martin Luther's Religious Thought* (Mountain View, Calif.: Pacific Press®, 1971), 139.

When two respected denominational leaders write in a book about Adventist beliefs that "we cannot be saved without keeping the law" and that "salvation is by the new-birth experience" and that *justification* is "both a legal act by which our guilt is abolished" *and* "an experience by which our hearts are cleansed from sin,"[19] I probably shouldn't compare their book unflatteringly to the Council of Trent's Declaration on Justification and point out the similarities between their theology and the theology of the *Counter*-Reformation. I should just take a deep breath and mutter something to myself about how these two good men are trying to say the same thing we're all trying to say.

But to tell you the truth, I don't believe we're all trying to say the same thing. I don't believe that our reluctance about grace is just a clumsiness, an imprecision of language. I know the pressure that is brought to bear on pastors and teachers, writers and publishers to go back to the way we used to do Adventism, to return to an earlier works orientation. "We must be careful not to overemphasize the grace of God," an editorial in the *Adventist Review* warns, "to the devaluation of the claims of the law of God."[20] There it is! That's the real fear. We're afraid that an emphasis on God's grace will lessen our commitment to obedience, to living the sanctified life, to keeping the commandments, to remembering the Sabbath day to keep it holy.

It's the same fear that Ronald Sider expresses in his recent book *The Scandal of the Evangeli-cal Conscience: Why Are Christians Living Just Like the Rest of the World?* when he complains that "many contemporary Christians act as if it is possible to divide Jesus up, accepting Him as Savior and neglecting Him as Lord."[21]

Sider is absolutely right in wanting Christians to be Christlike; to be responsible and accountable, to study the Bible and keep the Sabbath,[22] to feed the hungry and clothe the naked and to avoid hypocrisy, greed, and slander. But when he argues that a Martin Luther-like emphasis on justification "easily leads to a neglect of sanctification and holy, obedient living,"[23] he reveals a woeful distance not only from the Reformation rediscovery of grace but also from the biblical insistence that it is the reality of being saved by grace alone that motivates our desire to make Jesus the sanctifying Lord of our life.[24] If we Christians are doing poorly in our sanctification (and we certainly are), it is not because we are emphasizing grace too much. It is because we are not emphasizing grace enough!

This time the emphasis must hold: There never has been a more consequential time to insist that we get it absolutely right! When a pastor tries to amend his church's mission statement to talk about what people have to stop doing *before grace is extended to them,* we can't stay quiet any longer. When a book shows up in an Adventist Book Center claiming that "Romans 2:13 tells us that we must be *doers* of the law to be justified,"[25] failing to follow Paul's argument all the way to "therefore no one will be declared righteous in his sight by

---

19. *This We Believe* (Boise, Idaho: Pacific Press®, 1993), 163, 90, 88.
20. *Adventist Review,* July 23, 1992.
21. Ronald J. Sider, *The Scandal of the Evangelical Conscience* (Grand Rapids, Mich.: Baker Books, 2005), 67.
22. Ibid., 88.
23. Ibid., 58.
24. See the Grace Notes for chapter 9, "The Clothes of the Chosen."
25. *God's Law and God's Grace* (Roseville, Calif.: 2002), 34.

observing the law" (Romans 3:20) and missing altogether " 'by observing the law no one will be justified' " (Galatians 2:16), we must speak up. When people say they are attempting to attain perfection of character so Jesus will take them to heaven, we must feel the obligation to tell them about grace.

A man came up to me after a recent camp meeting sermon and said, "What I don't like about you preachers of grace is that you make fun of us who are trying to do good, to obey the commandments and live a good life. You've forgotten that there are some good things about legalism."

I'm sorry if a preacher of grace has made fun of someone trying to do good. I apologize for everyone who has laughed at those whose emphasis is on the keeping of the commandments. Those kinds of responses should never happen. But there is *nothing* good about legalism! Legalism is trying to get to heaven by our own works and on the merit of our own obedience, and there's *nothing good* and *nothing productive* and *nothing biblical* about such a course of action. It is as wrong to stay silent in the face of such shallowness as it is to make fun of it.

THE MOST IMPORTANT THING

This is the day for the good news. This is the time when every word we speak should be spoken with clarity and power and be "full of grace" (Colossians 4:6). This is the moment when every song we sing should soar with the melodies and harmonies of amazing grace, when every publication should announce "God's grace in all its truth" (1:6), when every ministry should proclaim, "Grace and peace be yours in abundance" (1 Peter 1:2). This can be the era of the everlasting "gospel of God's grace" (Acts 20:24) given to "every nation, tribe, language and people" (Revelation 14:6).

Charles Bradford, former president of the North American Division of our church, says: "A people will appear in time and history who will proclaim and model the kingdom of grace. Those who drink deeply at grace's fountain will present these living waters to all the people who dwell on earth. Seventh-day Adventists must be in the vanguard, foremost proponents, stewards of His matchless, saving grace."[26]

Dr. Fritz Guy preached at the La Sierra University Church for Homecoming Sabbath on March 9, 2002. "I have learned many things in fifty years as pastor, teacher, and theologian," he said. "But nothing else is as important as knowing that God's love is unlimited and unconditional—that we are truly loved—right here, right now, just the way we are. This is the meaning of grace.

"This is the proper center of all our Christian beliefs and Christian living. This is the most fundamental definition of *who we are.* When we know this—really know it, believe it, and live it—nothing else matters *decisively.* . . . Nothing else defines us as fundamentally as this: We are loved unconditionally by the Personal Source of all reality.

"Nothing—absolutely nothing—I have learned is as important as this."

TIME TO EMBRACE THE GOSPEL

When I was a young teacher just starting out, I had in my office at school a huge, colorful chart of the last days prepared by Gordon Collier, an Adventist pastor who had studied the end times like nobody else had ever studied them. Every possible reference to the Second Coming, the time of trouble, the death decrees, the persecution, and the

26. Charles Bradford, unpublished manuscript, "Only by Grace."

plagues appeared on the chart. It contained boxes and arrows and lines and exclamation points and color-coded themes. My eyes often would drift away from the material I was reading to prepare for my classes, or from tests I was grading up to the details. When students came into the office to talk, we often ended up exploring the chart and discussing what would happen before Jesus came to earth again.

After months of fascination with the chart, however, I realized that I had become so absorbed in its details that I hadn't spent significant time with the Person who was going to return and virtually no time at all celebrating the grace that made my standing in that day a certainty. Before long, I took the chart down, rolled it up, and put it away. It hasn't come out in a long, long time.

Then, just a few years ago, I spoke at an alumni homecoming church service at the little school in Arroyo Grande on the central California coast where I had attended the seventh and eighth grades. I talked about the *Valuegenesis* research that had revealed that Adventist young people knew the doctrine of salvation by grace but held on to a works orientation in their own lives. I spoke of how we had presented other emphases, even good ones like the Sabbath and the Second Coming, in such a way as to rob our youth of the assurance of salvation. I spoke of the necessity to share the gospel of grace until we fell so in love with Jesus that the Sabbath and the Second Coming became prized dynamics in our experience rather than dreaded ones.

After the church service, just as I was sitting down at the potluck, I looked across the room and noticed a man coming my way. It was Gordon Collier. He'd been there all morning. I leaned over to Karen and said, "I'm really going to get it from this guy."

Gordon was walking straight for our table, so, rather than wait for him to arrive, I got up, walked toward him, extended my hand, and said, "Gordon, it's good to see you."

"How do you know who I am?" he asked.

I told him about the chart I used to have hanging on the wall in my office and about all the time I had spent studying it and about how his name was there in the corner of the chart right in front of me.

"Oh, I'm sorry that's the way you know me," he said. Before I could ask him to explain, he said he had spent most of his life trying to find out all the details about the end of time. "But I found out, after all that study, that I knew more about the time of trouble than about the Person who was going to return and save me from all that trouble."

With a big smile on my face, I asked him, "What are you doing these days?"

I'll never forget his answer. "I'm going everywhere I can," he said, "to tell as many people as I can about the amazing grace of Jesus."

In that moment, Gordon Collier became a hero of mine. And an example of what I want to do with my life. And what I want the church to be. Whatever our emphasis has been before, whatever our fundamental focus, now is the time to put everything else in its proper place, to stop being afraid of God's enduring grace, and to fully embrace the everlasting gospel.

The treasure of grace will give us the definition of our self we so desperately need to know. It is grace that destroys our fear of God and establishes our relationship with Him. It is grace that builds the sure foundation to everything we do—our family life, our work, our church involvement. It is grace that lends wonder and relevance to our beliefs. It is grace that transforms us. It is grace that gives us lasting joy.

Now is the time to unlock the treasure once and for all.

Before our thoughts of truth and time, before the consultation;[27]
Before the furtive hopes displace a fear of records kept;
Before the righteousness of Christ our wonder could accept;
Before our awe, before our fear, before our hope, was grace.

Before the boundless wealth of God secured our souls' salvation;
Before the gospel's solid brace unlocked the treasure's seal;[28]
Before the jubilant refrains God's covenant reveal;
Before the songs, before the seal, before the gift, was grace.

# Grace in Question

## Chapter 18: The Everlasting Gospel

Chapter 18 concludes our study with a broad overview of the grace emphasis in the Adventist Church since the Minneapolis General Conference of 1888. Our focus on the righteousness of Christ has come and gone repeatedly, until we're left to wonder why we can't hold on to what's supposed to be central for us. Can our day, finally, begin the era of the everlasting gospel?

1. Think of a house in which your family has lived recently or a long time ago, and describe the architectural features of the house. What parts of the house make you think of God's grace?

2. Read the three "columns" of Bible passages on pages 243, 244. Do you see the progression from simple to sturdy to ornate? Why do you think all Bible verses on grace are not exactly alike? Why is there so much variety in the passages?

3. Quite a bit of this chapter details the falling away of Jones and Waggoner after they had performed such a service to the church in calling our attention to grace in the 1880s. Why is it essential to be grounded in the Bible's presentation of salvation instead of tying our hearts to some person with whom we've come to agree?

4. React to this statement: "The thief on the cross is the rule, not the exception." What meaning does it hold for you?

5. How can grace-oriented people best uphold their perspective in the face of detractors? How can we best approach people who want the church's emphasis to be on keeping the commandments instead of accepting God's grace? Why do you think there is tension between the two positions?

---

27. Concluding the prologue "Before the Beginning" (see page 13). "Truth and time" references the Sabbath and the Second Coming. For "the consultation," see pages 246, 247.

28. See the introduction, "The Buried Treasure," for the analogy about the unlocking of the treasure.

# GRACE NOTES
## REVELATION 14—THE NATURE OF THE GOSPEL

Q. Why do you believe that now is the time to unlock the treasure of God's grace?

Q. How can something eternal and everlasting begin in the present?

The Bible has a lot to say about what lasts. Translated from the original languages into English, the words used to describe what lasts all sound pretty much alike: *eternal* (Deuteronomy 33:27), *everlasting* (John 3:16), *for ever* (1 Kings 10:9), *for evermore* (Psalm 16:11).

God is *eternal* (Genesis 21:33); He has no beginning and no end. God's love to us is *eternal* (1 Kings 10:9). His ways are *eternal* (Habakkuk 3:6). He gives *eternal* life (Matthew 25:46). He is the Author, the Source of *eternal* salvation (Hebrews 5:9) and *eternal* redemption (Hebrews 9:12). God's word is *eternal* (Psalm 119:89); it cannot be changed or altered.

God's covenant with us is *everlasting* (Genesis 9:16); it remains in force as long as He exists. His kingdom is an *everlasting* kingdom (Daniel 4:3); it is endless, enduring, timeless. His righteousness is *everlasting* (Psalm 119:142). " 'With *everlasting* kindness I will have compassion on you,' says the LORD your Redeemer" (Isaiah 54:8, emphasis supplied here and in the following texts). He is the *"everlasting* Father" (Isaiah 9:6).

" 'The LORD will reign *for ever and ever*' " (Exodus 15:18). "The LORD is King *for ever and ever*" (Psalm 10:16). "God is our God for *ever and ever*" (48:14). " ' "The saints of the Most High will receive the kingdom and will possess it forever—yes, *for ever and ever*" ' " (Daniel 7:18).

The book of Revelation tells us about something that lasts forever: "I saw another angel flying in midair," John tells us, "and he had the *eternal gospel* to proclaim to those who live on the earth" (Revelation 14:6). Like the eternal pleasures we find at God's right hand (Psalm 16:11), like the eternal blessings we receive in His presence (Psalm 21:6), like God's Word, which has been true from the beginning (Psalm 119:160), like God's dominion, which is from generation to generation (Daniel 4:3), the gospel is everlasting. It stands settled from eternity to eternity. It endures forever.

The everlasting gospel insists that God chose us in Jesus before the beginning of the world (Ephesians 1:4), before our obedience or good works, before we had even responded to God. The gospel repeats the fact that our inheritance has been prepared for us since the creation of the world (Matthew 25:34), long before we were born. It reveals that God's love is *unfailing,* that it lasts *for ever* (Psalm 52:8).

The second thing Revelation reveals about the gospel is that the gospel is for everyone, for all those who live on the earth—for "every nation, tribe, language and people" (Revelation 14:6). Christ is worthy of eternal praise because He has "purchased" people for God " 'from every tribe and language and people and nation' " (5:9). That's the good news Jesus told us to preach

" 'in the whole world as a testimony to all nations' " before the end of time (Matthew 24:14). The result of the gospel will be a great multitude in heaven "that no one could count, from every nation, tribe, people and language, standing before the throne and in front of the Lamb" (Revelation 7:9).

The everlasting gospel—the good news that Jesus has been thinking about you and me since before the beginning of our world, that He's been planning your home and mine, the place where we'll be living ten million years from now, and that He has made it all possible by what He has done in our behalf—is the sum and substance, the alpha and the omega, the core and center and essence of why Christians are Christians and of why Christians so love to share their story with people who have not yet heard it. Everything else—our behavior, our doctrines, our medical service, our educational work, our sermons, our publications—*everything else* is the result of the gospel, a response to God's grace, a celebration of the good news.

Let's begin shouting out loud and singing together at the top of our voices. The endless treasure of the grace of Jesus is the one, great, central, fundamental belief around which all other truths cluster. It has been so from the beginning. It continues to be so for eternity.

# GLOSSARY

The following is a brief list with definitions of historical and theological words and phrases used in this book. Some of the terms have also been defined within the body of the book. The page numbers (in parentheses) refer to the first mention and to significant discussions in the text. The words in SMALL CAPS within the definitions are also defined in this glossary or identified in the Biographical Notes.

**Atonement** (20, 40, 45). "The sacrifice of Christ as an *atonement* for sin is the great truth around which all other truths cluster" (Ellen G. White, *Gospel Workers* [Washington, D.C.: Review and Herald, 1948], 315, emphasis supplied).

The state of reconciliation between a holy God and sinful humans. The means by which obstacles to reconciliation with God are removed.

The Old Testament sacrificial system provided one illustration for the Hebrew people of how God "covered" or "atoned for" their sins through the blood of the sacrificial lamb, in whose death they took part (Leviticus 17:11). Christians, realizing that a lamb's death can never reconcile us with God (Hebrews 10:1–11), believe those sacrifices point to Jesus, "the Lamb of God" (John 1:29) who was slain for us from the foundation of the world (Revelation 13:8).

**Attribute** (170, 171). "John the Baptist . . . is recognizable by his *attribute.*"

In religious art, each saint is characterized by an element, or attribute, to help identify him or her, such as Peter with his keys and John the Baptist pointing to Jesus. This "identifying code" of the saints, which is common from popular works to the most sophisticated masterpieces, has been defined over the course of a thousand years of Western art. It remained substantially unchanged from the Middle Ages on.

**Barbarian** (138). "The *barbarian* invaders all look alike to the citizens of Rome."

Originally, a foreigner—one thought of as uncivilized. The Romans applied the term to anyone who lived outside the Roman Empire, anyone who spoke a language other than Latin, anyone who was born into what the Romans considered an inferior culture.

**Bishop** (131). "*Bishop* Ambrose preaches 'the sound doctrine of salvation.' "

A high-ranking, ordained Christian clergy, usually given charge of the governance of a church in a particular city. An overseer or guardian. Essentially equivalent to a pastor today (see 1 Timothy 3:1–7).

**Book of the Dead** (54). "The Egyptian funerary text called *The Book of the Dead* explains the ceremony."

From as early as the sixteenth century B.C. in the Eighteenth Dynasty, the ancient Egyptians placed inside their coffins papyrus scrolls containing charms, passwords, and magical formulas to be used by the deceased in the afterlife. From these scrolls, which we call the Book of the Dead, we understand the nature of ancient Egyptian religion and especially the ceremony called The Weighing of the Heart, which details how the deceased person's fitness for eternity was judged.

**Catholic** (127). "The 'counter-church' 'rose up in every town . . . as a rival to the church *Catholic.*' "

*Catholic* means universal, general, all-inclusive. A *Roman* Catholic is a member of the worldwide Roman Catholic Church.

**College of Cardinals** (166). "The *College of Cardinals* [took] almost a year . . . to elect a new pope."

The body of all eligible Roman CATHOLIC cardinals that meets at the death of a POPE in a conclave to elect the next pope, or pontiff.

**Confessors** (119). "Below the martyrs in terms of importance are the *'confessors.'* "

Initially, one who had confessed to being a Christian at a time during which such a confession brought about persecution and even death. In between the sentencing and the execution of the death penalty, the confessor was held in prison and visited by church members. In time, confessors were asked to settle local

church disputes, and they were granted the authority to hear the confessions of the sins of church members.

**Contrition, Confession, Satisfaction, Absolution** (152, 153). "Without this entire process [of *contrition, confession, satisfaction, and absolution*], no guilty sinner could be assured of salvation."

Roman CATHOLIC THEOLOGY concerning forgiveness of sins describes how a church member is forgiven for sins committed after baptism. In order to be worthy of receiving the Sacrament of Reconciliation, one must first of all be genuinely sorry for his or her sins. This sorrow is known as *contrition.* The next step in the Catholic system, *confession,* is telling a priest how you have offended God since the last time you confessed. *Satisfaction* entails anything you are directed to do to make up for, or pay the penalty for, the sins you have committed. Once you have paid the penalty, the priest can grant *absolution,* which is pardon or forgiveness.

**Council of Trent** (180). Luther thought the *Council of Trent* was angry at God.

The immensely consequential ecumenical council of the Roman CATHOLIC Church held between 1545 and 1563. Frequently referred to as the most important council in the long history of the church, the council established Roman Catholic teaching on the DOCTRINE of JUSTIFICATION in opposition to the REFORMATION insistence on SALVATION by GRACE alone. The doctrines of the council are referred to as *Tridentine,* after Trent, the city in northern Italy where the council was held.

**Creed** (13). "Before a thousand years' erase of venerable *creed* . . ."

From the Latin *credo,* for "I believe." A formal statement of religious belief. The written teachings of a religious body, generally accepted by that group. Earliest Christian creeds were simple, such as "Jesus is Lord" (see 1 Corinthians 12:3). Later creeds developed into succinct but systematic statements of the faith, such as the Apostles' Creed and the Nicene Creed.

**Culture of Achievement** (40). *"The Culture of Achievement:* No pain, no gain, it's all in a day's work."

The approach to everyday life, deeply imbedded in American culture and throughout the world, which suggests we must work for whatever benefits come to us in our experience. From our childhood, we are taught we have to earn our allowance, work hard for good grades in school, conform to company rules to hold down a job, and even work for success in our relationships.

While this approach is productive, even necessary, in the world in which we live, it is counterproductive to understanding the way God grants SALVATION, which is by GRACE alone, freely given, without consideration of our works or MERIT.

**Developmental Theology** (130). "Augustine's theology is not so much inconsistent as it is *developmental."*

The fact that our views of God develop gradually over our lifetime rather than being handed down to us from heaven as one comprehensive understanding. Paul expressed this reality when he wrote, "When I was a child, I talked like a child" (1 Corinthians 13:11).

**Doctrine** (42). "When all the *doctrines* have been discussed, . . . the only thing that matters is Jesus." (David Newman, "Farewell," *Ministry,* September 1995.)

A principle or tenet that is held as a fundamental truth and taught, advocated, or presented for acceptance or belief, as by a religious group. A dogma.

A list of five "leading doctrines" of the Seventh-day Adventist Church first appeared in the *Review and Herald* in 1854. By 1872, the list had grown to twenty-five propositions and was referred to as a "synopsis of our faith." In 1889, the list was expanded to twenty-eight statements. From 1931 until 1980, Adventists used a list of twenty-two doctrines to explain the "principle features" of our faith. At the General Conference session held in Dallas, Texas, in 1980, a list of twenty-seven doctrines was approved.

At the 2005 St. Louis, Missouri, session of the General Conference, a twenty-eighth fundamental belief was proposed and accepted. (See "FUNDAMENTAL BELIEFS.")

**Donatists, Donatism** (128). No sinner can be a part of a perfect church, the *Donatists* claim.

"Donatism is the name given to the schismatic movement in the North African church which began with a disputed election to the see of Carthage, sometime between 308 and 311." (Allan D. Fitzgerald, gen. ed., *Augustine Through the Ages* [Grand Rapids, Mich.: Wm. B. Eerdmans, 1999], 284.)

Donatists believed that the only church that was a true church was one in which the "communion of saints" was a communion of genuine, perfect people. Their own "innocence," their ritual purity, their meritorious suffering, they proposed, were God's methods of preserving His chosen people. God would listen to their prayers alone.

**Eschatology** (42). " 'It is not grace, but our *eschatology* that makes us unique,' " the theologian said.

Eschatology is the branch of THEOLOGY that is concerned with the ultimate or last things, the end of the world, the *eschaton*. The explanation of Bible passages that prophesy "last-day events."

**Faith** (44). Salvation is by grace alone, through *faith* alone, in Jesus Christ alone.

Biblical faith is trusting that God means what He says, and that He has the power to keep His promises to us (Romans 4:20, 21). There is no MERIT in faith; it is, like GRACE, God's gift to us (Ephesians 2:8). "Faith is not our Savior. It earns nothing." (Ellen G. White, *The Desire of Ages* [Mountain View, Calif.: Pacific Press®, 1940], 175.) "Faith is simply believing God." (Francis Schaeffer, *True Spirituality* [Wheaton, Ill.: Tyndale House Publishers, 1971], 78.)

**Finished Work** (76). "When the *finished work* of salvation . . . was announced to the angels, 'inexpressible joy filled heaven.' "

The work that produces eternal SALVATION has been completed, finished, and accomplished by Jesus and is given to humans by GRACE alone through FAITH. It cannot be added to by any human effort, work, or MERIT, no matter how worthy or valuable or deserving.

**Fresco** (39). "The revolutionary *frescoes* break the stranglehold of the sterile, flat Byzantine conventions."

The art of painting by pressing pigments, dissolved in water, into fresh, wet plaster, as opposed to painting on a dry surface. In fresco, the painting actually becomes part of the surface on which it is painted.

**Fundamental Beliefs** (119). "No compelling statements about grace show up on the early lists of *fundamental beliefs.* "

The group of DOCTRINES closely held and taught by a denomination is often referred to as that church's fundamental beliefs. The summary or explanation of those beliefs as proclaimed by the church. (See the entry on "DOCTRINE.")

**Gnostics, Gnosticism** (120). *"Gnosticism* included the distinct, works-oriented teaching that *truly spiritual* believers don't need salvation."

From the Greek word for knowledge, *gnosis*. In early Christianity, a group of believers held a variant THEOLOGY concerning the value of a knowledge about God that they felt had been revealed to only a few. Understanding this information was for Gnostics the key to attaining SALVATION; "knowledge enables the divine spark, the *pneuma,* to return to the Source from which it originally had fallen."

In 1945, in Nag Hammadi, Egypt, archaeologists discovered fourth-century Gnostic texts from which, along with the attacks of early Christian writers, we derive most of our information about Gnosticism.

**Gospel** (32, 155). "That Sabbath morning, the *gospel* began to be an unassailable foundation for me."

The good news (the Greek word is *evangelion*) that our eternal SALVATION is sure because of the gift of God's GRACE (Ephesians 1:13), given to us in Jesus Christ (Romans 1:16). The *Gospels* are the four New Testament books (Matthew, Mark, Luke, and John) that tell us the story of the INCARNATION and the life, ministry, death, and resurrection of Jesus.

**Gospel of Grace** (77). "The *gospel of grace* is all about resting in the saving presence of Jesus."

A further clarification of the word GOS-PEL: "The gospel of Christ is from beginning to end the gospel of saving GRACE." (Ellen G. White, *Testimonies to Ministers* [Mountain View, Calif.: Pacific Press®, 1923], 92.) "Grace is the soul and the music of the gospel; without it, the gospel is silent." (Charles Spurgeon, *Grace Abounding in a Believer's Life* [Lynwood, Wash.: Emerald Books, 1994], 99.)

**Grace** (44)." 'There never was a moment when it was not the delight of the eternal mind to manifest His *grace* to humanity.' " (Ellen G. White, *Signs of the Times®*, June 12 1901.)

Grace is the divine acceptance that seeks and saves sinful human beings, doing for us that which we are powerless to do for ourselves. Grace is not the beginning point of the Christian journey; grace is the road upon which journeying Christians walk day by day, moment by moment. Grace is not a robe Christians put on in order to be correctly dressed, grace is the air Christians breathe in order to live.

**Grace Orientation** (52). "We set a *works* orientation over against a *grace orientation.*"

An approach to the Christian message that emphasizes the good news that our place in God's kingdom is assured because of God's undying, unquenchable love for us, not because of our MERIT or our good works.

**Great Awakening** (193). "Add to these factors a *'Great Awakening'* of religious fervor."

Two periods in American history that are characterized by a revival of religious interest and practice. The First Great Awakening took place in colonial America in the 1730s and 1740s, led by preachers such as Jonathan Edwards and George Whitefield.

The Second Great Awakening centered in the northeastern states in the 1790s and early 1800s, and spread through the mid-Atlantic states to the South and the frontier. Conspicuous in this movement were Timothy Dwight, Lyman Beecher, and Nathaniel Taylor. In upstate New York, the driving force was the noted evangelist CHARLES FINNEY.

**Great Controversy** (63, 64). "The first three chapters of Genesis effectively place the entire *great controversy* in the forefront of our thinking."

The continuing battle between God and the forces of evil, which began with the accusations of Lucifer against the character and government of God (see Revelation 12:1–9) and will end with the creation of a new heaven and a new earth and the destruction of all death, sorrow, crying, and pain (see Revelation 21:1–4). The irreconcilable warfare "between darkness and light, sin and righteousness, wrong and right, death and life." (Ellen G. White, *The Great Controversy* [Mountain View, Calif.: Pacific Press®, 1950], page iii.)

The conclusion of the great controversy results with "one pulse of harmony and gladness" beating through the vast creation, and "all things, animate and inanimate, in their unshadowed beauty and perfect joy" declaring "that God is love." (Ibid., 678.)

**Great Schism** (166). "Before the 'Great Schism' [was] over, a church council [met] in Pisa."

Also known as the Western Schism and the Papal Schism, this split in the CATHOLIC Church took place in 1378, following the return of the papacy to Rome, after almost seventy years in France. Two months after the election of an Italian POPE, the cardinals repeated of their decision and on September 20, 1378, elected a new, rival pope. A later church council resulted in the election of a third pope. The schism finally was resolved in 1417 at the Council of Constance.

**Illumination of the Scriptures** (150). "The monasteries also can be credited with much of the . . . *illumination of the Scriptures* that took place."

In medieval sacred art, illumination was the act of decorating a page of a Bible manuscript or ornamenting the initial letter of a page or section of the Bible.

**Incarnation** (14). "Before the gathered angels sang the wondrous *incarnation.*"

The Christian belief that the Second Person of the Godhead literally and miraculously became a human being and lived on this earth as the person named Jesus (see John 1:1–14). The purpose of the Incarnation was to reveal the God who "so loved" us already and to announce eternal SALVATION (John 3:16, 17).

**Infidel** (154). "Sinners could purchase a remission of a portion of the penalties for their sins . . . by participating in a crusade against the *infidels.*"

An infidel is one who has no religious beliefs, or one who is an unbeliever in respect to a particular RELIGION.

**Justification** (107, 108, 153, 168, 169). All "are *justified* freely by his grace through the redemption that came by Christ Jesus" (Romans 3:24).

The act by which God declares that He will treat sinners just as if they had never sinned. Justification is about God's GRACE forgiving us and accepting us and making us a member of His family.

**Lamentation** (39). "In the middle of the north wall . . . is Giotto's bold depiction of the *Lamentation.*"

An expression of sorrow and grief. An elegy or dirge. In biblical literature, a cry of mourning or loss (see 2 Samuel 1:17–27). In art, the moment at the foot of the cross of Jesus when His body has been removed from the cross and His family and followers have gathered around the body to mourn the loss of their Lord and dearest Friend.

**Legalism** (42, 251). "Isn't the pendulum swinging 'too far away from *legalism* toward grace?' "

The belief that our obedience, behavior, or MERIT contributes in any way, large or small, to our eternal SALVATION. Legalism is trying to get to heaven by our own works. From the perspective of the Christian GOSPEL OF GRACE, there is nothing good, productive, or biblical about such an approach to salvation.

**Merit** (41, 117) Christians [began] to define and distinguish their Christianity. . . *by the nobility and* merit *of their own behavior.*

That property of a specific good deed, or good works in general, that entitles the doer of the good works to receive a reward from the person in whose service the good work was done.

In medieval THEOLOGY, the church taught that God *owed* believers such a reward if the merit were sufficient, including the reward of eternal life for considerable merit. The more good works, the more the merit, and the greater the reward.

**Monastics, Monasticism** (149, 150). "The educational work of the *monastic* schools grew."

The religious practice of renouncing all worldly possessions and practices in order to fully devote one's life to a contemplative, spiritual existence. Men pursuing a monastic life are generally called "monks" or "brothers," and women monastics are usually referred to as "nuns" or "sisters."

**Moral Influence Theory** (151). "Abelard's theory has been called 'the *moral influence' theory.*"

The INCARNATION and death of Jesus are the highest expression and clearest communication of God's love. The effect of the Cross is toward humanity, not toward God. "According to ABELARD, what humanity needs is a new motive for action, not a compensation paid to God on its behalf." (Roger Olson, *The Story of Christian Theology* [Downers Grove, Ill.: InterVarsity Press, 1999], 328.) Captivated by the parable of the prodigal son, Abelard saw the Cross as God's running toward humanity, demonstrating His loving heart.

**Mother Church** (128). "The tension in North Africa between the *mother church* and the Donatists is raging."

In the most general sense, the stream of Christian belief and practice that flows from Jesus and the disciples and apostles, through the early administrative efforts of the believers, to the members of the primitive New Testament church, and ultimately, to all Christians today. From this stream, this "mother church," all branches of Christianity, historical and contemporary, have proceeded.

**Nahushtan** (82). "How often have we turned our sacred symbols into *Nahushtans*—into objects of worship?"

The ancient sacred symbol of a bronze snake on a pole commanded by God, shaped by Moses (Numbers 21:4–9), later referred to by Jesus (John 3:14, 15). The object was destroyed by Hezekiah (2 Kings 18:4) because the Israelites were worshipping the symbol, not the God to whom the symbol pointed.

**Negative Confession** (55). "While the defendant recited his protestations of innocence—his *'negative confession'*—his heart reacted on the scale."

In the ancient Egyptian BOOK OF THE DEAD, during the final judgment ceremony known as the Weighing of the Heart, the deceased is instructed to make a series of thirty-six statements to determine his or her fitness for eternal life. The *proper* statements were to be made in the negative: "I have not blasphemed a god"; "I have not made anyone sick." The statements came to be known as "the negative confession."

**Numidian** (126, 127). "The *Numidian* bishops teach that those who had given up their books are no longer worthy of being church members."

Numidia was an ancient kingdom in northern Africa (corresponding roughly to present-day Algeria) that became a Roman province. The people of North Africa became known as Numidians.

**Orthodox, Orthodoxy** (130). "They quote passages that obviously differ from *orthodoxy.*"

From the Greek words for *correct* and *teaching*. The accepted, traditional, or established DOCTRINE or belief. One who adheres to such doctrine. Those whose beliefs differ from orthodoxy are generally referred to by the church as *heretics* (heresy is the denial of defined doctrine) or *schismatics* (a schism is caused by the denial of authority).

**Osirian Doctrine** (54, 55). "The . . . rationale for this ceremony [is known as] 'the *Osirian doctrine* of self-justification.' "

Osiris was the Egyptian god of death and the underworld. He presided over the final judgment ceremony known as The Weighing of the Heart. (See the entry on the "NEGATIVE CONFESSION.") This ancient religious practice is typical of the belief, widely held in antiquity, that eternal life is dependent upon our behavior in this world.

**Pagan, Paganism** (120; 41, 56, 139). "At the foundation of every *pagan* religion is the principle that we can save ourselves." (See Ellen G. White, *The Desire of Ages* [Mountain View, Calif.: Pacific Press®, 1940], 35.)

Traditionally, a derogatory reference to anyone who is not Christian, Muslim, or Jew. One who has no RELIGION or who is polytheistic.

In this study, any adherent to a religious system emphasizing the human attempt to influence, persuade, or purchase the good will or favor of a god by sacrifice, behavior, or works. This "need to bargain with God" has been "the faith that has animated pagan religion ever since there was such a thing—namely, the belief that we can repair our own relationship with God by putting God in a position where he cannot say no to us." (Paul Tournier, *Guilt and Grace* [New York: Harper & Row, 1962], *xx*).

**Pelagians, Pelagianism** (Ch. 10). "The *Pelagian* writings on sin, free will, and grace turn the Holy Land into a cauldron of controversy."

Followers of PELAGIUS, who advocated a variation of the GOSPEL that emphasized not the good news of what Christ has accomplished for us but the basic good nature of human be-

ings and the freedom of their will to choose to do good. If God commands us to do good and not sin, Pelagius reasoned, then we must have the inherent capacity to do what God commands; we must be able to choose not to sin without the assistance of GRACE or any other spiritual force or persuasion.

Since PERFECTION is possible for humans, Pelagius insisted, it is obligatory. Because sin is not inevitable, and those who have not sinned do not need to be justified, a SALVATION not based on grace must be available for those who have lived a life of victory, perfectly keeping the commandments of God.

**Pendulum Argument** (42, 236). "Isn't the *pendulum* swinging 'too far away from legalism toward grace?' "

The argument put forward by many Christians that LEGALISM is at one inappropriate extreme of a religious pendulum swing (an extreme from which we must retreat), and that GRACE is at the opposite end of the pendulum (an additional extreme from which "balanced" Christians also retreat).

A GOSPEL understanding of the Christian faith proposes instead that it is not grace but *lawlessness* that is at the opposite extreme of legalism; grace is in fact at the central position of Christian THEOLOGY. It is grace that places the proper emphasis on law keeping, not for righteousness or in order to earn eternal life but out of respect and appreciation for the enduring love of God to us, expressed in the life and ministry of Jesus. It is grace that protects the Christian from the extremes of both legalism and lawlessness.

**Perfection, Perfectionism** (140). "Since *perfection* is possible . . . , Pelagius insists, it is obligatory."

The complete absence of error, sin, or wrongdoing. A quality of life many Christians think those who wish to be eligible for eternal life must achieve in this world before the second coming of Jesus.

**Plan of Salvation** (64; 32). "Nothing in the rest of the Bible [will improve] on this initial story as an explanation of how the *plan of salvation* operates."

The divinely originated arrangement to provide eternal life for sinful human beings, who, by their rebellion and estrangement from God, have forfeited the ability to earn a place in heaven. The plan, put in place before the creation of planet Earth (Ephesians 1:4; Revelation 13:8), assures us that it is the never-failing love of God for us that resulted in Jesus coming to this earth, so that "whoever believes in Him might not perish but have everlasting life" (John 3:16).

**Pope** (166). "Rioting breaks out in the streets of Rome as Romans demand that a Roman become *pope.*"

The leader of the Roman CATHOLIC Church. By at least the early fifth century, the terms *bishop of Rome* and *pope* had become interchangeable. The office itself is known as the *papacy,* or, in Roman Catholic writings, the *primacy of Peter.* According to Catholic reckoning, Pope Benedict XVI is the 266th pope.

**Protestant, Protestantism** (Ch. 12, 167). " 'Grace is the most important word in the *Protestant* vocabulary.' "

The branch of Christianity resulting from the sixteenth century REFORMATION, during which the Reformers *protested* against certain practices and doctrines of the church, especially the doctrine that proposed we can contribute to our SALVATION through good works or earned MERIT.

**Ransom Theory** (151). "Pope Gregory the Great explained the *ransom theory* in its clearest detail."

The ransom theory proposes that God the Father offers Christ's death on the cross in exchange for the right to save humans. Satan, according to the theory, was tricked into thinking he could keep Christ in the tomb forever and so accepted the ransom.

**Redemption** (40, 44). "In [Christ] we have *redemption* through his blood, the forgiveness of sins, in accordance with the riches of God's grace" (Ephesians 1:7).

The act of redeeming or the condition of having been redeemed. In Christian THEOLOGY, redemption is the assurance of a SALVATION that is based on the unending GRACE of God as demonstrated in the person and ministry of Jesus Christ (Romans 5:8).

**Reformation** (Ch. 12). The "rediscovery of God's grace provided the spark that lit the *Reformation* fire."

The sixteenth century movement that, in the minds of Reformers such as JON HUS, JOHN WYCLIF, MARTIN LUTHER, and JOHN CALVIN was to reform the church and correct the errors they saw in its DOCTRINES, the chief of which was the teaching that humans could influence their eternal SALVATION by their good works, their obedience, or by the MERIT of their deeds. The Reformation principles are often referred to as "only the Bible," "only by GRACE," and "only by FAITH."

**Religion** (51, 52). "*Religion* answers the questions of restless souls about the supernatural, the eternal, the spiritual."

Religion is from our perspective. It is a human attempt to make some sense of what happens in this world, to bridge the chasm between the experienced and the unknown, to forge some sort of relationship with whatever force or being or god there is out there.

**Retribution Principle** (57). "Eliphaz . . . lectures Job with words that reek of the *retribution principle.*"

The principle states that, in order for God to be just, He must reward and punish in this lifetime in proportion to the righteousness or wickedness of each individual. Prosperity is a reward for righteousness. Suffering is a punishment for wickedness. Great prosperity is a sign of great righteousness. And great suffering reveals great wickedness.

**Righteousness** (44). "The robe of Christ's *righteousness* 'has in it not one thread of human devising.' " (Ellen G. White, *Christ's Object Lessons* [Washington, D.C.: Review and Herald, 1941], 311.)

The state of full moral uprightness. The absence of all sin and guilt. The condition for entrance into heaven and the joys of eternal life. Righteousness is not about stopping sinning; it is about never having sinned at all.

For the GOSPEL-oriented Christian, righteousness is a quality of Jesus alone, which He gives by GRACE to all those who believe in Him. It is this "robe" of His righteousness covering our sinfulness that makes us acceptable in judgment. The righteous Judge sees only the character of Jesus and declares our JUSTIFICATION.

**Sabbath** (Ch. 5). "The finished work of Creation is celebrated with the first *Sabbath.*"

In both Judaism and Christianity, the day set apart, sanctified, and made holy at the conclusion of the Creation week (Genesis 2:2, 3). *Shabbat* in Hebrew; the seventh day of the week; Saturday. The Israelites were taught to honor the Sabbath through their experience with manna (Exodus 16) and commanded to remember the Sabbath in the Ten Commandments (Exodus 20:8–11; Deuteronomy 5:12–15).

The Sabbath celebrates the FINISHED WORK of creation and redemption, reminds us to rest in the presence of God, and declares our acceptance of GRACE by helping us to recognize that God also is in charge of our SALVATION (Ezekiel 20:20).

**Sacraments** (152). "The medieval conclusion emphasize[d] the *sacraments* . . . as the 'means of grace.' "

Those religious practices that convey the sanctity or sacred nature of the experience. Rites such as baptism, the Lord's Supper, and marriage.

In the Middle Ages, the doctrinal discussions concerning GRACE frequently emphasized the idea that no one receives grace unless they have first taken part in these rites. It was taught that the sacraments were *ex opere operato*—that is, that "by the work performed," the believer caused the grace of God to work and become valid, whether or not the one taking part in the rite actually understood what was taking place.

**Salvation** (31, 90, 91, 143). "What part [do] we play in the *salvation* dynamic"?

Deliverance from destruction. In Christianity, the full and final REDEMPTION from the penalty, guilt, and consequences of sin; and the gift of eternal life. Salvation is about what Jesus does for sinful human beings that assures us where we'll be ten million years from now (Isaiah 25:8, 9). Salvation is provided by God alone (Isaiah 45:17–22).

**Salvific** (63). "Seizing the *salvific* significance of the Creation story becomes crucial."

Having the power to bring about SALVATION or REDEMPTION.

**Sanctification** (153). *"Sanctification* is not about salvation."

The state of being consecrated, set apart for sacred use and purpose. Made holy. Purified.

The acts of God throughout our lives that help us overcome temptation and become more and more like Jesus. Sanctification is about growing up in the family, learning how to live a life of praise, and overcoming the temptations that so easily entice us to rebel against God (see Luke 15:11–32).

**Sanctuary** (Ch. 5). "The *sanctuary* . . . is all about learning to be at ease in the [central] presence of God."

The wilderness tabernacle, the tent of meeting, in which the visible presence of God dwelt with the Israelites during their wanderings in the wilderness (Exodus 25:8). In Hebrew, the *Mishkan.*

**Satisfaction Theory** (151). "Anselm proposed 'the *satisfaction theory* of the atonement.' "

"The theory says that Christ paid a debt that all humanity owes to God because of disobedience. God's justice demands payment of a satisfaction or else the order of the universe would be disrupted. The needed satisfaction is like a debt to God's honor that humanity must repay, but humanity is incapable of repaying it without suffering complete loss in hell. God in his mercy provides a perfect substitutionary sacrifice that satisfies his own honor and preserves the moral order of the universe." (Roger Olson, *The Story of Christian Theology* [Down-ers Grove, Ill.: InterVarsity Press, 1999], 324.)

**Scholastics, Scholasticism** (150). "In the eleventh century, the commitment to intellectual growth had become a movement we know as *Scholasticism.* "

The dominant western Christian theological and philosophical school during the Middle Ages, founded on the authority of the Latin Fathers and of Aristotle.

**Synod** (141). "By the end of the year [the local bishops] . . . convene[d] a *synod.* "

A council or assembly of churches or church representatives.

**Theology** (28). " 'Most *theology,* like most fiction, is essentially autobiography.' " (Frederick Buechner, *The Alphabet of Grace* [San Francisco: HarperCollins, 1970], 3.)

The study of the nature of God and religious truth.

**Thomism, Thomistic** (154). "The theology I was hearing was *Thomistic*—from Thomas Aquinas straight out of the Middle Ages."

The theological and philosophical system of THOMAS AQUINAS that harmonized the teachings of Aristotle with CATHOLIC doctrine. The Thomistic system dominated SCHOLASTICISM. "In the Roman communion his [Thomas Aquinas's] influence has never ceased." (Williston Walker, *A History of the Christian Church* [N.Y.: Charles Scribner's Sons, 1959], 245.)

**Wars of the Lord** (68). " 'The theology of the *wars of the Lord* is extremely simple . . . : God does it all.' "

The military battles commanded by Yahweh against the enemies of God's people who lived in and around the promised land of Palestine.

The strategy of fighting these battles is summarized in 2 Chronicles 20:17: " ' "You will not have to fight this battle. Take up your positions; stand firm and see the deliverance the LORD will give you." ' "

**Works Orientation** (168; 52). In this rampant *works orientation,* . . . people [were taught] to fear grace.

The belief that our place in God's kingdom is awarded to us, either in whole or in part, in exchange for, or in reward for, or because of, our faithful obedience, our proper behavior, our correct belief, the strength of our faith, our good works, the MERITS of our Christian life, our acceptance of Christ's offer of GRACE, or anything else, other than the wholly undeserved favor of God.

# BIBLIOGRAPHY

## BOOKS

Aeschylus. *Prometheus Bound.*

Allison, C. FitzSimons. *The Cruelty of Heresy.* Harrisburg, Penn.: Morehouse Publishing, 1994.

Anselm. *Proslogion.*

Aquinas, Thomas. *Summa Theologica.*

Ashe, Arthur. *Days of Grace.* New York: Alfred A. Knopf, 1993.

Assmann, Jan. *Ägypten. Eine Sinngeschichte.* Munich, Germany: Carl Hanswer Verlag, 1996; English translation *The Mind of Egypt: History and Meaning in the Time of the Pharaohs.* New York: Metropolitan Books, Henry Holt and Company, 2002.

Augustine. *City of God.*

Augustine. *Confessions.*

Augustine. *Psalms.*

Bainton, Roland H. *Here I Stand: A Life of Martin Luther.* Nashville: Abingdon Press, 1950.

Barth, Karl. *The Epistle to the Romans.* London: Oxford University Press, 1933.

Berkouwer, G. C. *Faith and Justification.* Grand Rapids, Mich.: Wm. B. Eerdmans Publishing, 1954.

Blake, Chris. *Searching for a God to Love.* Nampa, Idaho: Pacific Press®, 1999.

Bonhoeffer, Dietrich. *The Cost of Discipleship.* New York: Collier Books, 1963.

Braaten, Carl E. *Justification, The Article by Which the Church Stands or Falls.* Minneapolis: Fortress Press, 1990.

Brown, Peter. *Augustine of Hippo.* Berkeley, Calif.: University of California Press, 1967.

Brown, Robert McAfee. *The Spirit of Protestantism.* New York: Oxford University Press, 1961.

Buechner, Frederick. *The Alphabet of Grace.* San Francisco: HarperCollins, 1970.

Calvin, John. *Institutes.*

Capon, Robert Farrar. *The Astonished Heart.* Grand Rapids, Mich.: Wm. B. Eerdmans Publishing Co., 1996.

Capon, Robert Farrar. *Between Noon and Three: Romance, Law, and the Outrage of Grace.* Grand Rapids, Mich.: Wm. B. Eerdmans Publishing, 1997.

Capon, Robert Farrar. *The Parables of Grace.* Grand Rapids, Mich.: Wm. B. Eerdmans Publishing, 1988.

Carter, Jimmy *Always a Reckoning.* New York: Times Books, 1995.

Carter, Jimmy. *Living Faith.* New York: Random House, 1996.

Cassady, Neal. *Grace Beats Karma: Letters from Prison, 1958–60.* New York: Blast Books, 1993.

*The Catechism of the Catholic Church.* New York: Doubleday, 1995.

Chadwick, Henry. *The Early Church.* New York: Penguin Books, 1967; rev. 1993).

Chadwick, Owen. *The Reformation.* Baltimore, Md.: Penguin Books, 1964.

Chesterton, G. K. *Orthodoxy.* New York: Dodd, Mead & Co., 1908.

Chesterton, G. K. *Saint Thomas Aquinas.* New York: Doubleday, 1956.

Chilton, Bruce. *Rabbi Paul, An Intellectual Biography.* New York: Doubleday, 2004.

Cobb, Jr., John B. *Grace and Responsibility: A Wesleyan Theology for Today.* Nashville: Abingdon, 1995.

Coles, Robert. *The Spiritual Life of Children.* Boston, Mass.: Houghton Mifflin Company, 1990.

Collins, Kenneth J. *The Evangelical Moment: The Promise of an American Religion.* Grand Rapids, Mich.: Baker Academic, 2005.

Collinson, Patrick. *The Reformation: A History.* New York: The Modern Library, 2004.

Coupland, Douglas. *Life After God.* New York: Pocket Books, 1994.


Daniells, Arthur G. *Christ Our Righteousness.* Takoma Park, Washington, D.C.: The Ministerial Association of Seventh-day Adventists, 1926.

D'Auria, Sue H. "Preparing for Eternity," in *Pharaohs of the Sun.* Boston: Museum of Fine Arts, Boston, 1999.

Dawn, Marva. *Keeping the Sabbath Wholly.* Grand Rapids, Mich.: Eerdmans, 1989.

Dickson, Athol. *The Gospel According to Moses.* Grand Rapids, Mich.: Brazos Press, 2003.

Douglas, Herbert E.; Heppenstall, Edward; LaRondelle, Hans K.; and Maxwell, C. Mervyn. *Perfection.* Nashville: Southern Publishing Association, 1975.

Dreyer, Elizabeth. *Manifestations of Grace.* Collegeville, Minn.: The Liturgical Press, 1990.

Duffy, Stephen J. *The Dynamics of Grace: Perspectives in Theological Anthropology.* Collegeville, Minn.: The Liturgical Press, 1993.

Duguid, Iain M. *Living In the Grip of Relentless Grace.* Phillipsburg, N.J.: P & R Publishing, 2002.

Dulles, Avery. *The Assurance of Things Hoped For.* Oxford: Oxford University Press, 1994.

Durant, Will. *The Age of Faith.* New York: Simon and Schuster, 1950.

Dürer, Albrecht. *Diary of His Journey to the Netherlands.*

Dybdahl, Jon. *Old Testament Grace.* Boise: Pacific Press®, 1990.


Eno, Robert B. "Some Patristic Views on the Relationship of Faith and Works in Justification," in *Justification by Faith, Lutherans and Catholics in Dialogue VII,* H. George Anderson, T. Austin Murphy and Joseph A. Burgess, eds. Minneapolis, Minn.: Augsburg Publishing House, 1985.

Eusebius. *Ecclesiastical History.*


Farris, Stephen. *Grace! A Preaching Commentary.* Nashville: Abingdon Press, 2003.

Finney, Charles. *Finney's Lectures on Systematic Theology.* 1851.

Fox, Robin Lane. *Pagans and Christians.* New York: Alfred A. Knopf, Inc. 1986.

Froom, LeRoy Edwin. *Movement of Destiny.* Washington, D.C.: Review and Herald, 1971.

Frost, Robert. *The Poetry of Robert Frost.* New York: Holt, Rinehart and Winston, 1969.


Galli, Mark, and Olson, Ted. *131 Christians Everyone Should Know.* Nashville: Broadman & Holman, 2000.

Garwood, Julie. *Saving Grace.* New York: Pocket Books, 1993.

George, Timothy. *Theology of the Reformers.* Nashville: Broadman Press, 1988.

Gerrish, Brian A. *Grace and Gratitude: The Eucharistic Theology of John Calvin.* Minneapolis: Fortress Press, 1993.

Giorgi, Rosa. *Saints in Art.* Los Angeles: Getty Publications, 2003.

*God's Law and God's Grace.* Roseville, Calif.: 2002.

Goldingay, John. *Old Testament Theology: Israel's Gospel.* Downers Grove, Ill.: InterVarsity Press, 2003.

Gonzáles, Justo. *A History of Christian Thought, Volume 2, From Augustine to the Eve of the Reformation.* Rev. ed. Nashville: Abingdon, 1987.

González, Justo. *The Story of Christianity: Volume 2, The Reformation to the Present Day.* New York: HarperCollins, 1985.

Gonzáles, Justo. *A History of Christian Thought, Volume 3.* Rev. ed. Nashville, Tenn.: Abingdon, 1975.


Halley, Henry H. *Bible Handbook.* Chicago: Halley, 1924.

Hals, Ronald M. *Grace and Faith in the Old Testament.* Minneapolis: Augsburg, 1980.

Hamilton, Edith. *Mythology.* Boston: Little, Brown and Company, 1942.

Hardinge, Leslie. *Shadows of His Sacrifice: Studies in the Sanctuary.*

Hardman, Keith J. *Charles Grandison Finney: Revivalist and Reformer.* Grand Rapids, Mich.: Baker and Syracuse University Press, 1987.

Hemingway, Ernest. *The Old Man and the Sea.* New York: Charles Scribner's Sons, 1952.

Heppenstall, Edward. *Salvation Unlimited.* Review and Herald, 1974.

Heschel, Abraham Joshua. *Quest for God: Studies in Prayer and Symbolism* (New York: Crossroad, 1990).

Heschel, Abraham Joshua. *The Sabbath.* New York: Farrar, Straus and Giroux, 1951.

Hinson, E. Glenn. *The Early Church.* Nashville: Abingdon, 1996.

Hodge, Charles *The Way of Life.* Mark A. Noll, ed. New York: Paulist Press, 1987.

Hoekema, Anthony A. *Saved By Grace.* Grand Rapids, Mich.: Wm. B. Eerdmans Publishing Company, 1989.

Hoezee, Scott. *The Riddle of Grace: Applying Grace to the Christian Life.* Grand Rapids, Mich.: Wm. B. Eerdmans Publishing Co., 1996.

Holifield, E. Brooks *Theology in America: Christian Thought from the Age of the Puritans to the Civil War.* New Haven, Conn.: Yale University Press, 2003.

Homer. *The Iliad.* Book 18.

Horn, Siegfried H. *Seventh-day Adventist Bible Dictionary.* Washington, D.C.: Review and Herald, 1960.

Horton, Michael S., ed. *A Confessing Theology for Postmodern Times.* Wheaton, Ill.: Crossway Books, 2000.

Hovig, Thomas. *Art for Dummies.* Foster City, Calif.: IDG Books Worldwide, 1990.

Hudson, R. Lofton. *Grace Is Not a Blue-Eyed Blond.* Waco, Tex.: Word Books, 1968.

Hughes, John Jay. *Pontiffs: Popes Who Shaped History.* Huntington, Ind.: Our Sunday Visitor Publishing, 1994.


Jedin, Hubert. *Crisis and Closure of the Council of Trent.* N. D. Smith, ed. London: Sheed & Ward, 1967.

*The Joint Declaration on the Doctrine of Justification.* Grand Rapids, Mich.: Wm. B. Eerdmans Publishing, 2000.

Jüngel, Eberhard. *Justification: The Heart of the Christian Faith.* Edinburgh: T&T Clark, 2001.


Kalas, J. Ellsworth. *Grace in a Tree Stump: Old Testament Stories of God's Love.* Louisville, Ky.: Westminster John Knox Press, 2005.

Kelly, J. N. D. *The Oxford Dictionary of Popes.* Oxford: Oxford University Press, 1986.

Kenneson, Philip. "Visible Grace: the Church as God's Embodied Presence," in *Grace Upon Grace,* Robert Johnston, Gregory Jones and Jonathan Wilson, eds. Nashville: Abingdon Press, 1999.

Ketchum, Hank. *Dennis the Menace: Prayers and Graces.* Louisville, Ky.: Westminster John Knox Press, 1993.

Kinghorn, Kenneth Cain. *The Gospel of Grace: The Way of Salvation in the Wesleyan Tradition.* Nashville: Abingdon Press, 1992.

Knight, George R. *Angry Saints.* Washington, D.C.: Review and Herald, 1989.

Knight, George R. *From 1888 to Apostasy.* Washington, D.C.: Review and Herald, 1987.

Kugel, James L. *The God of Old.* New York: Simon & Schuster Free Press, 2003.

Küng, Hans. *Christianity.* New York: Continuum, 1996.

Küng, Hans. *Great Christian Thinkers.* New York: Continuum, 1996.

Küng, Hans. *Justification.* New York: Nelson, 1964.

Kushner, Rabbi Lawrence. *The Book of Words.* Woodstock, Vt.: Jewish Lights Publishing, 1993.


Lacey, Robert. *Great Tales From English History.* New York: Little, Brown and Company, 2003.

Lamott, Anne. *Traveling Mercies: Some Thoughts on Faith.* New York: Pantheon Books, 1999.

LaRondelle, Hans. *Christ Our Salvation.* Mountain View, Calif.: Pacific Press®, 1980.

Latourette, Kenneth Scott. *A History of Christianity, Volume 1: Beginnings to 1500.* San Francisco: HarperSanFrancisco, 1953.

Lewis, C. S. *The Four Loves.* New York: Harcourt Brace Jovanovich, 1960.

Lewis, C. S. *Letters to an American Lady.* Grand Rapids, Mich.: Wm. B. Eerdmans Publishing Co., 1967.

Lewis, C. S. *Poems.* New York: Harcourt Brace Jovanovich, 1964.

Lewis, C. S. *The Silver Chair.* New York: Macmillan Publishing, 1953.

Lindberg, Carter. *The European Reformations.* Oxford: Blackwell Publlishers, 1996.

Lowe, Harry. *Redeeming Grace.* Mountain View, Calif.: Pacific Press®, 1968.

Lucado, Max. *A Gentle Thunder.* Dallas: Word Publishing, 1995.

Lucado, Max. *In the Grip of Grace.* Dallas: Word Publishing, 1996.

Luther, Martin. *The Weimar Edition of Luther's Works.*


MacCulloch, Diarmaid. *The Reformation, A History.* New York: Viking, 2003.

McCumber, Harold O. *The Advent Message in the Golden West.* Mountain View, Calif.: Pacific Press®, 1946, 1968).

McGrath, Alister E. *Iustitia Dei, A History of the Christian Doctrine of Justification: The Beginnings to the Reformation.* Cambridge University Press, 1986.

McGrath, Alister E. *Luther's Theology of the Cross.* Oxford: Blackwell Publishers, 1985.

McManners, John, ed. *The Oxford Illustrated History of Christianity.* Oxford: Oxford University Press, 1990.

McNeill, F. Marian. *Iona, A History of the Island.* London and Glasgow: Blackie & Sons, 1920.

Manchester, William. *American Caesar: Douglas MacArthur, 1880–1964.* New York: Little, Brown and Company, 1978.

Manseau, Peter. *Killing the Buddha.* New York: Free Press, Simon & Schuster, 2004.

*Martin Luther's Religious Thought.* Mountain View, Calif.: Pacific Press®, 1971.

Marty, Martin. *Martin Luther.* New York: A Lipper/Viking Book, 2004.

Mauss, Marcel. *The Gift: The Form and Reason for Exchange in Archaic Societies.* W. D. Halls, trans. New York: W. W. Norton, 1990.

May, M.D., Gerald G. *Addiction & Grace.* San Francisco: HarperCollins, 1988.

Migliore, Daniel L. *Faith Seeking Understanding: An Introduction to Christian Theology.* Grand Rapids, Mich.: Wm. B. Eerdmans Publishing, 1991.

Miller, William. *To the Believers in the Second Advent.*

Moffatt, James. *Grace in the New Testament.* London: Hodder and Stoughton, 1931.

Moyers, Bill. *Genesis: A Living Conversation.* New York: Doubleday, 1996.

Muller, Wayne. *Sabbath.* New York: Bantam Books, 1999.


Nee, Watchman. *Grace for Grace.* New York: Christian Fellowship Publishers, Inc., 1983.

Niebuhr, H. Richard. *Christ and Culture.* New York: Harper & Row Publishers, 1951.

Noll, Mark A. *America's God: From Jonathan Edwards to Abraham Lincoln.* Oxford: Oxford University Press, 2002.

Nouwen, Henri. *The Return of the Prodigal Son: A Story of Homecoming.* New York: Doubleday, 1992.


Oberman, Heiko Augustinus. *The Dawn of the Reformation.* Edinburg: T & T Clark, 1986.

Oden, Thomas C. *The Justification Reader.* Grand Rapids, Mich.: Wm. B. Eerdmans Publishing, 2002.

Oden, Thomas C. *The Transforming Power of Grace.* Nashville: Abingdon Press, 1993.

Olson, A. V. *Through Crisis to Victory, 1888–1901.* Washington, D.C.: Review and Herald, 1966.

Olson, Roger E. *The Story of Christian Theology, Twenty Centuries of Tradition & Reform.* Downers Grove, Ill.: InterVarsity Press, 1999.

Ormerod, Neil. *Grace and Disgrace: A Theology of Self-Esteem, Society, and History.* Newtown, NSW: E. J. Dwyer, 1992.

Ortberg, John; Pederson, Laurie; and Poling, Judson. *Grace: An Invitation to a Way of Life.* Grand Rapids, Mich.: Zondervan, 2000.

Ortberg, John. *Old Testament Challenge: Discussion Guide.* Grand Rapids, Mich.: Zondervan, 2003.

Ozment, Steven. *Protestants: The Birth of a Revolution.* New York: Doubleday, 1991.


Packer, J. I. *Great Grace.* Ann Arbor, Mich.: Vine Books, 1997.

Pease, Norval F. *By Faith Alone.* Mountain View, Calif.: Pacific Press®, 1962.

Peck, M. Scott. *In Search of Stones: A Pilgrimage of Faith, Reason, and Discovery.* New York: Hyperion, 1995.

Pelikan, Jaroslav. *The Christian Tradition: A History of the Development of Doctrine, Volume 1: The Emergence of the Catholic Tradition, 100–600.* Chicago: The University of Chicago Press, 1971.

Pelikan, Jaroslav. *The Christian Tradition, A History of the Development of Doctrine, Volume 4: Reformation of Church and Dogma (1300–1700).* Chicago: The University of Chicago Press, 1984.

Peterson, Eugene. *Leap Over a Wall.* New York: HarperCollins Publishers, 1997.

Piper, John. *Future Grace.* Sisters, Ore.: Multnomah Books, 1995.

Placher, William C. *A History of Christian Theology.* Philadelphia: The Westminster Press, 1983.

Potok, Chaim. *I Am the Clay.* New York: Alfred A. Knopf, 1992.

Prejean, Helen. *Dead Man Walking.* New York: Vintage Books, 1993.

Pritchard, James B. *Ancient Near Eastern Texts Relating to the Old Testament.* Princeton: Princeton University Press, 1950.


*Questions On Doctrine.* Washington, D.C.: Review and Herald, 1957.


Rabey, Steve. *In Search of Authentic Faith.* Colorado Springs, Colo.: WaterBrook Press, 2001.

Rahner, Karl. *Foundations of Christian Faith: An Introduction to the Idea of Christianity.* New York: Crossroad, 2002).

Reardon, Bernard M. G. *Religious Thought in the Reformation.* 2nd ed. London: Longman, 1995.

Rice, Richard. *The Reign of God.* Berrien Springs, Mich.: Andrews University Press, 1985.

Rohr, Richard. *Radical Grace.* Cincinnati, Ohio: St. Anthony Messenger Press, 1993.

Rohr, Richard, and Martos, Joseph. *The Great Themes of Scripture: Old Testament.* Cincinnati, Ohio: St. Anthony Messenger Press, 1987.

Rosenblatt, Naomi H. *Wrestling With Angels.* New York: Dell Publishing, 1995.

Roy, James Charles. *Islands of Storm.* Chester Springs, Penn.: Dufour Editions, Inc., 1991.

Schaeffer, Francis. *How Should We Then Live?* Old Tappan, N.J.: Fleming H. Revell, 1976.

Schaeffer, Francis. *True Spirituality.* Wheaton, Ill.: Tyndale House Publishers, 1971.

Schaff, Philip. *History of the Christian Church.* Volume 2. Grand Rapids, Mich.: Wm. B. Eerdman's Publishing, 1910.

Schmidt, Peter. *The Ghent Altarpiece.* Ghent-Amsterdam: Ludion, 2001.

Scott, Donald. "Evangelicalism, Revivalism, and the Second Great Awakening," in *The 19th Century.* New York: City University of New York, the National Humanities Center, October 2000.

*The Seventh-day Adventist Bible Commentary.* Volume 6. Washington, D.C.: Review and Herald, 1957.

*Seventh-day Adventists Believe . . .* Washington, D.C.: General Conference Ministerial Association, 1988.

Sider, Ronald J. *The Scandal of the Evangelical Conscience: Why are Christians Living Just Like the Rest of the World?* Grand Rapids, Mich.: Baker Books, 2005.

Smith, Dan. *Lord, I Have a Question.* Nampa, Idaho: Pacific Press®, 2004.

Smith, Huston. *Why Religion Matters.* San Francisco: HarperCollins, 2001.

Soltau, Henry. *The Tabernacle, the Priesthood and the Offerings.* Grand Rapids, Mich.: Kregel Publications, 1998.

Spalding, Arthur Whitefield. *Origin and History of Seventh-day Adventists,* Volume 1. Washington, D.C.: Review and Herald Publishing, 1961.

Spitz, Lewis W. *The Protestant Reformation, 1517–1559.* New York: Harper & Row, 1985.

Spivey, Nigel. *Greek Art.* London: Phaidon Press Limited, 1997.

Spurgeon, Charles *Grace Abounding in a Believer's Life.* Lynnwood, Wash.: Emerald Books, 1994.

Spurgeon, Charles. *Grace and Power.* New Kensington, Penn.: Whitaker House, 2000.

Sweet, Leonard. *Post-Modern Pilgrims.* Nashville: Broadman & Holman Publishers, 2000.

Swindoll, Charles. *The Grace Awakening.* Dallas: Word Publishing, 1990.


Tillich, Paul. *A History of Christian Thought.* New York: Simon and Schuster, 1967.

Tillich, Paul. "Accepted," in *The Shaking of the Foundations.* London: SCM Press Ltd., 1949.

Tillich, Paul. *Morality and Beyond.* Louisville, Ky.: Westminster John Knox Press, 1963.

Tillich, Paul. *Systematic Theology.* Volume 2. Chicago: The University of Chicago Press, 1957.

Tillich, Paul. *Theology of Culture.* London: Oxford University Press, 1959.

*This We Believe.* Boise, Idaho: Pacific Press®, 1993.

Torrance, Thomas F. *The Doctrine of Grace in the Apostolic Fathers*. Grand Rapids, Mich.: Wm. B. Eerdman's Publishing, 1959.

Tournier, Paul. *Guilt and Grace*. New York: Harper & Row, 1962.

Tyner, Stuart. "Grace Orientation," in *The ABZs of Adventist Youth Ministry*. Riverside, Calif.: The Hancock Center for Youth and Family Ministry, 2000.

Tyner, Stuart. *The Colors of Grace in Our Homes*. Pacific Union Conference Resource Center and Advent Source, 1996.

Tyner, Stuart. *Walking on the Edge*. Riverside, Calif.: Hancock Center Publications, 1996.

van der Meer, F. *Augustine the Bishop*. Brian Battershaw and G. R. Lamb, trans. London: Sheed and Ward, 1961.

Walker, Williston. *A History of the Christian Church*. New York: Charles Scribner's Sons, 1959.

Walsh, Michael. *The Conclave*. Norwich, Norfolk, UK: Canterbury Press, 2003.

Wangerin, Jr., Walter. *Miz Lil and the Chronicles of Grace*. New York: HarperCollins Publishers, 1988.

Weaver, Rebecca Harden. *Divine Grace and Human Agency*. Macon, Ga.: Mercer University Press, 1996.

Weinberg, Rabbi Noah. "Shabbat—Heaven on Earth." http://www.aish.com/shabbatthemes/explorations.

Whidden II, Woodrow W. *Ellen G. White on Salvation*. Hagerstown, Md.: Review and Herald, 1995.

White, Arthur L. *Ellen G. White: The Early Years, Volume 1, 1827–1862*. Hagerstown, Md.: Review and Herald, 1985.

White, Ellen G. *The Acts of the Apostles*. Mountain View, Calif.: Pacific Press®, 1911.

White, Ellen G. *Child Guidance*. Nashville: Southern Publishing Association, 1954.

White, Ellen G. *Christ's Object Lessons*. Washington, D.C.: Review and Herald, 1941.

White, Ellen G. *Conflict and Courage*. Washington, D.C.: Review and Herald, 1970.

White, Ellen G. *Counsels on Health*. Mountain View, Calif.: Pacific Press®, 1923.

White, Ellen G. *Counsels to Writers and Editors*. Nashville: Southern Publishing Association, 1946.

White, Ellen G. *The Desire of Ages*. Mountain View, Calif.: Pacific Press®, 1940.

White, Ellen G. *Early Writings*. Washington, D.C.: Review and Herald, 1945.

White, Ellen G. *Evangelism*. Washington, D.C.: Review and Herald, 1946.

White, Ellen G. *Faith and Works*. Nashville: Southern Publishing Association, 1979.

White, Ellen G. *The Faith I Live By*. Washington, D.C.: Review and Herald, 1958.

White, Ellen G. *God's Amazing Grace*. Washington, D.C.: Review and Herald, 1973.

White, Ellen G. *Gospel Workers.* Washington, D.C.: Review and Herald, 1948.

White, Ellen. *The Great Controversy.* Mountain View, Calif.: Pacific Press®, 1950.

White, Ellen G. *Manuscript Releases.* Volume 5.

White, Ellen G. *Medical Ministry.* Mountain View, Calif.: Pacific Press®, 1963.

White, Ellen G. *Mind, Character and Personality.* Volume 1. Nashville: Southern Publishing Association, 1971.

White, Ellen G. *The Ministry of Healing.* Mountain View, Calif.: Pacific Press®, 1909.

White, Ellen G. *Patriarchs and Prophets* Mountain View, Calif.: Pacific Press®, 1958.

White, Ellen G. *Prophets and Kings* Mountain View, Calif.: Pacific Press®, 1943.

White, Ellen G. *Reflecting Christ.* Washington, D.C.: Review and Herald, 1985.

White, Ellen G. *Selected Messages.* Volume 1. Washington, D.C.: Review and Herald, 1958.

White, Ellen G. *Steps to Christ.* Mountain View, Calif.: Pacific Press®, 1956.

White, Ellen G. *Testimonies for the Church.* Volumes 1, 3, 4. Mountain View, Calif.: Pacific Press®, 1948.

White, Ellen G. *Testimonies to Ministers and Gospel Workers.* Mountain View, Calif.: Pacific Press®, 1923.

White, Ellen G. *That I May Know Him.* Washington, D.C.: Review and Herald, 1964.

White, James R. *The God Who Justifies.* Minneapolis: Bethany House, 2001.

Wilkinson, Richard H. *Reading Egyptian Art.* London: Thames and Hudson, 1992.

Williams, ed., Michael E. *The Storyteller's Companion to the Bible.* Volume 1. Nashville: Abingdon Press, 1991.

Wills, Garry. *Papal Sin.* New York: Doubleday, 2000.

Wills, Garry. *Saint Augustine.* New York: A Lipper/Viking Book, 1999.


Yaconelli, Michael. *Messy Spirituality.* Grand Rapids, Mich.: Zondervan, 2002.

Yancey, Philip. *What's So Amazing About Grace?* Grand Rapids, Mich.: Zondervan, 1997.

Burkle-Young, Francis A. *Passing the Keys.* Lanham, Md.: Madison Books, 1999.


Zoba, Wendy Murray. *Evangelical Christianity.* New York: Doubleday, 2005.

## Journals and Magazines

*Adventist Review.* August 24, 1989.
*Adventist Review.* July 23, 1992.

Anfenson-Vance, Deborah. "The Trouble With Grace." *Adventist Review.* January 7, 1988.

Christenson, Reo M. "Salvation: Faith Versus Works." *Ministry.* February 1999.

Forseth, Patricia A. "Hosea, Gomer, and Elective Grace." *The Reformed Journal.* November 19, 1985.

Hopps, James M. "Needed: Balance in Theology." *Ministry.* February 1999.
Horton, Michael. "Charles Finney vs. the Westminster Confession." The Alliance of Confessing Evangelicals, 1995.
Horton, Michael S. "The Disturbing Legacy of Charles Finney." *Issues, Etc. Journal.* Volume 2 (1997), no. 4.

Jones, A. T. *General Conference Bulletin.* February 13, 1893.

Litch, Josiah. *The Morning Watch.* April 24, 1845.
Logan, James C. "Grace Upon Grace: God's Mission and Ours." *Quarterly Review.* Spring 1988.

McGrath, Alister E. "Do We Still Need the Reformation?" *Christianity Today.* December 12, 1994.

Newman, David. "Farewell." *Ministry.* September 1995.

Ott, Helmut. "Another Look at Valuegenesis." *Ministry.* February 1994.

Schickel, Richard. "Dead Man Walking." *Time.* January 8, 1996.
*South Pacific Record.* June 8, 1991.
Spangler, J. Robert. "The Dynamics of Salvation." *Ministry.* February 1988.

Tyner, Stuart. "Are We Afraid of the Gospel?" *Ministry.* December 1999.

White, Ellen G. *The Day-Star.* January 24, 1846.
White, Ellen G. *General Conference Bulletin.* April 1, 1899.
White, Ellen G. *Review and Herald.* January 25, 1881.
White, Ellen G. *Review and Herald.* September 3, 1889.
White, Ellen G. *Review and Herald.* March 11, 1890.
White, Ellen G. *Review and Herald.* November 4, 1890.
White, Ellen G. *Review and Herald.* April 5, 1892.
White, Ellen G. *Review and Herald.* July 26, 1892.
White, Ellen G. *Review and Herald.* April 4, 1893.
White, Ellen G. *Review and Herald.* January 8, 1895.
White, Ellen G. *Review and Herald.* January 29, 1895.
White, Ellen G. *Review and Herald.* October 8, 1895.
White, Ellen G. *Review and Herald.* July 25, 1899.
White, Ellen G. *Review and Herald.* August 31, 1905.
White, Ellen G. *Review and Herald.* October 15, 1908.
White, Ellen G. *Signs of the Times.* July 1, 1889.
White, Ellen G. *Signs of the Times.* July 4, 1892.
White, Ellen G. *Signs of the Times.* September 5, 1892.
White, Ellen G. *Signs of the Times.* June 12, 1901.

Zackrison, Edwin. "A Theology of Sin, Grace and Forgiveness." *Journal of Psychology and Christianity.* Volume 11 (1992), no. 2.

# Letters and Manuscripts

Aristeides. *Apology.*
Athenagoras. *Legatio pro Christianis.*
Augustine. *Against the Letters of Petilian.*
Augustine. *Letters.*
Augustine. *Letter 186.*

Bradford, Charles. "Only By Grace" (Unpublished manuscript).

Clement of Alexandria. *Paedagogus.*
Cyprian. *Corpus Scriptorum Ecclesiaticorum Lainorum.*

*Epistle to Diognetus.*

Felix, Minucius. *Octavius.*

Hermas. *The Shepherd.*

Ignatius. *To the Magnesians.*
Ignatius. *To the Romans.*
Jerome. *Letter.*

Justin. *Apology.*

Laetantius. *On the Deaths of the Persecutors.*

Origen. *De Principiis.*

Pliny. *Letters.*
Polycarp. *The Letter of Polycarp to the Philippians.*

Tacitus. *Annals.*
Tertullian. *Apology.*
Tertullian. *De Praescriptione Haereticorum.*
Tertullian. *On Repentance.*

White, Ellen G. *Letter 27,* 1876, to James White.
White, Ellen G. *Letter 18,* 1879, to Willie White.
White, Ellen G. *Letter 24,* 1892.
White, Ellen G. *Letter 57,* 1895.
White, Ellen G. *Letter 224,* 1908.
White, Ellen G. *Manuscript 31,* 1890.
White, Ellen G. *Manuscript 36,* 1890.
White, Ellen G. *Manuscript 122,* 1897.
White, Ellen G. *Manuscript 156,* 1898.
White, Ellen G. *Special Testimonies.* March 12, 1901.
White, Willie C. *Letter to Dan Jones,* April 8, 1890.

Zosimus. *Letter.*

# Biographical Notes

Names in SMALL CAPS in the notes also appear as entries.

**Abelard, Peter** (1079–1142). French scholar, theologian and philosopher. Disagreed with ANSELM's "satisfaction theory" and proposed what came to be known as the "moral influence theory."

**Aeschylus** (*c.* 525–*c.* 456 B.C.). Greek dramatist, the literary predecessor of Sophocles and Euripides. Of his ninety or so plays, seven survive in full.

**Alaric I** (*c.* 370–410). King of the Visigoths, 395–410. Served Emperor THEODOSIUS I, then rebelled against Rome at the emperor's death. Alaric sieged and sacked Rome in 410 and died of an illness shortly after. He was buried with all his treasures in the bed of the temporarily diverted Busento River.

**Ambrose** (339–397). One of the DOCTORS OF THE CHURCH, Ambrose was educated in Rome and was made Bishop of Milan in 374 by popular acclamation. His eloquent sermons spurred the conversion of AUGUSTINE.

**Anderson, Harry** (1906–1996). American painter and illustrator who was a frequent contributor to magazines such as *Colliers, Good Housekeeping,* and *Saturday Evening Post.* Harry and his wife, Ruth, joined the Adventist Church in 1943. His first painting for the church was a portrait of WILLIAM MILLER. He enjoyed portraying Jesus in traditional clothing but in modern settings.

**Andrews, John N.** (1829–1883). Early Adventist believer and leader. Joined the Millerite Adventists in the early 1840s. Began preaching at age twenty-one in 1850 and was ordained in 1853. Served as the president of the General Conference and editor of the *Adventist Review and Sabbath Herald,* and became the denomination's first official overseas missionary in 1874.

**Anselm** (*c.* 1033–1109). Philosopher and theologian, and disciple of LANFRANC, whom he followed as prior and abbot of the monastery at Bec. Became Archbishop of Canterbury in 1093, following Lanfranc again. Known as the "father of Scholasticism," Anselm proposed the "satisfaction theory of the atonement," which replaced the church's "ransom theory."

**Anthony the Hermit** (*c.* 251–356). Egyptian "holy man" considered the founder of Christian monasticism.

**Aquinas, Thomas** (1225–1274). Italian theologian and philosopher, generally regarded as the greatest of scholastic theologians. A DOCTOR OF THE CHURCH. Introduced the work of Aristotle to the church and to medieval civilization. Major theological work is the *Summa Theologiae* (1265–1272).

**Aslan.** The noble golden lion who epitomizes the goodness and justice of Narnia in C. S. LEWIS's beloved *Chronicles of Narnia*. As the resurrected king of Narnia and the son of the Emperor-Over-Sea, Aslan takes on a Christlike presence.

**Athanaric** (?–381). Chieftain of the Visigoths. Fought against the Roman emperor Valens. Engaged in a civil war with FRITIGERN. Defeated by the Huns in 376.

**Attila** (406–453). Co-ruler with his brother of the Huns from 434 until 445, when he murdered his brother. King of the Huns until his death. At war with or receiving tribute from Rome most of his career.

**Augustine of Hippo** (354–August 28, 430). The greatest of the Latin CHURCH FATHERS. Born in Numidia, modern Algeria, to a pagan father and a devout Christian mother, Monica. Converted to Christianity and baptized in Milan by AMBROSE (386). Returned to North Africa, where he became bishop of Hippo in 396. Among his most famous works are *Confessions* (*c.* 400), *On the Trinity* (400–416), and *The City of God* (412–427). Among the first to be named, in 1298, a DOCTOR OF THE CHURCH.

**Barth, Karl** (1886–1968). Swiss pastor, theologian, and professor. His 1919 work on the book of Romans, *The Epistle to the Romans*

(translated into English in 1933), established his reputation. In 1935, he refused to take an oath of allegiance to Hitler and moved to Switzerland.

**Bates, Joseph** (1792–1872). The oldest of the Adventist pioneers, Bates was a retired sea captain and convert to the Millerite movement. His forty-eight-page tract on the seventh-day Sabbath (1846) influenced JAMES and ELLEN WHITE. Became the first Seventh-day Adventist local conference president (in Michigan, 1861).

**Bede** (*c.* 673–735). Known as the Venerable Bede. The English monk, theologian, and historian is best known for his book *The Ecclesiastical History of the English People,* published in 731, which has become a primary source for early English history. Bede also originated the B.C./A.D. manner of dating.

**Beza, Theodore** (1519–1605). Protestant French theologian. Founded, with JOHN CALVIN, the Geneva academy for the promotion of Calvinism. Succeeded Calvin as the leader of the Protestant Reformation in Switzerland.

**Bonhoeffer, Dietrich** (1906–1945). German Protestant theologian and anti-Nazi activist. After Germany cracked down on the church, Bonhoeffer took his ministry underground and eventually became involved in a plot to assassinate Hitler. He was captured, imprisoned, and executed by the Nazis. His most influential writings include *The Cost of Discipleship* (translated in 1948)—in which he worried about "cheap grace"—and *Ethics* (translated in 1965).

**Botticelli, Sandro** (c. 1445–1510). Florentine painter of the early Renaissance. Best known for his devotional paintings (*The Adoration of the Magi* and *The Coronation of the Virgin*) and his treatment of mythological scenes (*Primavera* and *The Birth of Venus*). Painted frescoes for the Sistine Chapel.

**Butler, George I.** (1834–1918). Early Adventist convert baptized by J. N. ANDREWS. Became local conference president. In 1871, elected president of the General Conference, then again in 1880. With URIAH SMITH, opposed the views of JONES and WAGGONER. Retired after the 1888 General Conference session. Returned to church administration after the death of his wife. In a change of heart, Butler publicly accepted the message of righteousness by faith he had so strongly opposed.

**Caelestius.** Young disciple of PELAGIUS, and a lawyer of noble descent. Traveled to North Africa with Pelagius after the sack of Rome. Branded as a heretic for six statements concerning original sin. Presented the case for himself and Pelagius to Pope ZOSIMUS who, for a time, defended him before bowing to the pressure of the emperor and banishing them both.

**Calvin, John** (1509–1564). Protestant Reformer, born in France, who fled to Switzerland to escape persecution. Published his *Institutes of the Christian Religion* in 1536, then joined the Swiss Reformers in Geneva, where ultimately he controlled most of the city's affairs from 1541 on. He systematized Reformed theology, organized the church, and wrote commentaries on most of the books of the Bible.

**Cassian, John** (*c.* 360–*c.* 435). Early monastic who taught that both grace and human efforts play a necessary role in salvation. His views, known as Semipelagianism, were dismissed by the Synod of Orange in 529.

**Charis.** In Greek mythology, a woman of remarkable, redemptive character, who, in full knowledge of HEPHAISTOS's sordid past, approaches him intentionally. Seeing through his unattractiveness, she embraces him. Desiring what is best for him, she marries him. She speaks in his behalf and sweetly invites her husband once again to occupy a place of importance. In English, we know her as Grace.

**Chemosh.** The god of war and the national deity of the Moabites. Solomon built a sanctuary to Chemosh east of Jerusalem. Josiah abolished that worship.

**Chesterton, G. K.** (1874–1936). Popular English writer who became a Roman Catholic in 1922 and after that date wrote mostly about religious subjects, including biographies of Francis of Assisi and THOMAS AQUINAS. C. S. LEWIS claimed that Chesterton was the first writer with a Christian perspective on history that made sense to him (*Surprised by Joy: The Shape of My Early Life* [New York: Harcourt, Brace & World, 1955], 223).

**Church Fathers.** Early, influential Christian theologians and writers, particularly those in the first five centuries of church history. Often divided into Apostolic Fathers (the first two generations after the apostles—Clement of Rome, Ignatius, POLYCARP, etc.); Latin Fathers (such as TERTULLIAN, AUGUSTINE, AMBROSE, and JEROME); Greek Fathers (including Irenaeus of Lyons, Clement of Alexandria, and Origen); and the Desert Fathers (such as ANTHONY).

**Columba** (521–597). Irish monk who traveled to the island of Iona in Scotland in 563 and established a monastery from which missionaries were sent to all of Scotland and England, and on to the Continent.

**Constantine** (*c.* 274–337). Known as Constantine the Great. In 306 acclaimed emperor by his troops. On October 28, 312, at the Battle of the Milvian Bridge, he defeated other claimants to the title, but he didn't become sole ruler of the Roman world until 323. Not only tolerated Christianity in the empire but also initiated moves that ultimately made it Rome's official religion.

**Daniells, Arthur G.** (1858–1935). Attended Battle Creek College. Missionary to New Zealand and Australia (1886–1900). Elected president of the General Conference in 1901. Reorganized the departments and moved the headquarters from Battle Creek to Washington, D.C. As secretary of the Ministerial Department, authored *Christ Our Righteousness* (1926).

**Diocletian** (245?–312?). Roman emperor from 284 to 305, the only emperor to retire from office. Of humble origin and a distinguished military career. Brought about administrative and military reorganization of the empire. His firm support of the old heathen religious practices brought him into sharp disagreement with emerging Christianity and led to severe persecution of Christians.

**Doctors of the Church.** Recognition, given posthumously and after canonization, to early Christian theologians whose works are held to have greatly benefited the church. Among those so honored are AMBROSE, AUGUSTINE, JEROME, ANSELM, and THOMAS AQUINAS. Currently, thirty-three theologians are thus designated.

**Donatus the Great** (?–*c.* 355). Bishop of Carthage in North Africa. The Donatist Christian schismatics took their name from him. Condemned as a heretic at the Lateran Council of 313.

**Dürer, Albrecht** (1471–1528). German painter and engraver known as the first great Protestant artist.

**Eusebius of Caesarea** (*c.* 260–*c.* 340). Historian of the early Christian church; his *Ecclesiastical History* records the main events in the church until 324. Became bishop of Caesarea in Palestine around 313. Attended the Council of Nicaea.

**Farel, Guillaume** (1489–1565). Protestant Reformer, born in France. He studied in Paris (during which time he converted to Protestantism), then fled to Switzerland to avoid persecution. Worked with CALVIN in Geneva.

**Finney, Charles** (1792–1875). Frontier preacher and revivalist in early twentieth-century America. Studied law but, following an emotional conversion (1821), was ordained a Presbyterian minister (1824). In the 1830s, he pastored in New York City, then became professor of theology at Oberlin College in Ohio (1835), where he served as president from 1851–1866. Finney has been described as a close friend of Millerite leader Charles Fitch. In his *Systematic Theology* (1851), Finney revealed a deep disconnect between himself and the Reformers on the doctrine of justification.

**Fritigern** (?–380). Visigoth chieftain and rival of ATHANARIC for leadership of the Goths. Adopted Arian Christianity to gain the support of Emperor Valens, against whom he later rebelled and, in 378, defeated and killed.

**Gamaliel** (?–c. 50). The most famous and influential of the first century rabbis, a Pharisee, and leader of the Torah school in Jerusalem attended by the apostle Paul.

**Giotto di Bondone** (c. 1266–1337). Italian painter, founder of the Florentine School of painting, and the artist who broke away from the sterile Byzantine style of the Middle Ages. His first mature masterpiece was the fresco cycle *The Lives of Christ and the Virgin*, in the Arena Chapel in Padua, completed in 1306.

**Hammurabi.** Sixth of eleven kings in the First Babylonian dynasty in the eighteenth century B.C. Best known for his code of 282 laws discovered by a French archaeological expedition in 1901–1902 at the site of ancient Susa in what is now Iran.

**Hephaistos.** Greek god of fire and crafts. Son of ZEUS and Hera, the crippled Hephaistos was disowned and expelled from his home among the gods in Olympus. Ultimately weds CHARIS, or Grace.

**Heppenstall, Edward** (1901–1994). English-born Adventist pastor, author, and educator, one of the church's leading theologians in the twentieth century. Taught at La Sierra College (1940–1955), the Theological Seminary at Andrews University (1955–1966), and Loma Linda University (1966–1977).

**Himes, Joshua V.** (1803–1895). Called by Spalding "the second most prominent Adventist in 1844," Himes was an early editor, publisher, preacher, and manager of the Advent movement. Though he never accepted the seventh-day Sabbath, Himes maintained a mostly cordial, and at times complimentary relationship with Seventh-day Adventists. His final illness, in his early nineties, was treated at the Battle Creek Sanitarium.

**Hodge, Charles** (1797–1878). Influential American Protestant theologian. Studied at Princeton and the Princeton Theological Seminary, and taught at the Princeton Theological Seminary. Edited the *Princeton Review* for more than forty years. Published his *Systematic Theology* in 1871 and 1872.

**Homer** (*c.* eighth century B.C.). Greek poet who gave us the great epics the *Iliad* and the *Odyssey*.

**Honorius, Flavius** (384–423). Youthful emperor of Rome (395–423) who is notable mostly for abandoning England to the barbarians and for losing Rome to ALARIC and the Visigoths in 410.

**Hus, Jan** (*c.* 1369–1415). Bohemian pastor and religious reformer born in what is today the Czech Republic. Lectured in Prague on theology, ultimately becoming chancellor of Charles University. Influenced by WYCLIF, Hus was excommunicated in 1410 from the Roman Catholic Church. Called before a general council, he was convicted and burned at the stake.

**Innocent I** (Bishop of Rome, 402–417). *The Oxford Dictionary of Popes* points out that Innocent "seized every opportunity of asserting the primacy of the Roman see, making more substantial claims for the papacy than his predecessors. As a result he not only proved one of the outstanding popes of the early centuries but has sometimes been saluted as 'the first pope.' "

**Jerome** (*c.* 342–420). Early Christian ascetic and scholar. Best known for his translation of the Bible from Hebrew and Greek into Latin (the Vulgate), which he accomplished in a cave in Bethlehem.

**Jones, Alonzo T.** (1850–1923). In his early twenties, Jones was baptized as an Adventist and began preaching in California. In 1885, he became editor of the *Signs of the Times.* With E. J. WAGGONER, preached about righteousness by faith at the Minneapolis General Conference session of 1888. While serving as editor-in-chief of the *Review and Herald,* Jones turned his attention to religious liberty. Ties with J. H. KELLOGG led to his separation from the Adventist Church in 1909.

**Julian of Eclanum** (*c.* 386–454). The most intellectual and eloquent of the Pelagian leaders, Julian refused to subscribe to the condemnation of PELAGIUS issued in 418 by Pope ZOSIMUS. Exiled from Italy (421), he carried on a literary attack on AUGUSTINE and his doctrine of grace.

**Kellogg, John Harvey** (1852–1943). American surgeon, writer, and health reformer. Superintendent of the Western Health Reform Institute in Battle Creek, Michigan, which he renamed Battle Creek Sanitarium. Developed nutritious breakfast cereals. Disfellowshipped from the Adventist Church in 1907.

**Knox, John** (*c.* 1505–1572). Protestant Reformer. Born in Scotland, ordained as a Roman Catholic priest. Joined the Reformation in the 1540s. After exile in Geneva, where he was influenced by CALVIN, Knox returned to Scotland in 1555, where he preached and founded the Church of Scotland.

**Küng, Hans** (b. 1928). Contemporary theologian and author whose teachings helped set the stage for Vatican II. Censured by the Vatican in 1979 and banned from teaching as a Catholic theologian. His works include *Infallible?* (1970), *Does God Exist?* (1978), and *Christianity: Essence, History and Future* (1996).

**Lanfranc** (*c.* 1005–1089). Italian clergyman who became a Benedictine monk at Bec and then became the prior there. In 1070, appointed Archbishop of Canterbury.

**Lewis, C. S.** (1898–November 22, 1963). Perhaps the most influential twentieth-century Christian writer, Lewis was born in Ireland, served in the British Army in World War I, then studied at Oxford, where he taught from 1925 to 1954. During the Second World War, he served as chaplain for the Royal Air Force and, through a weekly radio broadcast, became the second best known voice in England, behind only Winston Churchill. He became professor of Medieval and Renaissance English at Cambridge in 1954. Wrote *The Screwtape Letters* in 1942 and published the popular *Chronicles of Narnia* beginning in 1950. Lewis's only autobiographical work, *Surprised by Joy* (1955), describes his conversion to Christianity.

**Luther, Martin** (1483–1546). German religious reformer credited with beginning the Protestant Reformation with the publishing of his ninety-five theses at Wittenberg in 1517. Excommunicated, he appeared before a council in Worms in 1521. Later that year he translated the New Testament into German.

**Marcion** (*c.* 110–?). Early Gnostic reformer who protested the growing legalism of the church, which he connected with Judaism. He compiled a canon of sacred books composed of ten epistles of Paul and the Gospel of Luke, excising from them all passages that implied that Jesus regarded the God of the Old Testament as His Father. Excommunicated around 144.

**Miller, William** (1782–1849). American farmer and veteran of the War of 1812 who experienced a religious conversion around 1816. Became a licensed Baptist preacher in 1833, and began a movement that predicted the second coming of Christ in 1843, then 1844, then on October 22, 1844. Many of his followers were in the core of believers who founded the Seventh-day Adventist Church.

**Molech.** From as early as the third millennium B.C., the Canaanite god of fire to whom children were offered in sacrifice. The national deity of the Ammonites. Also worshipped by the Israelites on many occasions.

**Moody, Dwight L.** (1837–1899). American evangelist who founded the Moody Bible Institute in Chicago.

**Newman, John Henry, Cardinal** (1801–1890). English theologian, an ordained Calvinist, converted to Catholicism in 1845. Published his sermons, essays, and lectures as well as a spiritual autobiography, *Apology for His Life,* in 1864. Made a cardinal in 1879.

**Ockham, William of** (*c.* 1285–*c.* 1349). English Scholastic philosopher, a Franciscan. Studied at Oxford. Accused of heresy in 1324, he ultimately fled to Bavaria, where he remained until a couple of years before his death. Best known philosophically for "the rule of ontological economy," known as Ockham's razor.

**Osiris.** In the Egyptian Ennead (group of nine gods) of Heliopolis, Osiris was the son of Geb, the earth, and Nut, the sky, brother and husband of Isis, and the father of Horus. Osiris became the Egyptian god of the dead and the afterlife, where he presided over the ceremony known as the Weighing of the Heart, which determined a person's fitness for the afterlife.

**Pelagius** (*c.* 360–*c.* 420). British or Irish monk who settled in Rome around 400, then, after the sack of Rome, in Jerusalem. His preaching that salvation can be attained through the exercise of human willpower brought him into conflict with AUGUSTINE on the nature of grace. His theology was condemned by church councils in 416 and 418, and he was excommunicated and banished.

**Polycarp** (*c.* 69–*c.* 155). Bishop of Smyrna who learned from the apostle John and was the teacher of Irenaeus. Wrote the *Epistle to the Philippians*. Martyred in Smyrna.

**Reynard the Fox.** The celebrated main character of the medieval folk tales popular in Europe after the twelfth century. The satirical stories were a safe way for the peasants to criticize and show their contempt for the upper classes, the church, and the clergy.

**Smith, Huston.** Contemporary American academic, author, philosopher, and much sought-after authority on comparative religion. His works include *The World's Religions* (1991) and *Why Religion Matters: The Fate of the Human Spirit in an Age of Disbelief* (2001).

**Smith, Uriah** (1832–1903). Joined the Sabbath-keeping Adventists in 1852 and, because of his publishing experience, joined the editorial staff of the *Review and Herald*, becoming the editor of the church paper. Became the first secretary of the General Conference in 1863. Best known for his book *The Prophecies of Daniel and the Revelation*.

**Spalding, Arthur** (1888–1953). Adventist educator, author, editor, and historian. His major work, *Captains of the Host*, was revised, expanded, and published in the early 1960s as the four-volume *Origin and History of Seventh-day Adventists*.

**Stilicho, Flavius** (?–408). Roman general who rose to be the virtual ruler of Rome under Emperor Honorius. Won victories over Alaric and the Visigoths but was assassinated out of fear that he was plotting to overthrow the emperor.

**Sunday, Billy** (1862–1935). American Protestant evangelist. Joined the Chicago White Sox baseball team in 1883, was converted in 1887, retired from the White Sox in 1891, and went to work for the YMCA in Chicago. His career as an evangelist began in 1896.

**Tertullian** (*c.* 160–220). Early Christian theologian born in Carthage. Wrote frequently in Latin against heathens and heretics, becoming a strong and eloquent influence in the thought and language of the young church.

Became a leader of the Montanist sect around 207.

**Theodosius I** (*c.* 346–395). Roman emperor who attempted to rid the empire of paganism, successfully fought the Vandals and the Huns, brought peace with the Goths, and repressed Arianism in the empire while establishing Christianity.

**Tillich, Paul** (1886–1965). German theologian and philosopher and an ordained Lutheran minister (1912). During World War I, he served as a chaplain, then pursued an academic career. In the United States, Tillich taught at Union Theological Seminary, Harvard, and the University of Chicago. His principle works include *The Courage to Be* (1952) and *Systematic Theology* (three volumes, 1951, 1957, and 1963).

**Ulfilas,** also **Ufilas** (*c.* 311–*c.* 380). A Goth, or half-Goth, educated and ordained in the west. Returned to his people as a missionary, created a Gothic alphabet, and translated most of the Bible into the Gothic language. Believed that God the Father, but not Jesus, was "unbegotten."

**Van Eyck, Jan** (c. 1389–1441). The greatest Flemish artist of the fifteenth century. His major works include *The Adoration of the Mystic Lamb* (1432) and the *Arnolfini Wedding Portrait* (1434).

**Venden, Morris.** Influential Seventh-day Adventist pastor and writer whose books and sermons (especially to the collegiate congregations at La Sierra College and Pacific Union College in California, and Union College in Nebraska) champion the theology of grace.

**Waggoner, E. J.** (1855–1916). Became assistant editor of the *Signs of the Times* under his father, J. H. WAGGONER, then co-editor with A. T. JONES. Preached on the subject of righteousness by faith at the 1888 Minneapolis General Conference session. From 1892–1902, he led the church's publishing work in England. Waggoner's life ended in disagreement with ELLEN WHITE and the Adventist Church.

**Waggoner, J. H.** (1820–1889). Theologian, editor, health-reform pioneer, and a strong influence in religious liberty, Waggoner followed JAMES WHITE as editor of the *Signs of the Times*. Father of E. J. WAGGONER.

**White, Ellen Harmon** (1827–1915). Baptized as a young girl into the Methodist Church, Ellen became a follower of WILLIAM MILLER's Advent movement in the 1840s and survived the Great Disappointment. In August 1846, Ellen married JAMES WHITE. She became the spiritual leader of the young Seventh-day Adventist movement, speaking, writing, helping found schools, hospitals, and health-reform institutions. Her formal education was cut short after only three years, yet during her lifetime she wrote more than five thousand periodical articles and forty books, of which *Steps to Christ* is probably the most popular, with over twenty million copies printed.

**White, James** (1821–1881). Joined the Millerite Adventists, who recognized his executive talent and zeal. He married ELLEN HARMON WHITE in 1846 and with her helped found the Seventh-day Adventist Church. He published the first Seventh-day Adventist periodical (1849) and became the first editor of the *Review and Herald* (1850), the *Youth's Instructor* (1852), and the *Signs of the Times* (1874). Served three terms as president of the General Conference.

**Whitefield, George** (1714–1770). English Methodist evangelist. Associated with John and Charles Wesley at Oxford. He made several visits to America, where his preaching was a major influence in the religious revival known as the Great Awakening.

**Witz, Konrad** (*c.* 1400–*c.* 1445). German painter who spent most of his life in what is now Switzerland. His 1444 work *The Miraculous Draught of Fishes* is the earliest known recognizable landscape in European art and the first work to place a biblical scene in a contemporary setting.

**Wyclif, John** (*c.* 1324–1384). English religious reformer known as the Morning Star of the Reformation. Studied and taught at Oxford before entering the church. He became at odds with the church over ecclesiastical abuses and the doctrine of transubstantiation. In 1380, he published an English translation of the Bible—the first version in English.

**Yahweh.** One of the names of God in the Old Testament, occurring more frequently than any other divine name. Anglicized to *Jehovah*.

**Zeus.** The youngest son of Cronus and Rhea, Zeus was the supreme ruler of Mount Olympus in the Greek pantheon of gods. Father of Perseus, Hercules, and HEPHAISTOS.

**Zosimus** (?–418). Became bishop of Rome in 417 after the death of INNOCENT

I. Impressed by letters from PELAGIUS, Zosimus supported him, to the chagrin of AUGUSTINE. But under pressure from Emperor HONORIUS, Zosimus retreated and condemned Pelagius.

**Zwingli, Ulrich** (1484–1531). Swiss Protestant Reformer and preacher. Zwingli was opposed to the selling of indulgences and preached Reformed doctrines. Killed during a battle between Swiss cantons.

# Scripture Index

# SUBJECT INDEX

# IF YOU FOUND THIS BOOK INSPIRING AND THOUGHT-PROVOKING, YOU WILL WANT TO READ THESE OTHER BOOKS AS WELL.

## Searching for a God to Love
*Chris Blake*

This book is for thinking people who desire a belief system that goes beyond proof texts, anecdotes, and simplistic reasoning. It's for people who want to deal with the hurtful issues and irksome questions they have now. Share it with those you know who have trouble seeing God as Someone to love.

Book, paper, 256 pages.   0-8163-1719-4   US$11.99
Study guide, paper.   4-3330-0235-5   US$1.49

## A Strange Place for Grace
Discovering a loving God in the Old Testament
*Jon L. Dybdahl*

Do the Bible's stories reveal a hidden personality disorder in the Creator of the universe? Is He "sometimes up, sometimes down," exhibiting a happy-go-lucky, forgiving attitude of grace one day, but striking sinners dead the next? If you've struggled with to see how the stories of the Old Testament and the New can fit together to give us a consistent picture of God, you will find answers, here—not pat answers, but ones that really wrestle with the questions.

Paper, 144pages.   0-8163-2133-7   US$12.99

## Lord, I Have a Question
*Dan Smith*

Everything you ever wanted to ask God but were afraid to say out loud. The author wrestles with some of the hard questions and isn't afraid to leave some unanswered.

Paper, 240 pages.   0-8163-2016-0   US$13.99

Order from your ABC by calling 1-800-765-6955, or get online and shop our virtual store at www.AdventistBookCenter.com.
- Read a chapter from a book
- Order online
- Sign up for email notices on new products